THE WAY SCHOOLS WORK

SECOND EDITION

A Sociological Analysis of Education

Kathleen Bennett deMarrais
University of Tennessee

Margaret D. LeCompte
University of Colorado, Boulder

Longman Publishers USA

D0254493

The Way Schools Work: A Sociological Analysis of Education, second edition

Copyright © 1995, 1990 by Longman Publishers USA.
All rights reserved.
No part of this publication may be reproduced,
stored in a retrieval system, or transmitted
in any form or by any means, electronic, mechanical,
photocopying, recording, or otherwise,
without the prior permission of the publisher.

Longman, 10 Bank Street, White Plains, N.Y. 10606

Associated companies:
Longman Group Ltd., London
Longman Cheshire Pty., Melbourne
Longman Paul Pty., Auckland
Copp Clark Longman Ltd., Toronto

Acquisitions editor: Virginia L. Blanford
Production editor: Melanie M. McMahon
Cover design: Joseph DePinho, Pinho Graphic Design
Production supervisor: Richard C. Bretan

Library of Congress Cataloging-in-Publication Data

DeMarrais, Kathleen Bennett.
    The way schools work : a sociological analysis of education /
Kathleen Bennett deMarrais and Margaret D. LeCompte. — 2nd ed.
        p.   cm.
    Includes bibliographical references and index.
    ISBN 0-8013-1245-0
    1. Educational sociology — United States.   2. Education — Social
aspects — United States.   3. Education — Social aspects — United
States — History.   4. Educational sociology — History.   I. LeCompte,
Margaret Diane.   II. Title.
LC189.D36   1994
370.19'0973 — dc20   94-21574
                                                                             CIP

3 4 5 6 7 8 9 10-MA-98979695

We dedicate this book to four very special, talented women:
Rocklan McNeil
Elsita Leal
Amber Aguilera
Jennifer Walker

Contents

Preface

We initially wrote this book in order to have a text that would provide our own students with a critical perspective on the sociology of schooling—particularly those students without a strong background in social theory. We wanted to explore different theoretical perspectives and challenge our students to think about the major sociocultural and political issues related to schooling. We also wanted our students to examine their own notions of schooling in light of these perspectives, particularly a critical, transformative perspective.

A special feature of this book is its strong historical bent both in the information presented and the way developments in theory have affected the way we look at and interpret the impact of schools. We have couched our discussion of contemporary schools within the context of their historical development because we believe the way schools are currently organized has been powerfully influenced by events and social policies of the past. Similarly, although our own interpretations and conclusions are informed by critical and feminist perspectives, they are, like the viewpoints of all social scientists, built upon the theoretical models and analyses of the past—especially functionalism and conflict theory. Because this text is an introduction to the way sociologists think about educational processes, we weave both classical and contemporary critical perspectives into each chapter. Each chapter usually begins with a descriptive, functional approach and concludes with a more recent critical analysis. It is easier to know where we currently are if we understand where we came from.

The chapters derive from subfields in sociology: social theory, the sociology of organizations, the sociology of work and professions, the sociology of knowledge, and the study of class, race, and gender.

Chapter 1 examines the theories that underlie how people conceptualize the purposes for which schools are organized, whose interests schools serve, and what should be taught. These theories are divided into three categories: (1) *transmission theories* of function and conflict, which argue that schools rather passively transmit the patterns of society unchanged from one generation to another; (2) *interpretivist theories,* which describe the workings of schooling through a microlevel analysis and build a bridge between transmission and transformation theories; and (3) *transformation theories,* which argue that through critique and human agency, people in schools can play a role in transforming society.

Chapter 2 examines schools as social organizations. First it presents a historical analysis of school organization especially as it has been shaped by concepts from business and industry. Then it examines both the internal organization and patterns of control within schools and districts, and the external matrix of local, state, and national agencies that impinge on their operation. It emphasizes both the apparent ambiguity of patterns of authority and the influence of political as opposed to pedagogical concerns.

Chapter 3 is a detailed discussion of a group often overlooked—the students. It examines the impact of societal change on the way children experience childhood and adolescence, the special ways children relate to and resist the influence of school, and the impact of peer groups and youth culture on schooling.

Chapter 4 examines teachers, administrators, counselors, and parents. It describes the greater control being given to administrators, at the expense of teachers, and it questions the extent to which teaching is really a profession. The chapter also examines gender bias in the work force and its impact on the power and prestige of teachers.

Chapter 5 is an analysis of the relationship between social class and education. It traces changes in thinking about the origins of social class hierarchy, as well as what has led to the acquisition of social power. It also examines the impact of social class on the structure of society as well as on the achievements of individuals, and it raises questions about the degree to which contemporary educational systems really are "fair," meritocratic, and egalitarian. This chapter sets the stage for similar analyses in regard to minority status and gender.

Chapter 6 examines the curriculum, what is taught both openly and covertly. It looks at the differences in power and prestige attributed to various kinds of knowledge, and it examines how curricular differentiation, or tracking and ability grouping, serves to sort children into niches roughly similar to those occupied by their parents.

Chapter 7 discusses the relationship between minority status and schooling. It examines the role of the federal government in providing equal opportunities for minority students. It also analyzes various sociological and anthropological explanations for the failure of minority students. This chapter concludes with a discussion of minority student responses in the form of assimilation, accommodation, and resistance.

Chapter 8 is an analysis of the relationship between gender and schooling, in both formal and informal curricula. In regard to the formal curriculum is a discussion of gender-identified subject matter, staffing of schools, and the portrayal of women. In regard to the informal curriculum is an examination of the hidden messages sent to females and males through class organization, instructional technology, and class interaction. Following a discussion of gender differences in academic performance and occupational outcomes, the chapter concludes with a discussion of feminism as related to schooling.

Chapter 9 presents an examination of how sociological analysis and critical insights might be used to develop alternatives to the current system of education. Here we examine the changing balance of power in schools and propose alternatives for school structures, pedagogical practices, and teacher education.

NEW TO THIS EDITION

This book is a major rewrite of the first edition. We have added many new discussions about current theories and debates in education, moved the key concepts section to an alphabetized glossary in the back of the book, and sprinkled activities throughout the text to involve students. Our goal was to write a book synthesizing the most current thinking in the field.

Throughout the book are inserted illustrative boxes containing stories from students, teachers, and administrators to help bring the sociological concepts to life. Some were contributed by students and teachers with whom we work, and some are from published sources. The stories represent the experiences of people positioned in a variety of social class, ethnic, and gendered locations to illustrate the complexity of the concepts we are exploring.

Chapter 1 has been completely reorganized and clarified in light of students' and colleagues' responses to the material. We have added a chart, "Social Theories at a Glance," to help crystalize the assumptions, key concepts, and major questions of each of these perspectives.

In Chapter 2 we include a discussion of reform and restructuring movements currently changing the shape and structure of schools.

In Chapter 7 we added a section explaining our use of labels for particular ethnic groups and we challenge European American students to explore their notions of ethnicity. We've provided a more elaborate discussion of race and ethnicity.

We significantly enlarged Chapter 8, adding sections on sexist language, sexual harassment, and sexual orientation. We included a discussion of psychological development based on recent work by Lyn Mikel Brown and Carol Gilligan. We also updated the vignettes at the beginning of the chapter so that Susan, whose story ended with her high school experiences, is now faced with differential treatment in her college and adult life. The chapter now concludes with a discussion of feminism and the major feminist theories: liberal, radical, socialist, poststructuralist, and black feminism or womanism.

Chapter 9 has been totally restructured around the theme of "changing the balance of power." It has examples of new transformative practices that are now evident in many progressive schools. We have added a discussion of the major transformative pedagogies and a chart that summarizes the focus of each perspective. In this discussion we examine democratic education, multicultural education, critical pedagogy, and feminist pedagogy—a discussion unique to this book. We have also added a discussion about current networks that are forming around transformation of school structures and practices.

Acknowledgements

We thank the many people who contributed to this book through their reviews at different stages in its development and through more informal discussions with us. We are extremely grateful to:

William Armaline, University of Toledo

Robert Barger, Eastern Illinois University

Phil Frances Carspecken, University of Houston

Rodney Clifton, University of Manitoba

Diane Cudahy, University of Tennessee, Knoxville

Donna Dehyle, University of Utah

Kathy Farber, Bowling Green University

Nancy Greenman, University of South Florida

Jim Harvey, University of South Australia

Lynn Hutchinson, Walsh University

Sally Oran, University of Tennessee, Knoxville

Joel Spring, State University of New York at New Paltz

This book is much better for their thoughtful comments and critical insights.

Our thanks to the Association for School, College & University Staffing, Inc. (ASCUS) for their permission to use salary and teacher demand tables from their 1993 Report: Teacher Supply and Demand in the United States. Our students are always interested in these data.

We thank the Honolulu County Committee on the Status of Women for permission to use their wonderfully helpful "Do's and Don'ts of Non-Sexist Language."

We thank Naomi Silverman, the editor of the first edition of this book, who began as our editor and became a close and valued friend.

We appreciate the work of Virginia Blanford, editor of the second edition of *The Ways Schools Work,* for her help and support throughout the process. Our thanks to Melanie McMahon, Chris Konnari, Ilene McGrath, and Louise Capuano at Longman who helped with the development of this edition.

We owe special thanks to our students as well as the collaborating teachers and administrators who contributed to the book through their stories and discussions. Their lively criticism has helped to make this second edition much clearer. In particular we thank Theresa Apodaca, Bonnie Cadotte, Caelin Creasey, Pilar Ferreira, Anna Gildersleeve, Lisa McCoy, Rocklan McNeil, Barbara Medina, Andrea O'Conor, Leanne Ross, Duren Thompson, Jennifer Walker, Robert Whittfield, and Tracy Wood.

Finally, we wish to thank Paul deMarrais and Sergiu Luca for their continuing and cherished support of our work.

chapter 1

Theory and Its Influences on the Purposes of Schooling

INTRODUCTION

This book looks at schools and schooling from the perspective of the sociologist. Sociologists study the structure of society and the roles people play within it. Sociologists and psychologists think about schools and schooling differently in that psychologists tend to be interested in individuals while sociologists are interested in groups. Educational psychologists, then, are concerned with what goes on *inside* the minds of individual learners, while educational sociologists are interested in everything that happens *outside of* the minds of individual learners, including how learners interact with others and the characteristics of the settings in which they interact. Because most educational research has been done by psychologists, we believe that our sociological viewpoint will give a rather new perspective on schools.

Sociologists distinguish between *schooling* and *education.* The term **education** broadly refers to the process of learning over the span of one's entire life. Education begins at birth and continues in a wide variety of both formal and informal settings. Again, whereas psychologists study the psychological processes individuals undergo in learning and cognition, sociologists are more interested in the social or group aspects of learning.

Schooling is the learning that takes place in formal institutions whose specific function is the **socialization** of specific groups within society. Schooling is another name for socialization in schools, or the informal learning that groups of people, usually children, acquire about behavior in these schools. Sociologists who study schooling are interested in the characteristics of the people and institutions that make up educational systems, and particularly the dynamics of their interaction and operation.

As is the case with all social science disciplines, several different and competing theories exist within the sociology of education. While all sociologists share an interest in the same general phenomena, they use different theoretical lenses to interpret these phenomena. This chapter explores how sociologists with different theoretical perspectives explain the purposes of schooling. Keep in mind that these theories have evolved over time, growing from or in reaction to previous theories. They may share many concepts and methods. Some theories attempt to explain the way society works while others take these explanations, critique the current social order, and offer ways of working to transform the society. The principal questions addressed are the following:

What is the theory?

What are the purposes of schooling?

How does the theory relate to these purposes?

As you read this chapter, ask yourself which personal theories you use to explain the purposes of schooling.

The chapter begins with discussions of several key concepts, including the term *theory,* which will be used throughout the book. We then examine the various **theoretical frameworks** that have informed the sociology of education, showing how these frameworks alter interpretations of the purposes and impact of schooling. One of the primary theoretical issues addressed in the sociology of education is the process by which a society's ways of life, values, beliefs, and norms or standards for appropriate behavior are passed on from one generation to the next. Sociologists look at this process in two ways: as *social transmission* or as *social transformation.* In our discussion of transmission theories we explain **functionalism, structural functionalism,** and **conflict theory.**

Theories of transmission are concerned with description of the structural aspects of society (Parsons 1951, 1959; Weber 1947) and with how existing social structures facilitate the general functioning of society. For example, a sociologist might examine the social system within a school to understand how the values and behaviors of the society are transmitted and would find that American values such as neatness, efficient use of time, and obeying authority are emphasized in the daily routines of the classroom (LeCompte 1978b).

We then introduce **interpretive theories,** including *phenomenology, symbolic interactionism,* and *ethnomethodology.* These theories form a bridge to *theories of transformation,* which we discuss next. In the discussion of transformation theories we focus on **critical theories** and *feminist, postmodern,* and *poststructural* approaches. Transformation theories are less rigid than social transmission theories. Their central concern is the *transformation,* rather than reproduction, of the society (Burtonwood 1986). They also differ in how they view the role of individuals. While social transmission theories treat individuals as passive, transformation theories view individuals as having the capacity to become "empowered" (Ellsworth 1989). Rather than accepting the world as it is, they become agents for social action to improve their situation.

While many of these perspectives overlap, and many borrow heavily from each other, the primary difference between transmission and transformation theories lies in whether they concern *reproduction* or *production* of culture (Weiler 1988). Reproduction, or transmission, is concerned with how social structures are copied from generation to generation, regardless of external forces such as the activities or desires of groups or individuals. By contrast, theories of production, or transformation, give individuals' activities and desires an important role in the creation of culture. Theories of production describe the ways in which

> both individuals and classes assert their own experience and contest or resist the ideological and material forces imposed upon them in a variety of settings. Their analyses focus on the ways in which both teachers and students in schools produce meaning and culture through their own resistance and their own individual and collective consciousness. (Weiler 1988, p. 11)

WHAT IS THEORY?

In very simplistic terms, a **theory** is a world view, a way we organize and explain the world we live in. Theories are not necessarily impractical or complex. In fact, all human beings use theoretical thought every day.

> The informal explanations we use to guide our daily life as well as hunches we have about why things work as they do are *tacit* or lay theories. They derive from our own cultural background, academic training, life experiences, and individual personality traits. (LeCompte and Preissle 1993, p. 121)

We use theories about the weather to decide if we should take an umbrella to work, and "folk theories of success" (Ogbu 1987) to guide our career paths. Humans also have created theories to explain the operation of the natural universe, such as theories stating the relationship between energy and mass, or between moisture and the growth rates of plants. Similarly, we have developed theories to explain how the social world works, such as why job satisfaction and job performance are related and why people seem to develop conservative social attitudes as they grow older. We even develop theories about education, such as why higher occupational status usually is associated with higher levels of educational attainment, or why some ethnic minorities do poorly in school.

Social scientists generally use theoretical models or perspectives to organize their thought and inquiry. These models are "loosely interrelated sets of assumptions, concepts, and propositions that constitute a view of the world" (Goetz and LeCompte 1984, p. 37) or some significant part of it. Garbarino (1983) describes theory as a "statement of the principles presumably regulating observed processes, or one that accounts for causes or relationships between phenomena" (p. 5).

As we shall see, theory in both the natural and social sciences evolves because it is affected by historical and cultural developments. In general, theories change because we need more workable or accurate explanations for what we believe to be true. For example, science was guided for centuries by religious and philosophical theories that the sun revolved around the earth, and so all scientific inquiry was organized to support that belief. In time, however, as data amassed demonstrating that the earth revolved around the sun, support grew for a heliocentric view of our planetary system.

Social and cultural beliefs have similarly influenced theories about education. Throughout history people have observed that individuals who have higher levels of education tend to have higher social status, and a number of theories have been developed to explain this observation. At first they believed simply that the wealthy were smarter and capable of more education. Then, belief in the redemptory effect of education led people to believe that education would improve the human condition and help eliminate poverty, disease, and antisocial or immoral behavior. Schools, then, could make people better, if not actually wealthier. This belief justified the institution of schools for the poor, compensatory education programs, and a variety of social service practices. Later developments in social theory have changed our beliefs about the role and purpose of education. Now theorists believe that educational experiences, rather than leading to elimination of poverty and social differences, actually reinforce differences.

We all have acquired rather unscientific "pet theories" that we use to explain what goes on in the social world, including the schools. The poor performance of girls in mathematics is explained by a pet theory stating that math simply is more difficult for girls than for boys. A rationale for avoiding a Master's degree was the theory that school districts would not hire beginning teachers with a Master's degree because their salaries would be higher. Students who wanted to student teach only in a white, upper-middle-class district theorized that districts wouldn't hire teachers who had student-taught on an American Indian reservation or in the inner city.

Obviously some theories are more valid than others, but all of them help us to organize and understand our world. Many govern what we think about our educational experiences. At this point you might stop to consider some theories of your own. What theories do you use to answer the following questions?

> Why are some students or some teachers more successful in school than others?
>
> Why is teaching generally so little respected as a profession?
>
> Why is the public so dissatisfied with the public schools today?
>
> What leads some groups of students to be more successful in school than others?

We now begin a discussion of the three general categories of sociological theories that organize how sociologists think about schooling: social transmission theories, interpretive theories, and theories of transformation.

SOCIAL TRANSMISSION THEORIES

Functionalism

Functionalism, which has been the prevailing theoretical framework in the social sciences throughout the twentieth century, argues that society operates as does the human body: Like living organisms, all societies possess basic functions which they must carry out to survive.

For example, the human body is composed of many interdependent organs, each of which carries out a vital function. Every organ must be healthy and all must work together to maintain the health of the entire body. If any organ malfunctions, the entire body may die.

Similarly, societies, in order to survive, must carry out vital functions: reproduce themselves, recruit or produce new members, distribute goods and services, and allocate power. One of the most important functions is that of transmission. In the traditional functionalist view of social transmission, each elder generation passes on to each succeeding generation the rules, customs, and appropriate behaviors for operating in the society. They do so through the principal socializing institutions or transmitters of the culture, such as families, churches, and schools. By participating in these institutions, individuals accept their roles within the *social structure* of society. Functionalists identify not only the various functions within a society, but also the connections between the components of a societal system and the relations between different systems. For example, functionalists assert that if one socializing institution is not fulfilling its function, another will take over its role to maintain the equilibrium of the society. In today's society, functionalists would argue that as more families have both parents working, schools have taken over many of the functions formerly performed by the family.

Functional analysis has become an inescapable part of the training and worldview of all social scientists. Although they may not accept all the tenets of traditional functional social theory, all social scientists use its categories as basic analytic tools to describe social systems. However, functionalism has been criticized, both because it rejects conflict and change as viable and often valuable social processes, and because its proponents have asserted that it is the only approach that produces "objective," unbiased, or truly "scientific" findings. Functionalists may do this because their training has never presented alternative perspectives, and also because they are so steeped in the functional analysis approach that it appears to be the truth rather than merely one way of looking at the world. However, other theories are available, some of them variations of functionalism, and these may provide more adequate and/or critical explanations.

Structural Functionalism

An important variant of functionalism is **structural functionalism.** Based upon the assumption that human systems have an underlying but unobservable coherence based upon formal rules, signs, and arrangements, structuralists seek to understand human phenomena, such as systems of meaning, language, and culture, by identifying these underlying structures. Structuralists make inferences about underlying social structure based upon patterns observed in human life.

Central to structural functionalism is the conviction that social systems are like living bodies. Structures, like bodily organs, evolve to carry out vital functions in society, and they must maintain an equilibrium with each other in order for societal health to be maintained. Conflict, like an illness, is an aberration which the healthy system avoids and seeks to resolve as quickly as possible. Any change takes place only gradually in healthy systems, because it constitutes a disruption of normalcy. Revolutions and other forms of rapid change are signs of illness. Many structural functionalists came to believe that any social structure found in a system *must* have some function and probably serves some crucial need, even if that need is not immediately apparent. Some social scientists have used this argument to oppose change in general, especially in traditional societies, on the grounds that even practices that seem morally offensive, such as the cremation of Hindu widows upon the death of their spouses, must have utility within the given culture. They hold that to remove such structures might cause harm to the system and should, like surgery to the human body, be under-taken only with great care and in extreme circumstances. However, critics of func-tionalism contend that it ignores the notion—integral to conflict theories—that con-flict and contradictions are inherent in a social system and, in fact, stimulate its adapta-tion to new conditions.

Functionalists view educational systems as one of the *structures* which carry out the *function* of transmission of attitudes, values, skills, and norms from one genera-tion to another. Sociologists such as Robert Dreeben (1968), Emile Durkheim (1969), Robert Merton (1967), and Talcott Parsons (1951, 1959) have described this process. According to structural functionalists, educational systems perpetuate the "ac-cepted" culture. The concept of "accepted culture" implies that there is a consensus on which values, attitudes, and behaviors should be transmitted. When conflict over values does occur, adjustments are made to regain consensus and keep the system balanced. For example, in mid-twentieth-century America, conflict arose over whether school curricula should portray America as a white-dominated society in which immigrants were expected to assimilate, or a multicultural society in which differences were celebrated. The past several decades have witnessed a variety of adaptations in curricula, a reflection of attempts to arrive at a new consensus.

Functionalism and the Purposes of Schooling.   Functionalists believe that schooling serves to reinforce the existing social and political order. They assume there is consensus on the values and beliefs in society, especially on the allocation and use of power. Functionalism unquestioningly views the social system as benign and accepts existing class structures as appropriate. Because their perspective constitutes the current conventional wisdom about schools, the descriptions on the next few pages will seem quite familiar. We will soon examine other theories, however, and will see how interpretations of the purposes of schooling change when looked at through different theoretical lenses. Regardless of their particular orientation, though, theorists do not necessarily disagree with the functional description of how schools are organized; what they disagree on are the functions schools are said to have in society. They also differ in how they see the desired goals or purposes for schooling. The purposes attributed to schools fall into four general categories: intel-lectual, political, economic, and social. The following sections describe how these purposes are interpreted by functional theorists of education.

Divide your class into four or five groups. Have each group choose a differ-ent category of people to interview to determine what they consider to be the primary purposes of public schooling. Categories might include parents, students, teachers, administrators, community professionals, religious lead-ers, blue- and pink-collar workers, and others. Compare your findings in a class discussion.

Intellectual Purposes.   The three primary intellectual purposes of schooling are the following:

1. Acquisition of cognitive skills (reading, mathematics, etc.)
2. Acquisition of substantive knowledge
3. Acquisition of inquiry skills (evaluation, synthesis, etc.)

If you were to ask a parent, student, or teacher why children attend school, the most common response would be "to learn." They would mean, to acquire the knowledge and skills enumerated above. In 1988 the U.S. Secretary of Education stated, "American parents want their schools to do one thing above all others: teach their children to read, write, and speak well" (E. W. Bennett 1988). Businesses and industry also view schools as institutions whose job it is to impart both cognitive skills and a body of substantive knowledge in the natural and social sciences. Recent outcry over high school students' lack of knowledge (E. W. Bennett 1988; Bloom 1987; Finn and Ravitch 1987; Hirsch 1987) has been over alleged inattention to this purpose of education. As will be discussed in Chapter 6, neoconservatives have begun a campaign to limit the function of schools to imparting skills and knowledge through a "core curriculum" that provides the same traditional liberal arts education to all students.

Political Purposes.   Schools also are viewed as places that must produce future citizens and workers. To that end, they serve four major political purposes:

1. To educate future citizens for appropriate participation in the given political order
2. To promote patriotism by teaching myths, history, and stories about the country, its leaders, and government
3. To promote the assimilation of immigrants
4. To ensure order, public civility, and conformity to laws

Functionalists believe that schooling facilitates knowledge about and integration into the political system. It is a means by which common social and political values are transmitted to young people and others, like immigrants, who initially may not share them. This goal has been one of the most important of modern public schooling (Carnegie Council on Adolescent Development 1989; Durkheim 1969; National Commission on Excellence in Education 1983; Spring 1988a).

Early American leaders believed that republican forms of government were required to educate citizens so they could participate wisely in the political system — vote, run for public office, and make informed decisions about government. Hence they believed publicly financed schools should be provided for all — at least all white males.

One of the earliest plans for free elementary education to both males and females was introduced to the Virginia legislature in 1779 by Thomas Jefferson. In his "Bill for the More General Diffusion of Knowledge" Jefferson proposed that public elementary schools be established in each county so that all children would receive three years of reading, writing, and computation. The most talented boys would then go on for free education in regional grammar schools. A final selection of the most talented boy from all the schools would then attend the College of William and Mary at public expense.

Jefferson's plan, unlike those in the New England and other colonies, envisioned an *articulated system* of schools from elementary school to college. An articulated system links requirements from each lower level to prerequisites in each higher one; students must master preceding levels before passing on to the next. Jefferson's plan sought to elevate a few males from the lower classes to the ranks of potential leaders. However, the plan did not explicitly teach citizenship. It emphasized a classical curriculum of Greek, Roman, English, and American history, rather than government or civics. Jefferson believed that literacy and a free press were sufficient for making wise political decisions.

Jefferson's plan provided no equal opportunities for women or minorities, and it was never enacted. However, it did formalize the idea that schools were critical to the development of leadership in a democracy. This type of thinking continues to inform the way many people view schools today.

Horace Mann, often called the father of American education, believed that schools not only should produce leaders but also should train citizens. Foreshadowing John Dewey and others, Mann felt that a national political consensus could be developed through the teaching of common values and beliefs in public schools. During Mann's tenure as Secretary of the Massachusetts Board of Education (1837–1848), political tension, mass immigration, and class conflict were causing great concern. Mann was active in school reform; as editor of the *Common School Journal,* he advocated the establishment of publicly supported elementary schools, open to children of all socioeconomic classes, to provide basic literacy and to instill social and political values for a unified American identity. Such a Common School would be the key to reforming society and creating a more stable union. His plan was supported by leaders of the dominant culture—industrialists, church leaders, and the business community—who felt that instilling respect for a common order would build a productive and complacent work force.

At the end of the nineteenth century the influx of immigrants from southern and eastern Europe prompted educators' efforts to assimilate newcomers. "Americanization" programs were established to teach language, customs, and laws. Especially after World War I, schools were used not only to Americanize immigrants but also to stimulate patriotism in all children. Reciting the Pledge of Allegiance and singing patriotic songs in school were viewed as training for later allegiance and service to the nation (Durkheim 1969; Spring 1988a). Participation in student government and competitive sports was encouraged in order to develop school spirit, which later would be transferred to the country.

Current curricular trends differ little from those described above. High schools require Civics and Economics, with special emphasis on the "free enterprise system"; children still learn political history and myths, and they still recite the Pledge of Allegiance; and political education and English as a Second Language (ESL) classes are required for recent immigrants.

Economic Purposes.   Schooling serves two major economic purposes:

1. To prepare students for later work roles
2. To select and train the labor force

Schools prepare students for the work force in part by teaching attitudes, techni-cal skills, and social behavior appropriate to the work place, such as cooperation, conformity to authority, punctuality, gender-appropriate attitudes, neatness, task ori-entation, care of property, and allegiance to the team (Bossert 1979; Carroll 1975; Dreeben 1968; Jackson 1968; LeCompte 1978b). Schools also act as "sorting ma-chines" (Spring 1976), categorizing students by academic ability and then pointing them toward appropriate career goals. In this way, schools create a meritocracy, a hierarchical social structure organized by ability, and they distribute individuals to fill the diverse roles required by a complex industrial work force. Such a meritocracy assumes that no major external impediments stand in the way of success for able, hard-working individuals (Young 1971).

Schools' **stratification** of students and creation of an ability-based hierarchical ranking serves to link occupational to social class differences in society. As the United States industrialized near the turn of the century, the concept of "human capital" and "manpower planning" came to dominate educational thinking (G. Becker 1964; Blaug 1970). The human capital school of thought, which originated in the late 1950s, calculates the rate of return from "investing" in schooling; it is measured by lifetime earnings minus the costs of education, including "opportunity costs," or the amount of money *not* earned while in school (Miles 1977; Schultz 1961). Humans are viewed as economic resources, and their laboring ability is likened to physical capital such as money, coal, steel, or electrical power. Just as physical capital can grow by being invested wisely, the value of human capital can be increased through higher educa-tional levels.

Human capital theorists thus view young people as commodities in the labor market and view schools as the means of increasing the capacity of these resources by increasing their skill and knowledge. By supporting public education, industrialists invested in human resources just as they invested in physical capital and other kinds of resources. They also trained selected students for the work force. Industrial growth was believed to be intimately linked to a nation's ability to increase its supply of skilled human capital. School–business partnerships such as the "Adopt a School" program, whereby local businesses invest in schools, are a current example of the belief in human capital. This belief has been one of the strongest catalysts to the growth of educational systems in developing countries.

Social Purposes.   Schools serve three major social purposes:

1. To promote a sense of social and moral responsibility
2. To serve as sites for the solution or amelioration of social problems
3. To supplement the efforts of other institutions of socialization, such as the family and the church

In traditional societies the family, the churches, and the community transmitted social and moral values to youth for the maintenance of culture. As nations became more complex, children did not always follow the paths of their parents. More com-plex skills were needed for work, and schools were called upon more and more to assist in the training and socialization of children. Since the nineteenth century, schools have been viewed also as the primary institution for solution of social problems. In fact, in the 1890s the sociologist Edward Ross argued that the school had *replaced* the church and family as the primary instiller of social values, and he described education as an expensive alternative to the police (Ross 1901).

In the twentieth century, schools have been called upon to solve such problems as juvenile delinquency, poverty, child abuse, drug addiction, teenage pregnancy, sexually transmitted diseases, and highway safety. Social goals have become a very real and vital component of schooling.

Social services have been incorporated into schools on the grounds that well-fed, rested, and healthy children learn more readily and are less likely to drop out. They also are supported by the belief that children are more easily influenced in reform movements than are adults. Service programs also facilitate American egalitarian notions of equal opportunity and fair play.

This discussion of the purposes of schooling is a backdrop for exploring the various theoretical frameworks that have informed the sociology of education, particularly in the United States in the twentieth century. It is important to keep in mind that people interpret the purposes of schooling in accordance with specific theories about how schools relate to society. We have begun with the functionalist view, because it is the one with which people are most familiar. We now move to other views which, in our view, more closely correspond to the way schools and society actually are linked.

What do you think are the primary purposes of public schooling? How do these compare with the purposes of schooling discussed in this chapter?

Conflict Theory

Conflict theorists such as Karl Marx, Lewis Coser, Georg Simmel, and Ralf Dahrendorf believed that structural functional analysis, with its emphasis on social equilibrium and maintenance of existing patterns, is inadequate to explain the dynamism of social systems. They address questions not raised by structural functionalists, such as these:

1. What are the sources and the consequences of conflict in social systems?
2. How do conflicting groups organize and mobilize?
3. What are the sources of inequality in society?
4. How do societies change themselves?

Conflict theory, especially as developed by Marxists and neo-Marxists, states that the organization of a society is determined by its economic organization, and in particular by patterns of ownership of property. Inequality of property or of resource distribution, then, is the major source of conflict in societies. Insofar as schools are intimately linked to future economic opportunities, they too are institutions in which social conflict is played out.

Conflict theory has led to a rethinking of the relationship between schools, social class structure, and patterns of economic opportunity. Blau and Duncan (1967) first determined that the educational attainment of American males is a good predictor of their ultimate socioeconomic status. They further noted that the educational and socioeconomic status of sons tended to be the same as that of their fathers, indicating that status seemed to be inherited rather than transcended. Thus the system of class status seemed much more rigid than the egalitarian ideology of America purported. While interpretations differ as to whether it is the individual or the system that dictates one's ultimate destiny, the process of schooling clearly was linked to the structure of inequality as much as to opportunities, because of schooling's close ties to placement in the labor market. We now move to a discussion of reproduction as we examine the ways in which educational theorists explain how schools stratify—or rank-order—opportunity.

Reproduction Theory. The notion of reproduction represents the dark side of functional theories of transmission. Rather than viewing schooling as promoting democracy, social mobility, and equality, some theorists conceptualize schools as reproducing both the ideologies of the dominant social groups and the hierarchy of the class structure. In other words, schools serve as tools to keep wealth and power in the hands of the white middle- and upper-class groups.

According to these theorists (Boudon 1974; Bowles and Gintis 1976; Carnoy 1972; Carnoy and Levin 1985; Persell 1977), schools reproduce status in several ways. First, is the exclusive use of the formal language along with expectations for behavior of the dominant culture. This disadvantages the lower classes who do not speak the formal language, and also the middle and upper classes who engage in different behavior patterns (Bernstein 1977; Bourdieu and Passeron 1977).

Second, schools tend to magnify class differences by sorting individuals into occupational niches, not so much by their ability as by their social class origins. Thus children from middle- or upper-class families are thought to be more able and so are pushed toward professional or other desirable careers. Similarly, lower-class and minority children are viewed as less able and are placed in vocational curricula with lower job expectations. Children also are encouraged toward fulfillment of traditional gender roles.

Third, the status quo is reinforced by the fact that dominant groups control the major social and political institutions and they ensure that their power is never threatened. Giroux (1983a) summarizes this process of reproduction in schools:

> First, schools provided different classes and social groups with the knowledge and skills they needed to occupy their respective places in a labor force stratified by class, race and gender. Second, schools were seen as reproductive in the cultural sense, functioning in part to distribute and legitimate forms of knowledge, values, language and modes of style that constitute the dominant culture and its interests. Third, schools were viewed as part of a state apparatus that produced and legitimated the economic and ideological imperatives that underlie the state's political power. (1983a, p. 258)

Reproduction and the Purposes of Schooling.   The purposes seen by conflict theorists differ very little from those of functionalists. However, rather than accepting the status quo as natural, conflict theorists abhor the inequalities perpetuated by reproduction. Adherents to the concept of reproduction feel that public schooling operates so that the dominant class can maintain its place in a stratified society. Schools maintain class structure by preparing its members for stratified work roles, giving rewards for use of dominant language, and placing state regulation over most aspects of school life.

Three models of reproduction theory—economic reproduction, cultural reproduction, and hegemonic state reproduction—are used to explain how schools promote inequality and perpetuate class distinctions. Each model can be used both at the macrolevel, or schooling in the larger societal context, and at the microlevel, the more individual level of classroom and school practice. That is, some conflict theorists use large-scale quantitative analyses to study the relationship between reproduction and schooling, while others study interaction in small-scale settings such as classrooms to see how reproduction actually occurs.

Model #1: Economic Reproduction.   The economic reproductive model, which evolved from the work of Bowles and Gintis (1976), focuses on system blame, placing responsibility for social inequality on the schools. They link the failure of schools to reduce poverty and disadvantage to inequities in the economic structure of capitalist society (Carnoy 1972). This view, informed by traditional Marxism, states that power is in the hands of those who control wealth and capital and who maintain traditional class, ethnic, and gender inequalities. Stratification of work roles by race, class, and gender leave women, blacks, Latinos, American Indians, and other minorities at a disadvantage. The schools facilitate this stratification through their sorting and testing processes. Students are inculcated with skills, values, and attitudes considered appropriate for their later roles in the occupational hierarchy.

Correspondence refers to society's economic organization being mirrored in its institutions and vice versa. Thus if schools and churches resemble factories, this is so because the factory is the dominant form of economic organization in industrial society. Conversely, if schools are organized the way apprenticeships and workshops are, this is so because craftsmanship and skilled trades dominate the economic sectors. (See Chapter 2 for a discussion of correspondence between schools and factories.) Bowles and Gintis summarize the correspondence principle, which is central to their argument:

> The educational system helps integrate youth into the economic system, we believe, through a structural correspondence between its social relations and those of production. The structure of social relations in education not only inures the student to the discipline of the work place, but develops the types of personal demeanor, modes of self-presentation, self-image, and social class identification which are the crucial ingredients of job adequacy. (1976, p. 131)

Correspondence also refers to other aspects of societal organization being reflected in institutions such as schools. For example, schools tend to mirror the inequalities in society at large so that children learn, through both a hidden curriculum and an explicit curriculum, the skills and attitudes that will correspond to their later work roles. Jackson (1968) used the term **hidden curriculum** to describe implicit messages to convey "appropriate" values, beliefs, and behaviors to children. For example, by encouraging children to keep busy, complete their work neatly, come to school on time, wait quietly, and the like, schools teach behaviors needed in the labor market.

The hidden curriculum conveys different messages to children of different social class, ethnicity, and gender. Lower- and working-class children are socialized to accept authority, to be punctual, to wait, and to be compliant, while middle-class children learn to assume roles of responsibility, authoritative modes of self-presentation, and independent work habits. Teachers anticipate that middle-class children will need highly developed verbal skills but that lower-class children will not. Research in primary classrooms has confirmed that middle-class children are treated differently than are lower-class children. For example, during "sharing time," when children are encouraged to talk about themselves, teachers tend to give middle-class children feedback to enhance their self-presentation skills, while teachers of lower-class children tend to accept their students' presentation without correction or elaboration (Bernstein 1970; Labov 1972; Rist 1970).

Schools also reinforce gender differences. Studies show that males are called on more frequently, asked questions requiring higher-order thinking, given more criticism (both positive and negative), given more leadership responsibility, and generally provided with more teacher attention than are females (Sadker and Sadker 1985). The hidden message is that males are more capable and important than females. Researchers also have documented at the microlevel the connection between how social relationships in schools are organized and the implicit message about authority, work, and social roles and the values of the capitalist society (Borman 1987; Jackson 1968; LeCompte 1978b; Metz 1978).

In summary, the economic reproduction model provides insights into the relationships between social class, structural inequality in schooling, and reproduction of the social division of labor. It explains how initial class differences are reinforced by the structure of the school, so that students from lower-class backgrounds are relegated to lower-level jobs while middle- and upper-class students are rewarded with more desirable positions. However, this model has been criticized for its mechanistic, one-sided assumption that structure alone determines outcomes. Economic reproduction theory allows no room for individuals to act in behalf of their own destiny. It fails to explain **resistance** to authority, or the dynamics of relationships among students, teachers, and school staff. It is radically pessimistic, offering little hope for social change or alternative practices (Giroux 1983a, p. 266). This theory has also been criticized for omitting forms of domination based upon ethnicity or gender.

Model #2: Cultural Reproduction.   Cultural reproduction goes beyond transmission of the class structure alone. It examines how class-based differences are expressed in the political nature of curriculum content as well as in cultural and linguistic practices embedded in the formal curriculum. Bernstein's *Class, Codes and Control* (1977) analyzes these issues on both the macrolevel and microlevel. His studies, encompassing both the structures of and interactions in society, demonstrate that social inequalities begin in class-based differences in the family's linguistic codes, differences that are in turn reinforced by the schools.

According to Bernstein, the structure of society causes each class to develop a different family role system, each with its own mode of communication, which evolves as individuals participate in the shared assumptions and expectations of their class. Working-class life is organized around a family structure limited to traditional roles and positional authority based on age, class, and gender. It generates what Bernstein calls a "restricted" or "particularistic" code or meaning system, in which speakers use a shorthand communication, assuming that their intentions and meanings are understood by the listener. This code is described as "restricted" because its practitioners do not use an elaborate language system to make meanings explicit.

By contrast, the family structure of the middle-class is more open and flexible. It tends to rely on individual personality characteristics and personal relationships rather than on traditional, stereotypic roles. Because roles are negotiable, members of the middle class do not assume that meanings will be shared by listeners; hence they use what Bernstein calls an elaborated or universalistic language code to facilitate verbal communication. Differences between working-class and middle-class communication styles are illustrated by "How to Behave on a Bus" (see p. 16). Note the greater degree of directness and immediacy in the working-class dialogue. Working-class codes rely on the authority of the mother to obtain compliance, while the middle-class mother tries to obtain her child's compliance by means of rational dialogue.

Bernstein suggests that the elaborated or universalistic language patterns of the middle-class predominate in schools. Middle-class children are better able to participate in their own socialization processes because their language is similar to the language of schools. Since working-class students have less competence in the language of the school (or in Bernstein's words, have limited access to the elaborated codes of the socializing agencies), they often fail to understand exactly what is expected of them. They therefore respond inappropriately, perform more poorly, and reap fewer rewards for their efforts. Their poor academic performance leads them into preparation for vocational and blue-collar employment, whereas middle- and upper-class students are prepared for skilled and professional careers. In this way the class structure is maintained.

Pierre Bourdieu and Jean-Claude Passeron (1977) elaborated on Bernstein's notion of linguistic codes. Expanding on existing studies of class reproduction, they developed the concept of **cultural capital** to explain the function of schooling in the transmission of cultural and economic wealth. Cultural capital includes not merely language and social roles, but also the general cultural background, knowledge, and skills passed from one generation to the next. Cultural capital differs according to social class: Some has a higher "exchange rate" than others. High culture—that concerned with the arts, literature, and languages as well as communication skills, cooperative work patterns, creative endeavor, and what might be called "middle-class manners and behavior"—characterizes the middle and upper classes and is the most

---

How to Behave on a Bus

Working-Class Code:

MOTHER: "Hold onto the strap when the bus starts."
CHILD: "Why?"
MOTHER: "Because I said so!"
CHILD: "Why?"
MOTHER: "Sit down and do as you're told!"

Middle-Class Code:

MOTHER: "Hold onto the strap when the bus starts."
CHILD: "Why?"
MOTHER: "Because when the bus starts, you might fall down."
CHILD: "Why?"
MOTHER: "The bus jerks when it starts, and you might trip."
CHILD: "Why?"
MOTHER: "Sit down and do as you're told!"

---

highly valued. This type of cultural capital forms the basis of the overt and the hidden curriculum in schools.

Children go to school to add to their store of cultural capital, but working-class children find that their stock is undervalued. In fact, the capital they do have handicaps them. Since the schools embody the cultural capital of the middle and upper classes, children from lower social backgrounds who are not familiar with the codes will have more difficulty understanding the schooling process. The influence of cultural capital is especially pronounced in the first years of schooling, when their understanding and use of language is a major component in teachers' assessments of them. For example, students who respond in single words or short phrases rather than in complete statements will be perceived as less intellectually competent than their peers who speak standard English. They also will be judged less able if they do not make direct eye contact with teachers or if they use dialects such as Appalachian English, Black English (Labov 1972), American Indian English (Leap 1993; Spolsky and Irvine 1992), or the "village English" of Native Alaskan communities. These are the students who will be placed in reading groups for the "less capable" (K. P. Bennett 1986, 1991).

By contrast, students whose cultural and linguistic competence is congruent with school expectations will be considered academically superior. Schools reinforce the competencies already acquired by middle-class children, and since academic success tends to be associated with job success later on, this reinforcement in turn reinforces the existing class structure.

Model #3: Hegemonic State Reproduction.   A third model of reproduction is concerned with the complex role of governmental intervention in the educational system. The term **hegemony** refers to a social consensus created by dominant groups who control socializing institutions such as the media, schools, churches, and the political system; these institutions prevent alternative views from gaining an audience or establishing their legitimacy (McLaren 1989). The school is one of these agencies. Hegemony is created, at least in part, because schools reflect the ideologies advocated by the very state agencies that regulate the schooling process. For example, if state officials have mandated that sex education, AIDS education, drug education, driver education, or gun safety be taught in schools, districts must comply with those regulations.

Researchers in the hegemonic tradition argue that economic and cultural models of reproduction fail to consider how powerful the political intervention of the state is in enforcing policies that direct the reproductive functions of education. These researchers often refer to control by "the state," using "state" globally, without distinguishing among three kinds of "state" control in the United States—local, state, and national. Though these structures of power do not always coincide, Marxists would argue that all are products of a similar dominant culture and that the term "state" refers not to a political entity but to a general power structure. Giroux (1983a, 1983b) argues that hegemony is reflected not only in the formal curriculum, but also in school routines and social relationships and in the way knowledge is structured. The hegemonic model explains two functions which the state carries out in regard to schooling. The first involves the role of state and federal agencies in the actual production of knowledge taught in schools. The second involves state regulation of schools through certification requirements, length of compulsory schooling, and curriculum requirements.

THE ROLE OF THE STATE IN THE PRODUCTION OF KNOWLEDGE   At the national and state levels, government research reflects the interests of the party currently in power. According to hegemonic theorists, the state affects the production of knowledge by determining which types of research should be funded by the government. One of the earliest examples of federal involvement in educational research and the production of knowledge came in the 1950s following the Russian launching of Sputnik. Because federal officials believed that America was losing ground in the race to space, they encouraged talented students to study science and math. The National Science Foundation channeled funds into math and science curriculum-writing groups and, later, into summer institutes to train teachers in the use of new science and math materials. The National Defense Education Act also provided funds for college scholarships in science and mathematics, for new science and math equipment, and for purchase of curricular materials by local schools systems. Spring elaborates:

> . . . the National Institute of Education's main concern is the control of education by channeling of research interest into particular fields, which is ac-

complished by making available government funds for certain areas of research. The NIE, by designating priority areas for research, creates a potential situation wherein the production of knowledge about education is
guided, by the means of attracting researchers into desired areas with offers
of monetary support. (1985, p. 196)

The work of Anyon (1983, 1988), Apple (1979), Giroux (1983a, 1983b), Spring
(1988b), and others illustrates the extent to which the production of knowledge is
linked to the political sphere. A more detailed discussion of this process is presented
in Chapter 6, where we examine the school curriculum.

THE ROLE OF THE STATE IN THE REGULATION OF EDUCATION   Political influence is evident
in state control of teacher certification and assessment, compulsory education laws,
curriculum mandates, and mandatory testing. The trend is toward more and more
involvement by the states in the schooling process. For example, teachers in Tennessee, Texas, Georgia, and many other states are currently required to teach prescribed
sets of "basic skills" on which the students regularly are examined for mastery by
standardized tests. Where they are mandated, these basic skills constitute the major
portion of the curriculum taught by elementary teachers.

The regulatory function also is performed by state-mandated exit examinations in
reading, mathematics, and written composition, which are required for graduation
from high school. Many states also require pre-service teachers to pass a National
Teachers Examination for certification. Some states are considering ongoing competency testing to ensure that experienced teachers maintain their skills. As we shall
describe in Chapters 2 and 4, many of these policies directly affect students, parents,
teachers, and schools but are outside of their control (Giroux 1983a, 1983b; Spring
1985).

Hegemonic state reproduction theory, then, directs attention to the autonomy of
national and state governments in exerting pressure on schooling. Its critics argue
that while this theory attempts to explain macrolevel structural issues, it fails to consider the microlevel, or daily life in classrooms. It neglects the social relations among
teachers, students, and school staff and how these interactions help them accept,
accommodate to, or resist the role of the state in the classroom.

A Critique of Reproduction Models.   In summary, the three models for reproduction provide a structural view of the relationship between the work place and the
schools, a view of the relationship between the dominant cultural and linguistic codes
of the schools and those of the students, and an explanation of the effects of government on school policies and practices. In conflict theorists' view, the repressive economic, sociocultural, and political power of dominant groups reigns supreme and the
system is to blame for students' failure to succeed and for the schools' failure to ameliorate social problems. In this view, the hegemonic power of the state leads the individuals to accept official explanations for their failure and therefore to place the
blame on themselves.

Critics say that these theories are overly deterministic and one-sided. Some functional and conflict theorists have been criticized for their overreliance on quantitative research methods, for their unidimensional focus on social class and oppression based on ethnicity and gender (Clements and Eisenhart 1988; Delamont 1989; Ellsworth 1988), for the lack of empirical data in their analyses, and for their disregard of the power of individual human agency (Giroux 1983). Giroux explains that conflict theorists have "over-emphasized the idea of domination in their analysis and have failed to provide any major insights into how teachers, students and other human agents come together within specific historical and social contexts in order to both make and reproduce the conditions of their existence" (1983a, p. 259). Giroux argues that by avoiding a focus on human activity within social relationships, reproduction theorists offer little hope for change. While they have offered a different and often useful way of looking at schools as social and cultural transmitters, their view is a pessimistic one, giving no consideration to how individuals could interact to ameliorate or alter the constraints of the system.

Summary

Several themes emerge from our discussion of cultural transmission theories. Both functionalists and conflict theorists address the macro or structural aspects of schooling and its role in cultural transmission. The major differences between the two theories lie in their interpretation of cultural transmission. Functionalists believe in the existence of an underlying benign *consensus* on social beliefs and values and do not question its assumptions. Conflict theorists are critical of this assumption, arguing that social attitudes and values reflect the stratification in the society as a whole. They are concerned primarily with how schools serve the interests of dominant groups by replicating the existing social class structure and maintaining the division of labor necessary for a society stratified by class, ethnicity, and gender.

INTERPRETIVE THEORIES

Sociologists within the interpretive paradigm refer to themselves as phenomenologists, symbolic interactionists (Blumer 1969), or ethnomethodologists (Cicourel 1964; Garfinkel 1967). The common thread linking interpretivists is their focus on the *social construction of meaning* in social interactions. Interpretivists believe that human beings respond to each other and to their surroundings not so much on the basis of any objective or inherent meanings but on the basis of meanings assigned to people and settings by the people in them. Interaction and the assignment of meaning are affected by people's past experiences and beliefs, their current experiences in the given setting, and what they come to believe as interaction unfolds. This process is called the *social construction of meaning*. To interpretivists, reality is not fixed but is, at least insofar as it dictates human behavior and belief, negotiated in an immediate setting and depends upon the context. Such a fuzzy notion of reality might at first seem discomforting. However, consider how teenagers can be neat, helpful, well-behaved, and mature in *other people's* houses while remaining slovenly, slothful, irresponsible, and rude at home. Or how a perfectly well-disciplined class of students runs amok in the presence of a substitute. The construction of meaning is precisely why parents often transfer a child to a different school if the child has gained a reputation for being a troublemaker or a poor student. A chance to construct a new reality and new meanings often is all that is needed to transform a situation.

Interpretive Studies as a Major Shift in Research Methods

Interpretive researchers believe that the best way to understand human behavior is to examine real-world situations using qualitative or descriptive rather than experimental methods of inquiry. Interpretive approaches are a major departure from the quantitative studies which dominated the social sciences in the 1960s and 1970s, and the experimental studies which still dominate educational research. *Quantitative studies* use data from tests, surveys, or the census. These methods are indirect measures of actual behavior, since they ask people to recall what they did or to characterize their beliefs and actions in accordance with predetermined options designed by a researcher. *Experimental studies* try to place all elements of the research under the control of the researcher; anything the researcher cannot control is treated as bias or a threat to the integrity of the study. Neither quantitative nor experimental research is adequate for examining complex, uncontrollable, and multifaceted phenomena such as behavior in schools. By contrast, interpretivists rely heavily upon direct observation and open-ended interviewing in natural settings, frequently becoming participants; their major focus is on the details and nuances of interactions among people (Bogdan 1972; Erickson 1984; Glesne and Peshkin 1992; G. Jacobs 1970; LeCompte and Preissle 1993; Spradley 1980).

Interpretive inquiry has expanded tremendously since the late 1960s and early 1970s. It has grown beyond the discipline of sociology, and now researchers from a variety of disciplines are trying to understand the complex processes of schooling. Their studies are variously described as naturalistic, qualitative, descriptive, and ethnographic. Anthropologists of education, cognitive anthropologists, sociolinguists, and qualitative sociologists have begun to use the methods of interpretive inquiry. Their methods include long-term participant observation in classrooms, analyses of curricula, descriptions of methods and strategies used by educators, and extensive open-ended interviewing of those involved in schooling processes.

The three principal strands of inquiry that have influenced research in education are phenomenology, symbolic interactionism, and ethnomethodology. As we discuss them, note how each has influenced the others and contributed to an overall perspective in the social sciences.

Phenomenology

The key concern of phenomenologists is meaning. Phenomenologists study the social meaning of knowledge and what possessing various kinds of knowledge signifies. Phenomenologists such as Schutz (1972) and Berger and Luckmann (1967) viewed what we know, or reality, not as something given, but as constructed within the social interactions of individuals. This is so because people act upon their own definitions of reality *as if* they were fixed and true, not as if they were constructed and negotiable. Phenomenological researchers investigate these meanings that people construct in their personal interactions.

For example, researchers interested in the concept of a "good reader" can explore how meaning differs according to the actors and their social context. What a "good reader" is develops through interaction between teachers and students and varies from classroom to classroom. In Classroom A teachers may believe that being a good reader means being able to sound words out quickly and efficiently. In Classroom B the teacher may believe that being a good reader depends on how much of the text a child comprehends (K. P. Bennett 1986, 1991). A good reader from Classroom A would not necessarily be considered competent in Classroom B, because he or she might not conform to the meanings Teacher B assigns to good reading.

Symbolic Interactionism

Symbolic interactionists (Blumer 1969) link the construction of meaning to the roles that individuals and social structures play in creating meaning. While phenomenologists are concerned with *what* meanings are constructed, symbolic interactionists are concerned with *how* the meanings are made. To this end, they look closely at the processes of human interaction.

Symbolic interactionists state that people communicate meaning by using *symbols*—words, gestures, artifacts, signs, or concepts that stand for something else. Symbols are a shorthand and evoke a good deal more emotion or meaning than the actual object or concept. However, symbols can be confusing because they can have multiple meanings, which can differ from culture to culture, as the box on p. 22 indicates.

Symbolic interaction has introduced the individual into the study of social organization. Clearly, meaning is made by individuals. But society itself also is created by the meanings they make. As Blumer states:

> . . . social organization is a framework inside of which [individuals] develop their actions. Structural features, such as "culture," "social systems," "social stratification," or "social roles" set conditions for their action but do not determine their action. . . . Social organization enters into action only to the extent to which it shapes situations in which people act, and to the extent which it supplies fixed sets of symbols which people use in interpreting their situations. (1969, pp. 189–190)

Thus, unlike functionalists and conflict theorists, symbolic interactionists do not believe that people's actions and identities are dictated solely by their position in the social structure. Rather, what they do, who they are, and what they become are a product of what their past experiences have led them to expect is proper behavior. Personal identity incorporates all the things about them that give them a biological

Multiple Meanings in Symbols

Symbol	Meanings
A wink	—A physical reaction to an itch
	—A sexual invitation
	—An indicator that something stated as true actually is false
The American flag	—A sacred emblem of national honor
	—Fabric with which to make a shirt
	—A mark of oppression
Not looking directly into someone's eyes	—Shyness
	—Respect
	—Evasive or shifty behavior
A red sports car	—Transportation
	—An indication of wealth and status
	—An adventuresome lifestyle

and social uniqueness. People may have multiple identities. To fully understand who they are and how they act, one must piece together their past and current history (Braroe 1975, p. 30). For example, hard-working college students may also be frazzled parents, diligent employees, members of an ethnic group, and lovers of classical or rap music. Each of these identities affects performance in school.

By expressing themselves in particular ways, people can attempt to control the responses of others to them, thereby influencing a definition of the situation to make it favorable to them (Braroe 1975, p. 27). Problems arise when people do not share a common definition of the situation. If they cannot arrive at a consensus on meaning, each may view the behavior of the other as inappropriate, hostile, or even evil. These disagreements in meaning—and the conflicts they create—often characterize events in schools.

Although symbolic interactionists may hold perspectives similar to those of functionalist or conflict theory, they do not explicitly address political issues. Apple describes this stance as follows:

In the United States, England and France, it was argued that the questions most sociologists of education and curriculum researchers asked concealed the fact that assumptions about real relations of power were already embedded in their research models and the approaches from which they drew. As Young put it, sociologists were apt to "take" as their research problems those questions that were generated out of the existing administrative apparatus, rather than "make" them themselves. In curriculum studies, it was claimed that issues of efficiency and increasing meritocratic achievement had almost totally depoliticized the field. Question of "technique" had replaced essential political and ethical issues of what we should teach and why. (1982, p. 16)

Ethnomethodology

Ethnomethodologists are more narrowly concerned with rules by which people order their social interaction and with the way these rules are communicated. Like structuralists, they search for the underlying "patterns for behavior" (Jacob 1987) which give coherence to social behavior. Ethnomethodologists believe that human beings work diligently at making their own activities make sense to others. However, this work is done unconsciously, and its products are taken for granted or go unnoticed by members of society. The leading proponent of ethnomethodology, Harold Garfinkel (1967), in a series of "experiments," explored the content of this work and the rules that govern it. For example, he sent his students home with instructions to act not as children of the household but as tenants or boarders. The surprise, resentment, and open hostility that ensued provided clues as to the unconscious rules that parents and other relatives believe govern the social roles of children.

Ethnomethodologists also study discourse, or conversation, since it is through conversing that people communicate to others their sense of the world. They are particularly concerned with how people "fill in the blanks" in discourse, making inferences about what is unsaid or about unfamiliar people and situations in order to maintain proper interaction (Abercrombie, Hill, and Turner 1984). Problems arise, of course, when the inferences made are incorrect. For example, many Cambodian parents were accused of child abuse when teachers noticed black smudges, like bruises, on the children's bodies. The smudges were, in fact, charcoal marks made during treatment Cambodians use to cure minor illnesses. Among the processes ethnomethodologists have studied in schools are classroom conversations, patterns of turn-taking and participation, and the asymmetries in speech exchange between teachers and students (Atkinson, Delamont, and Hammersley 1988).

How Interpretive Theorists View Schooling

Interpretive theory views schools as places where meaning is constructed through the social interaction of people within the setting. The interpretive approach to the schooling process gained prominence in the early 1970s when Michael F. D. Young in England announced the "new sociology of education," an approach whose key concerns were classroom interaction, utilization of the analytic categories and concepts used by educators themselves, and sociological studies of the curriculum (Young 1971). Questions to be explored in the new sociology of education included the social meaning of various kinds of knowledge, what its possession meant, and how it was distributed.

Interpretive inquiry was stimulated by various studies of reproduction, particularly the work of Bernstein (1977), who was interested in describing exactly how the process of cultural reproduction took place. According to Karabel and Halsey, Bernstein's arrival at the London Institute of Education in 1963 "played a crucial role in stimulating the emergence of a new approach focusing directly on the content of education and the internal operation of schools" (1977, p. 45). It sparked the development of phenomenological studies of schools.

An early example of the use of interpretive approaches is the work of Nell Keddie (1971), who worked with Michael Young at the London Institute of Education in the late 1960s and early 1970s. She explored what teachers know about their students and what they consider suitable knowledge for discussion and evaluation in the classroom. Keddie examined the organization of the curriculum, teacher–student interactions, and the terminology or categories into which educators divided their world. Careful use of observational techniques revealed that meanings constructed by educators resulted in differential treatment of pupils assigned to different ability categories. The teachers, while denying that student ability was associated with social class, suggested in concrete cases an intimate relationship between the social background and ability levels of their students. Thus the categories of meaning (for example, "poor children are poor learners") used by teachers led to tracking of students. When placed in tracks, poor learners use remedial books and receive less instructional time from teachers and more from aides than learners who are defined as more able (K. P. Bennett 1986). Differential treatment of students affects the internal structure of the school by creating a rigidly differentiated curriculum according to the perceived ability of students. Keddie's study further illustrated how this differentiation of curriculum impedes the academic achievement of lower-class students (see also Barr 1982; Page 1987).

The Contribution of Interpretive Approaches

You will recall that conflict theorists also discovered that students from different social classes received different types of schooling. However, conflict theorists looked at the macrosocietal level, using large-scale quantitative data, whereas interpretivists shifted the emphasis to microlevel qualitative analysis of interactions within schools and classrooms. They produced detailed descriptive analyses of these interactions, since they were concerned primarily with demonstrating that qualitative methods would provide "objective" descriptions of classroom processes. Many researchers who define themselves as symbolic interactionists, especially those in America, are careful to maintain this "objectivist" stance.

Interpretive theorists have been criticized for their single-minded focus on microlevel analyses to the exclusion of macrolevel linkages to social, political, and economic constraints—such as discrimination by class, ethnicity, and gender—described by critical and reproduction theorists. They also have been faulted because of alleged subjectivity of their research; critics asserted that interpretivists could not excise their own biases from their observations. However, interpretivists drew their research methods largely from the ethnographic literature of anthropology. They were trained to "bracket" or suspend their own beliefs and biases so as to describe classroom happenings from the point of view of the participants.

Summary

Interpretive theorists such as phenomenologist and symbolic interactionists study social meanings at the microlevel through qualitative or descriptive research methods. They are the precursors to theories of transformation in that they view the participants in their studies as engaged in the process of constructing culture through daily interactions.

SOCIAL TRANSFORMATION THEORIES

In this section we discuss sociological theories based on transformation, rather than transmission, of culture. It is important to remember, however, that these theories have evolved from those we have already discussed. Sociological thought builds upon, rejects, changes, and reformulates what has come before. Thus interpretive and critical theories of education draw upon functional and conflict theory. Unlike transmission theories, interpretive and critical theories are active, rather than passive. Participants engage in the social construction of their own reality, and both emphasize the need for microlevel studies. However, critical theorists go beyond simply exploring the agency of actors as they construct the meanings that structure their lives. Critical theorists focus on the construction of oppression and how individuals can emancipate themselves from it. In so doing, they forge a link between individual acts at the microlevel and social processes at the macrolevel, which the interpretivists fail to consider.

Critical Theory

Central to critical theory is a kind of negative but objective judgment which transcends simple fault-finding. It uncovers hidden assumptions that govern society—especially those about the legitimacy of power relationships—and it debunks or deconstructs their claim to authority (Abercrombie, Hill, and Turner 1984). Critical theory examines the current structure of society, in which dominant socioeconomic groups exploit and oppress subordinate groups. Critical theorists refer to active involvement by participants as *human agency* and believe that despite the influence of oppressive reproductive forces, hope for transformation of society is maintained because of the existence of agency.

Critical theory has its historical roots in a number of theoretical traditions. First, it combines both macro and micro analyses of social phenomena. It uses the analytic basis and many of the concepts of both functionalism and conflict theory. It shares with conflict theory a concern for social and economic inequality and a conviction that inequality is determined by the economic structure, especially the ownership of property. Like conflict theorists, critical theorists believe that inherent in social organizations are *contradictions,* which act as destabilizing agents to force change. Often contradictions can be found between social myths and beliefs and actual social behavior. For example, there is a contradiction between the American belief in equality and the simultaneous promotion of practices that create inequality of various groups. Critical theorists believe that contradictions are points of leverage within oppressive systems. As individuals learn to identify the contradictions that affect their lives, they also can become aware of the forces that oppress them. With growth in awareness, they can begin to transform their lives.

Critical theorists also borrow from symbolic interactionism and phenomenology. They believe that social reality is constructed and operates at multiple levels of meaning. However, they consider knowledge and understanding of meaning to be a source of inequality insofar as they are distributed unequally by race, class, gender, and other ascribed characteristics. Questions that critical theorists ask include the following:

What are the sources of inequality and oppression in society?

How do individuals experience life in social organizations?

How can individuals achieve autonomy in the face of societal oppression?

How are language and communication patterns used to oppress people?

How do people construct positive and negative identities?

Historical Roots of Critical Theory

Social theorists entered into World War I believing that however terrible the conflict might be, it was necessary to clean the slate of social, political, and economic evils. Once the war was over, they believed that the insights and methodological skills of social scientists could be used to create a new millennium. However, by the 1930s the rise of Nazism, the Great Depression, and the demise of the Weimar Republic made it apparent that World War I had not set the stage for Utopian developments. Neither war nor the new natural and social sciences had solved age-old problems, and the world was on the verge of another horrible war. The despair over these conditions destroyed a conviction that the sciences could solve human problems, a conviction that had persisted since eighteenth-century Enlightenment. Scientists were left believing that existing social science theory and methods were faulty and in need of radical critique or wholesale elimination.

Some of the principal critics of contemporary theory are discussed in the following sections. We provide only a brief glimpse at the works of these theorists and how their work has affected educational thought, but we encourage you to explore these works further on your own.

The Frankfurt School.   The Frankfurt School refers to a group of social theorists and philosophers who worked in Germany at the Institute for Social Research (1923–1950), which was connected to the University of Frankfurt. Max Horkheimer was the director of the Institute from 1931 until he retired in 1958. He coined the term "critical theory" to contrast what they were doing with the positivism of Descartes and Saint Simon (Tar 1985). Among the best-known of these theorists were Theodor Adorno, Herbert Marcuse, Erich Fromm, and Walter Benjamin. Members of the Frankfurt School, many of whom were Jewish, relocated the Institute to Columbia University in New York during World War II because of Nazi persecution, returning to Frankfurt in 1949. Its members' participation in American academic life, where they conducted a number of landmark empirical studies of race and prejudice, influenced generations of American scholars. Their critical perspectives are the foundation for critical theorists today.

Much like current work in critical theory, what emerged from their work was no single shared theory, but rather a perspective with several common elements. The analysis of the Frankfurt School was a critique of traditional or bourgeois perspectives, which had assumed that social phenomena could be understood through scientific methods of description, classification, generalization, and quantification. This traditional view, referred to as *positivism*, is patterned after that used in the natural sciences (Phillips 1987; Popper 1968). Knowledge gained by means of this type of research is presented as objective, value-free, and "scientific."

Frankfurt School theorists were critical of the positivistic model on the grounds that human phenomena could not be understood in the same way that physical phenomena could. Whereas positivistic research tends to ignore historical antecedents, critical theorists consider historical analysis central to understanding of social phenomena. The Frankfurt School members believed that neither social phenomena nor research methods—and even the decision to use specific methods—could be separated from their social and historical context. Both were embedded in social values and therefore could not be considered objective but rather were expressive of a particular theoretical or philosophical position. Critical theorists advocate recognition of this subjectivity through a process of self-criticism and self-reflection.

The Frankfurt School was critical of the economic determinism of Marxism because the latter ignored the influence of culture in the perpetuation of inequality and oppression. However, they shared a concern for injustice, oppression, and inequality and looked toward the radical transformation of social arrangements in order to increase human freedom.

Antonio Gramsci.   Gramsci was an Italian Marxist, both a theorist and an activist, who is best known for his *Selections from the Prison Notebooks,* which he wrote during eleven years of imprisonment for political activities during the 1930s, and which was translated into English in 1971. One of his most important contributions was his notion of the individual as an active rather than a passive agent, even in the face of extremely oppressive conditions. Gramsci was particularly concerned with the struggles of the working-class men and women in Italy and the ways in which dominant ideology of the state shapes individual consciousness. He used the term *hegemony* to describe the process by which the worldview of the dominant state maintains control through the socializing activity of institutions. (Recall our discussion of the hegemonic state reproduction model earlier in this chapter.) Gramsci believed that the state had the power to oppress but that individuals are active learners who produce knowledge and culture in their interactions within institutions. Gramsci argued that social change could occur only when revolutionary consensus—for which intellectuals provided a catalyst—was fully achieved among subordinate classes. However, once that occurred, alternative institutions could be created which would change the hegemony of the dominant groups. An example might be a group of female elementary teachers who resist the oppression of a male-dominated administrative structure by working together toward a structure in which they share in the governance of the school.

Jurgen Habermas and Michel Foucault.   Two other theorists who have contributed significantly to contemporary critical theory in education are Jurgen Habermas and Michel Foucault. Both are concerned with the relationship between knowledge and power. These theorists believed that knowledge is as important a social resource as land, money, or legal position. Those who control access to knowledge also control access to the power structure.

Habermas examined how restrictions on the flow of information contribute to inequality in society. He argued that valid knowledge derives only from open, free, and uninterrupted dialogue. Not even science is exempt from this dialogue. Habermas rejected the idea of an authoritative, neutral, apolitical science as well as the possibility of separating facts and values, since each is a product of social and historical context. Foucault also suggested that knowledge or truth is never free from the effects of history, power, and entrenched interests:

> Truth is a thing of this world: it is produced only by virtue of multiple forms of constraint. And it induces regular effects of power. Each society has its regime of truth, its "general politics" of truth: that is, the types of discourse which it accepts and makes function as true; the mechanisms and instances which enable one to distinguish true and false statements, the means by which each is sanctioned; the techniques and procedures accorded value in the acquisition of truth; the status of those who are charged with saying what counts as true. (1980, p. 131)

Paulo Freire.   Freire is a Brazilian educator whose work translates the notions of agency and power into strategies useful for educators. Freire has spent his life working with students and educators to challenge the constraints and inequities of traditional institutions. He draws on the radical "Catholicism of liberation" theology, which emphasizes the role of individuals in understanding and creating their own salvation, free from the mediation or definition of Church authority (Cleary 1985). Liberation theologians taught literacy skills to peasants by having teachers and students engage in dialogue over texts that were meaningful to them in their daily lives. Learning to read and talk about the conditions in which they lived gave peasants the courage to speak up against powerful agencies such as the government, the police, and the Church. Speaking up, in turn, led to efforts to transform their conditions of life.

One of Freire's central beliefs is that teachers must respect the culture of their students by providing opportunities for them to participate in their own learning. Teachers and students also must be self-reflective in discovering the ways in which state hegemony has structured their experiences. Freire views teachers and students as active agents in understanding, criticizing, resisting, and transforming schooling practices that serve to maintain a society that oppresses large groups of people.

Critical Theory in American Educational Thought

Since the 1970s a number of educational theorists have applied critical modes of thinking to issues of race, class, and gender in American education (Anderson, Apple, Aronowitz, Britzman, Fine, Giroux, Gitlin, Lather, McLaren, Tierney). In the pages that follow we discuss the thinking of Michael Apple and Henry Giroux, two of the earliest and most prolific American critical theorists of education. Their work has been stimulated in part by the inadequacy of both reproductionist approaches and interpretive theories to encompass the relationship between schooling and society. Apple and Giroux contend that reproductionist approaches examine only the macro-structural concerns of schools and that interpretive theories are limited to microlevel examinations of interpersonal interactions. Despite the fact that the methods used by interpretive researchers were a real breakthrough in our understanding of *how* educators and students interact to create social reality, they did not ask *why* these interactions proceeded as they did. Apple and Giroux used critical theory to unite the macro and micro approaches into one lens through which to view and understand the schooling process.

Critical Theory and the Function of Schooling

Critical theory assumes that schools are sites where power struggles between dominant and subordinate groups take place. A major theme of this work is an analysis of how schools are used to help dominant groups maintain their position of power, as well as how subordinate groups resist this domination. On the macrostructural level, critical theorists view schools as places where a class-based society is reproduced through the use of the economic, cultural, and hegemonic capital of the dominant social class. Giroux elaborates:

> Reproduction refers here to texts [language and communication patterns] and social practices whose messages, inscribed within specific historical settings and social contexts, function primarily to legitimate the interests of the dominant social order. I want to argue that these can be characterized as texts, as social practices *about* pedagogy, and refer primarily to categories of meaning constructed so as to legitimize and reproduce interests expressed in dominant ideologies. (1983b, p. 157)

Informed by conflict theorists, critical theorists contend that the power of dominant groups is reinforced within schools. By means of academic selection, socioeconomic stratification, and government regulation of curricular and pedagogical modes, dominant, white, male, and middle- or upper-class cultural standards are imposed on children.

Human Agency and the Production of Culture

On the microlevel, critical theorists view schools and classrooms as sites of cultural *production,* where people interact to construct meaning, much like those working from the interpretivist theories. Issues of power and control are worked out in classrooms by individuals. If those involved in the schooling process are able to resist the oppressive practices of schooling, and if critical consciousness can be developed by teachers, administrators, and students, schools can become sites of social change rather than of social reproduction.

The Influence of Critical Theory on Pedagogy

Critical educational theorists are deeply concerned with the art and practice of teaching. They argue that teachers must become "transformative intellectuals" and "critical pedagogues" in order to resist the oppression of the dominant ideology and to produce a liberating culture within schools. In other words, teachers must continue to be active, questioning learners. They must have knowledge as well as critical ability, so they can question not only their own practice but school structure as well. Students also must be taught to become active, critical, and engaged learners in an environment made stimulating. Critical theorists believe that their task is to uncover the ways in which dominant ideology is translated into practice in schools and the ways in which human agency mutes the impact of that ideology.

Critical Theory and the Purposes of Schooling

Critical theorists and reproduction theorists agree that the purpose of schooling is to serve the interests of the dominant classes. However, critical theorists point to a way out, emphasizing the power of individuals to structure their own destiny and to ameliorate the oppressive nature of the institutions in which they live. In many ways, the focus that critical theorists place on the liberating qualities of critical thinking resembles that of John Dewey and other educational philosophers who felt that an educated citizenry would facilitate the preservation of a democratic and egalitarian society. However, critical theorists have been faulted for failing to put their theory into practice. Much of their work consists of theoretical writing, much of it in obscure language unintelligible to the very teachers and students whom they hope to emancipate.

> Imagine a group of teachers who were critical theorists. If they had the freedom to make any changes they wanted in their schools, what do you think they would do? What problems would they encounter and how could these be handled?

Critical Ethnography

We will now consider the research methods in the critical approach to understanding the process of schooling. The guiding concept is "collaboration," which means that these scholars attempt to work with the people being studied to help them achieve release from oppressive conditions, especially in the work place. In this stance, they resemble applied researchers everywhere; their research questions are guided by the interests of the clients rather than by notions of pure science or the interests of the researcher.

Researchers who call themselves critical ethnographers (cf. G. Anderson 1988, K. P. Bennett 1991; Gitlin 1989; LeCompte and McLaughlin 1994; Weiler 1988) approach schools from a critical perspective and also use qualitative research methods much like those used by interpretive researchers. They too draw on the ethnographic methods of anthropology and qualitative sociology, but they differ from interpretive researchers in their concerns and the questions they ask. Unlike interpretivists, who try to enter the field free from preconceived notions of what they will find there, so-called critical ethnographers *assume* and *explicitly state* that schools contain both empowered and disempowered groups of people. Many even advocate abandoning scholarly detachment for active confrontation with oppressive situations and individuals.

These researchers borrow from the **sociology of the curriculum** (discussed in Chapter 6) to explain how power is maintained through control of the flow of information, and how dominant groups use the curriculum, methods of instruction, and modes of evaluation to maintain their power. They also look at the way in which hegemonic state control at the macrolevel and the hidden curriculum at the microlevel serve to maintain social inequalities. Using the methods but not the detached perspectives of ethnography, they study the curriculum in an attempt to determine how hierarchically arranged bodies of knowledge (ability grouping and academic tracks) help stratify children to receive differential learning, marginalizing or disqualifying certain groups (including women, minorities, and members of lower socioeconomic classes) from positions of influence in society. Critical ethnographers study interaction to understand how dominant structures and practices are resisted by subordinate groups. By uncovering some of the ways in which school structures disempower groups, they hope to be able to propose transformative approaches to education.

Examine Table 1.1 to explore how functionalism, conflict theory, interpretivist theory, and critical theory explain students dropping out of school.

Other Social Transformation Theories

We have stressed throughout this chapter the fact that social theories change over time to reflect new ways of thinking and the impact of new information. The first challenge to accepted social science theories that is relevant here is conflict theory. The second challenge, begun in the 1950s, gave rise to the application of phenomenology and critical theory to educational and other issues. Called *post-positivism,* it attacked the notion that scientific knowledge, especially as exemplified in classical physics, chemistry, and mathematics, was the ideal toward which knowledge should strive, and the idea that scientists were infallible "paragons of intellectual virtue and fortitude, worthy of emulation by lesser mortals" (Phillips 1987, p. 17).

TABLE 1.1   Differential Theoretical Approaches to the Same Phenomenon: Dropping Out of School

Functionalism	1. What are the characteristics of the dropout population?
	2. What role do dropouts, as a group, play in the social system of the school?
	3. To what extent does dropping out serve to remove from schools those students for whom formal schooling is inappropriate or wasteful of public resources?
Conflict Theory	1. What are the social class origins of dropouts and at-risk students?
	2. To what extent are disadvantaged students overrepresented among dropouts?
	3. What structural sources of inequality lead to tension between students and teachers?
Interpretivist Theory	1. How do the patterns of interaction between teachers and students lead students to define themselves as failures?
Critical Theory	1. What patterns of resistance do students (and teachers) employ to resist the hegemony of the dominant order in schools?
	2. What processes operate within the school to push students out?

Postpositivists believe that knowledge consists no longer of true statements, but rather of "statements that have been rigorously tested-and-thus-far-not-rejected" (Bredo 1989, p. 4). As a consequence, reality cannot be immutable and fixed. Scientific truth is neither verifiable nor completely falsifiable. It consists of whatever can, for the moment, be subjected to rigorous empirical testing, compared with the results of other tests, and warranted to be the most complete and accurate explanation yet obtained (Dewey 1929; Phillips 1987; Popper 1968).

Because postpositivism questioned the infallibility of scientific inquiry, it facilitated an attack on the capability of scientists to be objective. No longer could scientific inquiry be viewed as "value-free." Researchers began to realize that their own points of view inevitably shaped the direction and results of inquiry. Critical theorists have used this position to question the methods, theories, and interpretations of functionalists. Further, postpositivism helped to legitimate the use of nonexperimental, qualitative, and naturalistic research—the kind carried out in the real world by ethnographers, qualitative sociologists, and symbolic interactionists.

In the middle and late 1980s critical theory came under its own attack by social theorists such as postmodernists, poststructuralists, and feminists (Delamont 1989; Ellsworth 1989; Lather 1986). If postpositivism questioned the hegemony of science and rationality, *postmodernism* questioned not only the authority of traditional science, but the legitimacy of any authoritative standard or canon—whether it be in art, music, literature, science, or philosophy. *Poststructuralism* is a corollary of postmodernism; it attacks the assumption that societies are made coherent by underlying forms and structures, which it views as a form of authority. What poststructuralists object to is the notion that any fixed, nonnegotiable, ahistorical forms determine the structure of social life.

Postmodernism holds that dominant groups have controlled not only access to knowledge, but the standards of which knowledge is valuable and legitimate. Since it is Western European males that have been dominant, all art, music, science, philosophy, and social life have been governed by their standards. Only when the standards of other groups are equally powerful will the kind of free dialogue—and the valid knowledge—Habermas called for be possible.

While these approaches differ in their emphases and are as varied as the researchers who espouse them, they all draw on the analytic constructs of earlier functionalist and conflict approaches, as well as the postpositivists' attack on "hard science." They also, like interpretive theorists, accept the premise that reality is constructed of the sum of the realities of individuals interacting in any given setting. These approaches place great importance on presentation of the "multiple voices" (Geertz 1988, 1989) of all participants—especially less powerful participants such as women, members of minority groups, and students.

These critics of critical theory share a belief that it has merely substituted another form of hegemonic domination—that of the working class—for the elitism of traditional capitalists or bureaucrats. Because critical theorists have been concerned primarily with oppression of the working classes, and because their models are based upon analyses in Western European societies, critical theorists are, consciously or not, biased toward a working-class European perspective. Included in this perspective are patriarchal, male-dominated aesthetic values and social organization as well as individualistic, rather than collective, forms of human liberation. Critics of critical theory believe that models of resistance to oppression that are appropriate for working- and middle-class males of European descent may be inappropriate for non-European, non-working-class, and non-male individuals.

Perhaps most important, critical theory presents an oversimplified view of asymmetrical power relationships. Critical theorists assume that the end result of resistance, confrontation, and open dialogue will be some kind of consensus. However, they have made no systematic examination of the barriers unequal power relations create to the kind of expression and dialogue they advocate. "Critical educators have defined 'student voices' in terms of . . . being different from but not necessarily opposed to the voice(s) of the teacher or other students" (Ellsworth 1989, p. 7). However, especially in matters of cultural difference, matters of truth, and questions of who is entitled to receive privileges, consensus may be impossible to achieve. Further, the emancipation advocated by critical theorists is predicated upon Western and European notions of power and group relations. Imposing this view on people who are not part of that tradition is no less authoritarian, say the critics, than other kinds of oppression (Burtonwood 1986; Ellsworth 1989; LeCompte and Bennett 1992).

Table 1.2 presents a summary of the main concepts and questions addressed by the principal sociological theories discussed in this chapter.

In this chapter we examined functionalism, conflict theory, interpretive theory, and critical theory as they relate to schooling. Choose two of these theories to compare and contrast. Which theory most closely resembles the way in which you view the schooling process? Explain.

TABLE 1.2 Sociological Theories at a Glance

	Functionalism	Conflict Theory	Interpretive Theory	Critical Theory
Focus	Analysis of social and cultural systems with an emphasis on how order and equilibrium are maintained. Goal is to identify social system components and to describe how systems work with an emphasis on how order and equilibrium are maintained and transmitted.	Expansion of functionalism with an emphasis on conflict and change rather than order and maintenance. Goal is to arrive at a more realistic portrayal of social reality, one that includes an explanation of change, social disruption, and conflict.	Analysis of the constructed nature of social meaning and reality. Goal is to understand how people construct meanings.	Individual response to social, political, and economic oppression; inadequacy of current social theory to improve human condition. Goal is to unmask sources of oppression, to promote understanding of causes and consequences of oppression, and to encourage participation in liberation.

Assumptions			
1. All social systems are composed of identifiable and interconnected structures and institutions. 2. Each social system, through its structures and institutions, must carry out certain functions to survive. 3. Each component contributes to the overall health and order of the system. 4. Equilibrium is viewed as normal; disorder and conflict are viewed as pathological.	1. All social systems are composed of identifiable and interconnected structures. 2. Economic organization, especially the ownership of property, determines the organization of the rest of society. 3. While the basic categories and analysis of functionalism are accepted, traditional functionalism fails to explain the dynamism of social systems. 4. Inherent in social organizations are contradictions which cause their opposite—conflict is inherent. 5. Conflict and change are normal forces within social systems and contribute to their health and adaptation.	1. Meaning is constructed through social interaction. 2. Individuals act on the basis of meanings they perceive. 3. Meanings change in the course of interaction because of different perceptions held by the actors. 4. Thus reality is not a prior given; it is based upon interpretations and it is constructed during interaction between and among individual actors. 5. Reality is not fixed but changes according to the actors and the context.	1. Analytic basis of functionalism and conflict theory as well as methods of interpretive theory are used. 2. However, conventional social theory is a bankrupt construction of ruling elites whose purpose is to perpetuate patterns of oppression in society. 3. Humans are oppressed because power is hidden or disguised in language practices, communication patterns, and information flow defined and dominated by ruling elites. 4. Social life operates at multiple levels of meaning; knowledge and understanding of meaning are stratified and differentially distributed.

TABLE 1.2 *(continued)*

	Functionalism	Conflict Theory	Interpretive Theory	Critical Theory
Assumptions *(continued)*		6. Inequality of resource distribution is the major source of contradiction and hence conflict in society. 7. Conflict is manifested in bipolar opposition and is designed to resolve dualisms. 8. Conflict is dialectical; it creates new sets of opposing interests to resolve.		5. People are essentially unfree, inhabiting a world filled with contradictions and asymmetrical patterns of power and privilege.
Major Concepts	System, functions, goals, latent and manifest functions, adaptation, integration, institution and structure, norms, values, cultural rules, social equilibrium, and order.	The same concepts as in functionalism, plus others including legitimacy, consciousness, domination, coercion, subjugation, contradiction, dialectic, correspondence, ideology, strain, deviance, change, and adaptation.	Self, self-concept, mind, symbols, meaning, interaction, role, actor, role taking, role expectations, construction of reality, discourse, scripts, texts, communication.	Resistance, human agency, oppression, hegemony, domination, subordination, subjectivity, political economy, consciousness (false and true), stratification of power by race, social class and gender, ableness, sexual orientation, deconstruction.
Levels of Analysis	Macrolevel (groups, collectivities and their relationships—structural rather than individual level)	Macrolevel	Microlevel (individuals in interactions with others)	Macro and microlevels (integration of individual interaction with macrolevel social analysis). Meaning in interactions and texts.

Major Questions and Topics for Investigation	1. What categories organize the social world? 2. What structures and institutions constitute a given social system? 3. How are they interrelated? 4. How do they work to maintain order?	1. What are the causes and consequences of conflict in social systems? 2. How do conflicting groups organize and mobilize? 3. Where does power reside and how is it exercised? 4. What are the sources of societal inequality? 5. How do social systems transform themselves?	1. What meanings—both overt and covert—do humans attach to behavior patterns and objects in their world? 2. How do varying interpretations of meaning, expectations, and motivations affect human behavior? 3. How does the process of constructing meaning take place? 4. What symbols and rituals do humans create to structure their interactions?	1. What are the sources of inequality and oppression in society? 2. What is the experience of individuals within social organizations? 3. To what degree and how can humans achieve autonomy in the context of societal oppression? 4. How are research and oppression linked? 5. What patterns of language use, communication, and interaction do people use to oppress one another? 6. How are positive and negative meanings and identities constructed?
Critique	Too static: focuses on order maintenance that justifies the status quo; conflict and change come to be regarded as aberrations. There is some question whether there is consensus in society and whether the transmission of core values is based on a consensus model.	Does not define what constitutes conflict. Cannot resolve the question of order—how a society constantly in conflict can create order and stability.	Remains at microlevel; seeks no connections to determinants in external, social structural variables.	Lack of objectivity and neutrality in favor of stance of advocacy for the oppressed.

TABLE 1.2 *(continued)*

	Functionalism	Conflict Theory	Interpretive Theory	Critical Theory
Contributors	T. Parsons, C. Levi-Strauss, A. R. Radcliffe-Browne, B. Malinowski, R. Merton, E. Shils, E. Durkheim.	K. Marx, G. Simmel, R. Dahrendorf, L. Coser.	H. Blumer, G. H. Mead, R. Park, C. Cooley, R. Turner, E. Goffman, M. Kuhn, H. Garfinkel, A. Cicourel, H. Becker, J. Dewey.	T. Adorno, M. Horkheimer, H. Marcuse, H. Gadamer, M. Foucault, J. Habermas (In education: H. Giroux, M. Apple, P. Freire, M. Fine, L. Weis, P. Wexler, P. McLaren, J. Dewey, I. Illich).

SUMMARY

In this chapter we have tried to give some idea of how the theories that underlie social science thinking affect our beliefs about the purposes and operation of schools. The remaining chapters will discuss schools, their organization, participants, and purposes, using the language of sociologists. In some cases, we will first present perspectives that appear rather traditionally functionalist in their orientation. This is done because we feel that the earlier works established the foundations and developed the vocabulary for later analyses. Each chapter ends, however, with the critical analysis that is closer to our own thinking. As you read, consider how you, or other social theorists, might explain or interpret what is being presented.

chapter **2**

The Social Organization of Schooling

INTRODUCTION

In Chapter 1, we presented the theoretical basis for a sociological analysis of schooling. In this chapter we present the organizational basis. We begin by describing the internal organization of schools as they currently exist in most school systems, as well as the many different groups that participate in the schooling process. As you read this material, you may find yourself thinking, "Yes, but I know schools that aren't so rigidly structured." We recognize there are schools today using less hierarchical organizations, alternatives to age-grading, and more developmentally appropriate curricula, particularly with current restructuring efforts. We hope you are fortunate enough to be working in such a setting. However, we want you to consider traditional school organizations first, as a backdrop to later discussions on restructuring and alternatives. On the microlevel we describe the degree of influence of various participants at different positions within the organizational structure. We also present a descriptive and historical analysis of how school systems came to be organized as they are in the United States. This background will set the stage for a later examination of the impact of schools on society. Finally, we discuss recent efforts to change or "restructure" the organization of schools.

First we use a rather traditional analysis, describing school organization in terms of their functions and structures that carry these out. We then look more critically at how the structure of schools has changed in response to conflicts among various community constituencies whose interests should be served by the public schools. We have used the work of critical, or revisionist, historians because, like critical theorists in sociology, they question the validity of traditional interpretations of past events, asking in particular how these interpretations help to perpetuate cultural myths such as the belief that schools can eliminate poverty and promote equality and mobility. Among the themes we discuss are how business and industrial ideologies have affected the schools, the degree to which schools are pressured to serve economic, social, and political goals rather than intellectual or cognitive goals, and how school organization facilitates resistance to changes not congenial to dominant groups in the system or society.

THE INTERNAL ORGANIZATION OF SCHOOL DISTRICTS

Examining the actual structure of schools in an unbiased fashion is very difficult because both you, the readers, and we, the authors, have already spent most of our lives going to school. We are far too familiar with them to be objective! To facilitate the task, we use a device often employed by anthropologists—"making what is familiar strange" (Geertz 1973)—that is, treating something we know very well as if we had never seen it before.

Imagine that scientists from another planet—Mars, for example—have been sent to study the social institutions of Earthlings. Not knowing the language, they begin by describing the things they *see,* knowing that the physical setting of a social system often determines the behavior and attitudes of the people who live in it. They would probably use some Martian form of structural functional categories to organize their description.

The alien scientists would first be struck by the sheer size of the educational enterprise. They would note that school buildings are among the largest edifices in most communities, housing at least 250–300 people, except in the very smallest communities. From this they would infer that whatever happens in these buildings must be of great importance to the communities that support them, since so many resources are devoted to them. In fact, in many communities the educational system is the biggest industry, and the largest employer.

Differentiation as an Organizing Principle in Schools

During their first day of field work the aliens would note that everything in the school buildings is *differentiated,* or divided into clearly defined chunks or categories. Every chunk of space or time, every type of person, task, reward, or training, has a distinct function. The setting seems to abhor ambiguity, and where it exists, as in open-space classrooms, people try to impose a framework. From the clearly framed (Bernstein 1970) social and physical environment, the Martians infer that there are strict rules governing the use of such a place and the activities that can and cannot take place in its various sectors.

Differentiation of Space

Analysis of the use of space indicates that work predominates in schools and that teachers control and direct it. Work space for children is subdivided into two types: classrooms for academic work, and workshops and laboratories for vocational and other subjects that need to be taught but that require more equipment than books, papers, and audiovisual materials. It is clear from the predominance of classrooms over other kinds of work space that whoever runs the schools gives primary importance to book learning. A look inside the classrooms also verifies the existence of hierarchical authority relationships. Although desks and chairs may be moved around from time to time, the children usually face front toward the teacher, who is in charge. Although each school has some sort of recreational space or playground for the children, purely recreational activities, for both teachers and students, are not given high priority and are often preempted for other activities. Playgrounds become parking lots, and teachers' lounges become offices when space is tight.

Martian social scientists might have trouble classifying the large amount of space devoted to athletic fields and gymnasia, especially in schools for older children. Later analysis would confirm that these reflect cultural preferences for community entertainment. High school athletics are a major source of civic pride in many communities, especially in suburbs and smaller towns. The games are widely attended and well supported by local businesses and other sponsors. Schools are pivotal community organizations in other ways. Often the school auditorium or gymnasium is the only space in the community adequate for concerts, plays, and other cultural events. Rooms in the school are used for public meetings and by civic organizations. At every election the voting booths are located in the school's lobby, halls, or cafeteria.

Schools also contain service spaces that are used by both children and adults. These include assembly halls, a lunchroom (often these are combined and include a stage for various presentations), parking lots, and the nurse's office. Other spaces are presided over by adults for service to children, such as counseling and testing rooms, the cafeteria kitchen, the boiler room, and the maintenance shop. Still others, like lounges and bathrooms, are segregated, not only by gender but by age and status— one for adults and one for children.

The location of administrative spaces or offices reinforces the authority hierarchy noticed in the classroom. Visitors must locate them to obtain permission to be in the school, even if these offices are not located near the entryway of the building. Sometimes the offices are difficult to find. They may be located far from where visitors are allowed to park. Front doors may be locked, and imposing entryways make many schools seem forbidding. The Martian scientists note that this geographical arrangement helps control what goes on in the school and is often used to keep out people whom educators view as hostile.

Differentiation of Time

The alien scientists then make a key observation about the episodic nature of activity in schools: time is segmented and encapsulated; no activity lasts longer than approximately 50 minutes. Of that, a good portion is devoted to organizing the beginning and ending of activities (LeCompte 1974, 1978b, 1981). Use of the buildings is governed by bells or buzzers. Bells ring at regular intervals throughout the day, and in response people move from room to room and from activity to activity. To control the movement of children, they line up by gender and size under the watchful eyes of an adult. The early morning is a very busy period as hordes of children and adults arrive. In general, adults can enter the building any time, but children must wait for the buzzer and can leave only with permission. This process is more or less repeated in midafternoon. Although some people stay later to participate in after-school activities or projects, most children and many adults are gone within 15 minutes after the closing bell.

Differentiation of People

Following observations of the physical and temporal layout of the school, the Martians would begin to examine the differences among human inhabitants. In Chapter 3 we will discuss in detail the characteristics of student participants in schooling. Our purpose here is to analyze the structural differences between the way children and adults participate in the educational process. The Martian scientists interpret phenomena as these odd humans do, that is, they use human canons for distinction rather than Martian ones. They initially note that people in schools are differentiated by age, training, ability, and their purpose for being there. Only later do they begin to notice more subtle forms of differentiation and segregation by gender, ethnicity, and social class.

The anthropological "making things strange" means being careful not to take for granted the simplest and most obvious things. As we continue to use a Martian perspective to "make school strange," we have the aliens carefully document that students and other people in schools differ most obviously by age. Students are younger than teachers and staff. Age alone, rather than intellectual ability, determines when children enter school and at what grade level. Children are divided into classes or grade levels by date of birth. This is done for administrative convenience in processing the masses of people involved, but it creates many problems for instruction, because intellectual development and chronological age may be only vaguely related in some children.

A second and less obvious pattern of differentiation is that children are grouped by ability. Whereas the admission-by-age criterion reduces differences among children, ability grouping amplifies them (Dreeben 1968). In some ways this grouping permits school staff to overcome the instructional heterogeneity imposed by age-grading. As we shall see, however, ability grouping creates semipermanent cliques of differing social status and self-esteem, which often predict the occupational and social chances of their members (K. P. Bennett 1986, 1991; Eisenhart and Borko 1983; Powell, Farrar, and Cohen 1985).

Both children and teachers are differentiated by gender. Certain activities are designated only for girls, others for boys. Some activities, such as physical education, are not only differentiated by type, but segregated, so that the two sexes do not engage in the activities together. Some activities, such as teaching math and science, coaching football, and being an administrator, are more likely to be done by male than female staff members. The Martians also notice some differentiation of activities by ethnicity or race. Asians are concentrated in high-level academic courses but not in sports. African-American students are overrepresented in remedial, special education, and vocational classes; they also predominate on the football, basketball, and track teams, but not in golf, swimming, or tennis (see Chapter 7).

We will address these kinds of differentiation in later chapters, but they are important to note here as components of the organization of schools. The organization of instruction and the availability of subjects is predicated largely upon characteristics of the student population (Oakes 1985). Minority-dominated schools often provide fewer advanced courses and offer fewer electives. They are often more oriented to vocational training than schools whose students are expected to attend college. Teachers in these schools may complain that they have to teach many sections of remedial classes rather than advanced courses in their area of specialization. In addition, such schools often provide more support services and feel the need for ancillary staff such as security officers.

Differentiation by Employment

Adult participants in school are differentiated by the type of training they have received and whether or not they are paid for their work. The Martians notice that women teachers are more prevalent than men in all schools, especially those where younger students are housed. However, males outnumber females in administrative positions. Some of the adults work part-time; these include consultants and teachers who "float" among several schools teaching music, art, and physical education. Special services instructors, such as those who help disabled students or students with limited proficiency in English, often serve several schools because individual schools are unable to support a full-time employee in those fields. The marginal presence of these staff members means that what they do has little impact upon the day-to-day operation of the school. Their influence often wanes as soon as they are out of sight. There are also adults in schools who are not paid for their work; these include volunteers, parents, observers, and student-teachers.

In Chapter 4 we discuss in more detail the characteristics of adults who make up the work force in schools. Here we are only noting how children are distinguished from adult participants in schools: in the way they enter or are recruited to schools, in the rewards they hope to reap, in their training, and in the ancillary organizations that support their participation.

Differentiation in Recruitment

Perhaps the biggest difference between children and other participants in schools is how they enter or are recruited. Our alien social scientists observe that children come to school because they have to. Every child, regardless of his or her mental or physical condition, must attend some sort of school from approximately age 6 to age 16. Everybody else comes voluntarily—with the exception of parents, who come because their children must do so—either because they have a job there or because they have some special interest in education (Bidwell 1965; Nadel 1957).

Differentiation in Rewards

Because people come to school for different reasons, they expect different rewards. Children are somewhat short-changed in the immediate rewards category. The best they can hope for is a stimulating environment that is socially comfortable and intellectually challenging. Many teachers work hard to provide an environment that is intellectually rich, fun, and emotionally supportive. However, most teachers are severely constrained by the structures of time, organization, and governance already described. School staff try to reinforce the idea that learning is intrinsically worthwhile and that the payoff has substantial material value. They do so primarily by dispensing symbols—grades, gold stars, praise and awards, and eligibility for extracurricular activities. As Chapter 3 will show, not all students find these symbols intrinsically or extrinsically rewarding. Some students see little connection between their school experiences and their daily lives outside school. They cannot envision how what they do in school will result in economic rewards in the workplace.

Think back to your own experiences in elementary and high school. What were your rewards for participating in classes?

Staff members, on the other hand, not only garner immediate extrinsic rewards in the form of regular paychecks and long vacations, they may also reap the intrinsic rewards inherent in doing a job they have chosen, in working with children, in associating with professional colleagues, and in performing a task they deem necessary and socially useful. These rewards may pale, however, when working conditions grow difficult and inhibit opportunities for teachers to use their knowledge, skills, and talents (see Chapter 4).

Differentiation in Training

Children are grouped by ability in schools, but adults are grouped by the length and type of their training. Children are not specifically trained for the student role when they enter school; they are, in fact, there because they are deemed to be *in need* of

---

**Summary of the Criteria
for Differentiating People in School Settings**

Age
Gender
Social Class
Race/Ethnicity
Intellectual Abilities
Physical Abilities (or Disabilities)
Education/Training/Certification
Full-Time Work/Part-Time Work/Volunteer Work

---

training. On the other hand, professional staff such as teachers, administrators, and counselors have already undergone the rather lengthy training that gives them claim to expertise and to a certain degree of autonomy vis-à-vis students. Their training and subsequent experience lead them to feel that other adults—even parents of their students—have little competence in instructional or administrative practices. This feeling can create tension and sometimes hostility between school professionals and members of the outside community. Service personnel such as custodians, secretaries, and clerks also have some degree of training, but it is not specific to schools. Unlike the training of teachers, their training equips them for similar jobs in many kinds of organizations.

THE GEOGRAPHY OF CONTROL

Having established the organizing principles that humans use to differentiate events and occupants of schools, the aliens would next examine the impact of spatial arrangements on how people work in schools.

Spatial Decentralization

First they note that schools seem to come in two basic architectural types—multistory, rectangular brick buildings or sprawling campuses with many detached or semidetached buildings. Despite external variations, they possess remarkable similarities inside, resembling motels, with long strings of equal-size rooms placed on either side of long corridors, each room capable of accommodating approximately 30–40 children and an adult. The rooms are categorized according to the kind of tasks carried out in them: *work* and *recreational* spaces for children, and *administrative* and *service* spaces for adults.

Administrative space is typically arranged in clusters around a larger central waiting area. The aliens notice that architecture often follows cultural fads. Consequently, they make note of some exceptions to the motel-like construction of schools. For example, some of the buildings contain open space loosely divided by bookshelves. In most cases, however, this arrangement seems to be a vestige of the past, since temporary and semipermanent walls have appeared to redivide much of the space into more conventional arrangements.

They also notice that in most communities the school systems are geographically decentralized. Schools and central administrative headquarters are usually dispersed throughout the community, so communication from building to building or from one part of a particular campus to another takes some time, even with telephones and other communications systems to facilitate the process. The physical decentralization of school systems leads to structural looseness, or what many social scientists have called *loose coupling* (Bidwell 1965; Metz 1978; Weick 1976). We will leave our alien social scientists at this point since they have served their function to help us "make the familiar strange," and we will move on to explore this notion of loose coupling.

Loose Coupling and Its Impact on Control

Loose coupling refers to the fact that direct supervision and control are difficult in school systems. Both the geographic dispersion of supervisory staff and the "autonomy of the closed door" (Lortie 1969) contribute to loose coupling. In contrast to other types of organizations, such as factories, hospitals, and prisons, school supervisors cannot directly monitor teachers because they work in the privacy of their classrooms. Principals and their assistants cannot be in every classroom each day and may show up only once a year for mandatory evaluations. Similarly, central administrators do not usually visit each school building daily; in large school systems they may visit a particular school only once a year.

The motel-like configuration of most schools tends to isolate teachers both socially and professionally. Dispersion and closed doors affect the camaraderie of teachers. Departmental meetings are infrequent and devoted to business, so teachers may interact only with the staff members whose classrooms are across the hall and on either side of their own. In general, teachers spend most of the day in their own separate classrooms. They cannot leave their students unsupervised and have little free time to talk to each other. Elementary school teachers must often supervise students during lunch hour and before school. If breaks or planning periods are provided, they are devoted to lesson-planning rather than to developing solidarity with other teachers.

Loose Coupling and Teacher Autonomy

Although the isolation of teachers inhibits interaction, some researchers feel it helps teachers maintain a semblance of professional autonomy because it inhibits monitoring by administrators (Lortie 1969). On one hand, teachers may use the "autonomy of the closed door" to engage in innovative practices not approved of by their supervisors and colleagues. On the other, unmonitored teachers can avoid conforming to administrative dictates regarding even salutary innovation and remain traditional.

Although loose coupling does make the control of teachers more difficult, there are still indirect ways in which teachers are limited in their autonomy. For example, some states require a certain number of evaluations each year, sometimes unannounced. Thus teachers know that a supervisor can walk in at any time. In some such schools teachers develop an efficient grapevine so the evaluator's arrival is usually made known by the time his or her car key is removed from the ignition.

Another example of this indirect control is the heavy emphasis put on state-mandated proficiency tests for students. Teachers' autonomy is restricted by administrative pressure to prepare the children for these tests, and by the use of students' test scores to evaluate individual teachers' abilities.

DIRECT AND INDIRECT INFLUENCES ON DECISION MAKING

Perhaps the most incomprehensible aspect of American schooling is the ambiguity in patterns of control and decision making. The American educational system operates within a system of direct and indirect controls. The direct controls tend to operate at the local level, but as one moves farther from the home community, controls tend to be regulatory and indirect, consisting of guidelines and "strings" attached to funds beyond those raised locally. Functionalists view the support and concomitant control of nonlocal agencies as simply part of the system. Critical theorists, in contrast, believe that school systems are oppressive to the extent that local individuals are unable to determine their own destiny; hence they view the influence of state and national agencies, whether private or governmental, as evidence of further penetration into schools of the hegemony of dominant groups.

Indirect control also consists of the pressures deriving from a matrix of competing constituencies, all with a legitimate interest in what goes on in schools. Some, like school boards, superintendents' offices, and building-level administrators, are charged with the day-to-day governance of the system. Others, like local, state, and national governmental agencies and national accrediting associations, exercise regulatory and watchdog power. Still others, like parent groups, teachers' unions and other professional associations, youth organizations such as Scouts, and social service agencies, have an interest in the welfare of the adults and children who participate in school activities. More distantly related are community organizations such as churches, local employers, taxpayer organizations, cultural associations, political interest groups, and the media. While these organizations can attract a great deal of attention, they serve primarily as lobbies; they cannot regulate school activities directly. Who, then, does establish policies for and regulate the schools? We will begin with an examination of control at the local level, including the school board and the superintendency, and then will discuss how state and national interests influence local activities.

The School Board and the Superintendent

At one level, school districts are run by officials elected by the community. They establish overall policy, prepare and/or ratify the budget, approve curricular and instructional directions, and oversee the hiring of personnel. Although school boards represent the community and set educational policy, the real power at the local level generally rests with the professional chief administrator, or superintendent, whom the board hires. Superintendents are hired generally because they represent a particular educational philosophy or have a track record that appeals to the board. They are supported by professional staff, usually located in the central office.

The philosophy of school boards tends to reflect prevailing business ideology. Business and professional people dominate school boards, constituting more than three-fifths of the members nationally. Homemakers, usually middle- and upper-class wives of professionals, account for 7.2 percent, while skilled and unskilled workers account for 9.4 percent. Boards in larger cities and appointed boards tend to have an even larger proportion of business and professional members (Fantini 1975). In 1987 women made up 26.5 percent and African Americans 2.4 percent of the elected school officials in the country (Cull 1989).

Board members tend to be more fiscally conservative than their superintendents, but they are more open to change in other respects than the people who elected them. Many also tend to view election to the school board as a springboard to a further political career (Cull 1989). However, most board members lack expertise on educational issues. As old board members socialize new ones, the board becomes allied with the superintendent and dependent upon his or her expert knowledge. The role of the board often becomes one of legitimizing the actions of the superintendent to the community (Kerr 1973). However, we need to look at the community context in order to understand how specific boards interact with superintendents. For example, there have been boards that took a strong position on a school policy or practice, even removing superintendents whose philosophies differed from theirs.

The whims of school board decision making are limited, however, by state and national dictates regarding curricula, aid for special categories of children, and requirements for graduation and testing. Ties to local interests can create conflict with state and federal authorities. In recent years some districts have ended up in litigation because the actions of their school board violated the U.S. Constitution in regard to separation of church and state and equal protection of all citizens.

Attend a school board meeting. Find out about the background of the members. Notice the interactions in the meeting. Who speaks, who introduces new measures, and which positions do members take on different issues? What special-interest groups are in attendance? What role does the superintendent play? What types of actions are on the agenda? Who determined the agenda?

Limitations on the Power of the Superintendent

Although superintendents in large districts find it easier to maintain administrative independence than those in small districts, their actions are still somewhat limited. First, superintendents do not have absolute control over the ideological direction of education—that responsibility resides with the school board. However, since superintendents are appointed by the board, they often share educational philosophies.

Second, regardless of the size of the district, superintendents must maintain the support of the school board, as the story of Goose Pond Alternative School (recounted later in this chapter) illustrates. Much depends upon the political ability of a superintendent to maintain a consensus regarding policies he or she deems most important. Longevity in office depends partly upon the superintendents' ability to manipulate the flow of information to school board members so as to justify expenditures and either yield acceptable test scores or convince the board that academic progress is being made (Fantini, Gittell, and Magat 1974). Since priority is placed upon achieving consensus before matters are officially considered by the board, open board meetings often seem desultory at best (Kerr 1973).

Third, decisions are constrained also because they are not made in the same way as they are in business and industry. Major decisions are not made on a day-to-day basis. Many, like textbook and budget adoptions and curriculum changes, occur once a year or biennially.

Fourth, lines of control in school districts, even within the superintendent's office, are blurred by distinctions between *line* and *staff* areas of responsibility. Line and staff offices create separate hierarchies, each reports to the superintendent, but they are not accountable to each other. **Line offices** are the positions in an organization located in the vertical supervisory structure. People in lower-line offices report to and are supervised by those directly above them, who in turn report to and are supervised by those above them. These workers carry out the actual tasks for which the organization exists. In school districts, line offices are held by teachers, principals, assistant superintendents, and superintendents.

Staff offices occupy horizontal positions in the reporting structure responsible for tasks which are ancillary or consultative to the overall work of the organization. Counselors, secretaries, curriculum staff, and media specialists are examples of staff members in schools. Many staff offices are concerned with curriculum and instruction. They provide advisory assistance and monitoring to school-level personnel. They are responsible for developing curricula and providing staff development and training in the various subject areas as well as in specialized areas such as education for children who are handicapped or who do not speak adequate English. Lacking line authority, these offices can provide advice, develop materials, and train teachers but they cannot supervise or enforce the use of their products.

The offices responsible for vocational, gifted, remedial, alternative, and handicapped programs also may blur the lines of administrative control. While these offices may have staff functions, they also run programs. Some almost constitute districts-within-the-district, in that they often have responsibility for their own special schools, including hiring of teachers and administration of budgets.

Voluntary Organizations

A major source of pressure on school personnel comes from voluntary organizations whose members have an interest in the school but are not directly affiliated with it. They have power over schools as voters and as potential candidates for school board positions. In addition, they can petition the school board, appear at public meetings, and campaign for the support of their agenda. These groups include unions, parents, taxpayer coalitions, ideological "watchdog" groups who monitor the curriculum, and groups that pressure the schools to add or delete a variety of subject areas, including drug and sex education and school prayer. The activities of these groups are episodic, usually generated in reaction to some event. Because they can be unpredictable, these groups are most problematic for school systems. They often represent conservative special interests critical of what educators view as good innovative professional practice. Although school administrators circumvent them by following safe political policies, these groups can act as a strong deterrent to bold innovation and reform.

Teachers' Unions and Professional Organizations.   The tension over whether teachers are workers or professionals with control over their work is echoed in arguments over status discrepancies: Should teachers be represented by professional associations or by unions? (See Chapter 4.) Here we will examine the origin of teacher efforts to act collectively and their impact upon control of schools. One faction of the educational profession—one that emphasizes the white-collar, professional nature of its work—has consistently pressed for an umbrella professional organization serving groups as disparate as classroom teachers, administrators, and college professors. The result, as we shall see, is not one big happy family, but a collection of warlike tribes who fail to further the interests of any of the participants. Another faction—this one conceptualizing the teacher–administrator relationship as one of management and labor—advocates *teachers' unions.* Teachers' unions have suffered identity problems because although their members are not blue-collar workers, the orientation of the organization, like that of steelworker and truck driver unions, is adversarial.

While teachers' unions have not generally wielded substantial power, their existence does serve as a check on excessive administrative use of power. Two watershed events, both in New York City, changed the pattern of relationships between unions and school managers. The first was the 1962 strike of the United Federation of Teachers (UFT), the largest teachers' local. It not only won raises for teachers, but kept the district from retaliating against those participating in the strike. The second was the Ocean-Hill-Brownsville strike in 1968, when an alliance of the UFT and the very conservative school administrators of the Council of Supervisory Associations fought off attempts to give control over hiring and firing of teachers to decentralized local school boards (Scimecca 1980).

Since these events, there is evidence that teacher militancy has initiated some important changes in patterns of control and power in education. While these changes are not universal, and their full effect is still unknown, they point the way to future shifts in the governance of education. First, the militancy of teachers' unions has tended to radicalize the National Education Association (NEA) and other more conservative organizations. Second, it has reduced the arbitrary decision-making power of school boards and administrators with regard to teachers. Third, it has made clearer the dichotomy between teachers' and administrators' interests. Fourth, it has greatly reduced the power of building-level principals. Because teachers can use their union representatives to negotiate directly with higher district officials, the principal can be circumvented (Scimecca 1980). Finally, because the teachers' unions have affiliation with national organizations, the growth in militancy may produce a more cosmopolitan outlook among teachers. It shifts teacher concerns from purely local problems and local solutions to state and national arenas (Brookover and Erickson 1975).

Invite a representative from your local teachers' association to speak to your class about the roles unions have played in the teaching profession. In preparation for this visit, develop a list of questions you would like this person to address.

Community Groups.   There are other adults in the community who may claim expertise in the field of education on the basis of special knowledge. Parents may claim expertise in children. Taxpayers may claim financial knowledge. Athletic boosters may claim knowledge of the sports programs. Consultants, textbook vendors, lobbyists, and special-interest groups such as churches and political parties may claim expertise in curricular materials and current issues. Businesspeople and local employers may claim expertise in vocational training.

At the local level, anything having to do with sexual behavior, religion, or finance can stimulate citizen protest. Groups might protest sex education classes, day-care programs for children of students, controversial books, tax increases, or school bond issues. These and many other issues pit school people against segments in the community and threaten school personnel control over educational matters. However, despite the energy of their involvement in schools, none of these groups is trained specifically for such a role in the educational enterprise. Unlike parents, they do not have an automatic and compelling voice in school operations, but they do represent the multiple constituencies whose interests penetrate the school.

Parent Groups.   The outsiders who do have a legitimate interest in the schools are the parents of the students. First of all, their activities can make a big difference in teachers' workload. Parents serve as volunteer aides, class parents, and librarians, provide transportation for field trips, sponsor extracurricular activities, and raise money for computers and other materials not provided by the budget.

Second, teachers, administrators, and researchers believe strongly that parent activity enhances pupil achievement. In Houston, schools where students had the highest achievement scores had five times as many parent volunteers as those with the lowest achievement (Tedford 1988). A strong correlation has been demonstrated between children's reading scores and whether or not their parents read stories to them (Boehnlein 1985). The War on Poverty of the 1960s and 1970s heavily stressed teaching parents how to help their children study. Further, success of the educational reform movement of the 1980s is believed to rest upon involving parents in their children's schooling.

However, the involvement of parents and other nonprofessionals is viewed with ambivalence by teachers and principals. They are truly comfortable only with volunteer efforts that they can control and that do not question their authority. They do not look favorably upon upstart student groups or underground community newspapers, unfavorable media publicity, or organized groups of reform-minded parents who are dissatisfied with their children's academic progress or the educational activities provided for them.

On one hand, parent groups can be perceived as a serious threat to the school because, as parents, they have legitimate access to school affairs. On the other hand, the tenure of a child in a school is relatively short, and if parents cannot be discouraged, co-opted, intimidated, ignored, or otherwise resisted, school personnel can always merely wait until the children move, drop out, or graduate. Stern (1987), for example, documented how public schools train African-American parents to accept unquestioningly the low evaluations given to their children, "cooling out" those who resist by locking the doors, canceling meetings, and retaliating against their children.

Identify community groups in your area that wish to influence education. What constituency do they represent? What changes would they like to see? What tactics and strategies do they use?

PATTERNS OF CONTROL BEYOND THE LOCAL LEVEL: THE PUBLIC SECTOR

State Jurisdiction

Each state has an educational agency whose organization parallels that at the local level. At the top is a chief officer or superintendent, a state board of education, and an executive branch or agency that carries out the activities of the department. State regulation specifies the scope of state support, establishes curriculum content and minimum time for each subject, sets minimum standards for student promotion and graduation, describes the rights and competencies of teachers, defines the characteristics of administrative structure, and creates rules for the physical safety of school inhabitants (Benson 1982; Wirt and Kirst 1974).

Examine your state's teacher certification requirements and compare them to your college's teacher preparation program. Examine the state curricular guidelines for students at the grade level or in the subject area of most interest to you.

Some state departments of education adopt curricular guidelines which teachers must follow, and many states approve a specific set of textbooks. State involvement in education was relatively limited until the mid-1960s. With concern for educational standards and accountability in the 1980s, we saw increased state involvement in the day-to-day workings in schools, particularly in regard to standardized testing and cur-

---

Attendance Policy

State law requires that all children between the ages of 7 and 17, both inclusive, be enrolled in day school. Excuses for absences for students in grades K–8 must be made in writing or in person by a parent or guardian. High school policies for excusing student absences vary from school to school. Students with as many as five unexcused absences will be referred to the attendance and social services department. Students of high school age may lose their driver's license for excessive absences. Aside from the obvious need for students to be present in school on a regular basis, absenteeism decreases state monies available to local school systems.

SOURCE: This quote is from a 1994 policy document, county school district, Tennessee.

---

ricula. It has become common for states to work with test developers to create proficiency examinations that are administered statewide to students at designated grade levels. These proficiency tests have a tremendous impact on the way teachers handle the curriculum.

The passage in 1965 of Title V of the Elementary and Secondary Education Act, which provided federal funds to bolster the professional staffs of state education agencies, greatly increased state-level educational activity. It led, for example, to increased research, media, and consulting services to local school districts, and administration of federal funds for compensatory education. These activities had two effects. First, they increased the level of bureaucratization at the state level, and second, they permitted the federal educational policies to penetrate closer to the local level, thereby shifting the location of control in school systems. While national agencies still have little influence over day-to-day behavior in the classroom, districts that accept federal funds find that they are constrained to use them in specific ways and to carry out systematic evaluation of their actions.

The Role of the Federal Government

While the primary, day-to-day activities of educational systems are subject to governance no higher than the state level, regional and national agencies in both the public and private sector influence these systems by means of financial incentives, certification, court enforcement of constitutional and other national laws, and federally funded research.

Despite the fact that primary responsibility for education in America is reserved to the states, there has long been concern that extreme decentralization might lead to great inequalities in the educational services provided by individual states. In 1867 educators overcame their distrust of federal influence and established the first federal Department of Education. Its charge was limited to providing statistics and information about educational matters and promoting the establishment of an efficient educational system (Butts 1978).

Since that time, federal influence has grown, especially in the enforcement of equal opportunity provision. The courts have been used to ensure that these constitutional provisions were applied in local school districts. Although the power of the federal Office of Education has varied as it has gone through a number of title changes, this agency has provided financial aid to states and local districts for specific programs and has sponsored research on topics felt to be in the national interest. These have included vocational educational programs and the teaching of science, bilingual education, English as a foreign language, and foreign languages. Federal funds have also been provided for research on testing and assessment, desegregation effects, improvement in instruction in basic subject areas, and improvement in techniques for teaching the disadvantaged. In addition, the federal government has financed research and evaluation staff to ensure that funds are being used as intended. Since the 1960s each federally funded project has had a mandated evaluation component, even those carried out by local staff.

The federal government has provided scholarships and loans to special classes of individuals. These have included veterans of military service, under the Servicemen's Readjustment Act of 1944 (the "G.I. Bill"); those who study certain subjects such as foreign languages and science, under the National Defense Education Act; ethnic minority students, under War on Poverty legislation during the 1960s; and trainers of bilingual teachers, under Title VII of the Elementary and Secondary Education Act. Individual undergraduates have received Pell grants, while graduate study has been encouraged under the Smith-Mundt and Fulbright legislation, the National Science Foundation, and other scholarship and loan programs.

In addition, federal regulations protect the educational rights and welfare of certain groups of students, including the poor, the handicapped, and those with limited proficiency in English. Members of these populations have been provided with school nurses, lunches, certain medical examinations, clothing, remedial instruction, and other compensatory services. The national government has also enforced laws regarding discrimination on the basis of race, gender, religion, and national origin and has placed constraints on using schools for religious purposes. Because of affirmative action and laws outlawing discrimination in public agencies, schools in particular have come under close scrutiny by the Office of Civil Rights and the courts.

PATTERNS OF CONTROL BEYOND THE LOCAL LEVEL: THE PRIVATE SECTOR

Regional Accreditation Agencies

State monitoring of local graduation standards and instructional quality is reinforced by regional accrediting agencies. During the nineteenth century secondary school courses were so diverse that universities had no way of knowing what and how much their incoming students knew. They therefore established the practice of certifying the curricula of given schools and then accepting their students without entrance examinations. Eventually these certification practices were institutionalized, and the resulting agencies visited high schools to approve their curricula, certify their students, and "accredit" their programs. These agencies have made secondary school course offerings more uniform, at least for college-preparatory programs; it also has created an external watchdog function which reduces the autonomy of schools and districts.

Private Research Institutes and Philanthropic Foundations

While private institutions have far less money to dispense than does the federal government, they are far more accessible to local school districts. Operated by state, regional, and local corporations or funded by the legacies of philanthropists, they are often directed by charter to sponsor programs in the schools, especially to provide small grants for teachers. A few very large private research foundations, such as the Rockefeller, Ford, and Spencer Foundations, have a pervasive effect not only on the topics and methods of investigation, but also on the use of research data. In addition, recipients of awards from these agencies form an elite network of intellectual leaders whose judgment is sought on educational matters in both the public and private sectors (LeCompte 1972).

The influence of local businesses and industries is particularly powerful. School-business partnerships have been promoted heavily as ways to help minority youth enter the work force and reduce their dropout rate (see, for example, Hargroves 1987). Corporations also have loaned executives to school districts to teach specialty areas such as math, science, and computer technology. Vocational curricula in high schools often reflect the dominant industries in the community. The schools do initial training and students then are preferentially hired by local businesses.

THE SCHOOL AS A BUREAUCRACY

How did schools evolve into their current patterns of organization and control? School enterprises today are a great deal more complex than the one-time individual classroom and building. In fact, schools are large, formal, social organizations, similar to hospitals, corporations, and factories. These organizations are called **bureaucracies.** The term "bureaucracy" is neither an insult nor a reference to red tape and frustration, but rather, a term used by sociologists to describe large, complex, multilevel social organizations which are run by full-time professionals.

A Formal Definition

A convenient way to begin to understand bureaucracies is through functional theory as it was defined in Chapter 1. Functionalists define bureaucracies in terms of the tasks they perform and the organizational structures that carry them out. One characteristic of bureaucracy is that each task (function) the organization does has an individual, department, or group of people (structure) to carry it out. Imagine a typical organizational chart, in which the president occupies a box at the top, the lowest levels of workers are arrayed in horizontal rows of boxes at the bottom, and other tasks and departments occupy the space in between. Organizational charts specify the goals of the organization, what jobs are required to achieve them, and who shall carry them out. In effect, organizational charts provide a functional analysis of formal structure.

Bureaucracies embody a division of functions, much like that of an automobile assembly line, where each area of responsibility is clearly defined. Line tasks or offices—those that actually do the work of the organization—are arranged hierarchically, so that people lower in the organization are supervised by those higher up. Staff offices operate laterally. For example, design departments and quality control officials in the automobile industry advise line personnel but are not involved with the direct production of cars.

Obtain a copy of the school organization chart from the central office of your local school district. What do you think of this organization? How does it compare with the organizational chart shown in Figure 2.1? What organizational changes would you suggest to your local district?

According to Max Weber, the first theorist who completely delineated the characteristics of bureaucracy, workers in bureaucracies must be full-time workers, not volunteers or part-timers with divided loyalties. They must be rewarded according to their skill and training. Those with more training and responsibility are usually paid more and hold higher positions than those with less training and responsibility (Blau and Scott 1962; Dalton, Barnes, and Zaleznik 1968; Weber 1962). They may receive merit pay for objectively assessed exemplary performance.

Bureaucracies operate by means of rules which rationally and systematically establish *what* each person is expected to do—and often *how* they are to do it as well. These rules are the basis for systems of accountability and apply to all job-holders without favoritism. The rules can be found in job descriptions, by-laws, guidebooks, operating manuals, and handbooks of various kinds.

Clearly, a formal, functional definition of bureaucracy does not describe how most organizations really operate. Their sheer complexity makes it impossible to specify every action that might be undertaken. Individuals take on tasks that are not in their formal job description, bypass people or offices that are roadblocks, and bend the rules when necessary. Informal practices outside of the "normal channels" evolve to facilitate work (Blau 1955). These informal adaptations are necessary for organizations to function smoothly.

It is no accident that schools resemble other kinds of bureaucratic organizations in modern society. However, because institutions do not exist in isolation, the social context in which they have developed must be considered. Their history and physical arrangements, as well as the characteristics of their inhabitants, shape how people behave within organizations and how they feel about themselves and others. Bureaucratic organizations have assumed the shape they did because policy makers gave priority to order, uniformity, and efficiency (Katz 1971). Schools developed and

FIGURE 2.1

1994 ADMINISTRATIVE ORGANIZATION CHART
COUNTY SCHOOL DISTRICT*
528 SQUARE MILES
COUNTY POPULATION: 335,749

BOARD OF EDUCATION

SUPERINTENDENT OF SCHOOLS

ADMINISTRATIVE SERVICES DEPARTMENT
ASSISTANT SUPERINTENDENT FOR ADMINISTRATIVE SERVICES
Coordinator of Food Service
Coordinator of Transportation
Supervisor of Food Service
Specialist—Food Service
Supervisor of Transfers and Disciplinary Hearings
Supervisor of Student Information System
Supervisor of Athletics
Captain of School Security

BUSINESS AND PERSONNEL DEPARTMENTS
ASSISTANT SUPERINTENDENT FOR BUSINESS AND PERSONNEL
Specialist—Payroll Administrator
Specialist—Administrative Assistant to Assistant Superintendent
Specialist—Assistant Business Manager
Director of Personnel
Supervisor of Elementary Personnel and Evaluations
Supervisor of Middle School Personnel and Minority Recruiter
Supervisor of High School and Secretarial Personnel and Substitute Teachers
Supervisor of Data Processing for Payroll and Personnel
Director of Maintenance and Operations

CURRICULUM AND INSTRUCTION DEPARTMENT
ASSISTANT SUPERINTENDENT FOR CURRICULUM AND INSTRUCTION
Director of Vocational Education
Coordinator of Research and Evaluation
Coordinator of Science
Coordinator of High Schools
Coordinator of Elementary Schools
    Supervisors (3)—Elementary Generalist
    Supervisor of Adult Home Economics
    Supervisor of Trade and Industrial and Technology Education

Supervisor of Social Studies
Supervisor of General Business, Office Education, Computer Labs and Vocational Improvement
    Program
Supervisor of Adult Basic Education
Supervisor of Language Arts (6–12)
Supervisor of Driver Education and In-School Suspension
Supervisor of Mathematics (K–8)
Supervisor of Mathematics (9–12)
Supervisor of Health Occupations, Home Economics, Marketing Education, and
    Cosmetology
Supervisor of Science
Supervisor of Physical Education and Health (K–8)
Supervisor of Physical Education and Health (9–12)
Supervisor of Gifted Education
Supervisor of Art
Supervisor of Music—Choral
Supervisor of Music—Instrumental
Supervisor of Adult Basic Education and Evening School
Supervisor of Computer Skills
Specialist—Alcohol and Other Drug Prevention Programs/Section 504
Specialist Foreign Language/ESL
Specialist—Computer Skills
Specialist—Teacher Center

PUPIL PERSONNEL SERVICES AND SUPPLEMENTARY SERVICES DEPARTMENTS
ASSISTANT SUPERINTENDENT FOR SUPPLEMENTARY STUDENT SERVICES
Director of Pupil Personnel Services
Supervisor of School Nurses
Administrative Assistant to Director of Pupil Personnel Services/Special Education Generalist
Supervisors of Resource and CDC Programs (2)
Supervisor of Psychological Services
Supervisor of Sensory Communications and Home/Hospital Services
Supervisor of Special Education
Supervisor of Consultative and Intervention Support Services
Supervisor of OT/PT
Supervisors of Chapter I Reading, Language Development, and Mathematics (2)

ADMINISTRATIVE ASSISTANTS

SUPERVISOR OF COMMUNICATIONS

SUPERVISOR OF BUSINESS PARTNERSHIPS

CHIEF NEGOTIATOR

* At the time this chart was constructed, the county district operated 88 schools: 55 elementary schools (building average enrollment of 451), 13 middle schools (building average enrollment of 892), 12 high schools (building average enrollment of 1,176), 1 center for dropouts, 2 vocational centers, 3 special education centers, and 2 early childhood development centers.

changed in response to these priorities in ways that paralleled the bureaucratization of large hospitals, governmental agencies, factories, and society in general.

Schools are a special kind of bureaucratic organization. While they share characteristics with other bureaucracies—such as the prisons, factories, and social service agencies with which they often are compared—other characteristics conspire to make them unique. In addition to the particular historical, cultural, and economic context in which they developed, they are differentiated in the type, specificity, and number of their goals. Schools also are unique in the ways people can participate in them, and in their multiple lines of power and control. In the sections that follow we will discuss the special characteristics of school organization, how they affect the people who work in them, and some of the political and social forces that were critical to the development of contemporary schools.

Think about the organization of the high school you attended. How was it organized? Who controlled the school? Who were the people in power positions? How did they maintain this power? Do you think this organization was effective? Why or why not?

Schools as Modified Bureaucratic Organizations

Schools, like many organizations, possess some, but not all, of the characteristics of bureaucracies. For example, while teachers and other school staff are in fact hired for their professional training and skill, and while they do have job descriptions that encompass most of their required duties, they generally are rewarded for longevity rather than for merit. In addition, their written job description may not include many of their required duties, such as grading papers after school and being involved in extracurricular student activities (see Chapter 4 for a detailed description of teachers' work).

Multiple Constituencies and Multiple Goals

Ideally, bureaucracies have clear and unambiguous goals, and their leaders possess fairly complete control over the means for realizing those goals. School bureaucracies clearly do not fit this model. Schools actually have many organizational goals—some ambiguous or diffuse, and others contradictory. For example, schools are expected to provide training suited to each individual child while adhering to instructional guidelines based on single texts, uniform procedures, and mandated mastery of specific content.

Schools have multiple goals because they have multiple constituencies and clienteles, each with their own agenda and each pushing their own goals. Added to this is the unique mix of national, state, and local financial control. Few educational systems in the world and few social service agencies in the United States are as subject to external pressures as are the public schools in America, where the electorate controls the purse strings. Most school districts depend upon revenue from local property taxes, much of which comes from people who have no school-aged children. Further-more, school officials cannot operate independent of their community because it is usually the public that chooses the school board. In addition, by law, school board meetings must be open to the public, and community and parent groups can exert powerful pressure regarding the content of textbooks and other instructional materials, as well as teaching techniques and extracurricular activities.

Local control encourages diversity in schools but it also makes them an arena in often bitter conflicts over cultural values. Tension is produced when the ideologies of the community are at odds with those of the school staff or of government agencies. Often these tensions arise over the substance and delivery of curricula. As we will discuss in Chapter 6, religious fundamentalists fight with advocates of secular education, and back-to-the-basics advocates vie with developmentalists and humanists for control over the curriculum. As Apple (1993) and Brouillette (1993) have described, these conflicts become especially heated in times of budgetary shortages. Hard choices have to be made among disparate goals: Closing the alternative high school for pregnant teens is balanced against the firing of 30 special education teachers, which is weighed against the elimination of reading and math specialists or the dismantling of the swim team and the choir. If compromise cannot be reached, the various interests may end up in court. Conflicts over school goals have been generated over bilingual education (*Lau et al.* v. *Nichols et al.* 1974) and ethnic studies, prayer in school (*Engel* v. *Vitale* 1962; *Abington School District* v. *Schempp* 1963), racial integration (*Brown* v. *Board of Education* 1955), free speech for students (*Tinker* v. *Des Moines* 1969), and the teaching of creationism and secular humanism (*Smith* v. *School Commissioners* 1987).

The real mission of schooling becomes blurred under the onslaught of so many constituencies, each seeking control over some portion of school activities. In many districts the result of such conflict is goal displacement.

Goal Displacement

Goal displacement (Sills 1970) is a common malady in bureaucratic organizations. It occurs when procedural activities—the dos, don'ts, and how-tos of organizational life—become more important than the reasons for which the organization was created. Goal displacement occurs when the resources intended for a given task are diverted to another purpose, or when the survival of a procedure or a group achieves greater importance than the purpose for which it was originally created. We also see goal displacement when the means become ends in themselves, that is, when some practice that was adopted to help solve a problem begins to interfere with the organization's original goals.

Goal displacement can be found, for example, in the proliferation of programs for assessing students and teachers. These were initiated to ensure that teachers were teaching what was required and that students had mastered the subject matter. However, in many districts such tests now drive the curriculum, taking up almost as much school time as teaching, and becoming the focus of instructional content.

Another example can be found in teachers' organizations' protecting tenure;

they have been accused of maintaining teacher jobs at the expense of quality instruction. Teachers resist the firing of colleagues for incompetence because the firing of one might call into question the competence of others. Schools may continue to employ teachers who are incompetent, or who are racists, or who do not like children, or who have come to detest teaching—because there are so many legal and institutional obstacles to firing them (see Dworkin 1985b). In these cases, more energy is spent in avoiding change than in carrying out the original mission of the organization.

Schools are particularly vulnerable to goal displacement. Many of the issues we discuss at length later in this chapter are illustrations. In considering the social organization of schools and the extent to which they resemble other modern bureaucracies, you may find it helpful to think about who controls the schools in your community and the extent to which patterns of control affect what schools ultimately can and should do. You also may wish to examine how the original intentions of innovative educational practices come to be subverted.

What examples of goal displacement can you describe from your own experiences with school organizations?

HOW SCHOOLS BECAME BUREAUCRACIES

A bureaucracy as a social organization is a relatively modern phenomenon which developed along with a capitalistic economic system, political nation-states, industrialization, and demographic shifts to urbanization. Small organizations with limited purposes do not need many employees and can operate under informal and unwritten rules. However, as they begin to involve more people and carry out more activities, additional levels of management and coordination are created. Specialized individuals are hired for complex, technical tasks. The process by which organizations increase in size and complexity, add levels of hierarchy and professionalism, and begin systematically to subdivide tasks is called *bureaucratization*. Bureaucratization is not limited to schooling; it has penetrated virtually every modern social institution.

Origins of the Common Elementary School

Schools have not always been structured as bureaucracies. The "little red schoolhouse" frequently had no more than one classroom, a coat room, a shed for firewood or coal, and a field outside for recess. Even in urban areas, school buildings housing hundreds of students were generally one large room with a teacher and monitors to help with the instruction (Spring 1986). The schools' services were limited to book learning. In elementary school the teachers instructed children in the basic cognitive skills of reading, writing, and computation. While there were no classes in science or social studies as such, textbooks like Noah Webster's *Blue-Back Speller* and the *McGuffey's Readers* contained heavy doses of instruction in these subjects, as well as in literature, morals, and social values such as thrift, hard work, cleanliness, patience, abstinence, and correct social behavior. Because educators were concerned primarily with transmitting cognitive skills and cultural knowledge, the number of nonteaching staff required was minimal. Teachers swept their own classrooms and lit the fires to keep them warm.

In 1848 John Philbrick introduced the Quincy School in Massachusetts, a radical new design with three floors containing multiple classrooms and a large assembly hall on the top floor. Each classroom was designed for a teacher and 56 students. This design was a step toward bureaucratization of schooling because it differentiated teaching and administrative roles. Tyack quotes Philbrick's specifications for staffing of this school:

> Let the Principal or Superintendent have the general supervision and control of the whole, and let him have one male assistant or sub-principal, and ten female assistants, one for each room. (1974, p. 45)

Tyack refers to this type of organization, with a male administrator and female teachers, as a "pedagogical harem." The Quincy School, with its sex-role differences and hierarchical bureaucratic structures, became the model for urban schools in the United States in the late nineteenth and early twentieth centuries (Spring 1986).

By the 1880s "school-keeping" practices had changed dramatically. A relatively coherent system of elementary, or "common," schools had been established in every state, and what we call the "service sector" of education had expanded exponentially. Growth in the service sector was a critical factor in the bureaucratization of schools because it rapidly expanded the number of functions that schools were expected to carry out.

Establishment of Public Secondary Schools

In the early years of the Republic the demand for education was fueled primarily by an educated elite desirous of passing their status on to their children by means of college-oriented liberal arts instruction. Beginning in the 1830s the middle and upper classes began to advocate that publicly supported instruction in basic literacy and morality be provided for economically disadvantaged children. The implicit purpose of this instruction was social control—to ensure the continuance of a productive labor force and to forestall the civil unrest, drunkenness, and immoral behavior to which it was felt an illiterate and unindoctrinated working class would be prone (Boutwell 1859; Mann 1842; Resnick and Resnick 1985).

Many industrialists, civic leaders, and educators supported mass education, as did the business community, which saw little difference between running factories and keeping school. Compulsory attendance laws became common between 1880 and 1920. Labor unions applauded the removal of competitive and inexpensive youths from the labor market. With the passage of the Smith-Hughes Act in 1917, secondary schools added vocational and non-college preparatory, or "general education," streams to accommodate advocates of "democratization." The comprehensive, nonselective public high school became known as a "poor man's college" and provided all the education most people needed.

By the end of the nineteenth century the general structure of the American public educational system, both elementary and secondary, had been established. The public sector provided free or nearly free instruction from elementary school through land-grant colleges and universities, although it was clear that only a minority would avail themselves of postsecondary schooling (Katz 1971). Bureaucratization had gradually developed from the increasing size and complexity of the educational enterprise. Schools acquired principals; superintendents were hired to supervise groups of schools; and standards for hiring teachers, certifying the quality of schools, and graduating students were put into place.

During the first three decades of the twentieth century, the school structure continued to evolve as supporters of a powerful industrial ideology urged the shaping of schools along the lines of the most efficient American factories. The following sections draw heavily on the work of critical and revisionist historians such as Michael B. Katz, Joel Spring, Clarence Karier, Raymond E. Callahan, and Marvin Lazerson, who have questioned the conventional view that schools were established to support democratic and egalitarian ideals. While these ideals did motivate some supporters of public education, critical historians note how schools acted largely to reinforce existing patterns of social and economic inequality and benefit members of the dominant culture.

Addition of the Service Sector

The service sector began to develop in the late 1800s as civic leaders, educators, industrialists, and the churches targeted the elementary schools for the monumental task of upgrading the social and moral level of immigrant and working-class children. Between 1865 and 1900, 14 million immigrants were known to have entered the United States. Between 1876 and 1926 over 27 million immigrated, a number that exceeded the 1875 population by 50 percent. Whereas the original migrants were from England and Northern Europe, most of the newcomers during this later period were rural dwellers from central, southern, and eastern Europe whose languages, skills, habits, and ethnicity differed drastically from those of the established residents (Butts 1978, p. 229). Immigrants have continued to arrive at a rate of about one million per year (Callahan 1962). Since the 1970s, the greatest pressure for entrance to the United States has been from Latin Americans and Asians, especially from Southeast Asia.

It is difficult to imagine the fear that immigrants and the working class struck in the hearts of the affluent. Whether they were the Irish of the early nineteenth century, the southern and eastern Europeans later in the nineteenth century, or the Jews who came even later, unassimilated immigrants were viewed in America with the same suspicion as card-carrying Communists were during the "Red Scares" of the 1930s and 1950s, and as illegal aliens were in the 1980s and 1990s. They were portrayed as vicious, immoral, mentally deficient, lazy, unhygienic, and a threat to the social and moral fiber of the nation.

Part of the fear came from culture shock. The immigrants differed from established residents in language, religion, standard of living, and customs. Most important, they were—and still are—accused of taking jobs from the native-born. They also had little power and few influential advocates in government to oversee their interests (Higham 1969; The Massachusetts Teacher 1851). Established residents viewed education as a way to counteract the threat that immigrants posed to the social order. The type of education advocated was, however, a departure from prevailing practice. As the characteristics and needs of immigrants changed, pressures to provide appropriate education for them have also changed the schools.

Principal among the factors mandating social services to immigrants and the poor was growth of class conflict during the late 1800s. It was exacerbated by an almost rabid fear dominant groups had of immigrants and the lower classes. Concerns for law and order fueled the desire of policy makers to "Americanize" immigrant children as quickly as possible and to indoctrinate the working-class children with middle-class values (Higham 1969). Service programs were used to accelerate this process.

The service sector of schooling includes a wide variety of noninstructional activities such as medical inspections (1894), health and nutritional services (beginning in the early 1900s), rehabilitation for the handicapped (the 1920s), and school lunches (as an emergency measure during the Depression and made permanent in 1946). Legislation that was part of the War on Poverty in the 1960s added programs to reduce racial prejudice as well as a variety of support services, including dental care, clothing banks, free or low-cost breakfasts, after-school care, sex education and drug abuse advice, programs for pregnant girls, and mental and physical health counseling. Provision of these services has contributed substantially to the transformation of schools into large, complex, bureaucratic institutions.

Several themes provided impetus for the provision of social services. One was custodial and came from the belief that poor families were unable or unwilling to provide proper care for their children (Gumbert and Spring 1974). Another was the humanitarian acknowledgement that sick, hungry, and poorly clad children were too preoccupied with their physical needs to study. For families living in one-room apartments and amid grinding poverty, schools and settlement houses often were the only places where children could be fed, bathed, provided warm clothing, and given minimal medical care (Albjerg 1974; Butts and Cremin 1953; The Massachusetts Teacher 1851).

Schools as Custodians of Children

Over time, the school has become an all-purpose child-care institution whose services go far beyond training in the "three Rs." As the custodial functions of schools grew, teachers and administrators took on more responsibility for the health, well-being, and good behavior of young people—even in areas once considered the exclusive province of families and the private sector.

Some of these services, like drug, pregnancy, and prenatal counseling, day care, and driver education, are attempts to alleviate social problems, such as the many students who drop out because they become parents and the rising incidence of automobile-related fatalities. Other services, such as training in the performing arts, are designed to provide opportunities once available only to the wealthy. Still others, such as free lunches and medical exams, attest to our recognition that sick and hungry

The Fate of Goose Pond Alternative Jr./Sr. High School

Discussion of Goose Pond, the Cottonwood District's well-respected alternative school, occurred when there had just been a significant shift in the composition of the school board. Goose Pond had served seriously at-risk students since the 1970s. It was integral to the District's major stated goal: success for all students. Housed in an historic school building, it offered an individualized student-centered program with a 15:1 student teacher ratio. Though effective, Goose Pond was an expensive school to run, and its building was in need of repair. While previous school boards had supported the school, the agenda of the new school board was fiscally conservative. Noting the need for general financial retrenchment, board members questioned the amount of money to be spent on the Goose Pond facility. Stating that the district should not delude itself into believing it could heal all the world's ills, they targeted the school for closure. Dr. Roberts, the superintendent opposed the closing as openly as his status as a school employee would allow, knowing it was pivotally important that he maintain good relations with board members. They, however, rejected his argument that more funding should be assigned to help those most in need, arguing that social work should be left to social work agencies. According to their view, achieving the greatest good for the greatest number of students meant maintaining strong programs district-wide. In time of financial austerity, they felt, the district could not afford to keep open what they considered to be an inefficient school, despite a strong consensus among Cottonwood staff that the alternative school should remain open.

SOURCE: Brouillette 1993.

children cannot learn. Finally, some, such as classes and support services for the physically and emotionally handicapped, are congruent with the belief that all children—regardless of their motivation, aspirations, or limitations—are entitled to an appropriate, free education until age 21 or graduation from high school. Adding social service functions, with the accompanying resources and staff, has hastened bureaucratization. It also has added controversy, because the many constituencies who participate in and finance the schools seldom achieve a consensus as to whether these programs are legitimate school functions—as the controversy over Goose Pond Alternative School illustrates (see box).

A distinct feature of bureaucratization of schools in America was that, since there are no explicit constitutional provisions for schooling, states assumed responsibility for public education. Unlike in most other countries, where there is centralized national control, state and local boards oversee educational responsibilities. Placing school finance and governance under the control of local boards laid the groundwork for racial and economic inequality, because rich communities had more resources than poor ones. The public school system co-existed with independent private schools, whose numbers varied by region and which generally served special interests such as religious groups, those favoring alternative education, and the wealthy.

Urbanization, Consolidation, and Scientific Management

After World War II, global changes in the distribution of population, natural resources, trade, the labor market, and technology, as well as urbanization, industrialization, and changes in the labor force (Chafetz and Dworkin 1986) affected every facet of human existence and gave birth to modern society. In addition, during the past two centuries industrialization has caused the poor and landless to migrate to cities in every corner of the globe. Urbanization of the poor has increased the percentage of the economically disadvantaged (Chafetz and Dworkin 1986). It has also profoundly affected the locally controlled "little red schoolhouse."

The little red schoolhouse model was sufficient for relatively homogeneous small communities, but today more than 75 percent of the U.S. population lives in cities, where economic and ethnic diversity has exploded both the myth of the middle class and the myth of the melting pot. Concentration of the population into cities was accompanied by pressure for universal and compulsory education, in part because American cultural ideology promoted education as a means to improve one's social and economic condition. Education was no longer viewed as appropriate only for the affluent. It was needed both for nation building and for provision of the skills requisite for an industrial nation. However, pressures to expand educational opportunities often were conservative. While public education was, in fact, provided for children of the working classes and the poor, its content was different from the classical liberal arts training for the wealthy; it was more practical, oriented to civic training, and geared toward job preparation. Educational reform was equated with creating social and economic stability. It was a way to avoid taking more radical steps to solve problems such as urban poverty and social disorder (Katz 1971; LeCompte and Dworkin 1991).

THE SCIENTIFIC MANAGEMENT OF SCHOOLS

At the turn of the century America's cultural heroes were industrialists—Andrew Carnegie, John D. Rockefeller, J. P. Morgan, and others. Belief in the efficacy and virtue of big business and industry saturated American life. It was a logical extension of the "can-do" spirit of the legendary pioneers. Americans firmly believed that success—defined in terms of material acquisition—was the result of honesty and hard work. In keeping with another cultural myth—that America was an egalitarian, classless society (see Chapter 5 for further discussion of the "myth of the middle class")—they also believed that success had very little to do with social background or education. Since Americans tended to believe that businesspeople had made America great, they also believed that the best way to solve all problems was to subject them to good business practice. This notion meant that the value of any commodity, enterprise, or person was measured by marketability, the tangible contribution to sale value, or the ability of someone to get ahead.

The Rise of Taylorism

These ideas were embodied in a philosophy called "Scientific Management," whose chief exponent was an industrial engineer named Frederick W. Taylor. Taylor first came to prominence in 1910 when his theories of management were used as evidence in a widely publicized hearing before the Interstate Commerce Commission. The railroads had asked for an increase in freight rates to compensate them for higher wages granted to railroad workers. The government's lawyer, Louis Brandeis, argued in opposition that the railroads were being operated inefficiently and that if they introduced Taylor's new techniques of scientific management, they would be able to increase wages *and* also reduce costs. Taylor also suggested that his approach would result in more productivity from fewer workers. His ideas took the industrialized world by storm and were applied to everything from baking cakes and sewing trousers to carrying ingots of pig iron and getting students to study harder. Taylor's "scientific" operating principles included the following:

1. Management must be responsible for analyzing, planning, and controlling every detail of the manufacturing process.
2. Management must use scientific methods to identify the best methods for performing each aspect of every task carried out in the plant.
3. Each step in each task must be standardized, and tools must be developed that are appropriate both to the task and to the workers who are to carry it out.
4. Planning departments must be established to develop the science of each job, including the rules, laws, and formulae for its execution. These rules will replace judgments made by individual workers about how their work should be done.
5. Detailed records must be kept of every activity and transaction so that accountability can be established and traced.
6. Managers must carefully train workers in the exact execution of their tasks and must closely supervise them to make sure that they are following directions.
7. Assessment procedures must be established so that performance can be measured and exemplary performance can be rewarded.

Taylor's system which placed all power in the hands of managers and planners, introduced a rationale for meticulous observation, testing, and recordkeeping, and wrested from workers any control over the execution of their tasks. While it was criticized by individuals in industry and universities, the voices of protest were drowned out by the chorus of enthusiasm for a process that appeared to increase productivity while reducing costs. The outcry coincided exactly with a wave of dissatisfaction over the public schools (Callahan 1962).

Waste, Inefficiency, and "Laggards" in Our Schools

If businesspeople were the most capable individuals in America, then it stood to reason that they should be intimately involved in public institutions such as schools. The political reform movement of the early 1900s, generated from distrust of political machines, encouraged a shift away from political appointment of administrators. Council-manager forms of municipal government, in which an elected council hired a professional city manager, became popular because they were congruent with the desire for management by scientifically trained professionals rather than amateurs. School districts soon followed suit. Instead of hiring teachers to run the schools, they chose "professionals"—graduates from colleges of education that provided what purported to be professional training for school administrators. Communities elected to school boards businesspeople who evaluated school operation by the same criteria they used for factories. Educators became vulnerable to the same kinds of criticism as factory workers and managers: Why couldn't the product be manufactured more efficiently and at less cost?

Report after report alleged that educators were sadly lacking in both business acumen and accounting skills. Many could neither account for nor justify their expenditure of the taxpayers' money to the satisfaction of their boards and communities (Callahan 1962). Schools also were criticized for retaining large numbers of "laggards," or children who were over the normal age for their grade level. No one examined whether the so-called "retarded" children were immigrants with insufficient mastery of English for the work at their age level or whether they had been held back because they had failed courses. School efficiency came to be defined in terms of how fast children could be pushed through the grades: An "efficient" school had every child on grade level for his or her age, regardless of extenuating circumstances. Double-promotion or skipping grades was widely used as a cost-saving measure. Course offerings were judged by their cost per pupil and their utility in moving students right into jobs, notwithstanding any measure of intrinsic worth or external cost. School administrators also were criticized for the amount of time their buildings stood unused—in the summer, during holidays, and at night.

Solving such problems by application of businesslike practices accelerated the process of routinization, specialization, and bureaucratization. Pressured by taxpayers and school boards, superintendents had to go back to school to learn new methods. At universities, they became steeped in scientific management, a doctrine wholeheartedly embraced by education programs. With their degrees in hand, newly minted professional school administrators altered curricula, supervisory techniques, and instruction accordingly (Callahan 1962).

The Legacy of Scientific Management

Most of the changes introduced from 1915 to 1930, the heyday of the efficiency expert, were major departures from the tradition of "school-keeping." These changes became permanent and have welded the educational establishment ever closer to the image of corporate and bureaucratic America. Perhaps the most obvious change was the addition of a management stratum to the hierarchy. Teachers could no longer rise into administration without special training. While administrators still come through the ranks—most educational administration programs require three years of teaching—the requirement of a "professional" credential is here to stay. It is nearly impossible to be hired as a school administrator without certification from an approved graduate program.

Other changes were made in recordkeeping to codify attendance procedures, financial records, curricula, and time allocations for instruction. Many of the changes were needed to introduce system and **rationalization** into an enterprise that had become increasingly chaotic (Butts 1978). However, they also were harbingers of the paperwork avalanche which often overwhelms today's school staff.

The impact of Taylorism was also felt in equipment and design. Time-and-motion study experts developed tools suitable to both the job and the worker—for example, chairs that fit children's bodies and are an appropriate size, lighting that is adequate for reading, left-handed scissors, and big crayons which are easy for small children to hold. The efficiency bureaus established in some districts have evolved into departments of research, testing, and evaluation.

The efficiency movement also left more mixed blessings. One is the continued interest in split sessions and the year-round school as a solution to overcrowded buildings. More pervasive is the "platoon school" or "Gary Plan." The Gary Plan, named after the city in Indiana where the experiment was implemented, was based on the idea that schools would be more efficient if no room ever were empty. Space could be saved if one group—or platoon—of students were outside on the playground at all times so their classroom could be used by another group. Implementing such a plan required subdividing of the students, careful scheduling, and constant movement of people among the available rooms. It subordinated instruction to the dictates of a time clock, interrupting instruction regardless of student interest or the difficulty of the subject matter. Teachers could no longer decide how to allocate their instructional time, and students were ever more rigidly divided into batches by age rather than ability or intellectual interest. The Gary Plan lives on in the hallways of today's middle and high schools, as students move in batches every 50 minutes to a different classroom.

Taylor's human cost accounting survives in practices such as treating teachers as "FTEs" (full-time equivalents, or the number of workers multiplied by the number of hours worked each day), and demanding that course offerings justify their existence not on the merit of the material or the rigor of the course, but on the basis of per-unit cost calculated in "credit hour generation," or the number of students enrolled per course. Other accounting survivors include determining graduation requirements by counting "Carnegie units" (a specified number of hours taught in a given subject area), and the per-pupil-expenditure figures which appear before every school election.

The practices that probably have had the most impact upon the daily life of students and teachers include "Taylorizing" the curriculum into easily taught, measurable objectives, and the massive systems of testing students, teachers, and even administrators for academic competency and achievement. These practices, often instituted as part of educational reform measures, act systematically to **de-skill** teachers, removing from their control decisions over how and what to teach, as well as their prerogative to evaluate student progress. We discuss the impact of these practices in detail in Chapters 4 and 6.

The Impact of Scientific Management on Teacher Autonomy

Perhaps the most ominous legacy of scientific management is the authoritarianism built into Frederick Taylor's insistence on three principles: (1) granting managers absolute control over the definition, assignment, and assessment of tasks; (2) breaking down tasks into discrete, measurable subunits, and (3) requiring the complete and unthinking acquiescence of laborers in everything employers asked them to do. When applied to schools, these principles ultimately removed jurisdiction over instruction from teachers and changed the pattern of control and decision making in schools.

By the time Taylorism hit the schools in the 1920s, some shifts of control already had occurred. Many of the most important curricular decisions were being made outside the classroom. For example, accreditation agencies, school boards, administrators, and textbook committees decided what courses should be taught and which books would be used. All that remained to the teacher were how to teach the material and how to manage the children. Proponents of scientific management proposed that even these decisions be made centrally. On the grounds that teachers worked inefficiently at best, and could not be trusted to cover material adequately and objectively, curriculum and instruction were increasingly made "teacher proof."

"Professional educators"—usually university professors and administrators rather than classroom teachers—broke down instructional tasks into measurable "behavioral objectives" and then prescribed how they should be taught. While these practices organized and standardized instruction and facilitated assessment of results, they also prevented teachers from deciding what, in their professional judgment, was most valuable to teach and how to teach it. Teachers also no longer could rely exclusively on their own judgment for assessment of student ability. Children were grouped for instruction on the basis of external tests. Teachers were assigned textbooks which might or might not match the ability levels of their students. They were given scripted lessons which prescribed children's answers, and tests with which to assess student progress. Good instructional objectives were those accompanied by specified reading materials. Usually these also required a great deal of recordkeeping by the teacher—records that ostensibly were used to chart the children's progress but also could be used to monitor the teacher's conformity with the curriculum.

These reforms had the effect of enforcing progress. Teachers had to move their students through a certain number of curricular units per semester whether or not they felt the material had been covered adequately. Teachers could, of course, resist the imposition of lock-step curricula to some extent by relying on the autonomy of the closed door. They also could—and do—wait until the current wave of new ideas passes, a new superintendent is hired, or a new set of reforms are set in motion at the national level.

Management by Objectives in Cottonwood

Dr. Roberts explained that during the years prior to his arrival, "the district had received national recognition for the implementation of Outcomes-Based education and Computer-Managed instruction. It was also very centralized. Most major decisions and plans for implementation evolved directly from the central office administrators with little opportunity for input by those expected to implement the decision [the teachers]." And, as a curriculum specialist recounted: "We 'Benjamin-Bloomed' everything. I don't know whether you remember that era when objectives were the thing. We were all trained in writing objectives. In fact, I've had a number of courses from various universities on instructional objectives, goal setting, that sort of thing. So the district ended up, in every discipline, with an entire objective based curriculum. We wrote in that 86 percent of the teachers had to support an objective or it was revised or deleted. That became our curriculum."

SOURCE: Brouillette 1993.

As you continue through this chapter, ask yourself the following questions:
    How is your daily life in schools affected by practices grounded in scientific management?
    Can you identify features of your experiences that are governed by principles of efficiency rather than of good teaching and learning?

Schooling and the Hegemony of Corporate America

Schools now are criticized for mirroring corporate America and for too closely resembling factories. We need to remember, however, that the forces that led to bureaucratization were unleashed because people believed they led to highly desirable outcomes. The tenets of scientific management were introduced to the schools under the banner of the best-intentioned democratic reform. The alacrity with which scientific management was embraced illustrates just how powerful external control or "hegemonic domination" over education can be, as we discussed in Chapter 1.

    Because educators had so completely accepted the legitimacy of business ideology, no force was needed to induce them to adopt the structure, language, and practices of business. They did not foresee that scientific management had other, less desirable consequences. While the factory model was marketed on the basis of fostering efficiency, hard work, and entrepreneurship, it did not, in fact, train entrepreneurs. On the contrary, it fostered obedience rather than the risk-taking and nonconformity of industrial capitalism's early heroes. For this reason, the factory schools were most popular in the industrialized central cities, where the majority of the poor and working class lived, where financial shortages mandated money-saving practices, and where a hard-working, obedient labor force was needed by industry. There, schools that mirrored life in the factories flourished. In more affluent areas the rigidities and excesses of Taylorism were blunted, and the extras that were deemed wasteful by the efficiency experts, such as foreign languages, Greek, and smaller classes, survived to differentiate the education of the rich from that of the poor.

RESISTANCE TO SCIENTIFIC MANAGEMENT: RESTRUCTURING AND REFORM

Schools have continued to resemble factories, even those in campus-like structures. In fact, school reform legislation in the 1980s, which concentrated on entrance and graduation standards and the content and structure of instruction, accelerated the process. However, counterpressures are growing. Teachers, principals, parents, and others are exhibiting growing disenchantment with centralized control and their disenfranchisement in the educational enterprise. As early as the 1960s, decentralization movements constituted a critique of the increasing consolidation of schools for the sake of efficiency. In the sections that follow we will recount a brief history of efforts to reform the organization of schooling and instruction.

A Definition of Restructuring

In the 1980s a new buzzword, **restructuring,** emerged to describe any number of efforts to reform the schools. As an approach to educational change, it has been called the "garbage can" of school reform (Elmore and Associates 1990) because of its capacity to encompass almost any kind of change imaginable, or a "garage-like approach" to reform (Goldwasser 1994) because, like a garage, one can fit almost any kind of reform in it. Critical to our discussion, however, is that restructuring efforts constitute a rejection of the centralized governance and reductionist curricula advocated by descendants of Taylorism.

In general, restructuring involves one or more of the following:

1. Changes in the distribution of power between schools and their clients or in the governance structure within which schools operate
2. Changes in the occupational situation of educators, including conditions of entry and licensing of teachers and administrators
3. Changes in school structure, conditions of work, and decision-making processes within schools
4. Changes in the way teaching and learning occur or in the core technology of schooling (Elmore and Associates 1990)

Interview a school administrator who has been in your school district for a long time about the changes in organization over the past decade or more. What are some of these changes? What does this administrator think about the ways the bureaucracy has changed?

Decentralization: The Predecessor of Restructuring

The original idea for contemporary restructuring probably can be found in the decentralization movements to counteract extreme bureaucratic rigidity in large city school districts (Elmore 1990; Hess 1991; LeCompte and Dworkin 1991; Rogers 1968; Tyack 1990). The focus of decentralization is the structure of school district governance. It attempts first to dismantle nonresponsive, alienating, corrupt, top-heavy and expensive bureaucracies (LeCompte and Dworkin 1991). Decentralization was designed to make educational systems more responsive and accessible by reducing the size of the unit that people had to deal with daily and by locating administration in the community it controlled. Furthermore, it represented a reversal of the consolidation movement that had drastically decreased the number of districts over the previous 50 years (Tyack 1990).

Ocean-Hill-Brownsville in New York City (Rogers 1968) and the Woodlawn Experimental School District (LeCompte 1969) were efforts at this type of reform and paved the way for other large districts to decentralize and become more responsive to community diversity. Movements for decentralization were particularly attractive to community groups because they included a strong push for community, especially parent, involvement.

During the 1960s and 1970s this kind of decentralization was encouraged by federally funded projects which required "maximum feasible participation" (LeCompte 1972) in the form of citizen advisory boards, community liaison individuals, and the encouragement of Parent Teacher Organizations as a condition of funding. However, participation usually degenerated into tokenism or the continual recruiting of the same few members of the community who could be counted on not to rock the boat (Deyhle 1992; Reyes and Halcon 1988; Stern 1987). Further, increased community control, even as radical an approach as that documented by Hess (1991), has not proved a sufficient remedy for the unresponsiveness of "pathological bureaucracy" (Rogers 1968) or for low pupil achievement.

The "Excellence Movement": Standards for Students

Much of the current rhetoric surrounding restructuring can be construed as a reaction to the "excellence movement" of 1983–1986, which initially blamed poor student performance for the alleged demise of American educational quality. The excellence movement was given impetus by a large number of federal commissions and study groups whose charge was to examine the supposed fragile state of education in America. Their influence was typified by the report of the National Commission on Excellence in Education, *A Nation at Risk: The Imperative for Educational Reform*

Graduation Requirements

In order to receive a regular high school diploma, students must correctly answer at least 70% of the questions in each of the two sections — mathematics and language arts — of the Tennessee proficiency test, and shall have attained an approved record of attendance and conduct. In addition, verified handicapped students must have completed an individual educational program as confirmed by a multidisciplinary team. Regular students must complete 20 units of course work.

SOURCE: Quote from county school district publication, Tennessee.

(1983), and the Holmes Group's report, *Tomorrow's Teachers* (1986). *A Nation at Risk* described the failure of American education as a "rising tide of mediocrity that threatens our very future as a nation and a people."

The first wave of the excellence movement attempted to improve student performance by increasing the standards (see examples of increased graduation requirements in Table 2.1) to be met for promotion and graduation and by ensuring the competency of teachers to provide high-quality instruction. The mechanisms instituted in all 50 states included (1) increasing requirements for student graduation, (2) intensifying standardized testing, (3) establishing minimal competency standards

TABLE 2.1　Graduation Requirements[a]

Students Entering Ninth Grade in School Years:	1983–84 through 1990–91	1991–92 and 1992–93	1993–94	1994–95
English Language Arts	4	4	4	4
Mathematics	2	2	3	3[b]
Science	2	2	2	2
U.S. History	1	1	1	1
Economics	$\frac{1}{2}$	$\frac{1}{2}$	$\frac{1}{2}$	$\frac{1}{2}$
U.S. Government	$\frac{1}{2}$	$\frac{1}{2}$	$\frac{1}{2}$	$\frac{1}{2}$
Physical Education	1	1	1	1
Health Education	$\frac{1}{2}$	$\frac{1}{2}$	$\frac{1}{2}$	$\frac{1}{2}$
Free Electives	$8\frac{1}{2}$	7	7	7
Limited Electives	0	$1\frac{1}{2}$	$\frac{1}{2}$	$\frac{1}{2}$
TOTAL	20	20	20	20

[a]Graduation requirements taken from 1994 Tennessee county school district publication. Limited electives are to be chosen from among Mathematics, Science, World History, World Geography, Ancient History, Modern History, and European History.
[b]Beginning with the 1994–95 ninth-grade students, one of the three mathematics units must be earned in Algebra I, Math for Technology II, or the equivalent in an integrated mathematics curriculum incorporating standards of the National Council of Teachers of Mathematics.

for both teachers and students, and (4) tying teacher accountability to standardized test scores. With the "tide of mediocrity" decried by *A Nation at Risk* came metaphorical secondary waves of reform, one of which was restructuring.

Teacher Competence: "Excellence" for Teachers

Calls for improved student performance were soon seen to be empty without concomitant improvement in instruction. As a remedy, the second wave of excellence proposed a major revamp of training programs—including eliminating the baccalaureate degree in teaching and extending the program by a year—and a variety of methods for stimulating better teaching, including differentiated staffing, merit pay, and other incentives. Finally it was proposed that incompetent teachers simply be fired.

Beginning in the 1980s state departments of education became heavily involved in testing teachers' competency—so that those who failed even after remediation could be fired (see Shepard and Kreitzer 1987)—and in mandating the establishment of "career ladders" for teachers. Some of these proposals are a legacy from Taylorism and the 1930s efficiency experts, but they also are linked to the national educational reform movement of the 1980s. The establishment of state test development offices along with staff for assessment and enforcement, like the compensatory programs in the 1960s, increased the bureaucratization of state-level agencies and reduced local control over recruitment and promotion of staff and students.

"Excellence" reforms have been quite popular because they are relatively easy to institute. They avoid attacks on entrenched political interests because they do not radically alter basic structure, and they affect only those with the least power: teachers and students. They also have demonstrated little real impact on academic achievement or teacher performance (Malen and Hart 1987). Many of the proposed reforms, especially competency tests for in-service teachers and some of the schemes for accountability, have actually been detrimental. Competency testing in particular has done substantial damage to teacher morale (Dworkin 1985b; Shepard and Kreitzer 1987). Further, attempts to transform instruction by changing standards for teacher training are ineffective because schools cannot really be reformed with *new* teachers. New teachers represent only a fraction of the teaching staff. Reforms must be implemented with the existing teacher cadre, many of whom disagree with or do not understand what is being asked of them, while many more are burned out, entrapped, disinterested, isolated, or uncaring (LeCompte and Dworkin 1991).

Site-Based and Shared Decision Making

Building-level decentralization has been termed school-based or *site-based management*. Its purpose is to increase creativity and responsiveness to community needs (LeCompte and Dworkin 1991). Site-based management has now been appropriated wholesale by proponents of restructuring, though it began long before the term *restructuring* had the currency it now enjoys.

Site-based management devolves authority to a specific building principal, who is given far more control over the selection of curricula and instructional techniques, and sometimes over hiring and firing and budgetary matters. Depending upon how it is instituted, site-based management may or may not involve *shared decision making,* which gives additional power to other constituents in the school—teachers, parents, and students. It is this form of decentralization—or restructuring—that has been the primary locus of rhetoric surrounding empowerment. Because it includes lower participants (Merton 1967) (such as parents, teachers, students, noncertified staff, and local businesspeople) in decision making, and even gives them some areas of at least partial authority, it constitutes a shift of power away from higher participants (such as central office staff or middle management). Hence it "empowers" the lower participants.

However, site-based management is not a clearly defined term, nor is it without controversy. A number of studies have shown that teachers, administrators, and policy makers disagree over what should be managed at the site and by whom (Brouillette 1993; Goldwasser 1994; Hart 1990; LeCompte and Wiertelak 1992). For example, Dr. Roberts of Cottonwood School District clearly distinguished between site-based *management* and site-based *decision making* (see the box).

When major decisions remain the province of administrators, however, teachers retreat, as they did in the Pinnacle School District (LeCompte & Wiertelak, 1992). Site-based management also contributes to difficulty in overall district-wide planning, especially if principals take seriously a mandate to run their own schools as they think best. As Brouillette's (1993) careful ethnohistory of a site-based school district indicates, some principals use the latitude this gives them to initiate programs that subvert or counter the philosophy of the superintendent.

Interview a veteran teacher about changes in the school organization since she or he began teaching. What were some of these changes and what does this teacher think about them?

Dr. Roberts's Distinctions

Since my background reflected a participative approach to management, one of the things I began to do during my first year was to talk about decentralizing decisions that traditionally had been associated with the central office. . . . But site-based *management* is a misnomer. Site-based management [implies] that teachers, community members and others are going to be involved in managing the schools. This is not the case with our site-based decision making. The management of schools is an administrative function and people should understand from the very beginning that this movement is not intended to move the managerial functions from building principals and other administrators to staff and/or members of the community.

SOURCE: Brouillette 1993.

A Teacher's Retreat from Management

Site-based management just means teachers have to do what administrators should be doing. We have enough to do without having to run the school, too. What we have here in our district is "room-based management," not site-based management. I don't have any power to run the district, but that's OK. They just leave me alone. And I'm free to manage my own classroom the way I think is best.

SOURCE: LeCompte and Wiertelak 1992.

Changing Control of Teaching and Learning

A third kind of restructuring is *not* organizationally based but involves altering relationships of control in the content and delivery of instruction, so that the experience, knowledge, and participation of children are given more weight in the learning process. Some of the most active restructuring of this nature has come in language arts, especially in whole language programs. Many whole language advocates have appropriated the rhetoric of empowerment. Assuming that functional literacy empowers individuals by giving them "voice," they utilize a number of strategies to increase children's ability to make decisions about how they learn. One common strategy is to involve students in the choice of what they do, either by providing a cafeteria of learning centers or by letting them write stories on topics (or even in the language [Reyes and Laliberty 1992]) of their choosing.

Proponents suggest that by increasing skill levels in critical reading, writing, and inquiry skills, individuals develop a greater sense of self-awareness, which in turn leads to empowerment. This empowerment permits not only *recognition* of the forces that oppose disempowered or oppressed individuals, but also a *showdown* between individuals and the social structures that oppress them (Apple 1982; Ellsworth 1989; Freire 1970, 1985; Giroux 1983a, 1983b, 1988; Gitlin and Smyth 1989; McLaren 1989). Literacy then serves as a vehicle to social reform or revolution, depending upon the orientation of the writer (LeCompte and Bennett 1992).

Both critical theorists and curriculum theorists have drawn on the language, if not the procedures, used by liberation theorists such as Paulo Freire to justify their approach (LeCompte and Bennett 1990). However, much of the actual practice remains rooted in instructional practice and is not informed by social science theory. Often these pedagogical approaches promote methods that are most effective for middle-class children and do not take into account the special needs of other groups, thus rendering the techniques useless if not actually harmful (Delpit 1988; LeCompte and Bennett 1992; Richardson et al. 1989).

Find out what school reforms currently are being advocated in your community. Who is backing them? What problems are they meant to address? Do you think they will be effective?

The Juxtaposition of Restructuring and Empowerment

Considerable attention has been paid over the years to changes in the structure and content of the curriculum (Kaestle 1983; Kliebard 1986; Liston and Ziechner 1991; Tyack 1990), but the current calls for change explicitly link curricular and organizational changes with the concept of empowerment. In the forefront are some school–university collaborative projects initiated by critical theorists as a way to train teachers to be change agents, "critical pedagogues," and "transformative intellectuals" (Giroux 1988).

These new projects almost always, and we believe erroneously, link the terms *empowerment* and *restructuring.* The latter term refers to structural change in *systems* and implies a change in the locus of authority; the former refers to the psychological change in *individuals,* which presumably occurs as a consequence of structural change. The problem is that educators often are unclear as to which comes first, and how either is supposed to be generated. Lack of empowerment (that is, oppression), as described by critical theorists, is a consequence of unequal social relationships, and the presumed remedy uses a structural change model. As described by educators, however, increasing empowerment among lower participants requires a mental health model. With its focus on individuals, it is often vague or silent on structural change issues. As a consequence, it can be held accountable to charges of "blaming the victims" of oppression for not having empowered themselves.

It is an open question whether or not these programs will have a major effect on the power structure of schools. A major impediment seems to be that empowerment is based upon a model of participatory democracy, which seldom has proven longlasting except in very small and homogeneous communities. And school districts and their constituencies, as we have noted in this chapter, are anything but small and homogeneous!

Two other factors mitigate against the success of entirely participative models such as those advocated by their two most active proponents, John Goodland and his I.D.E.A. model, and Theodore Sizer's Coalition for Essential Schools. The first, as Michael Apple (1993) suggests, is the general lack of cultural support for participatory decision making. Apple asserts that participatory democracy evolved in the small, homogeneous religious communities of New England and eventually became the town meetings still found in small communities in the region. However, the class and cultural patterns that facilitated this form of egalitarian decision making did not prevail throughout the United States. In no other part of the country did this secular form of governance succeed.

A second mitigating factor is the lack of support for shared decision making within the schools themselves. School practice has, for decades, emphasized a top-down form of management, whose justification is enshrined in standard business practice and embodied in scientific management. Furthermore, while "Small is beautiful" (Schumacher 1989) might have guided proponents of private schools, in the business of public education smallness has been expensive or impractical. Given these traditions, practices such as school-based management, which give principals and teachers primary control and empower communities to share in the overall direction of schooling, are unlikely to be viewed with open enthusiasm by the current educational administrations.

If you had the power to change the organization of schooling within a school district, how would you do it? Why?

SUMMARY

In this chapter, we have described the organization and control of school systems in America. Our goal has been to provide a context for the rest of the book, which describes the process of schooling and its impact upon participants. We hope that you have begun to understand that schools and educational programs are not neutral. In fact, they exist in a highly politically charged arena. Because schools have more contact with children than any other social institution (excluding the family), and because they are the single agency most amenable to public manipulation, the groups who control the schools have a profound impact on indoctrination and training of future generations. We believe that sociologist Max Weber is correct in stating that it is possible to tell a great deal about the power structure and patterns of social differentiation in a society if you can determine how the schools are organized, the content of instruction, and who benefits from attendance. In the chapters that follow we will explore these issues.

chapter 3

Youth Culture and the Student Peer Group

INTRODUCTION

Most sociology of education texts look at all aspects of schooling—curriculum, staff, hierarchy, buildings, unions, testing—except for the students for whom schools are intended. Notwithstanding, most studies of young people are carried out in schools, because that is where they are most accessible. Researchers seem to assume that schools are the only places children spend time. Perhaps this convenient fiction exists because schools are the aspect of the collective life of children most firmly controlled by adults.

Because researchers study children primarily in school, they have attributed far more prominence to school-related activities in children's lives than may be valid. Because we believe that the out-of-school events are at least as important as are those occurring in school, we will look closely at both types.

Until recently the voices of students simply have not been heard, even to describe what schools really mean to them. (See LeCompte & Preissle 1992 for a review of research on student perceptions of schooling.) As we shall see, how students actually feel about school often diverges widely from what educators would prefer. In fact, schools have lost a great deal of centrality in the attitudes and values of students. Furthermore, students' attitudes toward school are at least as important in shaping their educational experiences as how they are taught or how school is organized. An increasing number of children have become convinced that schools have little to offer them. In response they have become mentally, if not physically, absent from school more than they are present. For many, what goes on outside school is far more important. Teachers no longer can assume that their pupils share their views about the value of education. How long students stay in school, how committed they feel, and the quality of their performance often depend upon their social class, race, and gender as well as characteristics of the community, pressures from outside the school, and attributes of the school itself.

The term *student* refers to a social role and, unlike the term *child,* depends upon enrollment in an educational institution. Successfully enacting the role of "student" means mastering certain institutional requirements, whereas being a child does not. In this chapter we distinguish between children *as children* and children *as students,* in order to highlight the importance of out-of-school events to children and to their lives as students.

The first part of this chapter is devoted to the process of growing up and how it has changed. We define the terms **peer group, adolescence,** and **youth culture** and trace their development. We suggest that the cultural content of any given youth group is context-specific and that, while all young people face common developmental, economic, social, and cultural variables, how they respond depends on the circumstances in which they live.

It is clear that some special kind of energy exists between and among young people. In the minds of many social scientists this energy possesses enough force and longevity to generate a culture of its own. In modern society this culture conforms to its own internal norms, but it can be and usually is directed in opposition to the culture of parents, school, and adult institutions in general. On one hand, this opposition, however mild or intense, constitutes a way for young people to establish an identity separate from that of their elders. However, as a collective entity, the "student peer group" can be a major problem in schools for students themselves as well as for teachers and administrators.

Parents want their children to hang out with friends whose behavior and values are acceptable. Teachers are aware of the powerful influence friends have upon each other, and they separate children who habitually get into trouble when they work together. Social scientists cite studies demonstrating that one of the strongest predictors of a child's future is what his or her friends do. Police, probation officers, therapists, and social workers try to keep juvenile offenders away from the deleterious influence of their old friends.

In the next part of the chapter we look at how schools affect the lives of students and the impact of peer groups. We focus on young people's resistance to the inflexibility of their educational experiences, especially the social definitions and the standards imposed on them in school. Ours is a perspective most applicable to Western European culture and subordinate groups under its influence. Hence some of our assertions may not apply for some minority youth, such as Navajo teenagers. While these cultural biases should be kept in mind, the analysis provides a valuable perspective on the Western European definitions and cultural forms that dominate school life in the United States.

WHAT IS YOUTH CULTURE?

The two terms **peer group** and **youth culture** are often used interchangeably. However, they refer to quite different phenomena and have their origins in different social science disciplines. The term *peer group* comes from sociology and refers to a group of people who share special characteristics such as age, race, gender, or professional or social status. Peer groups are not synonymous with friendship groups, although friendship groups often consist of people who are peers.

Often the equality of peers is defined rather loosely. The phrase "a jury of one's peers" has generated many court battles over the degree to which the composition of a given jury really did equate with the social standing, race, gender, or ideology of the defendant. The same might be said of student peer groups. While they most commonly are defined as an age or grade-level cohort—a group of students who are the same age and in the same grade—that definition is too narrow. Many other factors, including differences in place of residence, social philosophy, dress, academic prowess, social status, race, religion, and interests, cross-cut similarities of age and grade level, so it probably is more accurate to speak of multiple peer groups rather than just one (Epstein and Karweit 1983). Leanne's story (see box on p. 86) reflects this multiplicity of peer groupings, as well as the widespread belief (discussed in Chapter 5) that we all are "middle class."

The term *youth culture* comes from anthropology and is a broader term than *peer group*. Anthropologists have defined *culture* variously as the way of life of a

Leanne's Story

This friend informed me that my family was the richest in ____ County. I figured if this was true, why did we always drink 2% milk? Plus, how come I never got one of those shirts with the alligators when I was in junior high? We never spent money. That's why I considered myself very middle class. So, on any given day, I am either middle class or upper middle class. In my mind, we had this ladder. There were a lot of people on the top, and even more on the bottom. I fit somewhere on the middle. Every day I moved up or down, or even stayed on the same rung. When I was in junior high, the thing I wanted most was to climb to the top of that ladder. That is where all of the "popular" people were. In junior high, I was not popular. I don't even think I was noticed. Now when I look back on it, I'll bet other kids felt the same way that I did. The social ladder: (1) popular kids, cheerleaders/jocks; (2) smart kids, nerds, but not a bad term; (3) me, I didn't really fit in any group; (4) druggers, head-bangers, really cool kids; (5) scuz, people who took vocational classes or woodshop. We wanted to fit in but didn't really. In high school my affections never laid with the popular kids. I did not fit in with them either, but they seemed to respect me. I was an artist and I dressed a little off-center, and I loved the group "Police." They were a big topic of discussion with these guys I liked who had a band. I also hung out at school with this guy who looked like John Belushi and wrote poetry. All of this was at school. I did not go anywhere after school with these people. I did not talk to them on the phone. Therefore, I wasn't really friends with them.

people (Linton 1945), what anthropologists have observed about the behavior of a group of people (Harris 1981), and everything having to do with human behavior and belief (Tylor 1958). In general, they agree that culture includes the entire body of attitudes, values, beliefs, and behavior patterns of a group of people (Spradley and McCurdy 1972). These include language, kinship patterns, rituals, economic and political structures, patterns of reproduction and child-rearing, life stages, arts and crafts, manufacturing, and technology (LeCompte and Preissle 1993).

Cultural development is profoundly affected by a people's physical environment. The environment strongly influences the possessions they make or buy, their family structure, religious beliefs, morals and sexuality, attitudes and behavior toward work and government, and patterns of dress, personal adornment, and recreation. The concept of culture also includes a historical dimension, because past activities of a group affect its current behavior, as do its beliefs about what will happen in the future.

Think back to your high school experiences. What were the student groups in your high school? Describe how these groups distinguished themselves from others. What did they call themselves? How did teachers and school administrators relate to each of these groups? Was there a relationship between social class background and peer group membership?

Can Youth Have a Culture?

Many scholars have argued that youth cannot have a culture, since individuals grow up and become non-youth; in the inevitable loss of their youth they lose the primary characteristic defining them as a part of the culture. Still other scholars argue that one can move into and out of cultures as one gains and loses the status that earns entry. For example, many professions, such as teaching, medicine, and the arts, and many institutions, such as prisons and religious organizations, develop sufficiently distinctive sets of attitudes, values, beliefs, and behavior patterns—even distinctive patterns of dress, personal adornment, and language—as to constitute cultures (Becker and Geer et al. 1961; Ebaugh 1977; Goffman 1959; Sykes 1958). In this view, individuals who cease to practice the given profession or who leave the institution are no longer a part of that culture, and in the same way youths grow up and leave the youth culture.

We do not feel that youth culture necessarily requires that individuals remain children, because youth culture can in fact be perpetuated as practices are passed from one generation of children to another. Bennett, Nelson, and Baker (1992), for example, describe the way succeeding generations of Yup'ik Eskimo girls learned cultural norms and folk tales through "storyknifing," a way of telling and illustrating stories by cutting pictures in soft sand or mud with a dull knife. Similarly, Lever (1976) discusses how gender differences in patterns of play teach children the social roles they will enact as adults.

We believe that *peer group* and *youth culture* are linked terms which must be used together. Youth culture is defined by those distinctive behavior patterns that children and adolescents develop, often in opposition to the power of adults and their institutions. These patterns differentiate young people first of all from adults, and then from other cliques and subgroups within their age cohort (for example, "punkers" are differentiated from "preppies" in American high schools). The peer group is the social entity that develops and practices youth culture. To the extent that the youthful peer group is defined by its relationship to school, we can speak of a student peer group. While peer group influence is important in the lower grades, it becomes more profoundly problematic for schools during adolescence, as Robert's story illustrates (see box on p. 88).

Developmental Factors in the Generation of Peer Groups

Conformity.   One of the characteristics of growing up is not wanting to be different from your friends. Children are fad followers. On one hand, they want to have the most up-to-date fashions, toys, and equipment. On the other hand, they don't want to be too different from their friends or to be caught liking or possessing something that others think is outrageous, outmoded, or stupid. Part of the herd instinct that afflicts young people involves role-modeling and trying on different identities exemplified by their friends or significant adult figures. Another part involves learning the norms and values of a group and trying to stay within them.

Robert's Story

Peer groups had a great deal of influence on me. I was a straight "A" student in elementary school. When I got to junior high, I became friends with a group of boys that wanted to be cool. Our leader was 16 and had a car in the seventh grade. My grades dropped somewhat to B's and C's. Looking back, I believe I did not want to be thought of as one of those "smart" kids. Most of the "smart" kids were from a higher class, or so I thought. I had no idea of going to college. When I got to high school, I began to run track and play football. My new peer group talked about going to college. My grades picked up somewhat, although I still did not want to be perceived as one of the brains. In my peer groups I was a follower, until I became more secure in athletics. However, by my junior year I was a leader in my group. Most of the guys wanted to do whatever I wanted to do.

It is important to note that the conformity of a young person is *internal* to the norms of his or her chosen peer group. Some kinds of youthful solidarity actually facilitate conformity to the norms of teachers and other adults, as was the case with the middle- and upper-class "earholes" described by Willis (1977). In other cases, such as Willis's working-class "lads" and Marotto's (1986) "Boulevard Brothers," peer group norms usually lead to the formation of groups that oppose the rules of adults.

Rebellion.   As much as most children abhor being different from others in their own clique, they find it equally distasteful to be similar to their parents. Rebellion against adult symbols of authority is an important component of growing up in modern urban societies, whether it consists of the cranky independence of a two-year-old or the outlandish dress and behavior of punk adolescents (Roman 1988). The rebellion of students of the 1980s may be seen in part as a conservative reaction to the radicalism of their parents in the 1960s, just as the worldwide student uprisings of the 1960s might be viewed as a reaction to the conservatism, alienation, and repression of the 1950s (Keniston 1968, 1971; Miles 1977).

The actual content and direction of student rebellion is hard to characterize, other than that it is in opposition to whatever strong adult presence, whether parental or institutional, is prominent in the lives of young people. Rebellion against authority may make these groups a mirror image of adult society: What is "bad" to adults becomes "good" to kids.

You hafta make a name for yourself, to be bad . . . [to] be with the "in" crowd. . . . It's just all part of growing up around here. . . . (McLeod 1987, p. 26)

He's the baddest, He shot a fucking cop. . . . That's the best thing you can do.
. . . (McLeod 1987, p. 27)

Idealism.   A third characteristic of young people that affects the formation of the
student peer group in Western societies is idealism and a sense of immortality. We
define *idealism* as a desire to transform the world and make it a better place. It is a

---

Jennie's Story

Especially during my high school years, I experienced a wide variety of peer
groups at school. There were many different groups, and divisions were often
based on one's interests. For example, one group was athletes and cheerleaders.
Another was R.O.T.C. members. Yet another was made up of students in more
advanced classes. There was a group of band members and one with drama
students. There was another of those who were not focused on school and
smoked, cut classes, and found themselves pregnant. Although there were some
students who crossed lines and fit into several groups, they seemed to have a
primary identity with one of the groups. I was probably most easily identified
with the group of kids in more advanced classes. I was in the band during my
freshman year and fit into that group until I quit. My sister was two years behind
me in school. She was a cheerleader and that gave me a foot in the door to that
crowd. I would have been called a "preppie" over a "punker" any day. I was
influenced somewhat by the group in the sense of conformity. I was motivated
to receive the high grades the others did, and to understand the information as
they did. In most cases I was able successfully to conform. These were positive
goals that I sought to achieve. I was influenced also by groups that made me
appreciate where I was as an individual. I was thankful not to fit in with the
crowd of pregnant girls, druggies, and dropouts, although they made up a good
number of the student body. Because I grew up in a family that was intact and
held high moral standards, I was somewhat of an exception to the norm, even
within my peer group. The peer group that affected my life the most was the
friends I had at my church. I felt that I fit in better with them than anyone at
school. Another factor that influenced the peer group relations was socioeconomic status. Although this was not an absolute divider, there were obvious
divisions within the student population. This factor caused me to realize that I
was better off than many people I was closely associated with in the same
school building. School peer groups were not a wonderful experience for me
because I did not have an absolute place to fit in. I followed an "acceptance"
response to surviving school and worked hard to make it a successful experience. Looking back on my high school years, I realized that I was not as bad off
as it seemed at the time. I continue to be a well-adjusted person with a variety of
friends in different peer groups.

tendency to simplify problems and look for unambiguous solutions. Doing so is a necessary stage in the development of a young person's personal philosophy (Belenky et al. 1986). While it allows them to be brave and capable of action on issues that adults, with their more sophisticated understanding of complexities, would sooner abandon, it also makes them prey to outrage and despair when solutions are delayed. Idealism also makes many young people indifferent to the dangers of practices such as truancy, drug use, reckless driving, and unprotected sex.

Their belief in invincibility, immortality, and high ideals permits young people to feel that they cannot be harmed by actions that would endanger most people. This confidence permits them to grow and to change in response to a changing culture by challenging existing definitions and ways of doing things. It also facilitates growth because it encourages risky behavior. In Western societies this attitude is important, because individuation and personal development are valued.

These characteristics of youth—conformity with peers, rebellion against adults, and youthful idealism—facilitate the growth of children away from their families into separate lives as mature adults. The desire for conformity leads to strong friendship groups of individuals who share (1) likes and dislikes, (2) attitudes toward work, family, school, and the opposite sex, (3) aspirations and expectations for the future, and (4) patterns of language, dress, and recreation. Cultural differences may cause variation in specific attitudes, but peer groups remain a major socializing force for young people in modern life. The relative indifference of young people to physical and emotional danger complicates their relationships with school, however, if the cultural patterns and attitudes of the peer group are antithetical or indifferent to behavior required for success in school.

Interview several high school students about the peer groups within their schools today. With the help of these students, make a chart to illustrate the status hierarchy of these peer groups. Which groups hold more power? How does this power get translated into privileges within the school and outside the school? How do these peer groups compare with the groups that existed when you were in high school?

Social and Historical Factors in the Development of Youth Culture

Certain structural characteristics of societies, such as age grades, clans, and schools with patterns of academic tracking, facilitate formation of youthful peer groups. In most cultures people identify throughout their lives as members of a generation or age grade. In some traditional cultures these groups have ritual significance and are recognized as one of the primary organizational structures in the society. Where each age grade performs specific tasks or functions integral to the support of the culture, as they do in certain East African and American Indian societies, the social structure of youthful groups does not promote opposition to the mainstream (Bernardi 1952, 1985; Bowers 1965; Evans-Pritchard 1940; M. Wilson 1963).

In contrast, in much of contemporary Western society youth groups oppose adult values and traditions. We believe that this has occurred because our system of schooling has changed the way young people grow up and caused them to develop and function with only limited contact with adult culture. In fact, in immigrant families adult–child relationships often are switched. Children become teachers to their parents, serve as interpreters, and act as intermediaries between the culture of origin and that of the new country (see, for example, Delgado-Gaitan 1988; Gibson 1988; Richardson et al. 1989; Sanjek 1992). Young people maintain stronger contacts with each other, the media, and their own youthful culture than they do with that of their families. In the pages which follow we will discuss how this situation has come about.

Socialization in Traditional Societies

Unlike animals, children are born without the knowledge or instincts to survive. Either by formal instruction or by watching others, they must be taught social, cognitive, and technical or mechanical skills. They also must learn the history and acquire the knowledge base of the people to whom they belong. This entire process is called **socialization.** In many pre-industrial, or traditional, cultures, where formal schooling is not the primary agency for socialization, children learn how to be adults initially by modeling the behavior of parents and family members. Later they may acquire more technical skills or sophisticated knowledge of the culture from indigenous specialists. Socialization takes place within and is controlled by the community and reflects its structure and values. Young people may "sow their wild oats," but they do not, as a *cohort* or a peer group, develop values and behavior patterns wildly at variance with those of their parents.

Puberty rites, whose purpose is to create a dramatic break in the developmental stream, signify a biological change from childhood to maturity, but there is no such clear distinction between youth and adult culture. Whatever culture young people have is a fairly close approximation of that of their parents. In these traditional cultures parents do not always tell children directly how to behave: It is assumed that they will learn by watching adults, and they do. Such education is not limited to learning how to herd sheep, make clothing, care for children, hunt seals, or farm. It also includes learning how to interact appropriately with others, participate in social life, and adhere to the moral precepts of the community. Only when children misbehave are they punished, and often then only indirectly, through the telling of stories or through gentle reminders (Basso 1984; Deyhle and LeCompte 1994).

Historically, children spent very little time in school. School learning was not necessary for most people, and only the very wealthy could afford the luxury of permitting male children to be out of the work force. Females, too, were needed at home, to help in child-rearing and household chores and to serve as adjuncts to the economic endeavors of women. For example, young Moslem girls in Africa, who are permitted to move freely in the community until puberty, facilitate the trading activities of their mothers, who are restricted by *purdah* to their family compounds (Schildkrout 1984).

To some extent these patterns still prevail. Until the twentieth century, American educators believed education to be wasted on girls. Even if they were intellectually capable of acquiring the necessary skills, jobs where they could use them were not open to females. Considerable doubt was cast not only upon the suitability of education for girls, but also on their ability to absorb it. As recently as the late 1880s the study of geography for girls was opposed because it might make them dissatisfied with their homes and inclined to travel (Curti 1971). Some educators—and even medical experts—believed math, science, and physical education to be so taxing as to cause mental and emotional deterioration and even damage to girls' reproductive organs (Fausto-Sterling 1985; Kaestle 1983). These beliefs—rather than patterns of discrimination or conflict between family responsibilities and careers in an era predating birth control and affirmative action—were used to explain why most of the few women who did become highly educated and had careers remained childless and unmarried. Women were relegated to the home, despite the fact that "careers" as sheltered-wife-and-mother-with-a-spouse-who-supported-her were always more myth than reality. Social beliefs ignored the fact that wars, the distant or intermittent employment of spouses, poverty, death, and abandonment left many women to a great extent responsible for taking care of themselves and raising families alone.

With the exception of a small elite whose male children did spend long years being educated, childhood for most remained a brief prelude to adult responsibilities (Aries 1962). In fact, until the 1920s, and then only in industrialized societies, adolescence for most young people, if it existed at all, was very short and included no more than a few years of schooling.

Adolescence as a Life Stage

Adolescence is a fairly recent phenomenon produced, as we shall see, primarily in modern industrialized societies. In traditional societies adolescence usually begins at the onset of puberty or the achievement of a certain age and is celebrated with special celebrations or rituals, such as a *bar* or *bat mitzvah* for 13-year-old Jewish children. It lasts only until marriage, the birth of the first child, or the point when the young person demonstrates economic self-sufficiency, mileposts that are achieved shortly after biological maturity. In these societies, youth are closely supervised by adults, and there are no great concentrations of young people. The period of youthful irresponsibility is short, and leisure time is limited or taken up by the need to work or to train for it, so young people have no opportunity to develop a distinctive cultural style separate from that of adults.

Adolescence as a Liminal State.   Anthropologists (Gennep 1960; V. Turner 1969, 1974) define *liminal* points as social or developmental transitions—a period after leaving one clearly identified social status and before entering another. Liminal people exist in a state that is "ambiguous, neither here nor there, betwixt and between all fixed points of classification" (V. Turner 1974, p. 232). Initiates in fraternal orders exist in liminal states. So do brides on the day of their wedding before the actual ceremony; they are, in a sense, neither married nor single. Their in-between state is a state of **liminality.** We consider adolescence to be a liminal state because adolescents are neither children nor grown up.

Attitudes about liminal people are somewhat ambivalent. As novices, they are "structurally if not physically invisible in terms of [their] culture's standard definitions and classifications" (V. Turner 1974, p. 232). They are often thought to be in need of protection because they have not yet been socialized to know how to behave in their new role and they might do something that would harm them. They also pose a potential danger to others, because they do not as yet know the rules governing their new state in society and hence they could violate those rules with impunity. Therefore, in most cultures special precautions are taken to protect liminal people from actions that would endanger them or their future status, and other members of society must also be protected from their potentially asocial actions.

In traditional societies, rituals of passage from one social status to another generally include a period of liminality. During this period the initiates may be subject to avoidance taboos, be required to wear special adornments, be placed in a kind of protective custody, be isolated from other people, and made subject to special ceremonies or training. Turner suggests that this segregation emphasizes the equality and comradeship of people who are in a liminal state. It promotes development of group norms, cultural values, and a sense of community.

We believe that in Western societies, schools, especially high schools, act as the segregating and custodial institutions where the rite of passage from early childhood to adulthood takes place. Borman and Spring (1984, p. 238) suggest that adolescence in modern society is a period of transition in which adult status is incrementally achieved. During adolescence, youth occupy "multiple and conflicting statuses." They go to school full time . . . but they also work. They can drive a car and join the army, but they cannot vote or buy alcoholic beverages. They are biologically old enough to procreate but are considered too young by many parents to be told the "facts of life." Schools isolate adolescents in much the same way that formal rituals of passage do in traditional societies. In this way, they act as an incubator for youth culture.

Interview several high school teachers about the peer groups in their schools. Find out how they perceive the relationship of these peer groups to their academic performance in school. What kinds of student do they think are more able?

Schooling and Adolescence

Aries (1962) suggests that the recognition of adolescence as a life-stage is directly related to the lengthening of the mandatory period of schooling. In modern urban societies growing up is a more complex process than in traditional, usually rural, societies, and going to school is a more important part of a child's life. While recent growth in the "home schooling" movement (see Pitman 1987 for a description of home schooling and its supporters) and an increase in private school enrollment are evidence of groups that oppose publicly controlled learning, for the vast majority, childhood instruction takes place in public schools.

Further, the more technologically advanced a society is, the more years children spend in school. We believe that the number of years spent in school is associated with the development of strong peer relationships. As a consequence, the longer a society schools its children, the greater will be the tendency for them to develop a youth culture that is in opposition to adults, even where students change schools frequently. This is so because it is only in age-graded schools that so many people of the same age and sex are forced by law to remain in close proximity for so long.

Compulsory Schooling.   By the end of the nineteenth century universal primary school attendance had been mandated in most of the Western world. By the middle of the twentieth century serious efforts had been made to institutionalize primary schooling worldwide. The subsequent expansion of day-care, pre-school, secondary, and postsecondary school, especially in urbanized and industrialized countries, reflected a changing labor market, especially for women, as well as changing attitudes toward children and child-rearing. As the knowledge base deemed necessary for survival became more complex, and as custody of the young increasingly came to be supervised by the state, instruction was separated more and more from what parents can teach. Parents came to be viewed as incompetent to teach the cognitive and technical skills their children needed, and the family came to be viewed as an inappropriate place for this kind of instruction (Coleman and Hoffer 1987; Durkheim 1969). Children began to spend less time exclusively in their family, neighborhood, and close community and a correspondingly greater proportion of their developing years in institutions of formal instruction. With the institution of day care before and after school, students might be dropped off at 7:00 A.M. and not picked up until nearly twelve hours later. In many countries children of working parents often begin "school" in infancy and continue into university more than twenty years later.

Age Grade Segregation.   In school, young people are concentrated by age groups and segregated from contact with all adults but teachers and other school staff. Compulsory schooling isolates youth in a way which, as V. Turner (1969) suggests, facilitates the development of group solidarity. Idiosyncratic youth culture, especially one that is more or less in opposition to that of adults, developed hand in hand with the expansion of compulsory schooling and the concomitant creation of adolescence (Aries 1962). Schools gave students something to do in the long interval between childhood and adulthood and also provided a way for society to maintain custody over large groups of people deemed too old to be children and too young for the responsibilities of adulthood.

Separation of Biological from Social Maturity.   In contemporary Westernized and industrialized societies marriage or pairing off and the ability to support oneself do not coincide with or closely follow puberty. Instead, during the gap between biological and social maturity which constitutes adolescence, children are kept in a legally enforced state of liminality during which they are emotionally and socio-economically dependent. Institutions, like schools, have substituted for the rituals of the traditional society, serving to protect liminal persons from themselves and society from them.

Protective Custody and Economic Dependence.   Part of the custodial function of schools has been to protect adult laborers from the cheaper, and hence "unfair," competition of youthful workers. In the Third World young urban shoeshine boys, apprentices, "tour guides," beggars and car watchers, tiny rural shepherds, gardeners, and child-care providers perform critical economic functions for their families. However, in the industrialized West young people are denied substantial access to the labor market and often are paid lower wages than adults when they do work. They cannot support themselves well even if they want to. While Groce (1981) states that rural children differ from urban dwellers in that the former must perform many tasks of gardening, animal care, and housework, even they usually are not left to fend for themselves. Traditionally, children in the urban Western world bear few basic responsibilities. Upper- and middle-class children there enjoy a prolonged childhood enforced by economic dependence upon their families.

A second aspect to custody involves inhibiting sexual maturity and premature adulthood. Aries (1962) suggests that the prolonged period of immaturity common in Western society fostered ideas of childhood as a time of innocence, when children should be protected and given time for play and irresponsibility. This idea is associated with the romanticized Victorian notion that children—especially girls—are sexually naive, gentle, and nonviolent and that parents should preserve their innocence, closely supervise their passage through adolescence, and prohibit them from entering into early marriage. In Western societies children spend this stage of their lives segregated in schools and the military, where they acquire a protective veneer of intellectual, social, and vocational skills in preparation for the work force. Protective custody reinforces prohibitions against early marriage, parenthood, and exploitation in the work force, activities that are considered appropriate in traditional societies but an impediment to future economic well-being in modern ones.

In the first half of the twentieth century full-time employment was postponed until after high school. High school graduation came to symbolize the rite of passage into adulthood. However, decreasing economic opportunity and a glut of diplomas have substantially weakened the impact of high school graduation. This situation is changing, as we shall see. Global demographic and economic shifts have meant that many young people now must feed, clothe, and house themselves. Increasing poverty has transformed many children into *de facto* adults.

YOUTH CULTURE AND MODERN LIFE

Growing up is more complex than in the past for several reasons. As we have discussed, the lack of clear-cut rites of passage has blurred the distinction between childhood and adulthood. Second, increased crime as well as social, economic, and cultural pressures have made growing up riskier. Third, there are many obstacles along the way. Finally, even though adulthood takes longer to reach and involves more training than previously, it may no longer offer rewards commensurate with the effort. In the following sections we shall discuss how children have responded to this situation.

Material Culture

Patterns of Consumption.   Children in most of the Western world and in the urbanized portions of the non-Western world grow up in a world in which the monetary
value of commodities is paramount. Children have become prime targets of advertis-
ing, because they have enough money to be consumers. For example, children in the
United States 12 years old or younger spend more than $6 billion a year of their own
money and influence more than $130 billion per year in household expenses (J.
McNeil 1992). They are a market for fashionable clothes, up-to-date cars, electronic
toys, and other consumer goods. The global village has spawned global patterns of
consumption for children. Youngsters in Tokyo, Lagos, and Los Angeles look remarkably alike. Sometimes fads are adopted specifically because they represent a collective
departure from the ways of parents. Fads sometimes go to school in the form of antisocial or antischool behavior, often constituting visible manifestations of an oppositional culture.

Youth Employment.   While children under the age of 18 in the United States still
are legally regarded as minors, their relationship to the work world has changed. Most
students from junior high through graduate school are employed. Prior to 1970 a
full-time student from the middle class seldom had a substantial commitment to the
work force. Working- and lower-class students often did, and still may have to work as
teenagers to help support their families. Now many middle- and upper-class students
become parents while still in school and must support their own children. Many more
affluent students now work, not so much for basic necessities of life or even to save
for college, but in order to buy clothes, cars, and other consumer goods their parents
are unwilling or unable to provide (L. McNeil 1983; Powell, Farrar, and Cohen 1985).
Regardless of their reason for working, more than 70 percent of 16-year-olds who are
in school now work, and they are spending more time on the job. In 1970, 56 percent
of the employed in-school male high school students worked more than 14 hours per
week (Steinberg et al. 1982, p. 363). As a result, the centrality of school in their lives
has been affected. Students now devote to working the time they used to spend on
homework and extracurricular activities (Powell, Farrar, and Cohen 1985).

Jobs may provide an alternative source of self-esteem and gratification for students who do not do well academically or do not excel in athletics, school government, or other extracurricular activities. In fact, some studies have indicated that
working a few hours a week may enhance performance in school. However, for the
majority, jobs tend to interfere with school, especially when the immediate financial
gratification supersedes the deferred gratification of success in school.

While students' jobs are not usually full-time, they may consume as many as 30
hours a week, often in the evening. However, schools still are structured for students
who can devote all of their time to school-related activities. Teachers are faced with
students who have little time out of class to read books, do projects, or work math
problems. They might fall asleep in class because they worked late the night before or
may refuse to let schoolwork interfere with their jobs. In response, teachers "dumb

down" or reduce the amount and complexity of assignments, lower their aspirations for students, and teach less (McNeil 1985; Powell, Farrar, and Cohen 1985).

Technology. Technological factors differ somewhat from other cultural factors in that they have habituated children to patterns of interaction, transmission of information, and communication radically different from those once common in schools. These advances have forced teachers and curriculum developers to change their expectations of what and how children will learn.

While television, video games, the telephone, calculators and computers, portable radios, and audio equipment are indeed cultural artifacts, their impact is more complex and powerful than the mere fact that some people have them and others do not. In fact, their presence has irrevocably altered human communication, and perhaps even perception and cognition. In the first place, these artifacts absorb a great deal—even the vast majority—of young people's leisure time. Teenagers on the telephone or with Walkmans glued to their ears, toddlers viewing the television set as their primary caregiver, and students who cannot do homework without the television or radio blaring—all are stereotypes that represent reality for a large percentage of children. The impact of these technological innovations is profound, controversial, and still being studied, but we wish to mention only a few.

First, these innovations eliminate face-to-face interaction. Telephone conversations lack the immediacy of visual, tactile, and olfactory contact, and answering machines are even further removed from communicants. In the classroom, computers and interactive video sometimes substitute for teachers, leaving children to work in isolation, each with his or her own keyboard.

Second, technological devices like calculators and video games shorten the period of attention needed to solve problems.

Third, they have most commonly been adapted for the simplest cognitive tasks. Instead of enhancing complex cognitive skills, computer-assisted instruction most often is used for simple memorization and recall. Simplifying knowledge to the presentation of single datum "factoids" and presenting them in the form of "sound bites" has penetrated many other aspects of life—entertainment, the media, and even religion. As a consequence, educators feel they must accommodate instruction to limited attention spans and simple solutions. No message or lesson can be longer or more complex than is considered manageable for the assumed attention span of a mesmerized child.

Fourth, use of technology further widens the gap between rich and poor. Schools in poor neighborhoods have fewer high-tech resources. Poor children cannot buy the computers that generate attractive term papers—and that many colleges require students to own.

Economics and Demography

Size and Urbanization. Because children today must deal with people and distance on a scale far larger than any other generation, they face a paradox. As the external world becomes more familiar and intimate, their immediate surroundings become larger and more impersonal. On one hand, they live in a shrinking world where areas once remote and inaccessible now can be viewed nightly on television and visited by tourists. On the other hand, urbanization has made the once familiar strange. Most people now live in urban areas and in apartments rather than houses. Even the ostensibly bucolic suburbs have become urbanized. Families are renters rather than owners as the cost of homes prices most of them out of the market (Cohen and Rogers 1983).

As the supply of moderately priced rental housing decreases, many are faced with the specter of homelessness (Joint Center for Housing Studies 1988). The situation is so serious that the majority of homeless in the 1990s are families with children. The typical homeless person in New York City in early 1989 was a 4-year-old boy (*New York Times,* January 17, 1989). According to U.S. Department of Education estimates, 220,000 school-aged children are homeless and 65,000 of them do not attend school (Reed and Sautter 1990).

Adventure has become too perilous to be challenging. International travel is too familiar to be an adventure; adventure closer to home is too dangerous to be permitted. Parks are dangerous and there are few fields or open spaces where children can run and explore unsupervised. Even shopping malls have become centers of gang-related or criminal activity. The attendance zones of schools are so large that walking to school usually is impossible. Friends from the same school may live so far apart that it's difficult to visit each other. As a consequence, children either see only those children in their immediate neighborhood, or spend a lot of time driving or being driven to activities and friends' homes. Young people may be quite familiar with the customs of people on the other side of the globe but not know anybody on their block. Inner-city children may be even more isolated. In the housing projects, shelters for the homeless, and blighted neighborhoods where many urban children live, a visit to friends next door or even down the hall may lead to an encounter with drug-related violence.

Children may find it difficult to participate in any school-related activities before or after school, since most must come and go in accordance with a parent's schedule, timing of the bus route, or car pool. This constraint further reduces the capacity of the school to be of central importance to their lives and leaves them subject to the same social isolation afflicting urban adults. Under these conditions, the peer group's attitudes and behaviors are influenced primarily by street life and the media.

Poverty. Even as school has lost its centrality, changes in families have made them less able to provide support and guidance. The increase in divorce and single parenthood means that the *normal childhood experience* will become life with one parent. The majority of children—59 percent of all children born in 1983, for example (O'Neill and Sepielli 1985, p. 3)—at some time in their lives will live in a single-parent home (Brown 1986). The percentage is even greater among many minority groups; 90 percent of African-American teenage mothers are unmarried.

More children than ever also are growing up in families that are very poor. In 1987, 25 percent of children under the age of 6 lived in families below the poverty line. One in six had no health insurance, and fewer and fewer were receiving public

---

Families in Poverty in the United States

* 23.3% of children aged 3 and under are poor.

* Nearly 22% of 3–5-year-olds are poor.

* Of children between the ages of 6 and 11, 19.9% or 4 million children are poor.

* Of children between the ages of 12 and 17, more than 16% live below the poverty line.

* Almost 50% of children living in a family headed by a person 25 or younger are poor.

* 56% of families headed by single African-American women are poor.

* Two-thirds of America's poor are white.

* Less than 9% of poor people live in the core cities of the United States; 17% of poor people live in rural communities and 28% live in suburban communities.

SOURCE: Reed and Sautter 1990.

---

assistance or food stamps (Children's Defense Fund 1988). Although at least 3 million children were eligible for Head Start in 1985, funds were available to enroll only 400,000 (Hodgkinson 1985). The rising incidence of divorce and unwed motherhood increased the number of children living below the poverty line, because female-headed homes are more likely to be poor. Of the children living in poverty in 1985, 50 percent lived in female-headed homes but only 12 percent in homes where a male was present. The situation is worse for minorities. Forty percent of all minority children live in impoverished homes, and the situation is worse in those headed by a female (Bayes 1988; O'Neill and Sepielli 1985).

Family Structure.   Even children in intact and "blended" nuclear families cannot rely upon the presence of a homebound parent, because maintenance of most households with children requires two incomes. What this means is that children are caught between the expectations of schools and the reality of their family life. Schools still operate as if most children have two heterosexual parents, one of whom is a full-time parent available for helping with homework, having parental consultations with teachers, making cookies, and other tasks. However, 51.9 percent of the mothers of children one year and younger are in the work force (G. Collins 1987). Up to 33 percent—over 4 million—of elementary school children are "latchkey" children (*Education Week* 1989; O'Neill and Sepielli 1985) who take care of themselves after school, get help with homework from a telephone hotline if available, and cope with overworked parents in the evening. They are expected to be emotionally mature and to demonstrate adult-like independence even in pre-school, because their parents have few economic or emotional reserves left after the pressures of daily survival (Woodhouse 1987).

Children are deluged with invitations to engage in illegal activities, use drugs and alcohol, and become sexually active. They find it easy to do so as drugs permeate all echelons of society. They see drug-related behavior where they work, on the streets, in their schools, and among their family members, and their parents often are too busy working to supervise them during their leisure time.

The Labor Market.   The economic context of growing up in the latter part of the twentieth century for most young people, regardless of where they live, is one of frustrated aspirations and limited expectations. As the lower-paying service sector of the labor market grows, opportunities for lucrative positions shrink and there is less room at the top of the economic ladder (Bluestone and Bennett 1982). Young people must reduce their aspirations in accordance with the reality of the more humdrum, less lucrative jobs available (Littwin 1987). Competition for desirable professional positions is keen, feeding both a ferocious battle for those willing to join the fray, and hopelessness among those who deem the costs of competing to be too high. It also feeds racism and bigotry, as members of the dominant white culture feel unfairly disadvantaged by affirmative action programs. The lower-income white young men whom McLeod studied typify these feelings:

> [SHORTY:] "He got laid off because they hired all Puerto Ricans, blacks, and Portegis (Portuguese)."
>
> SMITTY: "All the fuckin' niggers are getting the jobs. Two of them mother-fuckers got hired yesterday [at a construction site]; I didn't get shit. They probably don't even know how to hold a fuckin' shovel, either."
>
> FRANKIE: "Fuckin' right. That's why we're hanging here now with empty pockets. . . . hey, they're coming on our fucking land. . . . They don't like us, man, and I sure as hell don't like them."
>
> SHORTY: ". . . *Listen.* When they first moved in here [into the housing project], they were really cool and everything. We didn't bother them. But once more and more black families moved in, they said, 'Wow, we can overrun these people. We can overpower them.' That's what their attitude was." (1987, pp. 39–40)

Violence, Environmental Degradation, and Potential Annihilation.   Today's children have immediate personal and global survival on their minds as well. In addition to the interpersonal violence they witness daily in the media, children see themselves or people they know being abused by parents. Their own parents abuse each other. Their schoolmates use drugs and carry guns and knives. Children worry about how to get through the school hallway or back home safely. Children living in urban communities worry about drive-by shootings in their neighborhood. Consider these statistics from the National School Boards Association's *Violence in the Schools:*

- Firearms are the leading cause of death of African-American males age 15–24 and the second leading cause of death for all teens in the United States.
- About 10 percent of youth (age 10–19) report that they have fired a gun at someone or have been shot at.
- One-fourth of all suspensions from school nationally were for violent incidents committed by elementary school students.
- Approximately 135,000 guns are brought into schools every day.
- One out of five weapons arrests in 1991 was a juvenile arrest; between 1987 and 1991 juvenile arrests for weapons violations increased by 62 percent.
- About 3 million crimes occur on or near school property each year. (National School Boards Association 1993, p. 3)

Schools and communities are actively working toward ways for making schools safer through a variety of programs, which involve protective as well as preventative measures. Protective measures include closed-circuit TV, gun-free school zones, drug-detecting dogs, establishment of "safe havens" for students, locker searches, metal detectors, phones in classrooms, search and seizure policies, and security personnel in schools. Preventative programs include conflict resolution and peer mediation training, multicultural sensitivity training, staff development, support groups, parent skill training, and home–school linkages (National School Boards Association 1993).

Growing up in the shadow of atomic, chemical, and biological war clouds, children wonder how growing up can be considered a viable proposition. The whole world might be blown up before they have any say in the matter. They know that activism in the 1960s neither solved the social and economic problems being protested, nor caused a revolution. James Gleick has suggested:

the explosion of the first atomic bomb stands . . . as the central moment in the history of our time, the threshold event of an age. . . . Its prelude was [a belief in] an irreversible mastery of science over nature; its sequel was violence and death on a horrible scale. (1989, p. 1)

These conditions spawn apathy and egocentrism among young people. All of them have made growing up in the past few decades a very difficult process, one requiring young people to set out upon virtually uncharted waters. One response has been simply to avoid growing up for as long as possible.

THE POSTPONED GENERATION

Joan Littwin (1987) suggests that middle-class young people in America have responded to the factors enumerated above by postponing adulthood. We feel that her phrase, the "postponed generation," fits more than just middle-class youth.

Being grown-up in Western culture means having economic self-sufficiency rather than biological maturity. Self-sufficiency means the ability to pay for one's own home, to support oneself, and to acquire and support a family. Until the late 1960s it more or less corresponded with completion of high school or military service—somewhere between 18 and 22 years—when individuals were old enough to work full-time and most could make a decent living. Increments of success were predicated upon obtaining skills that were not widely held by others or that were in demand. Schooling gave a competitive edge, whether or not it corresponded to increments of skill, because years of schooling served as a proxy for ability. Unfortunately, this is no longer always the case.

Inflation of Educational Credentials

As more and more people possessed the basic complement of schooling, the increment needed to stand out and be competitive increased. As more and more people need more and more education to compete for jobs, a real labor market dilemma arises: People are overeducated for the work they do. The level of schooling required to *obtain* many jobs is higher than the skill level needed to do the work. Littwin (1987) calls this disparity a "job gap," or the degree to which individuals must work at jobs that are below the level they expected to acquire, given their education and training. The job gap eliminates job slots to which the poorly educated or less skilled once aspired because more highly educated people who have revised their job expectations downward have filled those slots. Especially for graduates in the liberal arts, social sciences, and humanities—fields that historically held the most promise for creative individuals—interesting and desirable white-collar jobs are becoming increasingly scarce.

The job gap is aggravated by two factors. First, "our economy is very good at generating new jobs—but most of them are low-paying service jobs which require little education" (Hodgkinson 1985, p. 8). Since the number of young people who have done well in school exceeds the supply of entry-level jobs fitting their qualifications, many of the most talented young people must wait a long time to get any job, let alone one related to their chosen field (Borman 1987; Littwin 1987). In 1983 one out of every five college graduates worked in a job requiring no college education at all (O'Neill and Sepielli 1985).

The second factor exacerbating the job gap is current population trends. High birth rates between 1946 and 1964 produced the generation known as the "Baby Boomers" (see Figure 3.1). These individuals are now in their prime working years, increasing the number of people competing for jobs.

All of these factors prolong adolescence, or at least the period of time young people must wait before they can begin their life work. They also must adjust to a

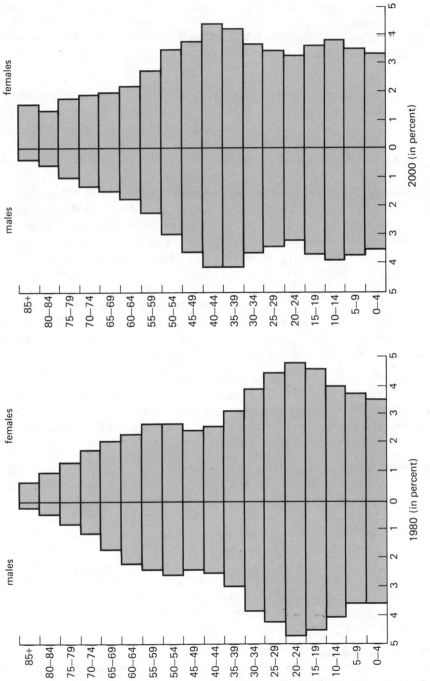

FIGURE 3.1 The Baby Boom Ages (Hodgkinson 1985)

lower standard of living than they expected, one perhaps lower than that of their parents, not only because of low-paying initial jobs (Borman 1987; Littwin 1987), but also because the jobs they ultimately get are less prestigious and lucrative than their aspirations indicated.

Postponed Maturation

The consequence is a "postponed generation." Its members start to grow up later than previous generations, and they take longer to attain economic independence. They may spend several years moving from one low-paying entry-level job to another (Borman 1987). They may be unemployable for long periods of time and have difficulty making a commitment to work that does not coincide with their aspirations. Both the academically successful and those who were less so and had lower aspirations suffer similar feelings of *ennui,* or boredom, because it is difficult for them to find gainful employment and to settle into family life.

Many also are unrealistic about what it takes to get and hold a job. Fine suggests that this is so because the schools do not provide them with information unless they are legally mandated to do so. As a consequence, students do not learn what it takes to get into college, join the military, or pass the GED. Fine's respondents, all dropouts, believed that "the GED is no sweat, a piece of cake . . . you can get jobs, they promise, after goin' to Sutton or ABI [trade schools and business colleges, most of which currently have dropout rates of close to 70 percent (Fine 1986; *New York Times,* June 28, 1989)] . . . in the Army I can get me a GED, skills, travel, benefits . . ." (Fine 1987, pp. 169–170). Hess et al. (1985), Powell, Farrar, and Cohen (1985), and others suggest that this situation is not unique to dropouts. An example:

> [To become a pediatrician] you have to go to community college for two years. Then you go to medical school for four years. After that you are an intern for two years. Then you are a regular nurse for two years. Then you do a residency, and after that you can be a doctor and start at $65,000 a year. (Firestone and Rosenblum 1988, p. 291)

Only the most motivated of students obtain realistic, adequate advice from school personnel (Cicourel and Kitsuse 1963; Powell, Farrar, and Cohen 1985; Sarason 1971).

A small decline in the job cohort in the 1990s may alleviate the situation somewhat, but there is evidence that although the Baby Boomers postponed having children for a while, their children will now create another population bulge. In addition, changes in the population will not affect the decline in professional jobs. The consequence for youth is that most will end up hitting a job ceiling at least for a while, and all will cope with extended periods of liminality.

Postponed Minority Youth

Most middle-class children eventually get back on track. However old they may be, they have a "safety net" of family connections and cultural knowledge which eventually helps most to work the system. Tobier (1984, quoted in Fine 1987) states that white high school dropouts living in affluent sections of New York are far more likely to be employed than African-American high school graduates from Harlem. The consequences of postponement for minority or disadvantaged youth are far more severe (see Table 3.1). They may never get started.

Many minority youth drop out of school, and many more graduate with minimal literacy skills. Even those who do graduate and are literate often find that no good jobs exist in their community (Wilson 1987). Deyhle (1991, 1992) found that high school graduation did not improve job opportunities for most reservation-dwelling Navajo youth, who ended up with the same low-paying menial jobs dropouts had. Minority youth in the inner city suffer from a flight of industry to the beltways and suburbs, and transportation networks often do not make it possible to travel easily to new work places, even if employers were willing to hire poorly trained adolescents. Some of the girls can become mothers, which is a culturally acceptable alternative (Deyhle and LeCompte 1994), but boys find themselves in a particularly desperate situation. In a society that values gainful employment above all other means of demonstrating self-worth, they find no jobs and nothing to do except drink and use drugs. Many die before the age of 30, often in ill-disguised forms of suicide such as substance abuse, fights, or motor vehicle accidents (see, for example, Conant 1988).

When they can find them, young minority men drift from one dead-end job to another. They often are unable to support themselves or a family except through illicit means—robbery, pimping for prostitutes, and the drug trade. These activities can land them in prison, if not in a morgue (McLaren 1989). The situation is worse on Indian reservations and in rural areas, especially where subsistence has been the traditional mode of life (Conant 1988; Deyhle 1988). These areas have no agricultural or industrial base and little hope for building one outside of the tourist industry, and most young people do not wish to follow traditional subsistence practices.

Although many middle-class youth postpone growing up by hanging out at home and working at make-do jobs they see as temporary, the poor, working-class, and minority youth may feel that they have no opportunity to grow up. Fine documents how minority youth know that "there ain't no jobs waitin' for me" (1986, p. 399). They pass their time hanging around street corners or other gathering places, talking, smoking, and drinking until they find some sort of work or get arrested (Marotto 1986). The hopelessness of their situation is illustrated by McLeod's description of the "Hallway Hangers'" reactions to a question about what they would be doing in twenty years:

STONEY: ". . . I could be dead tomorrow. Around here, you gotta take life day by day. . . ." (1987, p. 61)

FRANKIE: ". . . I live a day at a time. I'll probably be in the fucking pen. . . . I can work with my brother, but that's under the table. Besides, he's in [state prison] now." (Ibid.)

SLICK: "Most of the kids around here, they're not gonna be more than janitors. . . . I'd say the success rate of this place is, of these people . . . about twenty percent, maybe fifteen." (1987, p. 68)

TABLE 3.1 Civilian Labor Force—Employment Status, by Sex, Race, and Age: 1992[a]

Age and Race	Civilian Labor Force Total (1,000)	Percentage by Age Male	Percentage by Age Female	Male (1,000) Total	Male (1,000) Employed	Male (1,000) Unemployed	Female (1,000) Total	Female (1,000) Employed	Female (1,000) Unemployed	Percentage of Labor Force Male	Percentage of Labor Force Female	Percentage of Labor Force Male	Percentage of Labor Force Female
All Workers	126,982	100.0	100.0	69,184	63,805	5,380	57,798	53,793	4,005	92.2	93.1	7.8	6.9
16–19	6,751	5.1	5.5	3,547	2,786	761	3,204	2,613	591	78.5	81.6	21.5	18.5
20–24	13,703	10.5	11.2	7,242	6,357	884	6,461	5,799	662	87.8	89.8	12.2	10.2
25–34	35,103	28.0	27.2	19,355	17,847	1,508	15,748	14,594	1,154	92.2	92.7	7.8	7.3
White	108,526	100.0	100.0	59,830	55,709	4,121	48,696	45,770	2,926	93.1	94.0	6.9	6.0
16–19	5,744	5.0	5.6	3,019	2,464	555	2,726	2,297	429	81.6	84.3	18.4	15.7
20–24	11,539	10.2	11.2	6,097	5,462	634	5,442	4,993	450	89.6	91.7	10.4	8.3
25–34	29,538	27.6	26.8	16,510	15,364	1,146	13,029	12,222	807	93.1	93.8	6.9	6.2
Black	13,891	100.0	100.0	6,692	5,846	1,046	6,999	6,087	912	84.8	87.0	15.2	13.0
16–19	787	6.1	5.3	419	243	176	368	231	137	58.0	62.8	42.0	37.2
20–24	1,683	12.7	11.6	872	658	214	811	623	187	75.5	76.8	24.5	23.1
25–34	4,251	30.8	30.4	2,121	1,820	302	2,130	1,830	300	85.8	85.9	14.2	14.1
Hispanic	10,131	100.0	100.0	6,091	5,388	703	4,040	3,584	456	88.5	88.7	11.5	11.3
16–19	678	6.4	7.1	391	281	110	287	211	76	71.9	73.5	28.2	26.4
20–24	1,460	14.6	14.1	890	768	122	570	500	71	86.3	87.7	13.7	12.4
25–34	3,316	34.1	30.7	2,075	1,866	209	1,241	1,103	137	89.9	88.9	10.1	11.1

[a](For civilian noninstitutional population 16 year's old and over. Annual averages of monthly figures. Based on Current Population Survey. We have omitted data on workers 35 years old and over.)

SOURCE: U.S. Bureau of Labor Statistics, *Employment and Earnings*, January 1992.

JINKS: "I think most of them, when and if a war comes, they're all gone. Everyone's going. But for jobs—odds and ends jobs. Here and there. No good high-class jobs." (Ibid.)

The problem is that even those young men who try to join the military as a last resort often find that they do not qualify academically. The result is a youth culture of hopelessness:

FRANKIE: "We were all brought up, all we seen is our older brothers and that gettin' into trouble and goin' to jail and all that shit. Y'know, seeing people—brothers and friends . . . dying right in front of your face. You seen all the drugs. . . . We grew up, it was all our older brothers doing this . . . the drugs, all the drinking. They fucking go; that group's gone. The next group came, our brothers that are twenty-something years old. They started doing crime. And when you're young, you look up to people. . . . And he's doing this, he's drinking, doing drugs, ripping off people. Y'know, he's making good fucking money; it looks like he's doing good. So bang. Now it's our turn. What we gonna do when all we seen is fuckin' drugs, alcohol, fighting, this and that, no one going to school?" (McLeod 1987, pp. 117-118)

The entire social system has become less and less responsive to the varied and sometimes desperate needs of young people. The opportunity structure also provides good jobs for only a few disadvantaged young people. The remainder are systematically pushed out of schools, which continue to hold out fraudulent promises of a good job in return for solid effort. For minority and poor children, equality of opportunity is a myth. Schools simply reinforce and widen the gap between rich and poor. Most, like Fine's dropouts, internalize the reasons given by the dominant culture for their failure, believing the system and its values to be legitimate and the failure to be their own.

THE LESSONS OF SCHOOLING

Going to school represents a sharp break from being at home. First, going to school introduces a new role: Children become students—one of the first institutional roles they acquire. Second, schools are structured differently from home (Dreeben 1968; Durkheim 1969). Functional theorists have suggested that families and schools are structured differently because they have different purposes and represent different values. They believe that the discontinuity schools create between the past and present experience of children is both necessary and proper. Citing the differentiation of function that modernization brings to social institutions, they argue that in complex industrialized societies no one institution such as the family can hope to impart all of the skills children need for adult life. Therefore, a division of labor evolves whereby the tasks of socializing the young can be divided. Each institution in which young people participate carries out the task for which its structure is most appropriate. The family, which is smaller, more intimate, and idiosyncratic, is responsible for the development of individual personality, close relationships, and specific moral values. The larger, more impersonal, diverse, and universalistic school is responsible for technical training, including cognitive skills, and for preparing children to be responsible citizens and workers. Coleman and Hoffer (1987) summarize the functional position, arguing that schools explicitly were an

> instrument that alienated the child from the family, an instrument that benefitted the child by bringing it into the mainstream of American society, but at a cost to the continuity and strength of the family. The cost was not great when a school served [an ethnically and religiously homogenous] local community, for then the culture of the local community pervaded the school and made it consistent with the functional community of adults whose children it served. The cost was great, however, for cultural minorities in [heterogenous communities]. (p. 140)

This cost, functionalists argue, is warranted in the face of community needs for order and consistency.

Critical theorists agree that there are differences between school and family life, but they argue that what schools actually do is to maintain the existing power structure and reproduce the system of social classes by mobilizing a work force stratified by class, race, and gender. They hold that schools do not train citizens to govern themselves and work in a meritocratic, egalitarian society. As one dropout put it:

> In school we learned Columbus Avenue stuff and *I* had to translate it into Harlem. They think livin' up here is unsafe and our lives are so bad. That we should want to move out and get away. That's what you're supposed to learn. (Fine 1987, p. 164)

In the pages that follow we will discuss the structural and organizational differences between school and family and will indicate how these differences help to prepare the ground for development of youth culture and its opposition to adults. We will also describe how children resist the power of teachers and school staff, as well as how educators have created institutions within the school to counteract their oppositional behavior. We will begin with a discussion of what children encounter when they enter elementary school and what it teaches them. Many scholars refer to this as the "hidden curriculum" (Jackson 1968), or the "tacit teaching to students of norms, values and dispositions that goes on simply by their living in and coping with the institutional expectations and routines of schools, day in and day out for a number of years" (Apple 1979, p. 14). After a discussion of elementary school, we will move to an analysis of high schools and their relationship to students.

Becoming a Student: Elementary School

Schools are not organized to coincide with the natural impulses of children, and they seldom involve a child's favorite activities. Because we are so familiar with them, we tend to forget that the way schools are organized is not inevitable but has evolved under the impact of social and political pressures.

We also forget that children are conscripts. Whereas staff are voluntary recruits because of their skills and professional credentials, children are involuntary recruits because of their age status as minors (Bidwell 1965; Nadel 1957). Nowhere else is such a large group of noncriminals forced to remain in an institution for so long, a fact that makes children's attitude about their participation diverge markedly from that of adults.

Crowds and Noise. The organization of schools is very different from that of the family. In the first place, schools are much bigger. Many people, on returning to their elementary school, are shocked to discover how small it was. But to children, the school building, no matter how tiny, still is much larger than their house or apartment.

Physical size is not the only difference. There also are many more people, and they are apportioned differently. A family in Western society usually contains no more than 3 to 7 members, but classrooms usually contain at least 28 to 30. The adult-to-child ratio changes as well. Families usually contain at least one adult for every two or three children, but in the classroom the ratio is closer to 30:1. This means that children in school receive significantly less adult attention than in the family (Dreeben 1968). In fact, schools are crowded, noisy places where adults are far outnumbered by children (Jackson 1968).

Coping with Diversity. Schools also are marked by considerably more heterogeneity than families. Most parents belong to the same racial, ethnic, socioeconomic, and religious group. In schools, however, children begin to learn about people who are quite different from themselves. Because elementary schools are tied to neighborhoods, the student body is usually more homogeneous than junior and senior high schools, but as children grow older, the schools they attend bring them into contact with more and more diversity and challenging social situations (Dreeben 1968). Homogeneity is becoming less possible in public schools as minority populations come to outnumber whites in the Western world. Desegregation programs also have made inroads into patterns of educational and residential racial segregation.

Even where the students form a homogeneous group, they may have very little in common with their teachers, ethnically, socially, or economically. They probably do not even live anywhere near each other, and they may be totally unfamiliar with the lives each leads outside of the classroom.

Losing Individuality and Being Categorized. While most adults recall the size differential between home and school, they probably do not remember how it felt to lose the sense of demographic uniqueness that the family provides. Unless a family has adopted children or has twins or triplets, it seldom contains more than one child of the same age and sex. Treatment of individual children in the family is predicated upon these age and sex categories. Behavior is deemed appropriate or inappropriate according to whether one is old enough to carry out an activity, young enough to justify specific actions, and of the correct gender to participate.

In school, however, children learn to be treated as members of social categories. First is age. Children are initially grouped exclusively by their birth date, and they discover that there are many boys and girls of the same age.

While language patterns, physical attractiveness, and general deportment do affect teachers' reactions to individual children, teachers make few allowances for special characteristics, and all the children are expected to conform to rather standardized patterns of behavior. In fact, it is treatment and grouping upon the basis of similarity of category, rather than upon individual differences, that constitute one of the hallmarks of life in school.

Separating Roles from Persons.   School is the place where children begin to learn the difference between parents and all other adults as well as to distinguish between social roles and the people who occupy them. They learn, for example, that the social role—its expectations and obligations—of teacher remains constant from year to year, even if the occupants change. They also learn that their teachers do not respond as their parents do and that staff are not present to nurture their individual idiosyncrasies. Unlike parenting, teaching is a job, whose task it is to control children and to impart knowledge (Dreeben 1968). In fact, some researchers suggest that the differences between students and staff eventually diverge into "fighting groups" created from widely different interests in school and goals while there (Connell 1985; Waller 1932).

Learning to Achieve.   Another measure by which children are categorized is achievement. It is almost as powerful an influence on development as age, sex, and race (Dreeben 1968). This category begins to take shape before the child's arrival at school and remains almost immutable until school life ends, structuring the school experience and to a large extent determining the student's future occupational status. Children usually arrive at school already having taken "readiness" tests or with records of pre-school teachers and day-care workers. On the basis of these and sometimes additional tests, they are stratified for instruction according to their perceived ability to learn. The word "perceived" is an important one, because a child's ability is often subjectively defined and may have less to do with native intelligence than with behavior, ethnicity, and social class, as well as the teacher's affinity for the child and how a given school defines readiness (Eisenhart and Graue 1990; Graue 1994; Ortiz 1988; Richardson et al. 1989; Rist 1970, 1973; Rosenfeld 1971).

However they happen to be placed into ability groups, children are "tracked," "streamed," or "grouped" from the day they enter school. These groups are obvious to children, despite heroic efforts to disguise them. Tracks engender patterns of behavior and belief in children and play an important role in defining the kind of individual students believe themselves to be. An insidious characteristic of ability groups is that they construct failure. No matter how high the achievement of the lowest group is, children in it feel like "dummies," "retards," or "basics." Page (1987), for example, studied a "dream high school," where none of the students was disadvantaged, and even in this setting the lowest students—who might well have been the most advanced in an inner-city school—thought of themselves as "dregs" and a "circus," adopting the rebellious attitudes usually attributed to lower- and working-class students.

Ability groups are critical in the formation of student peer groups because they determine friendship groups. Study after study show that friendship groups form almost exclusively among students who study together and who share a common academic track record (K. P. Bennett 1986, 1991; Borko and Eisenhart 1986; Coleman 1961, 1965; Gamoran and Berends 1987; Gordon 1957). Students in the academic groups also tend to be the most popular students (Gamoran and Berends 1987, p. 427).

Evaluation and Gratification. Schools and families also differ in the relative emphasis they place on different modes of evaluation (Dreeben 1968). Whereas families evaluate children on the basis of their individual personality, schools evaluate them primarily on how well they achieve in school. Impulse gratification is also handled differently. Parents are warned that, since young people are oriented to immediate rewards, they should not promise rewards that cannot be given or that must be delayed; schools, on the other hand, operate on the premise of deferred gratification. Teachers encourage children to believe that hard work now will yield tangible rewards in the future. Grades only symbolically represent the material rewards which will ultimately come. This promise is, of course, not particularly compelling to many teenagers, for whom the future is far away indeed.

Cognitive knowledge is not the only kind of knowledge children acquire in school. In elementary school children learn about the separation of student and teacher roles and something about appropriate sex-role behavior (Goetz 1981). They internalize the rules of the organization and construct their own definition not only of how to survive, but of how well they can be expected to do. They have some idea of the degree to which their efforts will pay off in grades, and they may have learned how to "make deals" with teachers as to how much they will be taught (Borko and Eisenhart 1986; Powell, Farrar, and Cohen 1985). Most of them have acquired some rudiments of the cognitive skills, and they have fairly well-formed personalities and sets of social relationships. By the time they reach high school, they are interested in other matters.

Becoming Pre-Adult: High School

The Opposite Sex. In high school, students become deeply interested in working out their gender identity and relationships with the opposite sex. Especially for girls, sex complicates the development of attitudes and aspirations about work, careers, and their future. Weis (1988) and Holland and Eisenhart (1988) studied the "ideology of romance" (McRobbie 1978) which suffuses the lives of young women. Although Holland and Eisenhart (1988) studied college students, we feel that their analysis also applies to students in high school, who are only a year or two younger. Holland and Eisenhart stress the importance of the "world of peers" in the determining gender identity.

> [Students] spend most of their time around age mates, are constantly exposed to peer-organized activities, learn age-mate interpretations and evaluations of all aspects of . . . life . . . have most of their close, intimate relationships with age mates on campus, and learn ways to understand and evaluate themselves from those peers. (pp. 17–18)

Holland and Eisenhart (1988) suggest that the peer culture competes with schoolwork, derails some students, and affects even those who don't participate in it directly, because it creates a culture with which all students must cope. Whether they are identified as punks and badasses, greasers or jocks, preppies, nerds, or dropouts, young people cannot totally dismiss what the others say and feel about them, no matter how they try to distance themselves.

Most powerful of all pressures brought to bear on young people are those concerning traditional, gender-appropriate roles in romance, which have dampening effects on the self-image, aspirations, and efforts of young girls (Christian-Smith 1988; Brown and Gilligan 1992; Lesko 1988; Roman 1988b). We will talk more about self-esteem in young women in Chapter 8.

Getting Ahead.   Adolescents recognize that there are many areas of achievement. One is success in personal, social, and familial arenas. Another is demonstrated athletic prowess. A third is the status of conspicuous consumption. The fellow with the fancy clothes, expensive watch, and brand-new car smells of success, regardless of how these were acquired. A fourth, and the only one that schools are designed to facilitate, is success in academic and professional arenas.

Children go to elementary school to learn cognitive skills of reading, writing, and computation, and to high school to acquire both the knowledge base and the social skills and values that will fit them for various roles in the occupational structure. Their success in school is measured in terms of how well they do in these tasks, as measured by grades, teacher assessments, and standardized test scores.

Adolescents, however, know that the criteria for success in school are more diffuse and complex than just getting good grades. Two classic studies (Coleman 1961; Gordon 1957) demonstrated that grade point averages are of little importance in high school; extracurricular position or one's place in the juvenile social status system supersedes academic achievement. For boys the primary criterion was athletic prowess, followed by conformity to norms of in-school behavior, dating, dress, and recreation. For girls the highest positions went to the prom and yearbook queens. They gained this status by adhering to particular patterns of dress, giving service to the school, having a "good" personality and being friendly, being a leader in activities, and maintaining Puritan standards of morality. Grades still are relatively unimportant,

---

Amber's Dress Code

When I moved to College City from Denver, the kids all looked different from my old school. Like, they were all so . . . preppie! I like to look different . . . and I'm one of the only Hispanic kids. But the girls, they all had this thick straight blonde hair and little white tennies and tight jeans faded just right and white tee shirts and little gold chains. They all looked alike. I wear flannel shirts and baggy pants and boxers . . . [she laughs] . . . but under my pants! And I *don't* wear those little white tennies!

---

and although yesterday's teen queen wore bobby sox and pleated skirts whereas today's might "punk up" her hair, adherence to the prevailing adolescent dress code and standards for social behavior and recreation make all the difference in the status hierarchy (see box).

High grades alone are not sufficient to ensure a successful career in school even from the perspective of teachers, and conversely low grades will not always preclude students from feeling good about their life in school, being envied by their peers, and being defined as "successful" students. Many students consider social, personal, and familial achievement to be as important, if not more so, than academic achievement. They want very much to be accepted by their friends, and doing so means adopting the cultural values of their friends. If their friends do not value academic achievement, neither will they.

In point of fact, many can see little if any benefit, immediate or future, from the boring studies they slog through (McLaren 1980; McLeod 1987; Powell, Farrar, and Cohen 1985; Sizer 1984). Young people want to be in school, but less to study than because their friends are there. All they can do outside of school during the day is read, watch television, hang around on street corners and at shopping malls, and generally get into trouble. If their friends are anti-school, they may drop out, especially if they feel that conformity to school will alienate them from their peers. This circumstance is especially problematic for successful members of minority groups who are pressured to view conformity to school as selling out or "acting white" (Fordham and Ogbu 1986):

> People are afraid to show that they can speak grammatically correct English. When I do, my friends in my neighborhood will say, "you nerd!" or "Talk English!" or "Talk to us like we talk to you."
> I've been *per se* called an oreo because black as I am and bright, everybody thinks I'm too proper and talk white . . . and people tend to *tease* me. (Fordham and Ogbu, quoted in Erickson 1987)

An interesting reversal of acting white is the appropriation by rebellious *white* students of African-American hip-hop hairstyles and dress. Adoption of a stigmatized identity, or "acting black," led a number of white middle-school-aged girls to be spit upon and jeered at by their peers. Five dropped out, as did the few African-American students in their school (*New York Times* 1993).

Alienation from school is exacerbated when students respect very few of their teachers, because they feel either that teachers don't like or respect them or that they are incompetent to teach their subjects. Students form their opinions from the way teachers talk to them and treat them.

> Some teachers talk down to you like you're stupid when you ask questions. Some teachers embarrass you in front of the class. They make jokes about failed tests, poor grades, and things. (Firestone and Rosenblum 1988, p. 289)
>
> My teacher would put me on her knees in the corner and whip me with wet newspapers and the rest of the class would laugh. (Dixon, quoted by A. D. Greene 1989)
>
> The teacher laughed and said, "Well, here's a student who can't see how to get to class." [The speaker is a Navajo student whose name is Cantsee.] (Deyhle 1988)

Examples like these clearly indicate that the students' perceptions are sometimes correct.

The Extracurriculum

To channel the energy of young people and seduce them into school-related activities, educators have created an "extracurriculum" of sports, clubs, and entertaining activities to accompany the academic curriculum. These nonacademic functions of school help to contain the influence of the student peer group. They also fill the vacant time, which children are believed to have before and after school and on weekends, with activities sanctioned by the school. They reinforce academic standards because adequate academic performance and acceptable conduct are required for participation in these activities.

The extracurriculum also reinforces traditional gender roles. Activities for males emphasize what are considered appropriate male qualities of achievement, competitiveness, toughness, goal fulfillment in the face of pain and discomfort, and aggression. Girls' activities reinforce the fact that females are rewarded for having a pleasant, bubbly personality; neat, clean hair; a trim figure; and a calm, agreeable facade even under adverse circumstances, and for playing a supportive role to male activities (Eder and Parker 1987). Extracurricular activities also accustom students to the legitimacy of an unequal distribution of status and rewards in society, just as the academic curriculum does (Ibid., p. 205).

Visit a high school during its lunch period. What student groups can you identify? What distinguishes them from other peer groups? Discuss your findings in class.

Winners. The extracurriculum evokes a caricature of a white, middle-class American adolescent who does not have to work and whose life is filled with proms, sports, and cheerleading. Nevertheless, there are many students, of various social classes and ethnic groups, who "major" in the extracurriculum, finding the academic side of life too difficult or meaningless. They often are encouraged to do this by peers as well as by teachers and parents who believe that success in the extracurriculum is a boost to self-esteem. The importance of the extracurriculum to parents is highlighted by the practice of kindergarten "redshirting": Children who have the cognitive skills to begin school are held back a year so they will be more physically mature than their grade-level peers and can excel in sports (Eisenhart and Graue 1990).

The extracurriculum can even supplant academics: Athletes and other special students may be given undeserved passing grades to keep them eligible for outside-class activities. Controversy over this kind of pressure has led to the passing of "no-pass, no-play" legislation in many states, and to subsequent public outrage by coaches, alumni associations, students, beleaguered parents, and teachers on both sides of the issue.

What extracurricular activities did you participate in when you were in high school? Describe the students who participated with you in these activities by social class, gender, and race/ethnicity.

The dark side of extracurricular activities is the outgroups—the so-called wimps, nerds, losers, greasers, "badasses," punks, and delinquents—who cannot or will not participate. Until recently only the positive side of the caricature got attention. Studies conducted before the 1970s were concerned with suburban middle-class students or the white working class (Coleman 1961; Hollingshead 1949; Kahl 1953; Stinchcombe 1964). Parents and educators registered dismay at finding that the majority of students found academic work to have little intrinsic value and that, for most, the "gentleman's C" was the highest standard to which they aspired.

Yeah, if you're a straight A student, you get razzed. . . . (McLeod 1987)

[You have to] hang out at _____ 's. Don't be too smart. Flirt with boys. Be cooperative on dates. (Coleman 1961, p. 371)

Losers. Middle- and working-class white parents in the 1950s and 1960s assumed that teenage hijinks and aversion to work would dissipate with maturity and that students would settle down and become productive members of the community. Nobody examined what became of the high school underclass—minorities, dropouts, the unpopular, and the poor. This disaffected and dropout population is now garnering a great deal of attention, since it is much larger than was previously believed. In most large cities it makes up nearly the majority of the population (Hess et al. 1985; LeCompte and Goebel 1987; Powell, Farrar, and Cohen 1985). It also is much louder and more manifestly violent in its opposition to school than the mild underachievement believed characteristic of the middle class. Further, its members do not eventually assimilate into a semblance of middle-class life. Rather, they remain a disaffected, underemployed and unemployed underclass as adults. This phenomenon raises some important questions:

- Why are students in general and resident minority groups in particular beginning to believe that going to school will not help them to succeed?
- Why do they sense that the American Dream does not apply to them?

To understand this, it is necessary to recognize that schools do not exist in isolation from the world community and that not all of the problems in schools can be resolved by classroom instruction. Rather, it is necessary to look beyond the confines of any given school and its community into the larger world society. As we have seen, the failure of the disadvantaged actually acts to preserve existing patterns of domination.

SURVIVING SCHOOL

In the preceding pages we have described what life is like for contemporary teenagers and how they spend their days. We have defined peer culture and explained how it developed. We also have discussed some of the societal issues that complicate the process of growing up. We have suggested that a critical aspect in the maturation of children is their long period of schooling, during which they learn from each other and establish collective ideas about the world and how to live in it. We also have suggested that adolescents find the ideas of their friends and the media a much more powerful influence than those of most adults.

However, young people differ according to sex, academic achievement, socioeconomic status, ethnicity, whether they live in large cities, suburbs, small towns, or rural areas, and by neighborhood. They also respond differently to school, both individually and in groups. While factors such as economic status and teenage parenthood contribute to the alienation of young people from school, the impact of these factors is heightened by the extent to which their friends are similarly alienated. Even very bright and highly motivated students with parents who help and even push them find it difficult to study when none of their friends does. Conversely, if students already are in trouble because of family divorce, pregnancy, low grades, difficulty in finding jobs, or knowledge of the shrinking opportunity structure, their potential for disaffection from school still depends upon how many of their friends are in similar trouble.

Valli (1983), who studied young women planning to become clerical and office workers, suggests that there are three possible forms of response to cultural institutions: acceptance, negotiation, and resistance. Which form a young person will choose in reaction to school depends upon how much hope this individual has for the future, and to what extent school will contribute to the realization of his or her aspirations.

Acceptance

Acceptance involves internalization of the school's promise that academic success and educational longevity will pay off. Students who accept this premise struggle to believe the American cultural myth of the linkage between education and occupational status (LeCompte 1987b; LeCompte and Dworkin 1991). Some work hard to maintain the status inherited from their family of origin, to take their putative place in the top echelons of society; others, like Horatio Alger, believe in the "rags to riches" story as they struggle to do better than their parents did.

Children who adopt this response generally come from any of several kinds of families. Most obvious are those from the middle class or the affluent Anglo and dominant culture, or immigrant families who, like many Southeast Asians, are well educated and once were wealthy but lost their status when they became refugees (Dworkin 1974). Most of these parents have themselves benefited from education and they push their children to do well. Even if they are not themselves educated, most know how to exert pressure on the school system when their children have problems, to negotiate to have their children placed in the best classes, and to help them with their homework. They also obtain tutoring, psychological counseling, and other kinds of help when it is deemed necessary (Ziegler, Hardwick, and McGreath 1989). Others who tend to do well in school are children of immigrants whose present situation, however bleak it may seem to native residents, is infinitely more promising than the opportunities they might have had in their former homes (Gibson 1987; Ogbu 1987; Suarez-Orozco 1987; Valverde 1987).

The "immigrant psychology" of hope (Ogbu 1987) helps to explain not only the hard work and academic success of refugee children from Southeast Asia, but also the fact that fewer children who were born in Mexico and then migrated to the United States seem to drop out of school than do Mexican-American children born in the United States (Valverde 1987). The issue is not limited to migration across national boundaries. McLeod (1987) points out that while both groups of high school young men whom he studied were from similarly impoverished and crime-prone backgrounds, the "Brothers," who were African American, experienced relatively greater academic success and expressed greater belief in the efficacy of school learning than did the "Hallway Hangers," who were white. McLeod suggests that the difference may be that the Brothers' families had moved fairly recently to the mostly white public housing project in which both groups lived, and they saw the project as an improvement over life in the ghetto. To the Hallway Hangers, whose families had lived there all their lives, the project symbolized the impossibility of escaping a dead-end existence.

Negotiation

Negotiators seek to make a deal. Negotiation is not wholehearted acceptance of the premises of schooling but rather a recognition that, while the payoffs for completing school may not be monumental, the consequences of not doing so are worse. The reasons for staying are unimportant. Students might be motivated simply by the wrath of their parents. The important point is that schooling has extrinsic rather than intrinsic value.

Negotiators try to complete their schooling with minimum effort. They may feel that most schoolwork is boring beyond belief (Eisenhart and Holland 1988, 1992; Powell, Farrar, and Cohen 1985; Sizer 1984), but they will work hard enough and conform sufficiently to the rules to ensure that they will obtain the necessary diploma or degree. Fuller's study (1980) of black Caribbean women students in England demonstrates how these students consciously or unconsciously negotiate an exchange of reasonable work for reasonable demands from their teachers. Negotiators may seek to minimize work by "scoping out" their teachers to find out what is expected and how to get around them. They may take less advanced courses which still meet graduation requirements. They may even make deals with teachers so they will be required to do minimal work and in exchange they will guarantee an orderly classroom without harassment.

While the most active and overt negotiators are older students, some researchers have described the process in elementary school. Borko and Eisenhart (1986) demonstrated how second graders in the lower reading groups induce teachers to simplify their lessons. When asked questions they thought were too hard, the children would respond either with difficulty or very slowly. Their teachers then assumed the work was too difficult and would subsequently "dumb down" their teaching, revising lessons to include less material. The students thus achieved their objective of making school less taxing. L. M. McNeil (1988a, 1988b, 1988c) has suggested that an unforeseen consequence of this interaction is, however, that students are progressively more handicapped in school. As they learn less, they fall further and further behind their classmates.

Although we have described it as such, much of the negotiation is not actually a consciously struck bargain, like a union contract. In fact, most students accept the inevitability of adult expectations and institutional constraints. The procedures for negotiating survival evolve as cultural knowledge within the student peer groups, which pass it on to each succeeding generation. Insofar as the rules for negotiation still require conformity to minimal academic standards, teachers may complain about the loss of student proficiency and energy but they do not define their students as engaging in active resistance.

Both accepters and negotiators cause little concern to school staff because their conformity gives the impression that they have bought into the premises of schooling. They follow most of the rules and are likely to graduate. Other students, however, do not wish to negotiate on the school's terms. We define these students as *resisters*.

Resistance: Its Definition, Purpose, and Types

Resisters are a problem for schools because they cause trouble and are likely to drop out. Resistance to institutional constraints is more than simple misbehavior. It is principled, conscious, and ideological nonconformity which has its basis in philosophical differences between the individual and the institution. It involves "withholding assent" (Erickson 1987, p. 237) from school authorities. Students who resist may disagree with the way they are treated on the basis of their gender, ethnicity, or social class; they may disagree with the academic track to which they are assigned; or they may disagree with the esteem in which any of these categories is held. They become resisters when their disagreement is actively expressed.

Resistance can serve to salvage the self-esteem or reputation of the individual engaging in it. In some cases, the acts of resistance do not entirely sabotage the careers of students.

Assertiveness.   Schools consistently try to avoid, simplify, or deny the existence of resistance (L. M. McNeil 1988a, 1988b, 1988c; Page 1987; Powell, Farrar, and Cohen 1985). Some students, however, refuse to be silenced and demand the right to hold complex opinions or maintain contradictory consciousness (Gramsci 1971). Fine describes how Deirdre, a bright African-American senior, refused to accede to a teacher's demands that she decide whether the actions of Bernard Goetz, the New York City "subway vigilante" who shot four young men he thought were about to rob him, were right or wrong. From the supposedly silenced middle of the room, she declared:

> It's not that I have no opinions. I don't like Goetz shootin' up people who look like my brother, but I don't like feelin' unsafe in the projects or my neighborhood either. I got lots of opinions. I ain't being quiet 'cause I can't decide if he's right or wrong. I'm thinking. (1987, p. 164)

In another example, Rose (1988) was puzzled to find that African-American students in her college persisted in their use of Black English, even in written composition, despite the fact that they knew Standard English and realized that the practice would lower their grades. At first she thought it was a way to reinforce an African-American identity. The explanation the students gave, however, was that for their purposes, Standard English just did not sound right. Not using Black English was like not using inflection and punctuation. Standard English simply did not convey the meaning they wanted.

Hyperachievement: Beating Them at Their Own Game.   A few students choose to repudiate the negative labels the school assigns to them. A dramatic example is that of Carrie Mae Dixon of Yates High School in Houston. An economically disadvantaged African American, she had been an orphan with no legal guardian since kindergarten. She was pregnant, unmarried, and the mother of a two-year-old. In third grade her teacher called her dumb for repeatedly getting in trouble in school. But she also was at the top of her class in every grade since the end of elementary school and graduated high school as valedictorian. She was accepted to university, awarded two scholarships for the fall, and now wanted to be a chemical engineer. The turning point was a classmate's insult. "After that, I decided I would show her who was dumb and who wasn't. . . . In tenth grade is when I found out what the valedictorian is. They explained to me that this is the person with the highest grade point average and I said, 'OK, that's what I want to be.' "

Plans for her valedictory address almost went awry when her principal decided that a pregnant valedictorian set a poor example for other students and so she could not participate in the graduation ceremony. It took national media attention to change the minds of the school officials (A. D. Greene 1989).

The kinds of resistance just described are used by students who are more or less successful in school. They may win peer approval or, like some of the students who "act white," not encounter so much adverse response from peers that they drop out. Other forms of resistance, however, lead to further alienation from school. Students may define the academic part of school as meaningless. Some may disavow schooling altogether, insofar as they not only do not identify with the academic part of school but also fail to find its extracurricular aspects alluring. These students choose alternative avenues for achieving status, some of them sanctioned or at least accepted by the establishment, others not.

There are a number of ways students express their alienation from and lack of engagement with school. Before discussing these, we need to note that most students engage in at least some of them at some point. These acts do not constitute resistance, however, unless they involve active, conscious, and principled opposition to a specific way in which the school has chosen to define a student.

Resistance may begin with simple nonconforming behavior and then be transformed into resistance by the negative responses of school staff. Student behavior will diverge further and further from what school staff find acceptable and bearable. Under these conditions, students who are dropout risks become "push-outs"— forced out of school by an establishment that will not or cannot accommodate them. As teachers, counselors, and administrators mobilize to neutralize, isolate, or otherwise eliminate the behavior (and often, the student engaging in it), students may find themselves in an ever less congenial environment—detention, suspension, remedial classes, and repeated confrontations with parents and school staff. They also may find that nobody cares to rescue them and stop the process.

Talk to a group of elementary school students and then to a group of high school students. Ask them what strategies they use to "get back" at teachers, what kinds of tricks they play on teachers, and how they get around assignments. Would you define any of these activities as types of resistance?

Boredom and Alienation: The Initial Phase of Resistance.   Resistance usually begins when students stop studying or begin to engage in mild forms of smart-aleck behavior and vandalism. In an attempt to be considered more mature, they may begin to adopt what Stinchcombe (1964) calls symbolic adult behavior—use of drugs and alcohol, smoking, early dating and sex (Ekstrom et al. 1986). They get jobs, which make them feel good both because they involve some responsibility and because they provide funds to buy clothing, cars, and other goods with which to impress their friends. Girls may be happy to have a baby, despite feeling sorry because motherhood interferes with school and seeing friends (Deyhle and LeCompte 1994; A. D. Greene

1989; Sege 1989). Both jobs and babies can take so much time and energy that they seriously compromise a student's ability to cope with schoolwork.

Students who cannot get licit jobs or who find that they pay very little may engage in illicit ones—selling drugs, burglary, pimping, and prostitution. Alienated students often form gangs of similarly inclined peers and may go beyond simple vandalism and harassment to real terrorist tactics to intimidate both students and staff.

Tuning Out: Dropping Out in School. The ultimate form of resistance is to stop coming to school. There are many ways to accomplish this. Some students start simply by sleeping in their classes. Those who have after-school jobs may doze as a logical response to lack of sleep. Others begin to cut classes. They don't leave the school building, they simply ditch the classes they find most distasteful. Selective class cutting is increasingly widespread. Hess and his colleagues (1985) have documented what they call a "culture of cutting," wherein students spend more time in the hallways and hiding places of the school than in class. These students are in-school dropouts, or "tune-outs." They are likely to be average middle-class students and those whom we have called the "negotiators." While they have not yet actually cut their ties with school, they are disaffected, and they receive little more instruction than students who actually have dropped out. They are, however, increasing in numbers, and they are at great risk of becoming dropouts.

Dropping Out: Giving Up on School. Statistics on dropouts are notoriously unreliable. Even figures on the absolute number of students who fail to graduate are questionable. Some methods of analysis overestimate the dropout numbers, but most probably underestimate them significantly (LeCompte and Goebel 1987; Morrow 1986). However, since the 1960s at least 25 percent of any given age cohort in the United States failed to finish high school (McDill, Pallas, and Natriello 1985; Steinberg, Blinde, and Chan 1984). It probably also is correct that in most cities, and among what Ogbu (1978) has called "caste-like minorities"—African Americans, Latinos, American Indians—dropout rates exceed 40 percent and may be as high as 80 percent (Orum 1984).

It is even more difficult to determine *why* students drop out. Most dropouts do not appear at the school door to say goodbye. Like Carmen (see box on p. 122), they simply stop coming and eventually are placed in a "whereabouts unknown" category, then dropped from the records. Those who do announce their departure often lie about their plans. It is more socially acceptable to state that one has a job, is transferring to another school, or will join the military than to admit that one is simply giving up on school (Hammack 1986; LeCompte and Goebel 1987).

Most data on the reasons for dropping out consist of demographic correlations: Students, it is said, drop out because they are poor, are from minority or single-parent families, or are girls who have had babies. This descriptive data neither addresses the real motivations for leaving school, nor—because of its focus upon "victim characteristics" over which the school has little control—does it provide much assistance in remedying the problems. It is true that some young people must leave school in order to support their family or take care of siblings or their own children. However, the

---

Carmen's Story

By then I was hanging with a very rough crowd. My friends were into drugs, and soon I was doing the same. We shoplifted and stole everything we found that could be converted into cash. My parents were always on my case, and I ran away several times. I would come home only when I did not have any other place to crash. I would go to school while I was home, but my grades went down and I was not interested in school anymore.

   Nobody in school ever took interest in helping me or learning about what had changed me. They only were interested in me going to school on a regular basis. I don't even remember talking to the school counselor. I think they gave up on me, and when I left I never looked back. I never even considered going back to school until I came here and at the Employment Office they told me about the program for farm workers.

SOURCE: Velasquez 1993, p. 91.

---

evidence suggests that the majority who leave school do so because of school-related factors. Many already were part of the culture of opposition to school, a culture that acts to exacerbate their difficulties by inducing them to violate norms of behavior or to engage in activities that interfere with schoolwork. For others who had serious personal problems, school requirements became the final straw.

   In contemporary schools whose major task is the batch-processing and crowd control of huge numbers of children, little individual time and few resources exist for students with difficult problems, such as a need for child care or psychiatric care, or help for drug addiction or physical abuse. Many of these students with problems are defined as either intractable or just not the business of the school. For some, that indeed may be true. Schools cannot, for example, be expected to treat acting-out, psychotic students, or drug addicts.

   Most students, however, do not fall into such extreme categories. They are bored. They hate school. The work is too difficult or too easy. Their degree won't amount to anything when they get out. The staff told them they were failures or unwanted. Teachers didn't care, were incompetent, or didn't understand. They were pregnant and embarrassed to "show." They couldn't find a baby-sitter. Their guardian was dying and they were needed for nursing care. They had no car and couldn't get across town to the dropout center. In all cases, the school was too inflexible to accommodate to their needs (Delgado-Gaitan 1988; Deyhle 1988; Fine 1986; Holley and Doss 1983; LeCompte 1985; Valverde 1987; Wehlage and Rutter 1986; Williams 1987). We believe that most students who drop out are those who were already at risk and were pushed out altogether by an unresponsive institution. It wasn't that they didn't learn how schools work—following the rules just didn't work for them.

SUMMARY

In this chapter we have discussed the formation of youth culture and the student peer group in the context of global patterns of consumption, technological change, the labor market, family structure, and cultural survival. It suggests that the advent of compulsory schooling and the prolongation of adolescence facilitate the development of oppositional youth culture. It also describes how curricular and extracurricular experiences socialize children for participation in a society stratified by achievement but biased by race, class, and gender. Finally, it suggests that students respond differentially to the realization that the rewards of schooling are mirrored in the rewards of society. Some accommodate to school and survive, others resist and drop out.

It is important for us to consider the experiences of students in schools within the broader cultural contexts. We cannot hold teachers and other school personnel responsible for finding solutions to all the serious problems facing youth today. Teachers can, and often do, provide meaningful environments for students, but they must compete with all of the societal forces—mass media, material consumption, violence, poverty, changing family structures—that are tremendous influences on the way young people construct meaning in their worlds.

chapter 4

The Labor Force in Education: Teachers, Counselors, Administrators, and Ancillary Staff

INTRODUCTION

In Chapter 3 we suggested that children go to school mostly to work at tasks set for them by adults. In this chapter we discuss the roles of teachers, counselors, administrators, and ancillary school staff, whose qualifications for being in schools rest upon specific professional training. These adults relate to the school differently from students because they *are* adults, because their participation is voluntary, and because they are paid and, at least in theory, can be fired for poor job performance. Students, on the other hand, "qualify" for attendance in schools simply by virtue of their age. Students, required by law to attend, are "involuntary recruits" who are not paid for the work they perform and cannot be fired for malfeasance (Nadel 1957).

We will limit our consideration of adults in schools to "educators," that is, professionals whose primary tasks are defined by their direct relationship to the teaching of children. Security personnel, maintenance engineers, dieticians, cooks, janitors, bookkeepers and clerks, personnel specialists, bus drivers, and gardeners also work in schools and are critical to their smooth operation. In many cases the relationships these workers form with educators and students are of profound importance to the teaching and learning process. For example, in his classic book, *The Sociology of Teaching* (1932), Willard Waller argues that janitors, all of whom at the time of his study were males, are among the most powerful people in schools and often serve as role models for male students. However, such staff members perform work such as

---

Anna's Story

I really enjoy working with the students. I love seeing the little "light bulb" go on in people's heads. Kids feel good when they "get it," and I enjoy conveying how much I love language.

Duren's Story

I love to teach. I get high on it. I love watching a kid "get it." I enjoy doing my job well. It changes, the people change, and the subject matter changes. If you're good, you'll never teach the same thing the same way twice. You can get summers off, you can get to know some wonderful people (students and parents), and you can continue to learn. You and the students can explore the world together.

---

preparing food, cleaning buildings, and hiring workers, tasks that can be performed in many kinds of institutions and that do not involve teaching children. The work of educators, however, is centered upon schools and school-like settings. While it may seem all too obvious, the practice of their profession also requires the presence of students—the too-often forgotten recipients of educators' labor.

How Do Sociologists View Educators?

Sociologists view teachers—and other educators—in the context of their work. This context includes how educators and the society at large define what they do. We will first discuss the definition of professions in general and consider whether or not teaching should be considered a profession. We will then examine the characteristics of educators, addressing the following issues:

1. How has the historical evolution of the profession affected its current development?
2. What are the demographic characteristics—such as age, sex, socioeconomic background, and race—of educators?
3. Is the profession stratified by race, class, gender, and other demographic characteristics?
4. What relationship exists between the demographic characteristics of teachers and the specific tasks to which various groups of educators are assigned?
5. Does this relationship affect the way educators carry out their tasks and how they feel about them?
6. What distinguishes educators as a group from people in other professions?

Finally, we will discuss teachers' work. Questions we will examine are the following:

1. What is the nature of educators' work?
2. How do the characteristics of their work affect how they behave and how they feel about their jobs?
3. What kinds of power and control do teachers have over their work?

4. Is power differentially distributed among various kinds of educators?
5. How does the relationship of educators compare with the labor market experience of other kinds of workers?

Throughout the chapter we will call attention to the tensions and ambiguities of power and status which constitute both the political and social context of those who work in schools.

ISSUES OF STATUS AND POWER: PROFESSIONAL ESTEEM AND PUBLIC DISREGARD

Education professionals have an image problem. Whether university-level or elementary school teachers, counselors or principals, coaches or superintendents, all educators feel there is a gap between the status they would like to enjoy in society and the power they actually wield. Neither social analysts, policy makers, the public, nor educators themselves can decide whether educational practitioners are scholarly professionals, like doctors and university professors, or members of the laboring work force, like clerks, salespeople, or skilled laborers. In part this is so because teachers' salaries are discrepant with what they "ought" to get, given the supposed value of the work they perform. It is clear that income does not necessarily correlate with social standing. For example, artists—writers, poets, musicians—may live at the poverty line despite the value of their creative contributions. The community services of teachers are considered so crucial that their right to withhold those services is often denied by laws forbidding them to strike. However, the public repeatedly demonstrates its unwillingness to pay for these services by establishing low salary scales and rejecting school tax levies and bond issues. Table 4.1 depicts teacher salaries compared with salaries in other occupations.

Even though they are considered to be professionals, public school teachers are ranked only slightly above electricians and musicians in indices of social status, and far below doctors, lawyers, dentists, college professors, and airline pilots. Their ranking in scales of occupational prestige has fallen steadily (Hodge, Siegel, and Rossi 1966, p. 325).

Teachers are ambivalent about their field. While they insist that their professional training, certification, and expertise justify community esteem, they often denigrate teacher education courses as the least rigorous part of their education (Lortie 1969, p. 24). Reflecting this ambivalence, there is widespread public belief that "anyone can teach."

One factor contributing to this ambivalence is that careers in teaching have different status levels for different groups. They are considered to be socially desirable for women and, until recent years, one of the highest attainable occupations for African Americans, Latinos, and American Indians. However, teaching is an entry-level position for white men if they move to administration, but a low-status dead end if they don't (Lortie 1969, p. 20).

Differential status also is based on age of students, subject matter, and gender.

TABLE 4.1 Average Starting Salaries of Public School Teachers Compared with Salaries in Private Industry, by Selectec Position: 1975 to 1992[a]

Item and Position	1975	1980	1985	1986	1987	1988	1989	1990	1991	1992
SALARIES (dollars)										
Teachers[b]	8,233	10,764	15,460	16,500	17,500	19,400	NA	20,486	21,481	22,171
College graduates:										
Engineering	12,744	20,136	26,880	28,512	28,932	29,856	30,852	32,304	34,236	34,620
Accounting	11,880	15,720	20,628	21,216	22,512	25,140	25,908	27,408	27,524	28,404
Sales—marketing	10,344	15,936	20,616	20,688	20,232	23,484	27,768	27,828	26,580	26,532
Business administration	9,768	14,100	19,896	21,324	21,972	23,880	25,344	26,496	26,256	27,156
Liberal arts[c]	9,312	13,296	18,828	21,060	20,508	23,508	25,608	26,364	25,560	27,324
Chemistry	11,904	17,124	24,216	24,264	27,048	27,108	27,552	29,088	29,700	30,360
Mathematics—statistics	10,980	17,604	22,704	23,976	25,548	25,548	28,416	28,944	29,244	29,472
Economics—finance	10,212	14,472	20,964	22,284	21,984	23,928	25,812	26,712	26,424	27,708
Computer science	NA	17,712	24,156	26,172	26,280	26,904	28,608	29,100	30,924	30,888
INDEX (1975 = 100)										
Teachers[b]	100	131	187	200	213	236	NA	249	261	269
College graduates:										
Engineering	100	158	211	224	227	234	242	253	268	271
Accounting	100	132	174	179	189	212	218	230	235	239
Sales—marketing	100	154	199	200	196	227	268	269	257	256
Business administration	100	144	204	218	225	244	259	271	268	278
Liberal arts[c]	100	143	202	226	220	252	275	283	274	293
Chemistry	100	144	203	204	227	228	231	244	249	255
Mathematics—statistics	100	160	207	218	233	233	258	263	266	268
Economics—finance	100	142	205	218	215	234	252	261	258	271
Computer science[d]	NA	125	171	185	186	190	202	205	218	217

NA Not available.
[a]Except as noted, salaries represent what corporations plan to offer graduates graduating in the year shown with a Bachelor's degree. Based on a survey o' approximately 200 companies.
[b]Estimate. Minimum mean salary. Source: National Education Association, Washington, DC, unpublished data.
[c]Excludes Chemistry, Mathematics, Economics, and Computer Science.
[d]Computer science index (1978 = 100).
SOURCE: Except as noted, Northwestern University Placement Center, Evanston, IL, *The Northwestern Lindquist-Endicott Report* (copyright).

129

Rocklan's Story

I care about children, all of them, and throughout my schooling I saw injustices occur to children because they were poor, who their families were, and these things always made me angry. I see teaching as a way to make a difference in the lives of children. I feel that I have been given many gifts and therefore I want to give something back. I have a love for knowledge and discovery and I want to share that with children.

The highest status is accorded to those who teach the oldest students. University professors are at the top of the status hierarchy, secondary school teachers and instructors in technical and vocational schools occupy the middle, followed by elementary school teachers, and day-care workers occupy the lowest ranks. Within these levels, teachers are differentiated by administrative rank, demographics, subject area, and the age and gender of the students. Supervisors and administrators rank higher than instructors. In general, women and minorities enjoy less status than men and dominant-culture individuals in the same position. Teachers of the "hard sciences" outrank philosophers, vocational educators, and English teachers. Teachers of graduate students and fifth graders outrank those who deal, respectively, with undergraduates and kindergartners. Those who teach women and minorities have less status than those who teach males and members of the dominant classes. Finally, differential status is accorded to specific philosophical outlooks. Since school bureaucracies are conservative and slow to change, change agents are stigmatized and the highest prestige is accorded to those who deviate least from the norm (Aronowitz and Giroux 1985).

These ambiguities and status differentials come from contradictions in the structural and historical evolution of the profession, the nature of teachers' work, patterns of control and status in the profession, the nature of career paths and the reward structure of education, and the age, racial, and gender characteristics of educators. We will discuss these from both a traditional functionalist perspective and the critical perspective which informs our own thinking.

CONTRADICTIONS IN THE STRUCTURE OF THE PROFESSION

Functionalists compare the structure and organization of teaching with those of other professions. They describe how differences in structure create gaps between the esteem in which teachers would like to be held by the public and their peers, and the low status they actually have. These gaps come from the nature and organization of tasks in teaching, how people are trained to execute them, and how much control teachers have over their performance.

Definition of a Profession: The Traditional View

Professions can be differentiated in terms of the complexity of tasks performed as well as the type, rigor, and duration of training and the nature of control, power, and autonomy in the profession. The relationship between the actual work done and the physical context in which it is performed also helps to differentiate professions. Max Weber first delineated the characteristics of the "ideal typical" professional, taking as his models occupations such as medicine, law, and the priesthood. Weber wrote that professionals shared the following characteristics: they were self-employed providers of services, they entered their profession because they were "called" to it out of some deep personal commitment, and their qualifications were based upon their possession of "expert" and esoteric knowledge. In addition, their knowledge base could be acquired by only a select few who underwent long and rigorous study. Their services dealt with serious, often life-or-death matters, and they were remunerated by fees from clients. Communication between professionals and their clients was legally privileged so that courts of law could not require its disclosure. Most important, entrance to these professions was controlled by professional peers, who set requirements for entry, training, and certification. Boards of peers also developed review processes to maintain standards and competence (Weber 1947).

Weber did not make value judgments about the relative merit of occupations; he simply provided a set of descriptors against which occupations could be compared. Today the profession that most closely approximates this standard is medicine. Education, on the other hand, deviates substantially from this model. Teachers are salaried and their communication with students is not legally protected. Other important deviations from the Weberian model include the nature of the knowledge base and the training required to attain it, the degree of control over entry to the profession, maintenance of standards, and the depth of commitment teachers, as a group, have to their calling (Etzioni 1969; Lortie 1969; Simpson and Simpson 1969).

Training. One of the most obvious differences is in the training. Medicine, the priesthood, law, architecture, certified accounting, and other recognized professions require at least five years of training, including several years of rigorous study beyond college. Many also require a supervised apprenticeship or internship. In traditional teacher education programs, elementary and secondary school teachers typically spend only two undergraduate years in Liberal Arts courses. They then spend two years in pedagogical studies, where they learn how to teach the subjects they have just been taught. Only two years of content area instruction—equivalent to an Associate of Arts degree—and one and a half years of actual coursework in pedagogy are required. The remainder of the program is student teaching, which is experiential learning, located off-campus, and only lightly supervised by university personnel. In many colleges teacher training still resembles the normal school tradition, where teachers taught those just below their own academic attainment. One group of universities belonging to the Holmes Group (1986) now expects prospective teachers to complete a Bachelor's degree in Liberal Arts prior to a fifth-year Master's degree in teacher education.

The traditional knowledge base required for teaching, then, is not technical information requiring intellectually rigorous study, but rather experiential knowledge acquired primarily in apprenticeship or student teaching. Developing expertise involves adding to a "bag of tricks" rather than mastering complex levels of skill. Although the cumulative knowledge imparted to students is critical to one's functioning, no single piece constitutes a life-or-death matter.

It is illuminating to compare the "science" of education with the "science" of medicine. Both are applied fields that make use of information and techniques developed in the natural and social sciences (Ginsburg 1988), but one has high status and the other doesn't. The difference seems to be the seriousness with which medicine and other more traditional professions address the need for rigorous study prior to practice. Extensive advanced study in biology, chemistry, physics, and other background courses is required *before* the techniques of medical practice are learned. By contrast, the four years of teacher training are so crowded that there is little time, for example, for studies of the social and psychological anatomy of learning or the logical structure of mathematics and social studies. Students generally regard these courses as too theoretical, far less important than "how-to" methods for teaching discrete "factoids" (Morgenstern 1989) of reading, mathematics, and foreign languages.

National studies, including those by the National Commission on Excellence in Education (1983), the Rand Corporation (Darling-Hammond 1984), the Holmes Group (1986), and the Carnegie Task Force on Teaching as a Profession (1986), have questioned the quality of teacher training. Some have suggested requiring a fifth year of study in the "content areas" (The Holmes Group 1986). However, these suggestions, as well as others designed to make teacher education more rigorous, meet resistance both from university departments of curriculum and instruction, who see their control of teacher education eroded by course requirements outside their departments, and from students, who see that additional years of study produce no commensurate raise in pay.

Teacher education programs frequently are money-makers for their universities because they are cheap to operate. The per-student cost is less because the faculty generally are paid less than professors in other departments and because students do not use university facilities while student-teaching. Profits from education programs finance costlier programs, and universities are reluctant to reduce those profits by adding a year to the degree requirement.

Standards for graduation from teacher education are set by legislatures and are subject to the whim of fads and political pressures. For example, multicultural education courses, which were popular in the 1970s, virtually vanished in the 1980s. These are being reinstated in the 1990s with a renewed commitment to serving the needs of a diverse population.

Certification. Control of entry into the profession is another critical issue. In medicine and law, panels of doctors and lawyers set licensing standards. In contrast, it is market factors and legislative fiat that govern teacher certification. Furthermore, individual school districts can waive specific requirements if qualified personnel are not available. Teachers often are assigned to teach in their minor area of study, or in areas for which they have had no preparation at all. Certain subject areas, such as mathematics and science, bilingual education, and education for the handicapped, experience chronic shortages. Districts with shortages of certified bilingual or ESL teachers and large numbers of children who are not native speakers of English routinely hire English monolingual teachers on temporary certificates. These teachers are then paired, where possible, with bilingual aides or colleagues (LeCompte 1985). Where aides are used, they often provide the bulk of instruction to the poorest and most disadvantaged students (K. P. Bennett 1986, 1991; Ortiz 1988).

A national survey demonstrated how widespread these practices are. In some states the "percentages of high school classes taught by teachers who did not have a major, minor, or 20 quarter hours of preparation included Geography, 92%; Physics, 43%; Chemistry, 43%; Math, 36%; History, 32%; and English, 30%." Thus the areas most typically misassigned are in the core curriculum. Specialized offerings, such as fine arts and vocational education, are not so profoundly affected. The percentages in junior high schools and especially middle schools were even worse (Robinson and Pierce 1985). Table 4.2 presents data indicating that the shortage of qualified teachers will persist. Hospitals would never be permitted to hire a dermatologist to do brain surgery, no matter how severe the shortage of brain surgeons. However, such practices are routine in education.

Finally, a profession is considered a lifelong calling. However, as we shall indicate later in this chapter, teaching is treated as an interim career by family-oriented women, to be practiced at the convenience of marriage and child-rearing, and as an entry-level occupation for men and women who aspire to administrative jobs or other, more lucrative and less stressful careers. While many people do make teaching their life work, and while the rate of quitting decreases the longer a teacher remains in the profession, teachers on average have among the shortest career trajectories of all the professions. Individuals who actually begin teaching remain for an average of no more than about five years (Anderson and Mark 1977; Charters 1970; Mark and Anderson 1978).

Semiprofessions

Initial analyses of teaching equated it with the traditional "autonomous" professions. Functionalists next grouped teaching, along with nursing and social work, as a "semiprofession" (Etzioni 1969). Semiprofessions share some but not all of the characteristics of the classic professions. Like the traditional professions, they are white-collar occupations which provide services rather than produce goods. The training they require, however, is considerably less intellectually rigorous and time consuming. Their status is less legitimated. Their right to privileged communication is less well established, and their applicable body of knowledge is less esoteric.

The semiprofessions also have more supervision and societal control than the traditional professions. Practitioners are not typically self-employed; rather they are "bureaucratized," within formal service organizations. They receive salaries instead of client fees. They are "more" than clerks and secretaries, but "less" than doctors and lawyers (Etzioni 1969, pp. i–v).

TABLE 4.2 Relative Demand by Teaching Area and Year[a]

	1993	1992	1991	1990	1989	1976
Teaching Fields with Considerable Shortage (5.00–4.25)						
Special Education—Multiply Handicapped	4.40	4.47	4.42	4.39	4.14	—
Special Education—ED/BD	4.39	4.23	4.44	4.46	4.40	3.42
Special Education—LD	4.29	4.18	4.41	4.49	4.26	4.00
Speech Pathology/Audiology	4.28	4.37	4.53	4.41	4.25	3.63
Teaching Fields with Some Shortage (4.24–3.45)						
Special Education—Mentally Handicapped	4.22	4.33	4.47	4.48	4.29	2.87
Bilingual Education	4.18	4.15	4.15	4.35	4.45	—
Special Education—Deaf	4.17	4.41	4.21	4.34	4.12	—
Language—Other	4.04	3.53	3.67	3.41	—	—
Science—Physics	3.93	3.88	3.67	3.93	4.12	4.04
English as a Second Language	3.91	3.65	3.74	4.00	—	—
Science—Other	3.86	3.13	2.88	3.36	—	—
Special Education—Other	3.85	3.90	3.96	3.98	—	—
Special Education—Gifted	3.80	3.56	3.65	3.76	3.93	3.85
Science—Chemistry	3.79	3.68	3.84	3.62	4.01	3.72
Psychologist (School)	3.72	3.62	3.57	3.85	3.79	3.09
Language, Modern—Spanish	3.61	3.56	3.71	3.76	3.76	2.47
Teaching Fields with Balanced Supply and Demand (3.44–2.65)						
Library Science	3.43	3.61	3.53	3.76	3.60	—
Mathematics	3.43	3.53	3.58	3.91	3.83	3.86
Computer Science	3.41	3.25	3.36	3.84	3.75	—
Special Education—Reading	3.38	3.38	3.77	3.55	3.58	3.96
Counselor—Elementary	3.31	3.64	3.69	3.67	3.40	3.15
Science—Earth	3.24	3.14	3.33	3.15	3.55	3.44
Social Worker (School)	3.22	3.30	2.94	2.99	3.03	—
Data Processing	3.17	2.90	2.54	3.57	2.58	—
Counselor—Secondary	3.16	3.56	3.64	3.56	3.26	2.69
Science—Biology	3.16	3.08	3.04	3.17	3.35	2.97
Science—General	3.14	3.07	3.16	3.26	3.43	—
Language, Modern—French	3.13	3.13	3.24	3.22	3.51	2.15
Language, Modern—German	3.13	2.90	3.07	3.12	3.42	2.03
Technology—Industrial Arts	3.09	2.81	3.04	3.23	2.95	4.22
Agriculture	3.03	2.84	3.03	3.03	2.93	4.06
Music—Instrumental	2.91	3.09	3.27	3.23	3.20	3.03
Speech	2.88	2.85	2.72	2.78	2.95	2.46
Music—Vocal	2.81	2.95	3.10	3.12	3.00	3.00
Teaching Fields with Some Surplus (2.64–1.85)						
Home Economics	2.49	2.62	2.63	2.69	2.33	2.62
Journalism	2.46	2.64	2.59	2.66	2.76	2.86
English	2.44	2.94	3.05	3.28	2.97	2.05
Driver Education	2.42	2.31	2.82	2.57	2.71	2.44
Business	2.39	2.39	2.81	3.07	2.84	3.10
Art	2.25	2.11	2.21	1.96	2.24	2.14
Elementary—Intermediate	1.96	2.41	2.77	2.81	2.62	1.90
Health Education	1.89	1.90	2.17	2.02	2.03	2.27
Elementary—Primary	1.88	2.33	2.82	2.83	2.63	1.78
Teaching Fields with Considerable Surplus (1.84–1.00)						
Physical Education	1.61	1.70	1.85	1.72	1.78	1.74
Social Science	1.58	1.58	1.98	1.89	1.98	1.51

[a]Results for 1990 forward include Alaska/Hawaii; prior years are contiguous 48 states only.
5 = Considerable shortage; 4 = Some shortage; 3 = Balanced; 2 = Some surplus; 1 = Considerable surplus
SOURCE: From 1993 ASCUS (Association for School, College & University Staffing, Inc.) data supplied by survey respondents. In some instances, the averages are based upon limited input, and total reliability is not assured.

There is little agreement over standards for excellence in the semiprofessions. Both the establishment and enforcement of standards is affected by the needs of the employer bureaucracies. In addition, the knowledge base is applied and experiential rather than technical. While both professionals and semiprofessionals apply knowledge, semiprofessionals have less discretion over what they apply and how.

The authority of supervision over semiprofessionals is tenuous, since it is done by people who have had the same training, though more experience. This similarity in training is a source of tension and conflict. For example, school administrators all had to serve as teachers at one time, and teachers may question their dictates on the grounds that they do not have more training than the teachers. Another source of conflict is that teachers view administrators as management, not as colleagues or a respected reference group (Etzioni 1969, pp. v–xvi).

A Critical Note

Functionalists, in studying teachers' qualifications, compare teaching *up* to doctors, lawyers, and priests. Critical theorists, in contrast, focus on the character of teachers' work itself. They compare *down,* finding teachers to be more comparable to factory workers than to autonomous professionals. Both critical theorists and functionalists have examined the nature of control and power in the profession, including the fact that teaching is primarily a profession for women—a fact that they both use to explain many of the profession's unique characteristics. However, functionalists treat these asymmetrical patterns of control and power as understandable and unchangeable, while critical theorists view them as functions of the institutionalized patterns of oppression in modern capitalist society, conditions that perpetuate the weaknesses of the educational system—and that can and should be changed. We will next examine the themes of feminization, control, and work in teaching from both perspectives.

WHO BECOMES A TEACHER?

A Brief History of Women in Teaching

Teaching has not always been considered women's work. Until the middle of the nineteenth century most formal education, especially at the secondary level, was directed primarily at male students. For the most part, girls who were educated came from well-to-do families and were tutored in their homes. All teachers and administrators, whether of male or female students, were men.

Education Up to the Reformation.   During the Hellenic and Roman eras, military leaders, town governments, and royal courts encouraged the establishment of public schools for the teaching of arts, rhetoric, music, literature, and grammar. With the fall of the Roman Empire, the thriving municipal schools for grammar and rhetoric also collapsed. By 400 A.D. literacy had survived only within the priesthood and among a very few aristocrats (Boyd 1966; Marrou 1956). Monastic orders preserved the remaining libraries, produced teachers, and copied books. The very few universities were governed by canon, or church law. Most professors were priests, and both teachers and students were treated as if they were members of the clergy. Some families of the nobility employed tutors and established schools for their own children and those of their entourage. These teachers often were priests who, like dancemasters and troubadours, were high-status servants.

The Protestant Reformation served as a catalyst for broader-based literacy. As the use of Latin as a *lingua franca* began to be replaced by the ancestors of modern European languages, songs and oral literature were developed in these, not ancient languages. By the time of Martin Luther, Latin was used only by priests and scholars. Literacy in Latin, however, was the key to the power of the Catholic Church hierarchy, since the Christian Bible was available at this time only in Latin and only priests were permitted to read and interpret it. One of the tenets of the Reformation was to reduce the power of priests by translating the Bible into the vernacular, making it accessible to all who could read.

The Reformation drew its power from the gradually strengthening middle and lower classes, groups that previously relied upon family socialization and apprenticeship to prepare young people for adulthood. Schooling for their children was deemed essential by Protestant churches and political leaders alike to inculcate in them the virtues of religion and the laws of society. As was pointed out in Chapter 2, because education then, as now, was viewed as a cure for social disorder, especially that allegedly fomented by the working classes, religious and civic leaders advocated the establishment of schools to indoctrinate the children of the poor. However, the existing educational system was designed only for an aristocracy and linked to university-level training for boys. It included tutoring in the traditional curriculum of Latin, Greek, grammar, rhetoric, and mathematics, followed by university training in law, medicine, or theology.

Towns and religious orders responded to the call for mass education by setting up primary schools which taught the rudiments of literacy, the catechism, and sometimes a little arithmetic. Thus was created a dual system of education: One strand was oriented to Latin, Greek, and the classics and led to university training for the rich; the other was conducted in vernacular languages and linked to vocational training for the poor (Resnick and Resnick 1985). Teachers for the former were required to have secondary school or university training, while those for the latter needed only to be literate. At best, they had some formal classes in pedagogy and had achieved one grade higher than the grade they taught.

The Entry of Women. By the end of the 1600s, women were beginning to enter the teaching profession, although not in formal educational institutions. Dame schools, located in the women's homes, for neighborhood children, became a common way to learn the ABC's and the catechism. The English Poor Laws, enacted to ensure that poor children would not become public charges, encouraged apprenticeships. They also facilitated the education of orphans and girls from poor but respectable families, who learned to be governesses and tutors in the homes of well-to-do families, since, if unmarried, they would have no other respectable means of support.

Calvin E. Stowe Says Women Should Be Employed in the Elementary Schools, 1837

. . . Indeed, such is the state of things in this country, that we cannot expect to find male teachers for all our schools. The business of educating, especially young children, must fall, to a great extent on female teachers. There is not the same variety of tempting employment for females as for men, they can be supported cheaper, and the Creator has given [them] peculiar qualifications for the education of the young. Females, then, ought to be employed extensively in all our elementary schools, and they should be encouraged and aided in obtaining the qualifications necessary for this work. There is no country in the world where woman holds so high a rank, or exerts so great an influence, as here; wherefore, her responsibilities are the greater, and she is under obligations to render herself the more actively useful. I think our fair countrywomen, notwithstanding the exhortations of Harriet Martineau, Fanny Wright, and some other *ladies and gentlemen,* will never seek distinction in our public assemblies for public discussion, or in our halls of legislation; but in their appropriate work of educating the young, of forming the opening mind to all that is good and great, the more they distinguish themselves the better . . .

SOURCE: Knight and Hall, 1951, pp. 414-415.

Proponents of elementary school education, like Comenius and Froebel in Europe and Horace Mann in America, also encouraged the use of women as teachers of young children. Women were considered to be good influences on children. Their supposed motherly instincts, virtue, and less violent nature suited them for this work and served as a curb to the passionate, warlike nature of the young men they taught (Binder 1974, p. 124; Boyd 1966; Curti 1971). Perhaps more important, they were cheaper to hire than men (Boyd 1966; Curti 1971).

We need to remember that types of education were strictly differentiated by social class. The young children of the rich were taught at home and their education emphasized the classics, Latin and Greek. Older boys were taught by men at college preparatory academies and then were eligible to attend the university. If girls received any secondary training, it was primarily in the arts of homemaking and in those ornamental social skills deemed appropriate for upper-class women: French, fine needlework, music, dancing, and writing. Female teachers were restricted to teaching in their own homes, in the dame schools, or in those of the wealthy. Children of the poor received an education oriented to social control—sufficient literacy to understand the laws and contracts that governed their public life and labor and the doctrines of the Church.

The great influx of women into teaching began in the mid-nineteenth century through the Civil War period. The expansion of universal elementary schooling and the theretofore complete lack of schools for African Americans in the South, coupled with northerners' distrust of native southern teachers during Reconstruction, created a greater demand for teachers than could be filled by the available males. The "Yankee Schoolmarm" became a prototypical model for the female schoolteacher—single, dedicated, and often adventurous, willing to leave home and travel to hardship towns and frontier areas in search of the only jobs widely available for educated women (Kaufman 1984).

Teaching as Women's Work.   The events of the nineteenth century shaped many of the patterns that characterize teaching today, the most important of which was the feminization of teaching. While the teaching profession entered the twentieth century with a work force dominated by women, men held virtually all of the administrative positions—a situation that prevails today.

From early times in America, teachers earned low wages. In areas dominated by subsistence farming they earned hardly more than common laborers. Only those lucky enough to teach in cities or in secondary-level academies attended by the wealthy could eke out a fairly comfortable living. A college graduate could make more money in almost any other profession. As a consequence, most male schoolmasters avoided making a career of teaching (Main 1966). The entry of women into teaching furthered the practice of paying teachers poorly; women were hired because they were expected to work for less than men.

Teaching was held in low esteem because, in an era that valued hard manual labor, teaching was defined as "easy." It did not require the full physical efforts of a man. Nor was it considered to be mentally taxing, since qualified teachers needed to attain only the level of education immediately higher than their students. Elementary teaching became a female-dominated field by choice (for women) and by default (for a very few men). By the mid 1880s training consisted of attendance at a high school or normal school (Lortie 1969). The persistent problem of high teacher turnover was institutionalized in the nineteenth century by the failure to pay men—or women—a living wage and by the requirement that women leave their job upon marriage (Lortie 1973, p. 488).

There is a long history of male resistance to higher education for women, or to giving university status to programs like normal schools which were designed for the training of women (Ginsburg 1988). Such resistance was justified on both gender and class bases. Higher education was considered unsuitable to the nature of women and a threat to male hegemony. Teacher education programs were denigrated for diminishing the status of universities with which they were associated (Ginsburg 1988) because they recruited both women and people from the lower socioeconomic classes, both groups of low status.

Critical theorists believe that recognizing the feminized nature of teaching is crucial to understanding the political, economic, and ideological modes of control in the profession. It is not the nature of the work itself that is problematic, but the fact that it is performed by subordinated, *female* workers whose position can best be understood through analyses of the labor process and patterns of class domination (Apple 1986).

During the early part of the twentieth century women poured into the teaching

---

Tracy's Story

Ever since the third grade I have wanted to be a teacher. Mrs. Salcido, my third-grade teacher, really turned me on to reading. She inspired me to make myself a better student. The effect she has had on my life is one that I hope to share with my students. Teaching is a very giving profession and I have always had the urge to help people. I feel that I really want to be able to see my success in reaching children in the classroom by seeing them graduate from high school and possibly go on to some form of higher education. If I can affect one student in the tremendous way Mrs. Salcido has affected me, it will be worth more than any salary given to me.

---

profession. First, as the barriers prohibiting their enrollment fell, an unprecedented number of middle- and upper-class women began to graduate from colleges and universities. For example, female enrollment in higher education rose from 29 percent of the total in 1948 to 51 percent in 1980 (O'Neill and Sepielli 1985, p. 27). In addition, government scholarships and preferential loan programs encouraged men and women to pursue careers in teaching.

Finally, even highly educated women in the 1950s and early 1960s found that sex discrimination in employment still precluded them from virtually all professional positions but teaching. Table 4.3 illustrates the male domination of school administration. The few women who do attain administrative rank do so by means of career paths markedly different from those of men (Grow 1981; Ortiz 1981).

Men usually go directly from teaching and coaching to line positions as assistant principals or principals in middle or high schools, and from there go to central administration. Women, by contrast, go from teaching to staff positions as curriculum coordinators or directors to line positions as elementary school principals, then to upper division schools, and finally to central administration. Sometimes they go directly from a staff position to central administration, but not often. Their career trajectory is usually slowed down by beginning in lower status staff and elementary school positions.

Not only are the type of tasks performed by educators rigidly differentiated by rank, but routes to these ranks as well as the incumbents themselves also are highly differentiated by gender. We will first examine demographic characteristics of the people who choose to become educators, then will consider the nature of their tasks and the structures in which these tasks are carried out.

Demographic Characteristics of Teachers

The most salient factor about teaching is its predominantly female work force. In 1983, the average teacher was a white, married woman in her mid-thirties with two children. She came from a middle- to upper-middle-class family, received her training

TABLE 4.3 Public School Employment by Occupation, Sex, and Race: 1982 and 1990[a]

Occupation	1982					1990				
	Total	Male	Female	White[b]	Black[b]	Total	Male	Female	White[b]	Black[b]
All occupations	3,082	1,063 (34%)	2,019 (66%)	2,498 (81%)	432 (14%)	3,181	914 (29%)	2,267 (71%)	2,502 (79%)	463 (16%)
Officials, administrators	41	31 (76%)	10 (24%)	36 (88%)	3 (7%)	43	28 (65%)	15 (35%)	37 (86%)	4 (9%)
Principals and assistant principals	90	72 (80%)	18 (20%)	76 (84%)	11 (12%)	90	56 (62%)	34 (38%)	70 (78%)	13 (14%)
Classroom teachers[c]	1,680	534 (32%)	1,146 (68%)	1,435 (85%)	186 (13%)	1,746	468 (27%)	1,278 (73%)	1,469 (84%)	192 (11%)
Elementary schools	798	129 (16%)	669 (84%)	667 (83%)	98 (12%)	875	128 (15%)	747 (85%)	722 (83%)	103 (12%)
Secondary schools	706	363 (51%)	343 (49%)	619 (88%)	67 (9%)	662	304 (46%)	358 (54%)	570 (86%)	66 (10%)
Other professional staff	235	91 (39%)	144 (61%)	193 (82%)	35 (15%)	227	58 (26%)	170 (75%)	187 (82%)	30 (13%)
Teachers' aides[d]	215	14 (7%)	200 (93%)	146 (68%)	45 (21%)	324	54 (17%)	270 (83%)	208 (64%)	69 (21%)
Clerical and secretarial staff	210	4 (2%)	206 (98%)	177 (84%)	19 (9%)	226	5 (2%)	221 (98%)	181 (80%)	24 (11%)
Service workers[e]	611	316 (51%)	295 (49%)	434 (71%)	132 (22%)	524	245 (47%)	279 (53%)	348 (66%)	129 (25%)

[a]In thousands. Covers full-time employment. 1982 excludes Hawaii, District of Columbia, and New Jersey. Based on sample survey of school districts with 250 or more students. 1990 based on sample survey of school district with 100 or more employees; see source for sampling variability.)
[b]Excludes individuals of Hispanic or gin.
[c]Includes other classroom teachers, not shown separately.
[d]Includes technicians.
[e]Includes craftworkers and laborers.
SOURCE: U.S. Equal Opportunity Commission, Elementary-Secondary Staff Information (EEO-5), biennial.

at a public university, and was likely to teach in a suburban elementary school. She was not politically active and although she put in a slightly longer work week than the average blue-collar worker, she brought home a slightly smaller paycheck. She also was comfortable in her rather traditional gender role. She was older than her male counterparts by almost eight years, was somewhat less likely to have a Master's degree, and probably came from a family with somewhat higher socioeconomic status than the males (Feistritzer 1983; NEA 1963, 1972; D. Spencer 1986). Table 4.4 summarizes selected characteristics of public school teachers in 1990–1991.

Career Commitment: Teaching as a Second-Choice Job

Whether male or female, teachers are likely to have selected teaching as a second choice. The decision to teach is often made relatively late in college as students find that they lack the ability or financial and familial support to pursue a more desirable career (Holland and Eisenhart 1988; Pavalko 1970; Simpson and Simpson 1969). More college students transfer *into* education than out of it (Davis 1965).

Furthermore, most who enter teaching do not plan to make it their life work. One-third of those who are trained to teach never enter a classroom (Simpson and Simpson 1969). Sixty-five percent of beginning female teachers expect to leave within five years; 70 percent plan eventually to become homemakers. Although five out of six plan to return to teaching when their children are in school (Pavalko 1970), many do not. At any given time as many as 60 percent of those trained to be teachers are not in the classroom (Corwin 1965). In general, teacher turnover stands at about 17 percent of the cohort annually (Anderson and Mark 1977; Charters 1970; Mark and Anderson 1978). Increasing rates of divorce and single parenthood may have been changing this situation, however. By 1971 the number of female teachers with breaks in service had declined by 13 percent. In addition, attrition rates for both men and women tend to decline if they survive the first year or two of teaching (Charters 1970; Mark and Anderson 1978).

Commitment patterns for male teachers are similar, though for different reasons. Most men who enter teaching do not want to spend their lives as teachers; they plan to move into administration within five years. If they remain in the classroom, they express great unhappiness with their jobs by age 40 (Lortie 1973, p. 489). Another difference is in the percentage of male teachers with breaks in teaching service. Lortie found that the percentage increased by 6.6 percent, while the percentage of women who interrupted their teaching careers declined. These statistics indicate that men who remain in the profession try to leave it more often than women do, even given the female interruptions for child-rearing.

Intellect and Ideology

Although some studies indicate that those who enter education programs score higher on intelligence tests than the average college student (Pavalko 1970), many studies indicate that the standardized test scores and grade-point averages of teachers' college graduates are among the lowest of all college programs. This may be the case because the more able students drop out of teacher training. Pavalko (1971) indicates

TABLE 4.4 Public Elementary and Secondary School Teachers—Selected Characteristics: 1990–1991[a]

Characteristic	Unit	Age				Sex		Race/Ethnicity			Level of Control	
		Under 30	30-39	40-49	Over 50	Male	Female	White[b]	Black[b]	Hispanic	Elementary	Secondary
Total teachers[c]	1,000	312	732	1,003	514	720	1,842	2,216	212	87	1,298	1,264
Highest degree held:												
Bachelor's	Percent	84.1	56.4	43.8	41.6	44.7	54.7	51.5	50.8	61.0	56.7	46.9
Master's	Percent	14.4	39.1	48.8	49.9	47.0	40.1	42.7	42.1	32.9	38.7	45.5
Education specialist	Percent	1.2	3.4	5.9	5.9	5.3	4.3	4.5	5.0	4.3	4.1	5.2
Doctorate	Percent	—*	0.4	1.0	1.4	1.3	0.6	0.7	1.3	0.9	0.4	1.2
Full-time teaching experience:												
Less than 3 years	Percent	40.0	8.4	3.0	1.3	7.1	9.3	8.7	5.9	13.0	9.4	8.0
3–9 years	Percent	59.8	37.1	14.5	6.1	18.9	27.1	25.0	19.0	31.8	26.2	23.3
10–20 years	Percent	0.2	54.4	49.8	24.8	37.6	41.0	40.0	41.7	41.4	40.3	39.8
20 years or more	Percent	NA	0.1	32.7	67.8	36.5	22.5	26.4	33.6	13.8	24.1	28.9
Full-time teachers	1,000	283	650	925	481	666	1,273	2,015	199	81	1,170	1,169
Earned income (Dollars)		24,892	30,126	36,095	38,642	37,895	31,897	33,631	33,666	32,960	31,972	35,241
Salary (Dollars)		22,754	27,934	33,702	36,361	33,383	30,501	31,313	31,707	30,774	30,611	32,034
Supplemental contract during school year:												
Teachers receiving	1,000	121	231	313	122	353	434	701	49	25	238	549
Salary (Dollars)		1,675	2,045	1,914	2,088	2,663	1,357	1,977	1,664	1,709	1,172	2,276
Supplemental contract during summer:												
Teachers receiving	1,000	56	118	169	65	164	244	334	46	19	167	241
Salary (Dollars)		1,608	1,952	2,003	2,284	2,309	1,763	1,919	2,272	2,360	1,803	2,104
Teachers with nonschool employment:												
Teaching/tutoring	1,000	13	30	47	20	39	70	95	8	5	41	69
Education related	1,000	9	18	28	12	31	36	59	5	2	23	44
Not education related	1,000	32	63	91	42	130	99	203	16	5	52	147

[a]For school year. Based on survey and subject to sampling error; for details, see source. [b]Non-Hispanic. [c]Includes teachers with no degrees and associates degrees, not shown separately. *—represents or rounds to zero. NA = Not applicable.

SOURCE: U.S. National Center for Education Statistics, *Digest of Education Statistics*, 1993.

that of the women who did graduate and become teachers, those with higher measured intelligence were more likely to drop out of the profession. In any case, the appeal of teaching is not in its intellectual rigor. It appeals to the heart—to those who like working with people rather than ideas (Simpson and Simpson 1969)—or to those who have no more desirable alternative (see Dworkin 1986 and LeCompte and Dworkin 1991 for a discussion of teacher entrapment and "side-bets" which lure people out of the profession).

Teachers tend to be politically conservative: 16.9 percent describe themselves as conservative, while 43.6 percent describe themselves as tending to be conservative (NEA 1972). They also tend to be ambivalent about collective action in their behalf. In an early study, 21 percent felt that teachers should never strike and 64 percent believed that teachers should strike only in the most extreme cases, when all other means had failed (NEA 1970). More recently, when asked, "Do you believe public school teachers should ever strike?" only 10 percent said they believed teachers should be permitted the same right to strike as other employees (Ginsburg 1988).

Interview a leader of your local teachers' organization or union. What kind of organization is it? What has been the history of teacher organizations in your area? What obstacles have been overcome? How many teachers are active members?

Social Class Status

Data on the socioeconomic origins of teachers is mixed. Teaching traditionally has been thought of as an avenue for upward mobility. In 1911, 52 percent of teachers came from farm families and 26 percent had parents who were blue-collar workers, although the farm percentage has dropped steadily. By 1960 only 26.5 percent came from farm families and 30 percent from blue-collar families (Betz and Garland 1974). This change probably reflects a drop in the overall number of farm families and growth in the industrial sector, but it also reflects a substantial increase in the number of individuals from middle- and upper-middle-class backgrounds who chose to become teachers.

These figures, taken from Mason's (1961) often-quoted study, combined both rural and urban districts. They may somewhat underestimate the contribution of the urban middle class, since the impact of urban middle-class teachers is diluted by being combined with rural teachers. Rural teachers are fewer in number than urban middle-class teachers and teach in smaller districts. Consequently, they are less influential in education overall than the urban teachers with whom they were combined. Also, very importantly, the Mason figures are very old and reflect a time when there were more rural-origin teachers in the teaching labor force. As the country has urbanized, so has the teaching force, and the Mason figures don't reflect these changes (Hare 1988; Pavalko 1971). When figures from urban areas are examined, the contribution of the middle class to teaching is even higher, especially when figures for men and women are examined separately. The conventional wisdom that teaching is a career for those with blue-collar origins tends to be true for men as well as for the 5 percent of the teaching force that is Mexican American. However, white teachers, especially women, come disproportionately from professional, technical, managerial, and business backgrounds. Since the 1940s, African-American teachers increasingly have had similar backgrounds (Dworkin 1980). While women from upper-class backgrounds are overrepresented as new teachers, women from less-advantaged backgrounds are likely to continue teaching longer (Betz and Garland 1974). The reason may be that middle-class women have alternatives to teaching (Dworkin 1986). It also may be that women from the working classes, like men, see teaching as an avenue to higher status, or, as Maienza suggests, base their persistence in the job on the role model provided by their own working mothers (Grow 1981).

In any case, blue-collar children of both sexes seem to be encountering increasing difficulty in gaining access to teaching careers, perhaps because of both the rising cost of higher education and the curtailment of financial aid. Given the salary they can expect as teachers, few young people may want to burden themselves with the amount of debt a college education now requires. The consequences for the profession are that it will increasingly become a profession with white-collar and service-sector origins and that it will remain predominantly white and female.

Minority Teachers

While there are substantially fewer minority than white teachers, Gottlieb (1964) and Dworkin (1980) reported that turnover among minority teachers is much lower than for whites, perhaps because of their greater job satisfaction. Fewer desirable occupations were open to minorities, and these individuals are more likely to be upwardly mobile as teachers. While minority teachers were few and usually relegated to racially segregated schools prior to 1964, more African-American, Hispanic, and other minority teachers entered the profession during the period of educational expansion in the 1960s and early 1970s. Males, too, became teachers in increasing numbers to avoid being drafted. These changes, however, were temporary. When the draft was eliminated, the incentive for men to become teachers ended.

Curtailment of scholarships and other aid in the 1980s produced a drop in the number of minorities able to attend college at all, much less become teachers. Desegregation of school faculties in the 1970s and 1980s also contributed to the decrease in minority teachers. As segregated African-American schools were closed or consolidated with white schools, faculty slots were lost, and most commonly African-American teachers found that it was their jobs that were being eliminated or changed.

In addition, as discriminatory barriers in more prestigious fields eased, educated members of minority groups were no longer limited to teaching as the most prestigious occupation to which they could aspire. The result of all these factors is that the teaching force remains primarily white and middle class while school enrollments, especially in urban areas, become increasingly minority dominated (Hodgkinson 1985). More and more teachers are working with children whose background and ethnicity are radically different from their own. These conditions have important consequences for the amount of culture shock and stress teachers encounter on the job (Dworkin 1986; Dworkin, Haney, and Telschow 1988; LeCompte 1978a, 1985; LeCompte and Dworkin 1991).

What are the demographic characteristics of teachers and administrators in your local school district? How many males, females, and minority group members are represented in teaching and administration at each of the three levels: elementary, middle, and high school?

WHAT TEACHERS DO: CONTRADICTIONS IN THE NATURE OF TEACHERS' WORK

Teachers in the United States have inherited a "divided legacy." On one hand, education is believed to be essential to democratic citizenship, but on the other, it is housed in bureaucracies which subordinate individual learning to routine bestowing of degrees or "credentialing." Ironically, both notions are born of the same imperative. Democracy requires universal education, but the systems to provide it are so large that the complex, impersonal, and bureaucratic organizations required for their management are at cross-purposes with their educational goals (McNeil 1988a, p. 337).

Teaching also occupies a contradictory place in the occupational structure because it is neither an autonomous profession, like medicine, nor a bureaucratized occupation, like automotive assembly (Dreeben 1973, p. 453). Thus teachers are in what has been called a "contradictory class location" (Wright 1978). They are not blue-collar workers and cannot be expected to act like factory employees or clerks in large corporations. While many of them (especially men) have blue-collar origins, most do not adhere to working-class ideologies. At the same time, their status is not that of "real" professionals. The following sections will discuss the nature of these complexities and contradictions.

The Conditions of Labor

Contradictions in the status of teaching can be attributed, at least in part, to the type of work teachers do, the conditions under which they work, how their work is organized, and the differentiated sex ratio in the profession. We will begin with a functionalist analysis of the teaching profession, then examine what teachers do and what purposes these activities serve, and finally we will discuss how critical theorists conceptualize teachers and their work.

Classroom Conditions.   Forty-five percent of the teachers in the United States teach in districts that have from 3,000 to 25,000 students. The average teacher works for a white male principal. Teachers' jobs require them to be in their classrooms 37 hours per week, and they perform 8 additional hours of uncompensated but required duty. They teach an average of 181 days each year, and most do so without help. Only 5.5 percent had their own teacher aides, while an additional 24.7 percent shared aides with one or more teachers (NEA 1972). These figures, compiled in the 1970s, have remained more or less unchanged, though mandated reforms such as portfolio assessment and increased recordkeeping for accountability have intensified (Apple

1992) workloads in the 1980s and 1990s. At least in reform-minded districts, then, the number of unpaid work hours has increased (Apple 1986, 1992; LeCompte and Dworkin 1991).

Teachers have little respite from their classrooms. Few have free periods, and the number who do has declined. Teachers have no coffee or bathroom breaks. A daily lunch break of less than 40 minutes, which has declined as much as 5 minutes since 1950, is often combined with supervisory duties in the cafeteria. Many teachers feel lucky to squeeze a 25-minute "child-free" lunch period.

Teachers also are badly outnumbered. While pupil–teacher ratios have been declining to some extent in the past decades, most classroom teachers face some 27 to 35 students every time they enter their rooms. Jackson (1968) states that nowhere except in schools are humans required to spend so much time so physically close to one another.

Classrooms have been described as "three-ring circuses" in which the competent teacher serves as ringmaster (Smith and Geoffrey 1968). The school day is characterized by high rates of interaction and frequent changes in activities—as often as every 5 seconds in an active classroom and every 18 seconds in a quiet one. Changes in who talks can occur more than 174 times each lesson, totaling 650 to 1,000 interchanges daily between teachers and students. Teachers themselves initiate as many as 80 interchanges per hour with students (Dreeben 1973, p. 464). Under some circumstances, the teacher can feel like a stand-up comedian with an audience full of hecklers. At best, the teacher ends the day with sensory overload.

Divide the class into three groups and assign students to interview elementary, middle, and high school teachers. Ask the teachers to describe what they do each day. How much time do they spend teaching? How much is devoted to nonteaching duties? What do they perceive to be the rewards of their profession? What factors are most disagreeable? How many plan to stay in the profession? In a class discussion, compare your findings.

Fragmentation.   Teaching is fragmented by everyday life in schools. The flow of instruction is regularly interrupted by announcements over the intercom, lunch count, children asking to leave the room, others coming in with notes or requests from other teachers, fire drills, assemblies, athletic activities, fights, and other contingencies. Sensory overload is exacerbated by such fragmentation. The physical design of classrooms seems highly conducive to frequent disruption, particularly in the lower grades. A teacher's primary task becomes to design learning activities sufficiently engrossing that pupils find them more attractive than outlawed alternatives (Jackson 1968, pp. 85–90). Teachers spend only about half the school day in actual instruction (Adams and Biddle 1970, pp. 41–45). Elementary school teachers may divide their time equally between instruction and classroom management (LeCompte 1978).

Teachers' work is fragmented also by the way the curriculum is organized, by bureaucratic time schedules, and by complications of school life which interrupt the flow of teaching. School knowledge is divided into subjects, the subjects into courses, the courses into chapters and units, and these in turn into sets of objectives (L. McNeil 1988a).

Despite recent calls for integrated and multidisciplinary curricula, most subjects are treated as if they have little if any relationship with each other. Reading in math has nothing to do with reading in social studies. In fact, there is fragmentation even within subject areas: Students study European history and art without ever considering relationships these subjects might have with each other or with history and art in America.

Teaching activities are divided into discrete time allotments, taught at specific times of the day. Teachers have little latitude to teach longer to make a point, to combine related content areas, or to omit unimportant things. Most important, the schedule allows teachers no time at all to meet with one another to plan joint activities. It is difficult to be carried away into a "grand sweep of history" or general theory of mathematics.

Isolation. Teachers, unlike virtually all other professionals, work in almost total isolation from other adults. In the motel-like structure of most schools, teachers get to see their colleagues only between classes or at lunchtime, periods when they often are engaged in supervisory tasks. If they have a free period, it is occupied with school tasks and shared by only a few of their colleagues. These conditions are obstacles to collegiality, sharing of ideas, or collective organization. What teachers know and feel about their job and about how well they are doing it is deepened through introspection over their experiences, rather than broadened through sharing of experiences and ideas with colleagues. In a sense, teachers are taught by their own students in that they are left very much on their own to determine what they are doing right or wrong (Lortie 1969, p. 469).

Control of Students. Knowing one's subject is not sufficient. Teaching is contingent upon the good will of students (Connell 1985). Teachers cannot just enter a classroom and begin to teach. They must first achieve a minimum level of order and attentiveness, as well as an agreement by the students to internalize what the teacher presents. The rules for this agreement constitute a "hidden curriculum." The hidden curriculum is as important to teachers as to students because competence in teaching is judged more by how orderly the classroom is than by how much students learn— perhaps because quiet is easier to assess than achievement.

School policies require that teachers be "fair." This means that they must exhibit affective neutrality around their students and judge them by uniform and universalistic standards. Students expect that their teachers will not play favorites. They also expect their teachers to keep order, explain things carefully, and not be boring (Nash 1976). These role expectations constitute an unwritten contract, violation of which precipitates student retaliation. Teachers maintain control only by balancing personal forcefulness with intimate teacher–pupil relationships. In order to accomplish this, teachers allocate rewards so as to establish their own power base while weakening the power of student peer affiliations to sabotage their activities (Bidwell 1965, p. 1011).

Lack of Tangible Results.   Both the quality and quantity of what teachers do is difficult to assess. Connell succinctly describes this intangibility:

> Teaching is a labor process without an object. At best, it has an object so intangible—the minds of the kids, or their capacity to learn—that it cannot be specified in any but vague and metaphorical ways . . . [it] does not produce any *things,* nor, like other white collar work, does it produce visible and quantifiable effects—so many pensions paid, so many dollars turned over, so many patients cured. (1985, p. 70)

Because its product is elusive, teaching differs from both the factory work and the professional service sector to which it often is compared. Teachers can indeed count the number of their students who pass certain tests or courses, graduate from high school, or attain degrees. However, these measures are deceptive, because most teaching is cumulative and subjective. It is difficult to attribute to any one teacher the performance of any given individual or group of students.

Multidimensionality.   While the work of teachers ostensibly is teaching, they do many other things as well. They develop instructional materials, coach athletic teams, and supervise extracurricular activities. Teachers serve on committees related to the academic and administrative operation of schools, engage in tutoring and counseling, and perform social work for students' families. They do police work in school corridors, lunchrooms, playgrounds, toilets, and buses.

The multidimensionality of teaching keeps the job from being boring, contributes to its appeal as a career, and is one of its intrinsic rewards. However, these activities are time-consuming; when they are added to time spent teaching in the classroom, preparing lessons, and grading homework and tests, teaching becomes much more than an eight-hour-a-day job.

Stress, Burnout, and Victimization

Teaching has grown more and more stressful over the years. We attribute this increase to several factors. First of all, schools have changed so much as a consequence of societal changes that they are almost unrecognizable as the institutions of twenty or thirty years ago. Consolidation has increased the size of schools and districts. Urbanization and growth in minority populations have increased student heterogeneity. Finally, the whole social, economic, and cultural context of schools has changed radically during the professional lifetime of most contemporary teachers (LeCompte and Dworkin 1991). This means that historical models of teachers' roles are no longer appropriate. While teachers have always counted discipline and crowd control among their primary professional concerns, the student body has changed to the point that there is little commonality upon which teachers can build adequate working conditions in the classroom. The result is the potential for unprecedented social and psychological job stress.

There are many sources for teacher stress. One source of stress is the discrepancy between what teachers expect to find when they enter the profession and what they actually encounter. Stress also develops when the rewards do not seem commensurate with the effort expended. Work **intensification**—the sense that nothing ever is

---

A Teacher's Angry Voice

It was just a difficult situation. I was not angry, just scared. I was angry at the school system as a whole, because it happened due to one of my students being beaten, thrown to the ground, and kicked by a bully in another fifth-grade class, on school time, in the lunchroom. Apparently, it was very vicious. My student was a small little guy, and the bully was horrible. He brags about having access to drugs and guns, etc. This is fifth grade, different classrooms. I got in there when it ended and took both of them to the principal's office. She handled it by suspending the bully for two days and read him the riot act about being a bully. I talked to my student. He didn't cry. He didn't want to be held. He was stiff. He said he was okay. When he came back into the classroom later he said he was fine. I thought it was all over. I was amazed at how well he took all of this. I should have done more, but I didn't. I thought, "Well, I guess that's okay."

About a week later, just before noon, I picked up a coat from his desk. It felt heavy. I just smiled. "What did you bring to school, ____?" I thought it was a video game or something. He looked a little stricken, and I could feel right through his coat that it was a gun. I have never owned one, but I could tell. I just told him to go outside with me. I got the coat and had him sit in the hall with me. I got ____'s assistant and had her watch my class. I took him down to the principal's office and had to wait for 20 minutes for her to show up. I held the gun, in the coat, next to me, not thinking about if it was loaded. It never dawned on me. I talked to him as we were going down the hall. He told me how he was going to get even with [bully], and he first considered killing him, then decided how he would just blow out both of his kneecaps, and was going to do it on the bus on the way home. He would get off at [bully's] stop and shoot him there. Then he was just going to walk home, and that [bully] deserved it. His older brother used to take care of his problems, and he didn't want to ask him any more. He was old enough to take care of them on his own. In fact, one of his older brothers had been killed a year earlier, and so he was going to handle it himself. He never cried, he was very frank and open about it. I felt awful. If we had intervened more somewhere along the line, and really thought about how he'd been put down and recognized that something like this might have happened. I was just shocked and shaken.

A Teacher's Angry Voice

Well, we [teachers] would eat together, but kind of like in shifts, and since I was doing third grade then, I overlapped with second grade and fourth grade. It was such a small school, I think we all ate together—second, third, and fourth. It reached the point where I couldn't stand to eat with them anymore because they were racist, and the jokes and things that they would say—I had a hard time keeping my mouth shut. I knew that I was already in a precarious position there and just had to get through the year. If I became embroiled and said what I really wanted to say, it would become even more difficult.

I try not to be too outspoken, especially in the South. I've had a lot of teachers tell me, "Well, you aren't from the South. That's why you are willing to speak out and not sit back and let things happen." But I felt that I sat back a lot more than I am inclined to, and I don't think I got messed with nearly as bad as the other two teachers did. They didn't say anything; they kind of hunkered down and closed their door. . . . The people [in Seattle] are very outspoken and not willing to sit down for anything. Down here, it's kind of like, "Do what you will with me. It's okay. I'm here to be walked on." I found it very interesting. I have often had teachers say to me that they are just shocked that I would not accept some things.

subtracted from your job description—and **de-skilling,** the limiting of teacher autonomy through mandated curricula and policies developed at administrative levels, contribute to this kind of stress. Work overload and de-skilling lead to alienation.

Faced with stressful situations, teachers may develop a sense of inadequacy to carry out assigned tasks. What teachers conceive of as "add-ons" aggravate this sense of inadequacy. In today's context of school reform and restructuring, teachers are called upon to change their pedagogical practices. They may come to view innovation as something to be added to what they already must do. In large part, this interpretation is accurate, however, it impedes reform. Teachers finding it difficult to substitute a new strategy or task for an old one, simply do both. They define each innovation as potential work overload, therefore they can become particularly resistant to new ideas.

Burnout is a common name for a sociological concept called **alienation.** Alienation is a sense that life has become meaningless, that one is powerless to make the changes necessary to restore meaning to one's life and work. One can neither understand nor control one's destiny because the rules that once made life predictable are no longer effective. One is *personally isolated* and without allies to improve the situation, *personally estranged* from the kind of person one thought oneself to be, and *culturally isolated* from the community and context of which one is a part (Dworkin 1985b, p. 7; LeCompte and Dworkin 1991; Needle et al. 1980; Seeman 1959, 1967,

1975). All of these conditions characterize the working situation of an increasing number of teachers. The result often is that teachers "wear out" or "burn out" (Dworkin 1986).

Teachers burn out for a variety of reasons. Some burnout occurs as a consequence of the sensory overload described earlier. Teachers usually cannot take a restorative sabbatical from their jobs. Isolation also increases the likelihood of burnout in two ways. First, as we have indicated, the physical layout and scheduling constraints of schools give teachers few opportunities to blow off steam with other teachers. Second, because teachers tend to find most of their friends among other teachers, they get less input from people with other viewpoints (Ginsburg 1979). Expectations also play a role. People are attracted to teaching because they perceive teachers as catalysts for student learning. When they find that they are unable to make children learn—whether because of institutional or time pressures, student misbehavior, or interpersonal conflicts—they become subject to stress and burnout (Needle et al. 1980).

In addition, many teachers feel unsafe at work. Every year 12 percent of teachers report that they have been robbed at school. Twelve percent also say that they avoid confronting students because they are afraid of them. One percent per month are physically attacked at school. In a 1993 survey on school violence 60 percent of responding urban districts reported student assaults on teachers. Twenty-eight percent of all responding districts (urban, suburban, and rural) reported student versus teacher violence (National School Boards Association 1993). In another study 72 percent of the teachers felt concern about the vandalism and destruction of property in school (Phillips and Lee 1980). The majority of reported violence takes place in secondary schools, but elementary teachers are not immune.

While many reports have minimized the amount of actual danger in schools, perhaps more important is the dismaying feeling that "you might be next." Seventy-five percent of teachers knew someone who had been verbally abused, and 35 percent knew someone who had been physically attacked (National School Boards Association 1993). The installation of metal detectors in middle and high schools in both urban and suburban school districts, the use of police guards and drug-sniffing dogs in large urban districts, and the rising indices of drug use and crime among pre-teens give these feelings of victimization and vulnerability additional credence. The result is a widespread disaffection with the profession.

In a major study of teachers, nearly one-third indicated that they felt their work to be meaningless and that they felt powerless to do anything about it (Dworkin 1986). These feelings were most common among those in the demographic majority—female, white, middle class, under 30 years old, and with less than five years of experience. Elementary teachers were more likely to feel stressed than secondary teachers. Significantly, feelings of discrimination, victimization, and burnout were more likely to occur when teachers were "racially isolated," that is, in a school where the predominant race of the student body was different from their own (Dworkin 1986). As we have indicated, demographic change in the coming decades will likely aggravate the cultural estrangement engendered by racial isolation (Hodgkinson 1985) and consequently increase culture shock among teachers.

THE REWARD STRUCTURE OF TEACHING

Teaching traditionally has produced few extrinsic rewards for excellent performance. Most of its benefits are intangible, coming from classroom activity and interaction with children. Standardized salary schedules preclude bonuses or merit raises. (See Table 4.5 for the current average teachers' salaries by region.) Teaching also has a "flat" career trajectory. Teachers cannot be promoted for good teaching except by moving into administration, which means leaving the classroom. The only tangible rewards administrators can give to teachers concern working conditions: a desirable classroom, assignment to gifted students, a free period, permission to teach a specialty course, or time off to go to a conference.

Merit Pay

Many districts have tried a merit pay plan and discarded it. The major complaint about it is that the criteria for establishing merit are vague, subjective, and too prone to administrative manipulation. Teachers may not trust their administrators to be fair. Teacher organizations also reject the concept of merit pay, because it has taken them years to achieve equal pay for teachers across disciplines and grade levels.

Career Ladders

As a consequence of the reform movements of the late 1980s, many states have mandated "Career Ladder" programs, which attempt to eliminate the flat trajectory of the profession. These create levels in teaching based upon seniority, advanced preparation, and excellence in performance. Career ladders are a variation of merit pay but they attempt to avoid subjectivity by making the steps for acquiring merit very explicit. Systematization of career ladder steps has been criticized, however, for turning teaching performance into a rigidly prescribed and routinized activity. Current research indicates that career ladder programs have not fundamentally changed teachers' work roles, responsibilities, and reward structures. In fact, existing distinctions in rank among teachers became the basis for levels in the career ladder, with the result that those who had always been favored continued to be (Malen and Hart 1987).

Critical Area Pay

Incentive systems of a different kind have also been initiated. "Critical area pay" has been instituted to encourage certification in areas with few teachers, such as math, science, and bilingual education. Another form of critical area pay is given to teachers willing to work in inner-city schools or in neighborhoods with high crime rates. Critical area pay adds substantially to the remuneration of some teachers but does not enhance the profession overall. As Dworkin (1986) indicates, teachers feel that increases in pay are inadequate compensation for adverse working conditions.

TABLE 4.5 Estimated Average Annual Salaries of Total Instructional Staff and of Classroom Teachers, 1993–94

		1993–94 Average Salary of Classroom Teachers				
				All Teachers		
Region and State	Average Salary of Instructional Staff	Elementary School	Secondary School	Current $	% Increase Over 1992–93	Purchasing Power In 1984 $
1	2	3	4	5	6	7
50 STATES AND D.C.	$37,701	$35,258	$36,765	$35,958	2.7	$25,098
NEW ENGLAND	44,751	40,809	40,351	40,583	3.2	28,320
CONNECTICUT	51,100	48,900	51,000	49,500	2.4	34,548
MAINE	32,049	30,483	32,140	30,996	2.5	21,630
MASSACHUSETTS	47,774*	39,370*	39,370*	39,370*	3.0*	27,474*
NEW HAMPSHIRE	38,599	36,402	36,346	36,372	7.2	25,382
RHODE ISLAND	39,992	39,212	39,318	39,261	3.5	27,898
VERMONT	35,503*	36,043*	36,043*	36,043*	3.5*	25,152*
MIDEAST	46,132	43,845	46,031	44,853	4.9	31,300
DELAWARE	39,031	36,853	38,111	37,469	3.5	26,147
DIST. OF COLUMBIA	39,257	41,936	48,534	42,543	9.9	29,688
MARYLAND	41,755	39,101	41,067	39,937	3.1	27,870
NEW JERSEY	47,635	44,199	47,283	45,308	6.2	31,618
NEW YORK	47,800	45,800	47,800	46,800	4.0	32,689
PENNSYLVANIA	44,698	42,890	44,515	43,688	6.0	30,487
SOUTHEAST	31,642	30,055	30,858	30,364	2.6	21,189
ALABAMA	30,015	28,705	28,705	28,705	6.5	20,031
ARKANSAS	29,038	27,092	28,626	27,873	1.6	19,451
FLORIDA	33,423	32,020	32,020	32,020	2.7	22,345
GEORGIA	32,128	30,456	30,456	30,456	1.3	21,253
KENTUCKY	32,834	30,881	33,228	31,582	1.5	22,039
LOUISIANA	30,560	28,508*	28,508*	28,508*	3.2*	19,894*
MISSISSIPPI	26,162	24,816	25,744	25,235	3.6	17,610
NORTH CAROLINA	30,895	29,602	29,804	29,680	1.2	20,712

153

TABLE 4.5 *(continued)*

Region and State 1	Average Salary of Instructional Staff 2	1993–94 Average Salary of Classroom Teachers			All Teachers	
		Elementary School 3	Secondary School 4	Current $ 5	% Increase Over 1992–93 6	Purchasing Power In 1984 $ 7
SOUTH CAROLINA	30,730	29,690	31,230	30,190	3.3	21,068
TENNESSEE	31,173	29,520	31,380	30,037	3.7	20,961
VIRGINIA	33,928*	31,996*	34,794*	33,128*	2.5*	23,118*
WEST VIRGINIA	31,656	30,241	30,972	30,549	0.8	21,318
GREAT LAKES	40,277	37,775	39,775	38,746	2.6	27,088
ILLINOIS	42,335	39,042	45,789	40,989	6.1	28,604
INDIANA	37,331*	36,155*	36,372*	36,255*	3.4*	25,300*
MICHIGAN	46,392*	42,500*	42,500*	42,500*	-2.5*	29,658*
OHIO	36,000	34,500	35,900	35,700	3.5	24,913
WISCONSIN	37,543*	34,865	37,171	36,644	2.0	25,572
PLAINS	32,991	31,221	32,757	31,818	3.0	22,204
IOWA	31,880	29,714	31,684	30,760	2.1	21,465
KANSAS	35,640	34,178	34,178	34,178	4.0	23,851
MINNESOTA	37,309	35,566	37,761	36,146	3.0	25,224
MISSOURI	31,386	29,465	31,079	30,227	2.9	21,094
NEBRASKA	31,595*	29,564	29,564	29,564	2.8	20,681
NORTH DAKOTA	26,359	25,539	25,452	25,508	1.2	17,800
SOUTH DAKOTA	24,977	25,098	24,993	25,199	3.7	17,585
SOUTHWEST	31,446	29,534	30,563	30,036	2.1	20,960
ARIZONA	39,794*	31,680*	31,680*	31,680*	1.0*	22,107*
NEW MEXICO	28,383*	27,072*	27,989*	27,922	5.2	19,485
OKLAHOMA	27,730	26,086	27,571	26,749	3.2	18,666
TEXAS	31,046	29,912	31,136	30,519	2.0	21,297

ROCKY MOUNTAINS	31,650	29,946	31,226	30,581	1.7	21,341
COLORADO	34,911*	33,236*	34,439*	33,826	0.8	28,605
IDAHO	28,994*	27,593*	28,084*	27,803*	2.9*	19,402*
MONTANA	29,358	28,024	28,535	28,210	2.1	19,686
UTAH	29,068	27,235	28,630	28,056	3.0	19,579
WYOMING	31,200	30,250	30,370	30,310	0.8	21,151
FAR WEST	42,078	33,020	40,109	39,095	0.6	27,282
ALASKA	46,649*	46,581*	46,581*	46,581*	1.2*	32,506*
CALIFORNIA	44,210*	38,628*	42,436*	40,289*	0.6*	28,115*
HAWAII	37,671	36,564	36,564	36,564	0.3	25,516
NEVADA	35,603	33,355	34,799	33,955	-0.5	23,595
OREGON	38,500	36,500	38,120	37,150	3.5	25,911
WASHINGTON	37,468	35,478	36,417	35,860	0.3	25,024

*Data estimated by NEA.

SOURCE: National Educatition Association Research, 1994. 1993–1994 Estimates of School Statistics. Washington, D.C.: NEA. Reprinted with Permission.

DE-SKILLING, ROUTINIZATION, AND THE
ENFORCEMENT OF BUREAUCRATIC CONTROL

Teachers control only certain aspects of their classrooms. Lortie says that teachers' decision making is characterized by "variable zoning" (1969, pp. 13–15), meaning that they have "hard" jurisdiction in areas where their judgments will not be questioned and "soft" jurisdiction in other areas. Lortie and other functionalists suggest that the privacy of the closed classroom door ensures that instructional decisions can be "hard" ones for teachers, though they have less discretion over recordkeeping and other administrative matters. This area of "hard" decisions, teachers' area of discretion or autonomy, is one that strengthens their sense of professionalism. However, to the extent that teachers have discretion or empowerment in classrooms, "that which is most central and unique to schools—instruction—is least controlled by specific and literally enforced rules and regulations" (Lortie 1969, p. 14) and also is least under surveillance by the administration.

As schools have become increasingly bureaucratized, critical researchers have noticed erosion in the "harder" areas of teacher discretion. Apple describes the degree to which decision making about curriculum and instructional matters has passed out of the hands of teachers, leaving as their exclusive province only the control of behavior in their classroom (Apple 1982, 1988). He calls this phenomenon "de-skilling." It accompanies "teacher-proof" technological innovation in the delivery of instruction—computer-assisted instruction and other pre-programmed forms of teaching—as well as behaviorally based curricula with pre-specified teaching programs and lessons "bits." De-skilling strips from teachers the ability to make decisions about what and how to teach, the ability to utilize their training and expertise. De-skilling most often affects work typically performed by women—secretaries, clerks, and nurses in addition to teachers. Of particular note is that de-skilling is often associated with intensification of the teacher's workload.

Cuban suggests that teachers directly influence only five areas of classroom decision making, all related to the groupings and spatial arrangements:

1. Arrangement of classroom space
2. The ratio of teacher-to-student talk
3. Whether most instruction occurs individually, in small groups, or with the entire class
4. Whether or not learning or interest centers are used by students as a normal part of the school day
5. The degree of movement students are permitted without asking the teacher (1984, p. 5)

These are all basically management concerns and deal with matters other than the content of instruction. Decisions about curricula and content are made by local and state educational agencies, which mandate the subjects to be taught and the time to be allocated to each. State textbook committees also generally provide a list of ap-

---

A Teacher's Angry Voice

I can remember one [experience of anger in school]. It happened just before the end of school, and the reason I took it so hard was because I was tired. I had been through a lot all year, and we had all of the children in our school outside in the heat of the afternoon watching. The city police brought their dogs and they brought samples of drugs. They were showing how the dogs would hunt out the drugs. At other schools, they bring in clowns; at (name of school), they bring in dogs and drugs, right? That angered me in the beginning.

---

proved textbooks. Individual school districts may use teacher committees to help choose books from the list, but individual teachers may not select alternatives. Even teachers' choice of supplementary books may be restricted by community watchdog committees and district regulations.

The use of standardized subject-area criteria and normative testing also excludes teachers from decision making about curricula. In response to calls for improved standards, accountability programs have been instituted in almost every state. Much reform in the 1900s is, in fact, driven by assessment. To the extent that school districts gear course content toward externally developed tests, teachers lose control of daily classroom instruction. This is especially true when promotion, retention, and graduation of students is tied to performance on the tests.

Loss of control over content is a serious matter, because it prevents teachers from using skills they developed in their area of specialization. However, de-skilling can take even more insidious forms. Teachers may even lose control over *how* they teach. "Teacher-proof" curricula come not only with instructional objectives, but with lesson plans, mandated readings and exercises, pre- and post-tests, and supplementary activities. Such curricula routinize and bureaucratize the teaching process, hedging it with rules and regulations and making it difficult for teachers to improvise, create, or follow up on what they think is important.

L. McNeil's (1988c) case study comparing the attitudes and behavior of teachers before and after institution of educational reform programs amply documents the effect that de-skilling has upon enthusiastic and dedicated teachers. She describes how, in the name of improving student performance, the content of courses in one large school district was "taken apart, sequenced, numbered, and sub-numbered," not by teachers but by central-office test producers in a manner "perhaps unwittingly modelled on the activity analysis which efficiency experts used for pacing activities on an assembly line." Their purpose was to create measurable objectives for each component of the curriculum, then develop tests that assessed student mastery. Ultimately, uniformity of instruction and assessment of students was to be ensured for each student in the district. The result was to transform the tasks of the teacher into a set of "generic behaviors."

McNeil states that these curriculum reforms generated an immense amount of new work for teachers. Not only were they required to teach what they perceived to be much more material (the value of some of which they questioned), but both the instructional management systems and the preoccupation with administrating and grading tests generated a massive volume of paperwork. Teachers felt they had become little more than assembly-line workers or clerks, whose job was merely to organize, disseminate, and process predeveloped tasks.

Many of the teachers in McNeil's study engaged in principled resistance to this bureaucratic control. Some left teaching. Faced with an overwhelming volume of content to cover, some gave up on good teaching. They eliminated written composition altogether. Teachers engaged in omission of controversial issues, and compression or "defensive simplification" of complex topics. They taught students simply to recognize concepts rather than to understand them, and they presented outlines and lists to be memorized rather than analyzing and synthesizing the material. While these strategies undoubtedly made instruction less onerous, they also made teachers feel unprofessional and made them less credible in the eyes of students. Teachers neither answered serious questions from students nor seemed to have any demonstrated expertise (L. McNeil 1988b).

Reskilling and Alienation

The educational reforms of the 1980s not only increased teachers' workload but also changed the content and focus of tasks. While being "de-skilled" as they lost control over instructional matters, they were "reskilled" to manage complex technological and behavioral systems for students. Many responded, at least initially, with enthusiasm and competence. Apple (1986) attributes this reaction to the fact that they *were* learning new skills, even though these skills were clerical and out of their areas of competence. The process of learning new things, as well as the fact that they were in fact working long, hard hours, made teachers feel as though they were doing a good job. Because most teachers also believed that American education is in need of reform, they also believed they were participating in exciting educational innovation. They felt that they, in conjunction with external reformers—district administrators and state agencies—were defining the problem and working toward a mutually satisfactory way to solve it. Their efforts might have been illusory, however, because as the examples in Chapter 3 from Cottonwood School District indicate, the ultimate effect of centralized curriculum management is to remove control from teachers.

McNeil, by contrast, found meaning to be constructed in a different way. Teachers in the school she studied already had been defined by themselves and the district as excellent teachers in an exemplary magnet school. They interpreted the district's imposition of a reform program as an indication that they were no longer considered experts, and they resented the loss of status and control. We feel that the situation McNeil describes is more common. However, Dworkin's research (1985b, 1986) on teacher burnout indicates that principals and other administrators can lessen alienation in these circumstances. Regardless of the level of stress they encounter, teachers who view their principals as supportive are less likely to resist activities or experience burnout.

More recent innovations in education are centered on teacher empowerment and shared leadership. Whole language, the reading and language curriculum based on the natural language of students, and integrated curricular approaches place teachers at the center of decision making in their own classrooms. Democratic leadership or shared school governance movements encourage teachers to work with administrators regarding school policies and programs. We will talk more about these alternative and innovative approaches in Chapter 9.

Brainstorm with your colleagues a list of the satisfiers and dissatisfiers of teaching. Discuss both the difficulties and rewards of a career in teaching.

ADMINISTRATORS AND ANCILLARY STAFF

Having outlined the general conditions under which teachers work, we now move to a discussion of the work of administrators and ancillary staff. Initial experience as a teacher is the common denominator for all professional-level staff in public schools.

Administrators

Virtually all school administrators, whether they supervise teachers, counselors, bus drivers, evaluators, or recordkeepers, are required to have teacher certification. Entrance to administration programs in universities, which is required for most public school administrators as well as faculty in colleges of education, typically requires at least three years of teaching in elementary or secondary schools. This requirement guarantees a certain uniformity of outlook in the educational profession. It also ensures that a large proportion of professional staff will be drawn from the same pool of recruits.

Administrators do not constitute a representative sample of teachers, however. While they resemble teachers in social status, political views, and religious affiliation, administrators differ radically by gender. For example, 93 percent of U.S. high school principals in the mid-1970s were male (Boocock 1980). While searching for respondents for a survey of female U.S. school superintendents, Frasher et al. (Grow 1981) were able to locate only 131. Of the 82 who responded to the survey, over 70 percent served in school districts with an enrollment of fewer than 3,000 students. Although more women are moving into school administration, they continue to be underrepresented in these leadership positions. For example, in 1990, 38 percent of the principalships and assistant principalships were held by women (U.S. Equal Employment Opportunity Commission 1990). In 1990, 33.7 percent of all local school board members were women. In 1991, only nine of the fifty chief state school officers were women (American Association of University Women 1992).

Male and Female Career Patterns. In addition to the dramatic difference in numbers, male and female school administrators appear to follow different career patterns once they move from the classroom. While there have been few comparative studies of male and female administrators, Maienza's study (Grow 1981) indicated that men who enter administration appear to have decided to do so early in their careers. Male administrators typically taught for a little more than six years, started and completed graduate school in their thirties, and had about eight years of administrative experience, usually as a secondary school principal or in an upper-level central office post, before attaining their first superintendency.

By contrast, females did not decide to become an administrator until after finishing the Master's degree. They entered and completed graduate school in their forties or fifties and attained their first superintendency after almost thirteen years of lower-level administrative experience. Only five years of the delay in career advancement seem attributable to breaks for child-rearing. (In fact, while most male administrators are married, women, especially at the superintendent level, tend to be single — either widowed, divorced, or never married [Good 1981].) Women's careers lead through lower-level central office positions to elementary principalships, not from secondary principalships and upper-level central office positions to the superintendency (Gaertner 1978). As Ortiz puts it:

> Men are more likely than women to occupy those positions with greater potential for power and opportunity as well as those at the upper levels of the hierarchy. Male mobility tends to be vertical through a series of line positions entailing the administration of adults. . . . Women tend to move through positions involving instruction and interaction with children from which vertical movement is rare. (1981, p. 81)

Minorities.   Ortiz also points out that members of minority groups tend to be limited either to instructional duties or to supervision of other minorities. Because they are viewed as specialists in minority problems, as principals they tend to be assigned to schools defined as "problems" because of their large minority enrollments. Reyes and Halcon (1988) call this "type-casting" and the "Brown-on-Brown" taboo. They suggest that the very fact that minorities are considered experts in the problems of their own people disqualifies them as experts on the problems of others. They are regarded primarily as crisis managers rather than administrators capable of handling the broad range of responsibilities required in higher positions (Ortiz 1981). This perception limits the appointment of minorities to "one per pot" (Reyes and Halcon 1988) and reduces their chances for promotion.

Counselors and Ancillary Staff

Like teachers and administrators, counselors also must first be certified as teachers. Like administrators, counselors are not a representative sample of the teaching population. They tend to be older, male, and white. While we tend to think of schools primarily in terms of the activities of teachers, both the number of counselors and other ancillary staff in schools and their importance in educational functioning have grown dramatically in the past decades. In 1980 there were over 32,000 counselors in the United States (Boocock 1980). Their presence "bears witness to at least two things. There are problems in the school, and the usual personnel cannot, or have not been able to, resolve them" (Sarason 1971, p. 127). They are an indication of the growth in what in Chapter 2 we called the "service sector" in education.

Counselors often are counted as instructional personnel, so their numbers tend to deflate statistics on pupil:teacher ratios. However, counselors do not teach, and their career paths are different from that of teachers. They generally acquire a Bachelor's degree in teaching and experience in the classroom, followed by a Master's degree or doctorate, usually in guidance and counseling or school psychology. The relationship of counselors to overall administrative control in schools is more ambiguous than that of teachers, as is their status. While they have more education than most teachers, they do not acquire it in instructional areas. They have substantial power over students (Cicourel and Kitsuse 1963; Sarason 1971) but they are peripheral to the predominantly instructional life of the school.

The Contradictory Role of Counselors. Feelings of discrepancy between role expectations and actual accomplishments probably are greater for counselors than for any other school professionals. Originally, counseling was designed for academic purposes only. Counselors were placed in secondary schools as curricular offerings differentiated into more than one academic stream. They were responsible for the clerical function of ensuring that students were placed in appropriate classes and fulfilled the necessary requirements for graduation. They also helped students find and apply to appropriate colleges and universities. However, today both their training and the expectations parents, students, administrators, and the public have of them have broadened considerably.

As educators became aware of the importance to cognitive learning of social, emotional, and psychological factors, counselors were expected to engage in "social work," attempting to solve the psychological problems that kept students from learning. Their graduate training came to reflect a more clinical or therapeutic orientation. Counselors were customarily assigned 200 to 300 students in a given grade level. Now, student-to-counselor ratios of 420:1 and 350:1 are commonplace. Powell, Farrar, and Cohen (1985, p. 49) report that administrators in a school with a 200:1 ratio felt that their situation approached the national "ideal."

Even with a 200:1 ratio, the burden for seeking help falls primarily on students, who may not even know that they need advice. Even when students do get an appointment with a counselor, their average visit is less than ten minutes. Often the counselor has not had time to review student records before seeing them. Paper work is overwhelming. Though counselors are charged with seeing that eligible children receive appropriate special-needs programs and that the multiple standardized test scores are recorded, many students do not get placed in programs appropriate to their capabilities and minority children fail to get the encouragement and guidance they need to stay in school and aspire to college. Fully 75 percent of counselors' time can be consumed with these clerical duties, leaving little for the therapeutic interactions which they prefer and are trained to do. The result is that only those students with serious problems, aggressive parents, personal persistence, serious discrepancies in their records, or visibly flamboyant misbehavior will receive attention. Even many normally achieving students reach their senior year without realizing that they have serious deficits in their transcripts which will prevent them from graduating.

Functionalists view the activities of counselors as part of the status allocation function in society. That is, counselors help the school to function as a mechanism for social differentiation, sorting students by perceived abilities into academic, vocational, or remedial curricula commensurate with what is believed to be their occupational role (Cicourel and Kitsuse 1963). While the decisions are supposed to be made on objective grounds, from indisputable data such as test scores, Cicourel and Kitsuse demonstrated how other, more subjective measures played a role in student placement. These include counselor judgments of student social class and whether or not the student was perceived to be popular, a good athlete, a trouble-maker, or an underachiever. These judgments are critical, because they can conclusively bar students deemed unable to perform—for whatever reason—from the courses of study that they want or that would help them achieve their potential.

More problematic is that the increasing power of counselors over a student's academic—and occupational—destiny is not distributed equitably. Students whom counselors see most are those who need it least: those with a high level of academic achievement and extracurricular participation, who are from the middle and upper classes and have seldom been in trouble (Armor 1969). Shultz and Erickson (1982) describe how this process takes place, suggesting that the differentiation is facilitated by language patterns. Counselors can avoid spending much time with students by manipulating them to ask certain questions and to give answers that fail to elicit the needed help. Fine (1987) calls this a "policy of enforced silencing" (p. 167) and discusses how information about the consequences of dropping out is systematically withheld from students. We submit that enforced silencing also precludes disadvantaged students and women from getting adequate information about courses to take, job requirements, and ways to get into colleges and other forms of higher education. We will talk in more detail about the relationship of social class, race, and gender to academic differentiation in Chapters 5, 7, and 8, where the impact of variable treatment of students by teachers, administrators, and counselors will become apparent.

THE NATURE OF ADMINISTRATIVE WORK IN SCHOOLS

The daily routine of school administrators is almost as multidimensional as that of teachers. As we have indicated, school administrators are recruited from the ranks of teachers. Promotion is based upon further examination or experience as a school administrator, a practice that closes off the system to outsiders and non-school administrators (Fantini, Gittell, and Magat 1974). Historically, administrators served as instructional leaders. Some still return occasionally to the classroom, and many districts require that they do. Labor in the schools, however, has been increasingly subdivided both functionally and temporally. The resulting bureaucratization has created a rather wide split between instructional and administrative duties (Bidwell 1965). Those at the bottom of the chain of command—teachers and principals—find it difficult to make daily decisions without constantly looking upward for approval, but those in the central office are so removed from building-level activities that actions constantly are delayed or postponed. Sometimes this delay is deliberate as bureaucrats use the structure to avoid making decisions they would rather avoid (Rogers 1968). Distance leads to distrust. Central office staff believe that building-level personnel, especially teachers, are too close to the action to maintain objectivity and flexibility while teachers and principals see the central office staff as being in an ivory tower far from the firing line (Rogers 1968).

A number of researchers have described the daily activities of typical school administrators (Cuban 1984; Borman and Spring 1984; Wolcott 1973). Because of the great diversity of schools as well as recent changes in how administrators are expected to do their work, we shall outline the categories of responsibility for school-based and central office administrators. In so doing, we will illustrate the tensions and ambiguities inherent in these roles.

Loose Coupling and Variable Zoning

The gradual change from instructional to administrative responsibility has created contradictions between the role of educational managers and what Lortie (1975) called "zoning" in their areas of legitimate authority. On one hand, because they have been teachers, administrators claim special understanding of teachers and instructional problems. On the other hand, they are viewed by teachers as management, not labor, and as lacking expertise in the teachers' own subject areas. Teachers readily accept principals' authority as legitimate only in noninstructional matters. These include financial matters, parent relations, and contacts with agencies outside the school (Becker 1953).

This division produces constant tension in matters of control and supervision, aggravated by the loose structure or "coupling" of schools (see Chapter 2). Because of the closed classroom door and scattering of buildings and personnel, top administrators have little day-to-day contact with teachers, and therefore limited capacity for direct daily supervision (Bidwell 1965; Dreeben 1973, p. 452).

Principals also have limited power over hiring and firing of teachers. They must choose from among those screened by central office staff and sometimes must take teachers transferred from other schools. They can fire teachers only in the most extreme circumstances. In most cases, undesirable teachers can be transferred to another school only if a willing recipient can be found.

While schools resemble bureaucracies to some degree, the decision-making routine of top administrators differs substantially from that of chief executive officers in corporations. In the first place, decision making in schools is scheduled and routinized. Budgets are established annually or biennially, and the remainder of the fiscal cycle consists of administering decisions that were made long before. Hiring is done at the beginning of the school year. In the second place, school officials have little control over fund raising, other than lobbying for tax increases or state or corporate beneficence. How much revenue schools receive is in the hands of taxpayers.

Some researchers have attributed to this routinization the relative lack of crises and emergencies in school decision making. However, it is our belief that neither the periodic nature of fiscal and personnel decisions nor the absence of crises over sales, marketing, and procurement mean that schools operate peacefully, especially in urban areas. The crises that occur are of a different nature and require different, largely human relations skills.

Maintenance of Fiscal and Professional Standards

One area of potential crisis for school administrators is fiduciary; school leaders, as public officials, are caretakers of public funds. They also are responsible both to governmental agencies and their public constituencies for maintenance of appropriate standards, both professional and personal, of school staff. These are the touchiest areas for school people. Instructional mismanagement is not dramatic and takes a long time to be noticed, but fiscal mismanagement or behavioral impropriety creates the kind of scandal that topples superintendents and causes principals to be fired.

Quality Control versus Autonomy

At the same time that their managerial and fiscal functions have expanded, school administrators are experiencing pressure from policy makers to exercise more supervision over instruction. Responsibility for quality control, coordination, and monitoring to ensure uniform competence among high school graduates falls to administrators, from building-level principals to the central office. However, the structural looseness of schools and the long period of time over which cohorts of students are trained provide many opportunities for exercise of autonomy in teaching. Administrators are therefore pressed to institute rationalization and routinization of instruction and assessment (Bidwell 1965, pp. 976–977), thereby further bureaucratizing schools and removing control from teachers.

A number of reforms, including restructuring and site-based management, have encouraged administrators to exercise more control over instruction. Their increased control has had two effects. First, administrators, like teachers, experience work overload and burnout. Many feel that they cannot adequately supervise instruction and also carry out all their administrative duties. Second, serious monitoring of instruction contributes to de-skilling. It is resented by teachers, who see their "hard" area of jurisdiction over instruction eroded. Principals are caught in the middle, like factory supervisors who must enforce reform upon an unenthusiastic work force (Borman and Spring 1984).

Business Managers. Schools also have experimented with dividing the duties of the principal. Principals would become "instructional leaders" or "headmasters" who supervise teachers and help implement the curriculum. A specialist trained in business administration rather than education would handle the business aspects of schooling, especially those dealing with finances. While this plan is congruent with the efficiency movement described in Chapter 2, it has had a mixed reception. Principals are uneasy about the loss of control over budgetary matters, especially if the business manager reported directly to the central office. Teachers worry about more direct supervision by principals. We can expect to see more of these innovations in the future, but their impact upon overall school governance still is unknown.

A further issue is the impact of such division of duties on the principal's role and authority. While these proposals seem a sensible way to lighten the load for building-level supervisors, it also promises to subject them to the same de-skilling and loss of control that afflict teachers.

Relationships with the School Board and Community

Public relations is among the most important functions of school administrators. Principals must establish relationships with the parent–teacher organization and cope with those parents whose children are problems. Blumberg (1985, p. xiii) suggests that conflict is the most appropriate orientation for understanding the nature of a superintendent's work. Superintendents must maintain the uneasy balance between advice and control with their lay school boards. This task is made more difficult by the fact that, until recently, school boards exercised direct managerial control over district activities. Boards have been reluctant to relinquish this power, and since they can fire superintendents who dissatisfy them, one of the primary responsibilities of superintendents is to maintain good board relationships. Doing this can be difficult where racial and economic divisions produce disagreement over educational goals and procedures.

Principals and superintendents develop a range of strategies to maintain consensus and to prevent community conflicts from interfering with school operation. These strategies include lobbying board members on important issues in advance of meetings and/or peppering them with so much information before meetings that they cannot assimilate it all and must rely upon the judgment of the superintendent. Superintendents may hide important policy issues in meeting agendas laden with personnel, budget, and other diversionary topics. A cardinal rule is to see that open conflict never erupts in public meetings. As a result, many decisions are made first in executive sessions (Fantini, Gittell, and Magat 1974; Kerr 1973; McGivney and Haught 1972).

SUMMARY

In this chapter, we have outlined the contradictory nature of the teaching profession. We have suggested, with the functionalists, that the work of educators really does not equate with that of the traditional professions. We also have traced the development of forces that are removing teachers and building-level personnel from the center of control.

The patterns of control and training that prevail in teaching make it difficult for teachers to acquire the pay and prestige they desire. The fact that teacher work has come to be defined as female work acts to reduce its status.

Control of standards also is an issue. How teaching is carried out and who is permitted to teach is more a function of external political, ideological, and economic pressures than of concerns over expertise and technical skill. Teaching is work deemed critical to the operation of society, but often for reasons irrelevant to pedagogy. While critical theorists have argued that teachers must transform the conditions of their work, we suggest that the proportion of teachers actually trying to do so is minuscule. Teacher militancy at the collective level seems limited. A hopeful sign, however, is the fact that teachers engaged in union activity are more concerned with increasing their autonomy and control over curriculum and with respect to administrators than they are with bargaining over wages (Falk, Grimes, and Lord 1982).

The crisis in urban education of the late 1980s and 1990s (Kozol 1991) bodes well for the possibility of change. We share the caution articulated by Michael Apple (1993), who believes that while there is much about public schools in the United States that needs reform, attacks alleging that *all* public schooling is defective are dangerous. Public schooling, whatever its flaws, is a democratizing institution, which provides considerable opportunity for the underclass to achieve upward mobility. An all-out assault on the public schools provides ammunition for a conservative political movement whose agenda is privatization of schooling and subsequent sequestering of privilege for the more advantaged members of society. We challenge readers to examine each critique and each accolade leveled at the schools for its immediate as well as its long-term consequences for education in the United States.

chapter 5

Social Class and Its Relationship to Education

INTRODUCTION

In the previous chapters, we have discussed the characteristics of schools and the people who participate in them. We now turn to an examination of the impact schools have on children. This chapter begins with a discussion of social class, for several reasons. First, the variable social class constitutes perhaps the single most powerful source of inequality in society. Second, social class was one of the first factors, besides intelligence, examined by modern sociologists as a possible source of the differences in achievement. Explicating the relationship between social class and education has been one of the most important contributions sociologists have made to our understanding of education.

Notions of social class are so inextricably linked to our thinking about ethnicity, race, and gender that it is difficult to discuss them separately. This is especially true in the United States, where we tend to ignore social class origins, placing more emphasis on race and ethnicity. Most people in this country see themselves as middle class. In Europe and Australia people tend to differentiate social class positions more clearly. The experiences of women, people of color, and people from impoverished and working classes have long been neglected in the literature. Nevertheless, it is important to consider all aspects of a person's experience. We have attempted to disentangle them in this chapter as well as Chapters 7 and 8, to clarify their individual impact and to show the complexity of the interrelationship among education, class, ethnicity, and gender.

The first section of the chapter discusses the history of the concept of class and some of the most important thinkers who have contributed to its development. Next we look at the way social class and education interact to stratify society into a class structure. Finally, we examine some of the mechanisms in systems of education that lead both to reproduction of the existing class structure and social class bias in what purports to be a meritocracy based upon achievement.

WHAT IS SOCIAL CLASS?

Before we can talk meaningfully about the relationship between social class and education, we must understand what the term *social class* means and how it has become a key concept in how we think about our world. A *class* of things is a category—a number of things grouped together because they share common characteristics. Social scientists define social classes as groups of people who share certain characteristics of prestige, patterns of taste and language, income, occupational status (though not necessarily the same jobs), educational level, aspirations, behavior, and beliefs. Social classes are **stratified,** arranged in a pyramid-shaped hierarchy according to members' wealth, power, and prestige. *Wealth* refers to the control of material resources or economic clout, *power* refers to authority in the political realm, and *prestige* refers to the control of ideological resources or cultural influence. One's place in society depends upon the amount of superiority he or she has in all of these realms.

Throughout history, thinkers have had different opinions as to why certain kinds of people have occupied high positions in the hierarchy and others have occupied the bottom levels. As we shall explain, the social scientific view based upon socioeconomic status is a relatively new way of thinking about class.

To which social class do you think your family of origin belonged? What social class do you think you belong to now? What evidence do you use for giving yourself a particular social class assignment?

The Historical Perspective: A Hierarchy of Class and Virtue

People confuse a hierarchy of social class with a hierarchy of moral virtue and intelligence. Historically, this confusion has had a profound impact upon social and educational policy. It comes from the fact that the concept of social class is a very old one, predating by centuries the social science disciplines of sociology, economics, political science, and anthropology, which use it as an analytic concept.

The historical perspective is based upon notions of aristocracy. Until very recent times philosophers, religious leaders, and politicians, as well as the general population, believed that class status was determined by how valued, wise, and virtuous a person was. These ideas were reinforced by the concept of the "divine right" of kings to rule. People from the highest social classes were considered, merely because of their birth rank, to be the brightest and most virtuous, and therefore the most capable of ruling. For example, it was believed that kings and queens were anointed by God and ruled with God's permission, and they were held up as behavioral exemplars. The American Puritans too felt that wealth and prestige in this life were indications of God's favor and a guarantee of salvation in the hereafter. High levels of wealth and prestige, as well as of educational attainment, were seen as resulting from hard work, great spirituality, or moral superiority rather than, as was more often the case, from family inheritance.

In reality, many gentlemen were not very gentle, nor were all kings kingly, nor all ladies ladylike. Characteristics that were attributed to a superior intellect and morality often simply were functions of superior wealth. It was a great deal easier to be clean, kind, gentle, well educated, cultured, and generous if one were fortunate enough to be born into an affluent family. The illiteracy, social deviance, crime, moral depravity, lack of hygiene, brutish behavior, and general lack of culture common among the lower classes were believed to be innate or hereditary tendencies rather than a function of environmental influences.

This kind of thinking had a powerful influence on popular thinking. It argued against both social welfare programs and attempts to include the poor in decision making in their own behalf since they were not thought to be capable of such elevated behavior. Social Darwinists even argued that social policies to help the poor would be harmful, since they would only encourage the reproduction of people who were mentally or morally defective and would waste resources that could better be used for more deserving populations (Spencer 1851, 1898; Sumner 1883). The only rational response was to learn to live with poverty, rescuing those few "deserving poor" whose values could be shaped to resemble those of the middle and upper classes. This kind of thinking still exists today and impedes serious attempts to eliminate poverty and oppression.

Because class status was considered to be hereditary, few philosophers or social theorists considered that the association between affluence and virtue, leadership ability, literacy, and the like might be circular. However, their beliefs did not hinder attempts to use the schools as a means of social control. Educators developed curricula designed to teach obedience to the law, temperance, sexual restraint, good hygiene, thrift, and punctuality—all values acceptable to the upper and middle classes. In fact, some of the earliest educational sociologists felt that schools were the only appropriate place to learn civic virtues. As was explained in Chapter 3, Durkheim believed that as societies modernized, parents no longer could prepare their children adequately for adult life. Families had to specialize in what they could do best—developing the individual personality—while to the schools fell the task of nation building, that is, developing citizens capable of adhering to the laws of the land and carrying out their responsibilities to the state.

Durkheim developed his ideas in a 1901 treatise called *Moral Education* (1969), which was based upon a series of lectures he delivered to pre-service teachers. His ideas of moral education are echoed in contemporary theories of poverty which describe the incompetence of poor families to raise and educate their children. Courses in citizenship, health and hygiene, free enterprise, and other virtues are still popular, representing an effort to use the schools to create a consensus on acceptable ways of relating to the political order.

The Genetic Perspective: A Hierarchy of Intellect

Traditionally, then, social class was associated with morality. A modern variation has been to equate it with intelligence, as measured on so-called intelligence tests. People observed that the poor usually were badly educated, and they assumed that poor people and minorities had low educational attainment because they lacked intelligence. This conventional wisdom, coupled with the racism of the nineteenth and early twentieth centuries, led to a considerable volume of "scientific" research supporting a causal relationship between intelligence and social class. Studies of brain size and shape, or "craniometry," "proved" that women, lower-class people, African Americans, and other minorities had inferior brains with less cranial capacity than or different construction from those of Europeans. The connection between class and intelligence was bolstered by the advent of IQ testing, since lower classes and minorities scored lower on these tests.

Samuel George Morton, for example, attempted to show that Asians, Africans, and Native Americans were intellectually inferior to Northern Europeans because their brains were smaller. His research method was to weigh the amount of birdshot poured into the cranial cavities of skulls from various ethnic groups. Unfortunately, whenever he obtained results counter to his claims, he manipulated the data. The results of these studies have since been shown to be based upon misinterpretation or fraud (Gould 1981). Gould feels that Morton intended no fraud, however: "All I can discern is an *a priori* conviction about racial ranking so powerful that it directed his tabulations along preestablished lines" (1981, p. 69). The work of others, however, was not so innocent.

Sir Cyril Burt (1883–1971) was one of the most influential educational psychologists of his time. He was a pioneer in testing and mental measurement, and from the beginning of his career believed that intelligence was an innate and immutable characteristic. Nature, not nurture, determined one's destiny. Furthermore, people were poor because they—and their parents—were less intelligent. The observed differences in achievement between social classes were the consequence of hereditary intelligence. Not until after his death did investigators determine that the vast majority of Burt's research was based upon data flawed by inadmissible carelessness, fakery, omission, and outright fraud (Gould 1981, p. 235).

Despite the flimsiness of their work, these researchers have left a powerful legacy. As late as the 1970s Arthur Jensen (1969), William Schockley, and Richard Hernstein (1973) could publish articles in respectable scholarly journals advocating educational and social policies based upon the premise that the intellect of minorities, especially African Americans, was genetically inferior to that of whites.

The Sociological Perspective: A Hierarchy of Wealth

As sociologists, we reject the notion that class status and virtue are synonymous or that class is a function of innate intelligence. We also reject attempts to teach children to accept the status quo as the only legitimate alternative to social chaos. While we do believe that class status and associated behaviors and attitudes are, to some degree, inherited, this heritability consists not so much in genetic factors as in the fact that a child's environment has a profound effect upon his or her development. Furthermore, because our work is informed by critical theory, rather than treating class status and its attendant inequalities as a given, we view class identity as "constructed"— that is, we believe it develops through interaction with other people over time. A child *becomes* an upper-class prep school graduate with medical school aspirations, or a lower-class teenage mother about to drop out of school, not because they were born into a particular kind of family but because their background set up expectations for their behavior and also influenced how others would react to them. The net of mutual expectations is not totally inescapable, but it does, to a large degree, affect the direction of individual development.

Examine your family's genealogy. Were there changes in social class status over the generations? To what do you attribute these changes?

Sociological Definitions of Class, Status, and Power.   When sociologists look at the inequalities that rank-order groups, they distinguish among class, status, and power. *Power* refers to the ability to realize one's will, even if others resist. Weber suggests that power legitimated by others constitutes *authority,* while power not legitimated is *coercion* or force. The term *status* refers to a state of being or position. In sociology it connotes the distribution of prestige (Gerth and Mills 1953) based upon what people have—including material goods, where they live, who their family and friends are, the extent and type of their education and training, and their occupation. Status is associated with culture. Status groups

> subjectively . . . distinguish themselves from [one another] in terms of categories of *moral evaluation* such as "honor," "taste," "breeding," "respectability," "propriety," "cultivation," "good fellows," "plain folks," etc. Thus the exclusion of persons who lack the in-group culture is felt to be normatively legitimated. (Collins 1977, p. 125)

Sociologists believe that status and power are a function of *social class.* They define class as groups of people who share similar economic life chances because they have similar opportunities in the labor market. For Weberians, class is positional, a function of one's occupation, income, and to some extent educational level. For Marxists, class is relational, a function of one's interaction with others in the processes of production. Specifically, one's class is determined by the amount of political and cultural power as well as the extent to which one both owns the means to one's own livelihood and can hire or control the labor of others.

Some sociologists divide the social hierarchy into six classes: upper-upper, lower-upper, upper-middle, lower-middle, upper-lower (or working class), and lower-lower (Bensman and Vidich 1971). Marxists divide it into three strata, according to the kind of work their members do and how much control they have over their own labor. At the bottom are the *proletariat,* workers, or manual laborers, who own no part of the places in which they work, whose tasks are completely controlled by their supervisors, and who have to sell their labor to others. The *ruling classes* consist of two groups: (1) *capitalists,* who own their means of production, do not sell their own labor, and do purchase the labor of others; and (2) *petty bourgeoisie,* who own their means of production, do not sell their labor, and also do not purchase that of others (Wright and Perrone 1977). Capitalists, who include landed aristocrats, benefit from the "surplus capital," or profits generated by workers. In this formulation, teachers are considered to be workers, because they neither supervise labor nor own their means of making a living (Wright and Perrone 1977).

Marx wrote at a time when land ownership as a source of power was diminishing. His description of society better fits an eighteenth-century factory and industrial pattern than it does today's technologically oriented economy, where managers and professionals replace traditional capitalist owners, and manual labor and heavy industry have lost importance to service sectors in an "information" society. However, his ideas about social organization and the origins of power, inequality, and conflict are still powerful. Table 5.1 summarizes and to some degree updates Marx's ideas of social class structure.

Regardless of their orientation, sociologists agree that people with the most wealth, power, and prestige are at the apex of the social class pyramid and are influen-

TABLE 5.1. Expanded Marxist Criteria for Class

	Criteria for Class Position			
	Ownership of the Means of Production	Purchase of the Labor Power of Others	Control of the Labor Power of Others	Sale of One's Own Labor Power
Capitalists	Yes	Yes	Yes	No
Managers	No	No	Yes	Yes
Workers	No	No	No	Yes
Petty Bourgeoisie	Yes	No	No	No

SOURCE: E.O. Wright and L. Perrone, "Marxist Class Categories and Income Inequality," *American Sociological Review 42* (1977), p. 34.

tial in controlling policies and practices that maintain their position. While power comes from various sources—the political structure, business, the media, and the military (Domhoff 1967; Mills 1956)—these sources tend to overlap. The degree of overlap, as well as the means of exercising control, often are not obvious to the majority of the population.

The Material Conditions of Life.   Peter McLaren uses a Marxist definition of *class:* the "economic, social and political relationships that govern life in a given social order." He states that inequality in society is based upon the concept of *surplus labor* and the unequal access people have to it. Surplus labor is the work done beyond what is necessary for the workers' survival, and the subsequent profits that others earn from their efforts. According to Marxist or critical analysis, surplus labor is the genesis of social class variation. Social class relations "are those associated with surplus labor [or profit], who produces it, and who is a recipient of it" (McLaren 1989, p. 171). The amount of surplus labor is a measure of the degree of exploitation in a capitalist society, because it represents the extent to which those who profit from it are not those who produced it.

The critical perspective that informs this book stresses that social classes originate in the material, and specifically the economic conditions of life. These are at the center of human activity. They involve using the forces of production—or levels of technology, land, labor, capital, and available energy—and the social relations of production—or how human effort is organized—for productive activity (Persell 1977).

Membership in a social class is determined by the way people relate to the economic and material conditions of life, how much of them they control, and how much they are beneficiaries of the productive efforts. Those individuals who control more of or who benefit more from the economic order are those at the top of the pyramid. Those who control less and benefit less are toward the bottom. Because stratification patterns are patterns of social and cultural domination and subordination, it may be more accurate to use the term *structure of dominance* (Weber 1947, p. 426) than the common sociological term *social stratification* when referring to economic and social hierarchies. Those who control more and benefit more also have more power or more capacity to dominate others.

Social classes, or the structure of power and domination, are differentiated by the prestige and status ascribed to them within the hierarchy as well as by the actual power they wield. Members of a social class do not need to know one another, although they usually choose their friends and associates from their own class. Nor need they be aware that they are a member of a class to belong to one. Some theorists would argue that class cannot exist without class consciousness—people have to know that they belong to it for a social class to exist. Others argue that one purpose of educational ideology is to keep people from being aware of their class position so that they remain satisfied with the status quo. Critical theorists believe that as people become conscious of their class membership, they begin to develop opposition to the oppressive practices that have masked class differences and preserved the status quo. One of these practices is to foster social beliefs that deny the existence of oppression and inequality.

The Mythical Middle Class: Control through Ideology.   *Ideologies* are "way[s] of viewing the world . . . that we tend to accept as natural and common-sense." They provide the categories, concepts, and images through which people interpret their world and shape their behavior (McLaren 1989, p. 176) and, in doing so, they are instruments of **hegemony,** a kind of domination without the use of force.

Hegemonic domination operates through "social forms and structures produced in specific sites such as churches, the state, schools, mass media, the political system, and the family" (McLaren 1989, p. 173). There is no need to institute more stringent means of social control—such as exclusionary laws, imprisonment, and torture—when there is general agreement that the status quo is legitimate, even if not personally satisfactory.

Class consciousness is very low in America because our cultural ideology describes us as an egalitarian society. Americans generally refuse to assign each other to a hierarchical social ranking. Traditionally, most describe themselves as "middle class," regardless of their actual income, occupation, or education (Persell 1977). You might ask your friends or classmates to identify the social class that most accurately describes their own background to see if our argument fits them.

The consensus that everyone is "middle class" is one way in which actual class differences are hidden in the United States. Hegemonic domination is facilitated by this "myth of the middle class," because this social ideology maintains the domination of the existing class system. The common belief that any differences are only a matter of degree is a convenient fiction that allows us to ignore extremes of wealth and poverty. It is facilitated by the low visibility of the rich in America, who are segregated in private neighborhoods, schools, social clubs, and occupational circles (Persell 1977, p. 31) and the equal invisibility of the poor. Until recently, it cost middle- and upper-class Americans very little effort to avoid an encounter with homelessness or abject poverty. However, during the 1980s and 1990s the myth of a relatively "classless" society has been exploded by the growth and visibility of the poor, especially the underclass of the inner cities (Wilson 1987). That the poor do not revolt against their condition is a function of the power of ideology. Members of the underclass have internalized what schools have taught them: that people are rewarded for hard work. Even if they do not believe that they live in an egalitarian society, they tend to feel that they, not the system, are responsible for their plight. Either they weren't lucky enough, didn't have the ability, or just didn't work hard enough.

That is why schools play such an important role in maintaining existing patterns of domination. They perpetuate a middle-class ideology which states that status and social mobility in American society are based upon merit, earned competitively, and facilitated by schooling. These attitudes achieve legitimacy because some individuals actually do benefit from the system. However, those for whom the system pays off most are those who already were advantaged—white middle- and upper-class males (Rosenfeld 1980; Wright and Perrone 1977).

Think back to your experiences in elementary and secondary schooling. Were you aware that children came from different social classes? How? How did differences in social class status affect children's school experiences? Give specific examples from your own experiences.

THEORETICAL BEGINNINGS: MARX, WEBER, AND BOURDIEU

Both Karl Marx and Max Weber were concerned with the relationship between class and education, though from different vantage points. Both felt that educational systems were a reflection of the societies in which they were embedded. They differed as to what they felt was the basis of that society. For Marx, the structure of society and of domination and subordination was based upon the economy, or the production and distribution of goods and services. Weber, however, felt that domination was based upon more than economics. Critical to his analyses were politics and government, or the organization of power and authority, and their relationship to educational systems in a variety of societies, industrialized and others. Bourdieu rejected the Marxist emphasis on the economy as the only basis for class structure; he added the correlate of power, which comes from acquiring specialized forms of social and cultural knowledge. In the following sections we explore these notions more fully.

The Contributions of Karl Marx

Marx never treated education extensively. He considered that educational systems, like systems of esthetics and religion, were simply a part of the societal superstructure which came from and corresponded to the economic base of society.

Class Analysis.   Marx made explicit the relationship between social class and economic power and demonstrated how it creates a hierarchy of classes within a society. His analysis was so powerful that social scientists have been "Marxists" ever since, at least insofar as class and stratification have been critical to their analysis of social structure. Marxist analysis initially focused on class and caste at the structural level; it did not examine either the relationship of education to class or the functioning of schools as organizations. Later Marxist theorists did posit a relationship, stating that the educational system provided a legitimizing function for capitalist systems (Bowles and Gintis 1976; Scimecca 1980). Schools acted to defuse class antagonisms, as we shall explain later, because they indoctrinated students to accept the belief that the position they attain is the best they can achieve (Scimecca 1980, pp. 9-10). In this way, the school system was critical in reproducing the social class structure from one generation to another. This position has been adopted by critical theorists as well.

Marxists and neo-Marxists also believe that there is a tight causal link between and across subsystems, so that changes in one subsystem directly lead to changes in the others. The supposed existence of such links can be applied to education to bolster the argument that education is closely linked to generations of economic inequality. While most people who wish to use the schools to solve social problems are reformers rather than Marxist revolutionaries, using an education–economy link to eliminate poverty and other social ills has had powerful appeal to educators, policy makers, and social scientists. Especially with regard to education, however, current research has shown the links to be indirect and weaker than reformers would hope (LeCompte and Dworkin 1991). We will talk more about this later in this chapter.

Dialectical Analysis.   Perhaps most important to Marx's approach is the use of *dialectical analysis.* This is a method by which all assumptions are assumed to contain their own contradictions or opposites. Propositions believed to be true are analyzed as if they were false. For example, dialectical analysis would permit us to question the truism, "All men are created equal," asking what was meant by the terms *men, created,* and *equal.* We then would determine if all men—or women—were equal and under what circumstances, if any.

Dialectical analysis provided a framework by which the legitimacy of all conventional assumptions about the relationship between wealth and power could be questioned, including assumptions that made moral virtue the basis of social class hierarchy. Dialectical analysis also made it possible to identify sources of inequality, exploitation, and oppression and helped to forge an understanding that wealth was not necessarily a sign of superior effort or morality. On the contrary, Marxists looked at possession of great wealth in a bourgeois society as a sign of ill-gotten gains, attainable only through the exploitation of others.

Critical theorists have used the concept of dialectical analysis to raise questions such as the following:

- Why is it that working-class children get working-class jobs while the children of doctors and other professionals become professionals?
- Could it really be true that the reason 40 to 70 percent of minority children in many major cities drop out of school is that they lack sufficient intelligence or ambition to graduate?

- Do the rewards of the educational system really go to those with the most intellectual merit?
- Why is it that schools in poor urban neighborhoods or rural communities are desperately underfunded, while neighboring suburban schools offer a wide variety of programs to children in clean, safe, and well equipped schools?
- What are the consequences of educational reform? Will it really improve the achievement of minorities and the poor?

Alienation. Another major contribution of Marx has been a socioeconomic rather than a psychological definition of *alienation.* The sociological approach to alienation has contributed greatly to our understanding of why teachers burn out and students lose interest in schoolwork (Dworkin 1985b, 1986; LeCompte and Dworkin, 1991). Marx felt that workers could find meaning only in work that they directly controlled and in places whose ownership they shared. They were "alienated" to the extent that they had no control over what they did and how it was done.

However Utopian that notion may sound in a world of multinational corporations, accelerating buyouts, and consolidation of companies, alienation remains a powerful concept to explain industrial sabotage, teacher burnout, and other forms of occupational disaffection. To Marx, alienation simply meant that one's work place is so far removed from those who actually control the work, and so far removed from those who use the products, that the daily activities become meaningless. To cope with this boredom and meaninglessness, people may engage in self-sabotage in the form of shoddy work or rudeness, or may even destroy equipment, products, and materials.

Marx's concept of alienation is reflected in critical theorists' concept of de-skilling and its impact on teacher morale. Chapter 4 examines the impact of de-skilling through works by Apple (1986), Dworkin (1986), and LeCompte and Dworkin (1991).

The Contributions of Max Weber

Unlike Marx, Weber discussed education at length. He was especially interested in the curriculum and the types of students. He felt that each society created educational systems uniquely suited to indigenous systems of power and authority. These systems were used to select and train the leaders of the society. An analysis of schools' characteristics and populations would reveal who got into school and how, and an examination of what was taught would reveal what kinds of information were deemed important for different groups in the society.

Education and the Structure of Authority. Weber distinguished among three kinds of authority: traditional, charismatic, and rational-legal. They were found in different kinds of societies but were not predicated entirely upon the existence of a particular economic structure. Each type of authority required a different leadership style: Traditional societies produced kings; charismatic authority was that of the hero or guru; rational-legal forms required bureaucrats and civil servants. Each leadership type mandated differences in modes of training and education for elites (Persell 1977; Weber 1947, pp. 426–434). Weber used three case studies to identify the different systems: the Mandarin Chinese (traditional), Christianity (charismatic), and the industrial civil service of late nineteenth-century Europe (rational-legal).

A key contribution of Weber was his understanding of (1) the degree to which the educational system could facilitate the succession of elites through merit and rationally assessed competence, rather than through inheritance or some other nonrational means of selection; and (2) whether or not the curriculum could be standardized and graded. Only rational-legal forms of authority with their emphasis on competence and expertise required such standardization. If authority were based on charisma, leadership could not be taught; it was based upon "discipleship," and one could only wait for leadership capabilities to be awakened and demonstrated in some sort of trials or magical rites. And traditional kings were not trained; they ruled, competent or not, by virtue of "divine right" and their ability to survive attempts to remove them from the throne.

Merit and Achievement.   Weber understood that societies based upon meritocracy (Young 1971) could recruit able individuals for positions of wealth and power regardless of their initial social standing. Where achieved merit was the basis for rewards, it was possible to use educational systems to facilitate social mobility and exchange of ruling groups. Even within these societies, however, those who benefited most from the educational system were those who already were somewhat advantaged.

The Contributions of Pierre Bourdieu

Having determined the basis for the establishment of social classes, sociologists then turned to an examination of the dynamics and impact of class structure. Among the questions they asked were the following:

- What characteristics distinguish people in various classes?
- Can people move from one class to another, especially to a higher class?
- What rigidities stand in the way of movement from one class to another?

In Chapter 1 we discussed class differences in language and communication patterns. But class differences are based upon differences more profound than language and communication alone. To understand fully what differentiates people in one social class from those in another, we must examine the concept of cultural capital.

Distinctions between Class and Culture.   The terms *class* and *culture* are often confused. For sociologists, class is a position in the hierarchy or status. Culture is the way people express that status, or "the particular ways in which a social group lives out and makes sense of its given circumstances and conditions of life" (McLaren 1989,

---

Javier's Story: Former Migrant/Current ESL Teacher

School was someplace where I didn't have to go. It was a memory born in Del-Icias, Texas, and since we had left El Paso [It was] an activity that only happened now and then. School was a world of children's games, more gringos than I ever seen, and spanking by someone called the principal, who punished children for things they said. . . . School was the place where I was ridiculed for my clothes, my way of reasoning, and for my neck, my elbows, my hair, and my hands, which were cleaned by my mother and judged by the school.

School was Mrs. Peters, who enjoyed so much to march the kids from the migrant camp out to the water fountain in the hall, hand us a bar of soap, and then bring out the whole class to watch as she ordered us to wash our necks. "Look, don't you know how to wash your neck? It is filthy." It amazed me that Mrs. Peters could assume that there was plentiful water for bathing; my view of the world was that water for this purpose was limited everywhere, not just as it was at the camp. She led me out to the water fountain and gave me a small piece of soap. As I stood there scrubbing, she went into the classroom and brought out some kids to stare at me. Her voice echoes in my ears: "His mother must live like a pig . . . pig . . . pig."

SOURCE: Velasquez 1993, pp. 106–107.

---

p. 171). Culture includes the distinctive language, ideologies, behavior patterns, attitudes and values, artifacts, dress, and shared historical experiences of a group of people. Javier's story (see box) illustrates how culture and class work together to shape social perceptions.

Cultural Capital.   Taken together, all of these cultural patterns constitute *cultural capital* of a group—the ways of talking and acting, moving, dressing, socializing, tastes, likes and dislikes, competencies, and forms of knowledge that distinguish one group from another (Bourdieu 1977). Cultural capital is a resource, and just like natural resources, not all forms of it are valued equally. The social value of cultural capital is a function of the prestige of the group that possesses it; or conversely, the prestige of individuals depends upon how much of what kind of cultural capital they own. In Chapter 1 we discussed cultural reproduction, explaining how children in school are evaluated on how closely their cultural capital mirrors that of the dominant society, the latter reflected in the requirements for success in white middle-class schooling. Those who do not meet the school's standards for whatever reason—dialect, communication style, manners—may be perceived as being less capable than those who do.

Cultural capital is an important concept to critical theorists, because it is made up of factors to which people react in social interaction and which shape the construction of social beliefs and social realities. Insofar as members of subordinate groups refuse to conform to the norms or to value the cultural capital of dominant groups, differences in people's cultural capital can provide a starting point for the development of resistance and oppositional culture.

SOCIAL INEQUALITY AND THE STRUCTURE OF SOCIETY

Marxian and Weberian analysis laid the foundation for our understanding of the complex relationships between schools and societies, both at the macrolevel of societal organization and at the microlevel of the organization of teaching and learning. Educational sociologists have been concerned at the macrolevel in the following areas: (1) social mobility, (2) relationships between classes, (3) academic achievement and educational attainment, (4) social stratification and patterns of inequality, and (5) the occupational structure. Until the 1970s, sociologists were concerned primarily with effects: how "inputs" to education—such as parents' education, occupation, and income, and certain attitudes such as college and occupational expectations—affected "outputs" of education—such as test scores, high school completion, college entrance, and occupational attainment. What went on *inside* the schools was of little concern (Hargreaves and Woods 1984; LeCompte 1978b, 1981).

Since 1970 greater attention has been paid to the microlevel of schooling, that is, what actually happens in schools to create the inequalities school attendance seems to produce. We will discuss processes at the microlevel later in this chapter and in Chapters 6, 7, and 8.

Social Mobility

Social mobility refers to the movement of individuals and groups up or down from the social class of their birth to others. Mobility takes place through intermarriage or by acquisition of the cultural capital associated with the new status.

Up the Social Ladder. In a meritocratic society, education has been the key to upward mobility. It takes place in two stages. First, one must acquire at least some of the characteristics of the upper class, most important of which is a level of education that will provide competence in higher-status jobs and give a luster to social and intellectual interaction. Second, one must learn the social graces and habits of behavior of the class to which one aspires. Practicing for status is called *anticipatory socialization* (Srinivas 1965). It is reflected in the desire of parents to send their children to the "right" schools.

Americans tend to conceive only of upward mobility, and they encourage their children to get as much schooling as possible so that they can do better than their parents. Poverty in the lower classes has been attributed to an absence of the ambition or necessary ability to acquire an adequate education. However, upward mobility can exist only where there is room for expansion on the socioeconomic ladder. Room at the top is created when those at the top stratum are removed or decreased in number, either by lower birth rates among the elite, social upheaval, or geographic relocation of those hoping to move upward—in the past, for example, by moving to the colonies or out on the frontier—or by the creation of new economic opportunities, such as the computer industry. It has been possible for generations of Americans to ignore the possibility of downward mobility, both because the economy offered a wide range of opportunity and because social status has been heavily based not upon cultural standing, which had to be inherited, but upon economic wealth, which could be earned. The United States was blessed with expanding economic and geographic frontiers which provided opportunity for some people to escape their original destinies. The prestigious cultural goods associated with upper-class life could, in large part, be purchased once wealth had been acquired.

This model is, however, deceptive, because it is based upon a limited number of "deviant cases." Strategies that worked for a few who did "make it" were applied indiscriminately to everyone. Hence the Horatio Alger stories, in which a poor boy's hard work and diligent study won him wealth and the hand of the factory owner's daughter, became the model to which the general population aspired. The Alger stories contributed to hegemonic myths which held that if you didn't get rich and inherit the factory, you just hadn't worked hard enough.

Down the Social Ladder. The fact is, however, that not everyone can move up. Most societies are fairly stable and there usually are as many individuals moving down as are moving up. Where room at the top constricts, the net mobility downward may exceed movement up, no matter how much education people can acquire. This phenomenon appears to be occurring in the United States, as the society decapitalizes, industry moves to developing countries, and high-paying jobs in the industrial and professional sectors are reduced in number or replaced by lower-paying, less-skilled jobs in the service sector (Bluestone and Bennett 1982).

This situation is a real problem for the United States for several reasons. First, it devalues education, exploding the myth of the payoff for hard work in school. It creates educational inflation as increased educational attainment in the face of fewer appropriate jobs makes diplomas less valuable than before. College degrees are now required for jobs that once needed only high school diplomas. The prospect of downward mobility weighs particularly heavily on middle-class and poor students, for whom education represented their only hope to maintain status or escape proletarianization, or a descent into the working class (Miles 1977).

It also affects patterns of reward and control in school. Teachers no longer can promise their students that if they work hard to learn and if they respect the teacher, they will be rewarded with a good job. Finally, the anticipation of downward mobility can lead to student alienation and unrest as the promised "good life" seems further and further out of reach to an increasingly large group of young people (Keniston 1971; Miles 1977).

Caste and Class

Up to now we have been talking only about social *class*. Membership in a social class is not fixed, even though in many societies movement from one class to another is limited and often takes place only through marriage. However, where *castes*, rather than classes, structure a society, movement may be existent.

Membership in a caste is rigidly hereditary and is defined by occupational status. Caste members inherit the occupations of their fathers and are forbidden by law and social custom from engaging in any other profession unless it has the same assigned social status. Social interaction between castes is limited and intermarriage is forbidden. Often caste differences are highlighted by differences in dress, patterns of food consumption, ethnicity, language, and religion. Low-status castes often are stigmatized; anything associated with a low-status caste is considered polluting to a member of a higher caste. As a consequence, people from different castes cannot eat together or live in the same neighborhood.

Caste-based societies provide little opportunity for individual mobility. Using the case of India, Srinivas (1965) and Rudolph and Rudolph (1967) describe *group* mobility; certain low-caste groups have begun to raise the status of their group by becoming educated, changing their occupation, becoming vegetarians, and adopting the religious observances of Brahmins. The Rudolphs' research indicates that an increase in education is not sufficient. These groups had to change their *cultural capital* as well.

Castelike Minorities. Castes usually have not been thought to exist in the United States. However, Ogbu (1978, 1983, 1987) points out that the status of native-born, stigmatized minorities, such as Mexican Americans, American Indians, and African Americans, is "castelike." We might also argue that Appalachians could be included in this listing. Ogbu believes that the systematic patterns of discrimination these groups have experienced over many generations have transformed them into a virtually hereditary underclass of impoverished people. They do poorly in school as a group, regardless of the special programs set up for them, and are able to obtain only those jobs at the lowest end of the labor market. They share a fatalistic perspective: Since no amount of work will lead to a better job, why try?

Ogbu also makes the important point that the disabilities under which castelike minorities labor are contextual rather than inherent. When members of these groups escape to a society that does not discriminate against them, they can be as successful as any other migrant group. As Gibson's work with Punjabi students in California demonstrates, they often can do this without forswearing many aspects of their traditional culture (Gibson 1988).

In Chapter 7 we will further discuss minorities, education, and inequality and will also provide an update of Ogbu's perspectives on minority status and failure. Some scholars have criticized Ogbu's analysis for its overly simplistic and deterministic view of the impact of labor market structure (Erickson 1987). Others argue that his analysis fails to account for the fact that minority children often conform to, rather than behave antagonistically toward, the authority structure and norms of the school (D'Amato 1987). His discussion, however, points out that schools are among the primary locations where the process of social differentiation takes place. Children who start out there with ostensibly equal capabilities end up sorted into groups whose achievement is markedly different. Furthermore, these differences in achievement are explained, in large part, by differences in social class (or castelike status). Regardless of their ethnicity, poor students tend to study with poor students and rich students tend to study with other rich students. The remainder of this chapter will discuss how this process occurs and what its consequences are.

Occupational Attainment

Functional theorists in the sociology of education felt that educational systems played three roles in the larger society. First, they attributed to schools the functions of socialization for citizenship and social control (Durkheim 1969). Second, they believed that schools were sites for the meritocratic selection and training of leadership cadres (Weber 1947). Finally, they believed schools were where individuals were meritocratically selected and trained for specific occupational roles.

The last function is accomplished by means of two mechanisms: (1) the differentiated curriculum, which prepares students either for vocational careers or for higher education and professional training, and (2) the system of grading and ability grouping, by which students are placed into curricula appropriate to their ability and interests and to their ultimate career. In the United States sociologists and educators preferred to believe that status was based upon achievement. To do so, they had to demonstrate that social status was not inherited. Therefore, education, not family background, would have to be the most important predictor of educational and occupational attainment.

The Blau and Duncan Model.   Blau and Duncan's (1967) landmark study of young men examined the relationship between family background variables, including father's occupation and education, and the level of education and occupation attained by their sons. Blau and Duncan tried to develop a model to predict mathematically how much education contributed to individual occupational attainment. Their model had a profound impact upon the way social scientists thought about the relationships among education, occupation, and socioeconomic status. They did find that the impact of all educational factors combined—including mother's and father's education, the individual's educational aspirations and actual years of education completed, and the individual's motivation as measured by grades and standardized test scores—was the single largest contributor to one's life chances.

However, there were some significant limitations to their work. First, they looked only at white males. More important, the correlations were not overwhelming, indicating that education contributed only about 30 percent of the total predictive power to the model. Other sociologists then attempted to improve the predictive power of the model by adding other factors. Perhaps best known of these attempts was the work of Sewell, Haller, and their associates.

The Status Attainment Model.   The so-called "Wisconsin Model" (Sewell, Haller, and Portes 1969, 1970; Sewell, Haller, and Ohlendorf 1970; Sewell and Shah 1967; Jencks, Crouse, and Mueser 1983) asked the following questions:

1. What are the relative effects of family background and schooling on subsequent attainments?
2. What is the role of academic ability in the attainment process?
3. How do aspirations and motivations determine attainment and what is the role of family and school in providing support for aspirations? Do

social psychological variables merely transmit the effects of family background and/or ability or do they have an impact of their own? (Campbell 1983, p. 47)

These sociologists suggested that attitudinal factors in family background and aspirational variables were important links between ascribed (or family background) status, educational attainment, and ultimate occupation. In other words, family influence was not just passive. Families transmitted to children an active desire toward certain occupational goals and an expectation of reaching these goals. They also examined the influence of "significant others"—teachers and parents. Some sociologists even interviewed children and their parents to trace the impact of parents' aspirations for their children (Kahl 1953).

However, these studies did not explain why families from different social classes produced children with different goals, nor did they examine the constraints on occupational attainment imposed by both market conditions—supply and demand for given services—and by patterns of discrimination—both legal and customary (Persell 1977).

The Rosenfeld Model: Race and Gender Bias. As was mentioned earlier, Blau and Duncan's model looked only at whites, failed to examine the impact of mothers on sons, and did not discuss daughters at all. R. Rosenfeld (1980) replicated both Blau and Duncan's work and the status attainment models for women and African Americans. As she suspected, the model was not nearly as good a predictor for women or for African Americans as it was for white men. In the early stages—the first six years after completing school—white men and women receive about the same wage and status returns on their investment in education. However, after six years the picture changes dramatically.

At their potential, white men receive greater returns to their human capital [education and training] than white women. They receive higher returns in terms of both status and wages to their years of formal schooling, get greater returns in terms of status to their white collar training, suffer less of a status disadvantage from having some formal preparation for a blue collar job, and receive considerably greater wage returns from both kinds of training. (R. Rosenfeld 1980, p. 604)

Only nonwhite males do worse than white women.

The most important factors in ultimate occupational attainment for women are related not to education but to the labor market. They include previous work experience, the types of jobs available, and the degree of discrimination encountered.

The Contributions of Occupational Attainment Researchers. Despite their limitations, the work of these investigators clarified several important ways that the meritocratic model did not work as predicted. Blau and Duncan and the status attainment researchers found that the impact of education on achievement could not be explained without one's taking social background into account. This was so because the most powerful predictor of educational level obtained was found to be the social class background of parents, as measured by their income level, occupation, and education.

Their work also called into question the American view of meritocracy, which assumed that intelligence or ability was equally distributed throughout the population, not skewed by social class. If a meritocracy really existed in America, researchers would have found that each social class was represented in the various ability groups in proportion to the percentage in the population. For example, if 10 percent of students were recipients of public assistance, then 10 percent in each of the ability groups in the school—remedial, vocational, and college prep—should be students from welfare families. The same should be true of the representation of wealthy children. However, what researchers found was that children from higher socioeconomic status families were greatly overrepresented in classes for high-achieving students as well as in college preparatory schools, higher education, and professional jobs. Similarly, there was a significantly higher percentage of lower-class students in the remedial, vocational, and non-college preparatory classes than their percentage in the school population.

This measure of over- and underrepresentation meant that something was impeding the smooth operation of meritocracy. It became an indicator of inequality and class bias. Rosenfeld confirmed that the same indices of over- and underrepresentation among women and minorities meant meritocratic criteria also did not apply to them.

The Marxist Model: Class and Income Inequality.   Very few studies of the causes of social inequality have used Marxist categories of analysis. However, one important study (Wright and Perrone 1977) does examine three classes—workers, managers, and employers—to see what impact social class, in Marxian terms rather than in education, occupation, and family background, has on economic inequality. This study demonstrated that the class model is more powerful than status attainment models in predicting where a person will end up in the class hierarchy. Class matters more than education, and even overrides the effects of education.

Even with high levels of education, working-class children will not achieve as much prestige as children from the upper classes. This is so because working-class children, handicapped by their background, cannot translate their education into as much occupational prestige and economic success as can upper- and middle-class children with the same education or less. Studies like these provided a catalyst for identifying the mechanisms by which biases against the poor and working class impeded their performance.

THE MECHANISM OF CLASS BIAS IN EDUCATION

Discussions of the relationship between class and educational achievement are almost inextricably meshed with discussions of race, since castelike minority status, poverty, and low rates of educational achievement are highly correlated. However, we will argue that while patterns of discrimination create castelike conditions for some people and certainly systematically disadvantage women, nevertheless social class or patterns of economic domination and subordination create far more important distinctions among people. Hence, rich people, of whatever race, religion, or gender, are far more similar to one another than they are to poor people of their own race, religion, or gender. These differences are created, supported, and enhanced by participation in educational institutions.

Test Scores

Initial studies of social class impact used student test scores on standardized tests as a data base. This research was quantitative in that it looked at test scores as output measures and tried to predict them by looking at a variety of independent measures, such as sex, type of curriculum, mother's education, father's education, income, and race. All of these studies indicated that test scores are stratified by social class, ethnicity notwithstanding.

Ability Grouping

Test scores, however, proved to be insufficient to explain why differential learning according to social class existed, because they could not uncover the processes by which children were differentially treated. In the 1970s a strong interest in microlevel observation of classroom interaction developed. This work began to demonstrate how profoundly social class affects the placement of children in ability groups, because it showed the extent to which teachers grouped students on the basis of their *perceptions* of how able students are, rather than entirely on the basis of assessed competence. These perceptions are based on daily interactions with others and negotiations with teachers and are complicated by children's gender and cultural identities. Because lower-class children often lack the cultural capital congruent with school life, they are judged to be less able. Teachers classified children who were clean, were quiet, and acted respectfully as brighter. Teachers also tended to favor children who shared their own values, regardless of the student's measured ability. Sometimes teachers were notably poor judges of actual ability. They also had difficulty giving failing grades to students they liked. Unfortunately, since most teachers either were born into or have acquired the cultural capital, habits, and aspirations of the middle class, they now find many students in their classrooms who do not share their values (Brophy and Good 1970; Delgado-Gaitan 1987; Heath 1983; Ortiz 1988; Rist 1973; G. Rosenfeld 1971; Spindler 1987).

It is fair to say that teacher *perceptions* of a student's ability are a far more accurate predictor of a child's group placement than is measured intelligence or even standardized test scores (Cicourel and Kitsuse 1963). While all teachers take into account a child's past record—often too seriously—they may disregard evidence they disagree with, citing their own professional diagnosis skills as authoritative (Richardson et al. 1989).

As we will point out in Chapter 6, tracking or ability grouping acts to differentiate students further because it profoundly affects the amount and type of learning made available. Tracking affects the kind of control teachers exercise over their pupils. The treatment students receive in school also reflects the kind of cultural capital they bring to school.

Teachers interact far more with high-track students, for whom they hold higher expectations. These students are praised more when they are correct and criticized less when they are wrong than are students for whom teachers have low expectations (Allington 1983; Brophy and Good 1970; Grant and Rothenberg 1986). They are far more likely than lower-track students to be given autonomy in doing their school work, are more often expected to work independently, have better opportunities to engage in higher-order thinking skills, and are given access to innovative programs such as computer programming. They will be punished less for infractions of the rules, and will be given more chances and greater encouragement if they do poorly, if only because teachers fear the adverse reaction of middle- and upper-class parents.

By contrast, teachers of lower-class students employ custodial forms of behavior management. While much money and effort may be poured into special programs to enhance achievement, the programs often are remedial and simply repeat previous material. Where computers are used, they are used simply for drill-and-practice. Less capable students in the lower tracks get fewer hours of actual instruction and less rigorous coursework. "Pull-out" programs of special tutoring actually diminish the time spent in regular instruction (K. P. Bennett 1991; Delgado-Gaitan 1988). Teachers of the poor do not expect their students to do well and, assuming that they will fail, interact with them less, give them less encouragement, and worry less about the drop-outs. These findings have been confirmed in studies of classroom interaction (Borko and Eisenhart 1986; Rist 1970); in interview studies with low-achieving students (Fine 1986; McLeod 1987; Valverde 1987; Williams 1987; Willis 1977); and in analyses of curriculum distribution and content (Anyon 1990; K. P. Bennett 1991).

All of these findings are complicated by race, but one can find the same patterns of neglect and custodialism in schools serving poor white students as are found for poor African-American and Latino students.

Structural Inequalities in Funding

Social class backgrounds of students are often replicated in the schools they attend. In his powerful book *Savage Inequalities* (1991), Jonathan Kozol carefully documents the inequalities in how schools are financed. The formula for school funding is based on local property taxes so local districts support and govern their own schools. According to the "foundational programs" introduced in the 1920s, supplemental state funds were provided to help equalize funding in poorer districts, with these state funds being based on attendance. In addition, federal funds are provided for federally mandated programs such as special or bilingual education programs. On the average, school districts in the United States rely on local property tax for 40 to 45 percent, the state for 40 to 45 percent, and the federal government for 7 to 10 percent of their funds. Wealthier districts are able to provide better facilities and more programs. They are able to offer higher salaries to attract better teachers and administrators.

Dissatisfaction with these methods of financing schools began in the 1960s in a class-action suit filed in 1968 by Demetrio Rodriquez and other parents in San Antonio. The families lived in the city's Edgewood District, which was primarily poor and 96 percent nonwhite. Despite one of the highest tax rates in the area, the district could raise only $231 per pupil, even with state supplements. Another section of the city was able to raise $412 per pupil with a lower tax rate, plus state and federal funding. In 1971 a federal district court in San Antonio ruled that Texas was in violation of the equal protection clause of the U.S. Constitution because the equalizing effects from the state aid "do not benefit the poorest districts" (Kozol 1991, p. 214). This decision was later overturned by the U.S. Supreme Court on the basis that education as a right is not explicitly protected by the U.S. Constitution and "the Equal Protection Clause does not require absolute equality" (Kozol quoting Justice Lewis Powell, 1991, p. 215).

Observe two primary school classrooms, one in a poor urban area and one in a middle-class suburb. Pay particular attention to factors that help to identify children according to social class backgrounds. Can you distinguish between differences attributable to class and those that are a consequence of minority status? Observe the children in both classroom and playground situations. From your observations, what role do you think social class plays in the school experience of the children? Compare the two settings. What do you think of the school experiences provided to each group of children?

It is state constitutions rather than the U.S. Constitution that refer specifically to public education, usually saying that the state will provide common public schooling for all its children. Lawsuits filed in the 1980s in states such as New Jersey, Kentucky, and Tennessee have attacked the funding formulas used for schooling on the basis that inequalities in these states are in violation of their constitutions. The disparity in school funding from poor to wealthy districts acts to reproduce social class because it results in inequitable education for children already stratified by their family's social class. Even *within* districts, funding disparities exist. For example, in his analysis of school funding in Chicago, Hess (1991) found that the schools with the poorest students actually received less per capita funding for instruction than schools with the wealthiest students.

The Social Construction of Identity

Some very early studies pointed to the ways social class was inherited. In his study of "Elmtown," Hollingshead (1949) suggested that children who grew up on the "wrong side of the tracks" remained there, as did *their* children. In the late 1970s critical analysts began to look even more closely at classroom interaction in an attempt to explain the processes by which social class is replicated. They used the methods of symbolic interactionists (see Chapter 1), an approach holding that people do not simply react automatically and unconsciously to any "stimulus or pressure they are subjected to, but they make sense of these pressures in terms of frameworks of meaning they have built up through their lives" (Hargreaves and Woods 1984, p. 2). The symbolic interactionists have discovered what these frameworks of meanings are, how to get people to talk about them, and how they reciprocally affect behavior and beliefs as people engage in social interaction. They have explained the *reflexive,* reciprocal nature of human behavior as people "work at" constructing reality around them.

H. S. Becker (1953), for example, described teachers' notions of the "ideal" student and showed how teachers treated pupils in accordance with how closely they approximated that ideal. Poorer, more disadvantaged students were far from the ideal. For them, teachers lowered standards for performance, spent more time in discipline and less in instruction, and taught more slowly. (See also Firestone and Rosenblum 1988; Page 1987; Powell, Farrar, and Cohen 1985.) As a consequence, the students became even more academically disadvantaged as the school year progressed. Other researchers have demonstrated how students treated in this manner pay less attention in class (Eder 1982), come to define themselves as "poor students" or "slow learners" or simply as "not college material," and adjust their performance standards and aspirations accordingly (McLeod 1987; McLaren 1986; Page 1987; Willis 1977). Erickson (1987, p. 336) has described this occurrence as "school failure," a reflexive process by which "schools 'work at' failing their students and students 'work at' failing to achieve in school . . . [school failure, in this sense, is] something the school does as well as what the student does." Elsi's story (see box on p. 90) describes how one bright student was turned into a failure in this way.

Interview a teacher. What is the teacher's social class background? What is the social class background of her or his students? Does this teacher believe that social class background plays a role in students' schooling experiences? In what way? Write a personal reaction to this interview.

Resistance.   Schools do not fail all students with whom they are mismatched, and some students actively "withhold assent" (Erickson 1987) to educators' attempts to "cool them out" of the system. Early work by critical theorists blamed teachers for the failure of students, focusing on how their labeling of students destroyed students' self-esteem and stunted their intellectual growth. Data elicited from students bolstered the attack on teachers, detailing conflict and hostility among pupils, teachers, and other staff.

More recent studies have examined the patterns of mutual interaction between the inhabitants of schools. Researchers have begun to describe how people "work at" school, how both teachers and students come with preconceived notions and definitions with which they mutually construct the reality of their life in school. While much of the empirical research in this area has looked at negative effects—how negative self-concepts for both teachers and students are constructed and how they both resist being defined in ways detrimental to a positive self-image (see the discussion in Chap-

Elsi's Story: From Gifted Third Grader to High School Dropout

Elsi's mother, Maria, came from Guatemala when she was 15 to work as a maid for a wealthy family in the Southwest. She separated from Elsi's father, a Mexican American, shortly after Elsi was born. Life has been hard since. "Sometimes that lady, she just calls me the day before and says, 'I don't need you today, Maria.' And for her, it's OK, but I have to find somebody else's house to clean. That's why I want Elsi to stay in school. She can get her education and have a better life."

Elsi did very well in school, and in third grade she was tested and accepted for the SIGHTS (Supplemental Instruction for Gifted and High-Achieving and Talented Students) program at her school. SIGHTS provided pull-out instruction in science, art, and other enrichment areas three times a week. Elsi blossomed in the program. "I love SIGHTS," said Elsi. "I want to be a scientist and SIGHTS is the only place I get to study science." At the end of the year SIGHTS was eliminated in favor of a "school-within-a-school" gifted program which, though a full-day program, could accommodate only one-third as many students as SIGHTS had. The school held a lottery to fill its places and Elsi wasn't chosen. Back in a regular classroom, she was crushed, and her grades fell. "I really miss science. That's what I really liked to do. Maybe I'm just stupid." By fifth grade Elsi had given up, and by eighth grade she had failed English, Math, and General Science. Worried that Elsi was hanging out with a "bad crowd" and distraught over her grades, Maria tried unsuccessfully to transfer her to a parochial school nearby. After interviewing Elsi and Maria, the principal of the nearly all-white, middle-class school declared that Elsi "just wouldn't fit in" and that Maria "just wouldn't feel comfortable" in the support activities required of all parents. In tenth grade Elsi dropped out of school to help her mother clean houses.

ters 3 and 4)—a number of ethnographic researchers have begun to explore ways in which "working at" school can be turned from a negative to a positive process.

One perspective which focuses on ameliorating the impact of cultural as well as class differences is typified by Erickson (1984, 1987) and scholars from the Kamehameha Early Education Program in Hawaii and the Center for Cross Cultural Studies at the University of Fairbanks, Alaska (Au 1979, 1980; Au and Jordan 1981; Barnhardt 1982; Jordan 1984, 1985; Moll and Diaz 1987). These researchers identified aspects of the child's natal culture which could be utilized in classrooms to help students bridge the mismatch between home and school culture.

Empowerment. Another approach which concentrates more on a social class perspective is a recent branch of "critical pedagogy" (McLaren 1989, p. 162) which views the mutual construction of meaning as an opportunity for manipulating interaction in school. It advocates using schools to promote empowerment of subordinated and marginalized groups within society, especially teachers, minorities, the poor, and women.

These researchers believe that schools can be used to help people become conscious of the forces that oppress them and learn strategies to overcome them, thereby becoming "empowered." They emphasize the importance of researcher collaboration with teachers as a means to raise the consciousness of teachers and students. Their efforts so far have been limited more or less to individual schools and classrooms. Translated into a curricular philosophy, this work involves believing

> in conceptions of learning as something that happens to an individual as an internal and subjective action, as a process of inquiry and discovery; knowledge as something that can only be personally acquired and not given; as truths in each of us rather than as fixed and finite truths "out there"; of development as personal growth, as the transformation of powers already present; of classrooms as communities of learners helping each other . . . for the enhancement of all. (Ashcroft 1987, p. 155)

As Chapter 9 points out, this perspective also is limited. While it develops awareness of patterns of hegemonic domination, its efforts are constrained by its focus on microlevel and psychological processes rather than larger political and structural correlates of oppression (LeCompte and Bennett deMarrais 1992).

SUMMARY

In this chapter we have demonstrated how our ideas of social class have changed over time, and how even scientific explanations of why people are rich or poor were affected by social and cultural traditions. Social class status is inextricably linked to educational achievement and occupational attainment. The work of sociologists, however, has exploded some of the beliefs of educators. We now know that what appears to be intellectual merit may actually be the product of special treatment in the schools, given because of one's social class status. Similarly, what appears to be a student's lack of ability may be a product of teacher perceptions, based on the student's lower-class status, plus the student's response to negative assessments by the school system.

The process by which students fail—or achieve—in school is composed of a complex set of factors. It is insufficient to say:

> Kids are lazy—or poorly prepared.
> Teachers are incompetent—or hate kids.
> Parents don't care—or don't know how to help their kids.

All of these explanations may contain some truth. But the reality of inequality in education is a mixture of many things, all of which are played out reflexively in the arena of schools and classrooms.

In the chapters that follow we will look more closely at how the curriculum widens the differences between students of different social classes. We also will discuss the impact of race and gender on educational achievement.

chapter **6**

What Is Taught in Schools: Curriculum and the Stratification of Knowledge

INTRODUCTION

Think back to your own experiences of schooling. What subjects were you taught in elementary and secondary school? How were the subjects taught? How were students grouped for instruction? How did your teachers organize this instruction? How did they choose what to teach? How did you interact with your teachers in different classes? How was your learning evaluated or assessed? What kinds of learning activities did you engage in? You might consider these questions about your own schooling as you read this chapter on curriculum and the stratification of knowledge.

We begin this chapter with a consideration of traditional notions of curriculum theory which have dominated how educators viewed what is taught in schools. We then consider **curriculum** from a critical sociological perspective, using concepts from the **sociology of knowledge,** a subdiscipline of sociology which is broadly concerned with notions of what counts for "knowledge" in a society (Berger and Luckmann 1967). Critical theorists believe that dominant groups in society define legitimate knowledge. Since curriculum represents the knowledge taught in school, the **sociology of curriculum** is concerned specifically with school knowledge and relationships among the curriculum, schools, and dominant groups in society (Giroux 1988). In this chapter we contrast the sociological view of curriculum with that of traditional educational curriculum theorists.

We then provide a discussion of formal and hidden curricula and the stratification of curricula for different groups of students. In so doing, we will address the following questions:

1. What is curriculum?
2. What types of curricula are used in American schooling?
3. What knowledge is included in these curricula?
4. What values and attitudes are taught through the curriculum?
5. How does the curriculum change over time in response to sociocultural needs and political interests?
6. Who determines what is taught in schools in the 1990s?

WHAT IS CURRICULUM?

A curriculum, usually thought of as a course of study or a plan for what is to be taught in an educational institution, is composed of information concerning what is to be taught, to whom, when, and how. Consideration of the curriculum must include its purpose, content, method, organization, and evaluation (J. McNeil 1985).

A simpler but more comprehensive way to think about curriculum is that it is *what happens to students in school.* More than the formal content of lessons taught, it is also the method of presentation, the way in which students are grouped in classes, the manner in which time and tasks are organized, and the interaction within classrooms. The term *curriculum* refers to the total school experience provided to students, whether planned or unplanned by educators. By conceptualizing the curriculum this broadly, we are able to include its intended as well as unintended outcomes.

Traditional Curriculum Theory

Traditional curriculum theory comes from psychology and subject area studies in pedagogy rather than from sociology. Traditional curriculum theorists assume that the body of knowledge to be taught is a given, objective and free from biases. The assumptions about traditional curriculum theory are summarized by Giroux:

> (a) Theory in the curriculum field should operate in the interest of lawlike propositions that are empirically testable; (b) the natural sciences provide the "proper" model of explanation for the concepts and techniques of curriculum theory, design, and evaluation; (c) knowledge should be objective and capable of being investigated and described in a neutral fashion; and (d) statements of value are to be separated from "facts" and "modes of inquiry" that can and ought to be objective. (1988, p. 13)

Traditional curriculum theorists are concerned with determining the best ways to impart a given body of knowledge to people. Rather than focusing on what knowledge is to be taught, they emphasize how a given body of facts, concepts, and understandings can be transferred effectively and efficiently directly from teachers to learners. Colleges of education have curriculum specialists who train pre-service teachers and graduate students in the "science" of curriculum design. The history of traditional curriculum theory is a history of the application of rational, scientific principles to the management of "objective" bodies of knowledge. Models for the development of curriculum are produced by these specialists. They view knowledge as something to be managed by state departments of education, school boards, administrators, and teachers and to be given to students, usually in the form of prepackaged designs, kits, formulas, approaches, materials, and/or lists of skills and objectives. Educators categorize and manage knowledge, and students are required to master it.

Sociologists of knowledge, the "new" sociologists of curriculum (Giroux 1988; Liston and Zeichner 1991), and **reconceptualist** curriculum theorists (Pinar 1989; Shaker and Kridel 1989) challenge these assumptions made by the traditional curriculum theorists. The central questions for critical theorists of curriculum is not *how* to manage knowledge, but what kinds of knowledge are included in the curriculum and whose interests are served.

Sociology of Knowledge and Sociology of Curriculum

The term *sociology of knowledge* was first used by the German philosopher Max Scheler in the 1920s (Berger and Luckmann 1967). The sociology of knowledge is concerned with definitions of knowledge, particularly with how knowledge is constructed through the social interactions of individuals. In their classic book *The Social Construction of Reality: A Treatise in the Sociology of Knowledge,* Berger and Luckmann state:

Common sense "knowledge" rather than "ideas" must be the central focus for the sociology of knowledge. It is precisely this knowledge that constitutes the fabric of meanings without which no society could exist. The sociology of knowledge, therefore, must concern itself with the social construction of reality. (1967, p. 15)

Implicit in the sociology of knowledge is the fact that humans construct and modify knowledge within their social interactions. Knowledge is not an "objective" body of facts but is constructed by humans and therefore is value-laden.

Critical sociologists assume that knowledge is power and that different types of knowledge are provided or withheld according to one's place in the social structure of society. They ask questions about whose knowledge is in the curriculum and whose knowledge is omitted. As we will illustrate later in this and subsequent chapters, certain kinds of knowledge are provided to or withheld from certain groups of people on the basis of gender, race, ethnicity, and social class status. Those in power can use their influence to advocate inclusion of certain types of knowledge in the schooling process.

Rather than a conspiracy by one group over another, the transmission of a particular curriculum occurs as a result of a complicated system of historical and cultural beliefs, hegemonic ideologies, pressure groups, and textbook markets. For example, in the 1980s and 1990s tensions arose among policy makers, educators, and the popular media as groups worked to replace the traditional Western liberal arts curriculum in colleges and universities, which were centered largely on the experiences of white males, with a multicultural curriculum more representative of the experiences of women and people of color. These efforts were countered by a conservative backlash (Apple 1993) whose "official knowledge" is composed of a "core" curriculum based on what is purported to be the best that Western civilization offers (E. W. Bennett 1988; Bloom 1987; Hirsch 1987). Two central concerns in the sociology of knowledge, then, are: (1) what knowledge is valued? and (2) how do certain types of knowledge become reality in the everyday lives of individuals within the society through social interaction in schools?

Research on the *sociology of curriculum* began in the early 1970s. Berger and Luckmann's definition of the sociology of knowledge provided a theoretical framework for subsequent studies of the knowledge taught in schools. School knowledge became the focus of studies known as the *sociology of the curriculum,* or sometimes the *new sociology of education* (Giroux 1988). Michael F. D. Young (1971) announced a marked shift in the sociology of education when he proclaimed the emergence of a "new sociology of education" at the Institute of Education in London. His edited volume, *Knowledge and Control: New Directions for the Sociology of Education,* was instrumental in promoting the sociological study of the school curriculum, and with its publication, the "importance of [this] area of sociological study came to be widely recognized" (Whitty 1985, p. 13).

The sociology of the curriculum examines how different types of knowledge are provided for different groups of students, or how curriculum is organized and stratified. It views curriculum within the social context of schools and as a reflection of interest groups within the broader society. For example, in examining the curriculum, sociologists ask:

1. How do schools group children for instruction?
2. How much and what kinds of knowledge are presented by the teachers in these groups?
3. How do teacher–student interactions differ from one level group to another?
4. How are different people in society represented in school texts?
5. Are there differences in the amount of information and types of content provided in the curriculum according to the ethnicity, social class, and gender categories of students?

Sociological research on knowledge and curriculum has added much to our understanding about how schools work. We have learned that in addition to the formally stated, explicit curriculum, there is an implicit, or **hidden curriculum** that imparts beliefs and values to students. The following sections will explore both the formal and hidden curriculum of schools.

Ideological Interests in the Formal and Hidden Curricula

A central concern of critical theorists is uncovering the ideological interests embedded in both formal and hidden school curricula. Giroux explains that there are two kinds of **ideology:**

> Theoretical ideologies refer to the beliefs and values embedded in the categories that teachers and students use to shape and interpret the pedagogical process, while practical ideologies refer to the messages and norms embedded in classroom social relations and practices. (1983b, p. 67)

The former addresses explicit curricula; the latter is concerned with hidden or implicit curricula.

In order for us to understand the various and competing ideologies inherent in schooling in the 1990s, we need to look at the formal curriculum as it developed throughout the twentieth century. In the next sections we will look at what is taught in schools from the perspective of both formal and hidden curricula. The following questions asked by critical theorists guide our discussion:

1. What counts as curriculum knowledge?
2. How is such knowledge produced?
3. How is such knowledge transmitted in the classroom?
4. What kinds of classroom social relationships serve to parallel and reproduce the values and norms embodied in the accepted social relations of other dominant social sites?

5. Who has access to legitimate forms of knowledge?
6. Whose interests does this knowledge serve?
7. How are social and political contradictions and tensions mediated through acceptable forms of classroom knowledge and social relationships?
8. What compromises are made among dominant and subordinate interest groups in the selection of a curriculum that represents the official knowledge to be taught in schools? (Apple 1993, p. 68)
9. How do prevailing methods of evaluation legitimize existing forms of knowledge? (Giroux 1983b, pp. 17–18)

WHAT IS TAUGHT: THE FORMAL CURRICULUM

The debate about what knowledge should be included in the curricula of American public schools is as old as public schools themselves. Since schools are highly political institutions, the content and form of instruction depend in large part upon which socioeconomic interests wield power in society. Since different groups disagree both over the relative value to be accorded to different kinds of knowledge and over the appropriateness of various kinds of knowledge for different groups of people, there *never* has been a consensus over which body of knowledge was appropriate for all the children in all the schools.

Today many interest groups compete to influence what knowledge is transmitted in schools and how this transmission takes place. Spring's (1988a) discussion of the textbook publishing industry provides an excellent examination of the conflicting interest groups and their effects on educational policy and practice. He describes how the particular textbooks chosen determine what curricula will dominate in a school system, since textbooks often serve as the curriculum. These choices are powerfully influenced by negotiations among the textbook publishing industry, state and federal educational policy makers, special-interest groups (teachers' unions, associations of school administrators, parent-teacher associations, religious organizations, etc.), and corporations. All of these interest groups differ radically in their beliefs about the purpose of schooling, its role in transmitting ideas and values, and which ideas and values should be taught. Publishers, interested primarily in making a profit by capturing a large share of the lucrative textbook market, take seriously the challenges of special-interest groups. Anything in the texts that may offend particular groups can eliminate their books from a state's textbook adoption lists. Therefore they produce inoffensive books lacking both controversial material and varying perspectives on issues. Although these textbooks present what appears to be "objective" knowledge, they actually contain selective information considered "safe" by the publishers. Educators are not warned that, as critical consumers of texts, it is crucial for them to determine whose knowledge and perspectives are represented and whose are omitted.

During the 1980s and 1990s conservative religious groups targeted textbooks for careful scrutiny regarding content they believed to contradict the teachings of the

---

Hawkins County Textbook Controversy

Vicki Frost, spokesperson for the parents, explained her view of the way the Holt Basic Reading Program portrayed traditional gender roles:

> I see . . . the *terrible* dominance of role elimination and pro-feminism without any balance for traditional. I mean, every fairy tale was turned into a modern-day women's liberation movement in the story. And there was not one traditional fairy tale where they had the princess bein' rescued. But they made a point in the teacher's manuals to say . . . "We're bringin' you a modern-day fairy tale. And we're gonna contrast it in the teacher's manual to the old traditional one." And the old traditional fairy tale makes the princess look like she's frail and weak. But the modern-day princess is strong, not particularly pretty. She's clever. And she always saves the king or the kingdom or kills the dragon. And . . . you just think, "well, what's a fairy tale?" But it's what's behind . . . the moral or the lesson taught. And when you have that constantly fed, that at the end of seven years, . . . when you hear they have to write about "What do you think about the ERA?" . . . And when you've been given just one point of the issue, how will they respond? You know, that's the concern . . . the greatest concern's there's no balance. No balance whatsoever.

SOURCE: Dellinger 1991, p. 130.

Bible. For example, in a series of events from 1983 to 1988 known as the Hawkins County textbook controversy, a group of fundamentalist Christian parents in Hawkins County, Tennessee, challenged the content of the 1983 Holt Basic Reading Series *(Mozert* v. *Hawkins County Public Schools).* The parents, under the leadership of Vicki Frost, claimed that the reading program adopted by the county schools taught values that violated their personal religious views. They opposed, for example, teachings about evolution, magic, other religions, pacifism, rebellion against authority, situational ethics, promotion of human autonomy (as opposed to the primacy of Christ), feminism (see quote from Vicki Frost in the box), and one-world government. In December 1986 U.S. District Court Judge Hull decided in favor of the plaintiffs, awarding them approximately $50,000 in compensatory damages and stating that their children could attend school without attending reading classes where the Holt readers were used. In August 1987 the Sixth Circuit Court of Appeals reversed this decision, and in February 1988 the U.S. Supreme Court denied further appeal. This particular controversy illustrates the seriousness with which the content of textbooks is scrutinized by special-interest groups. It is easy to see the impact such a case might have on the textbook publishing industry—or on school districts faced with the need to maintain multiple sets of textbooks to satisfy multiple-interest groups.

Despite the lack of consensus about what should be taught in schools and how it should be delivered, identifiable trends in curricular knowledge appear throughout the history of American schooling. Kliebard (1986) has described these trends in *The Struggle for the American Curriculum: 1893–1958.* He illustrates how the formal curriculum has always been the result of conflicting ways of interpreting the goals of schooling (discussed in Chapter 1). Kliebard argues that four major types of curricula have dominated twentieth-century schooling: humanist, social efficiency, developmental, and social meliorist.

The Humanist Curriculum

The humanist curriculum is the model for the so-called "traditional liberal arts" program. Humanists view schools as the "guardians of ancient tradition tied to the power of reason and the finest elements of [Anglo] Western heritage" (Kliebard 1986, p. 27). They believe that the purpose of schooling is to develop the intellect by transmitting a core of the finest elements of this heritage to all members of society. This position was argued in 1983 by Charles W. Eliot, president of Harvard University and chairman of the National Education Association's Committee of Ten. The committee's report emphasized a K–12 curriculum that would increase students' reasoning power through traditional academic subjects (foreign languages, mathematics, literature, sciences, history, and the arts), which would be offered to all students whether or not they intended to go to college. The Committee of Ten believed that being taught a common core of subjects in the best possible ways was the best way to prepare all students for life (Kliebard 1986).

This same humanist viewpoint is embodied in E. D. Hirsch's *Cultural Literacy: What Every American Should Know* (1987) and was promoted in 1988 by former Secretary of Education William Bennett in his pamphlet, "James Madison High School: A Curriculum for American Students" and in his guidelines for "James Madison Elementary School" (1988). Bennett's curriculum proposals are designed for "mastery of a common core of worthwhile knowledge, important skills, and sound ideals" (E. W. Bennett 1988, p. 7). His plan prescribes a curriculum of seven core academic subjects. The core for high school includes four years of English; three years each of social studies, mathematics, and science; two years each of foreign language and physical education/health; and one year of fine arts (music history and art history). Bennett's plan for grades K–8 proposes a similar curriculum consisting of English, history, geography, civics, mathematics, science, foreign language, and fine arts. The curriculum ignores the literature of non-European cultures and includes twentieth-century American art and music only "if necessary."

While this assemblage of subject areas seems appropriate, what is problematic in a multicultural and multiethnic society is that it would, in traditional humanist style, emphasize only an Anglo-American cultural heritage. Such an emphasis reflects functionalist assumptions that a consensus on what should be taught in schools does exist and that the purpose of schooling is to transmit this knowledge from one generation to the next.

The Social Efficiency Curriculum

Among the most profound influences upon pedagogy has been social efficiency theory. As Chapter 2 described, social efficiency theory was developed from principles of scientific management, a movement based upon studies of organizations and industrial psychology. Social efficiency theorists believe that schools should facilitate the smooth functioning of the nation's economy by sorting citizens into job slots according to their abilities. Advocates of social efficiency believe that applying techniques of industry to the management of schools will make them efficient, smooth-running machines for transforming students into workers well equipped for a well-run economy. In Chapter 2 we examined the political context by which educators came to link schooling with work-force training and social engineering, as well as how scientific management affected the scheduling of the school day and the use of school buildings. Here we will examine the form and content of a "scientifically engineered" curriculum.

Rather than advocating the development of a core curriculum for all students as humanists do, the social efficiency curriculum prescribes different programs of study according to differences in students' abilities as measured by standardized testing. Programs of study usually include a college preparatory program, composed of the same academic core advocated by the humanists—literature, social science, natural science, mathematics, and foreign languages—and separate programs for students whom educators consider to lack the ability or interest to master the academic curriculum. These students, who are not "college material," are placed in vocational, commercial, and general courses that will prepare them for jobs not requiring a college education. Many of these courses have the same names as academic subjects in the college preparatory program, but they are presented less rigorously and at a lower conceptual level.

The tenets of the efficiency movement also affected how knowledge was conceptualized and evaluated and how learning tasks were organized. Cognitive skills and substantive knowledge were broken down into component parts, and learning was organized around the mastery of sets of behavioral objectives based upon those components. For example, in reading, curriculum specialists organized phonetic skills into lists according to perceived level of difficulty. Beginning consonant sounds were to be taught before short and long vowel sounds, which were to be taught before vowel diphthongs. These lists of skills were then written into behavioral objectives which teachers checked off as children mastered the skills. Study of more advanced skills was predicated upon mastery of earlier ones. In primary grades and remedial classes in particular, these practices persist. The teaching of phonics has played a significant role in the reading curriculum. However, this system disadvantages children who do not respond well to such an intensive phonetic skills approach to reading.

Elimination of "waste" also became a critical concern in the social efficiency curriculum. Students were to be moved through school as quickly as possible, and to that end, the degree to which children could be kept "on-task" became a measure of effective teaching. "Waste" also was defined as spending time on the teaching of "unnecessary" subjects. Necessary or useful knowledge was defined as that which could be used immediately in a job setting; hence subjects like Latin, history, and foreign languages were viewed with suspicion. In his article "Elimination of Waste in Education" (1912), John Franklin Bobbitt argued that students should be scientifically measured to predict their future role in society so that they could be taught only what they would later need to fulfill this role. A differentiated curriculum would solve the problem of "waste," since knowledge and skills that would not be used would not be taught.

Gender, too, played a role in curriculum planning. Since males and females would fulfill different social and vocational roles, student instruction should be tailored to gender-based adult roles. The training suggested for females generally was limited to general literacy and homemaking skills. (See Chapter 8 for more detail on the gendered curriculum.)

Development of the differentiated curriculum relied upon "scientific" and "objective" methods of testing, assessment, and measurement. In the 1920s and 1930s I.Q. testing came to be viewed as an accurate, scientific measurement by which children's native capacities could be determined. Educators considered it to be an effective way to determine how to place students in school programs appropriate both to their abilities and to their anticipated occupation (Kliebard 1986, p. 109).

By the mid-1960s testing had become a major part of the school curriculum. Continued routine use of standardized testing and curricular tracking provide evidence that the influence of the social efficiency experts is alive and well in American schools. Currently all 50 states have laws mandating state-regulated testing (D. Brown 1990). Increasingly these tests represent high stakes as rewards and sanctions for schools are being based on students' performance on state-mandated tests. The tests are used to provide evidence of school, program, and teacher effectiveness. They are used to justify accreditation of school districts and certification of students for completion of specific grades (Brown 1990).

In Tennessee, for example, teachers in second through tenth grades must administer the state-mandated Tennessee Comprehensive Assessment Program or "T-CAP." A Tennessee teacher describes the role these tests play in her teaching:

> When I came up to fifth grade, I really didn't know everything that would be covered in the fifth grade, so one of the teachers said, "Well, this skill will be on the achievement test, and you'll find this on the achievement test, and you'll find this on the test." And I know to teach my children survival skills that I had to teach those. Let's just face it, that's just the way it is. You know, I tell them, "This may be on the achievement test and this is something that I really want to stick." (Brown 1990, pp. 102–103).

Tennessee Comprehensive Assessment Program scores are released to the media, and scores of schools across the state are compared in local newspapers. One teacher described how these comparisons profoundly affect what is taught:

One of the neighboring county's scores were higher than ours last year, so there were problems here. Our principal came back from a principals' meeting and said, "Your test scores *will* come up. We will do a better job in this or this area " And he said, "I want you to pay attention especially in reading and math."

The National Center for Fair and Open Testing, operated by a consumer group which refers to itself as "Fair Test," estimates that American elementary and high school students take more than 100 million standardized tests yearly. Approximately 44 million of these tests are intelligence and admissions tests. The rest are measurements of achievement and basic skills (Fiske 1988). American educators and public officials continue to believe that standardized testing is an accurate method for monitoring students as they move through schools. In the elementary schools tests are used to place children in reading ability groups, special education classes, and gifted and talented programs. In high schools students are tested to determine their placement in either the general, college preparatory, or vocational curricular track. A later section entitled "Stratification of the Curriculum" presents a complete discussion of testing and tracking.

The Developmentalist Curriculum

The developmental curriculum comes from clinical and developmental psychology and is the only one of Kliebard's curricula that is "student-centered." Its focus is the individual learner rather than the needs of society or the importance of a particular body of knowledge. It also is concerned with helping people understand knowledge both experientially, that is, in the context of the real world, and intellectually, abstracted from the real world (Reisler and Friedman 1978). Developmentalists believe that curriculum should be designed to meet the needs of individual students throughout their stages of intellectual, social, and emotional development. Central concerns are the motivation, interests, and developmental stages of students. Students should be taught when they are intellectually and emotionally ready to learn rather than in accordance with their chronological age. Learning also should be structured so that children enjoy what they are doing while learning.

The developmentalists mandated a radically different role for teachers. They were to be partners with children in the learning enterprise rather than bosses. Some metaphors used for teachers provide clues to this shift in pedagogy. Teachers are described as advisors, supporters, observers, learners, facilitators, and senior partners (Silberman 1973). Experiential education, the open concept school building, the open classroom, middle-school philosophies, and cooperative and collaborative decision making and instruction all are legacies from the developmentalists.

Because of his emphasis on child-centered activities, John Dewey is one of the theorists most often associated with this type of curriculum. Both A. S. Neil's school, Summerhill, established in the 1920s, and the alternative or "free schools" of the 1960s were based upon these ideas. Spring (1989) notes that of Kliebard's four types of curriculum, the developmentalist has been the least influential on American public school curricula, even though colleges of education rely heavily on theories from developmentalists such as Rousseau, Dewey, and Piaget in the training of pre-service teachers. One sees little evidence of this approach in the daily activities of public schooling.

Despite its limited impact on public schooling overall, developmentalism survives in private and alternative schools and increasingly surfaces in special programs in the public sector. A contemporary example of a developmentalist curriculum is the "whole language" approach to the teaching of reading and writing skills in elementary schools. Drawing on their own language experience, children learn to read by telling and writing their own stories rather than relying on basal reading textbooks. The whole language philosophy includes the notion of an "integrated curriculum" in which language arts, math, social studies, sciences, fine arts, and other subjects are taught together through thematically organized units. For example, a teacher and students exploring a unit on zoo animals could integrate geography, children's literature, art projects, language skills, and knowledge from the sciences and social sciences to explore this topic. In recent years the whole language curriculum has gained greater support from teachers and administrators because it uses the developmental stages of children rather than standardized measures of ability to guide instruction. Current research in alternative forms of assessment, particularly portfolio assessment, has contributed to administrators' acceptance of this approach.

Another example of the developmentalist curriculum is in the work of the National Association for the Education of Young Children (NAEYC), summarized in the publication, "Developmentally Appropriate Practice in Early Childhood Programs Service Children from Birth Through Age 8" (1987). This work contrasts a developmentally appropriate curriculum to the traditional curriculum in primary schools. Other concerns about the inappropriateness of the traditional curriculum recently have surfaced among advocates of middle schools (Carnegie Council of Adolescent Development 1989; Connors and Irvin, 1989; Wiles and Bondi 1981; Williamson and Johnson 1991).

In the 1990s developmentalists in curriculum planning and implementation have achieved clear and strong—albeit minority—voices in public schools and colleges of education. American education is still far from using developmental curricula as the primary approach to teaching/learning processes in schooling.

The Social Meliorist Curriculum

Second to the efficiency movement in its impact on American education is social meliorism. Its tenets constitute a counterpoint to the tenets of social efficiency. According to social meliorists, schools should facilitate social change by producing students who will fight inequities and oppression and make the world a better place. The social meliorist curriculum came to the forefront of educational reform during the early 1930s as a reaction to scientific management, although it already had a long history among philosophers in Europe and America from Martin Luther and John Locke to Horace Mann and John Dewey. While Dewey provided inspiration to the

---

Components of Appropriate and Inappropriate Practice for 4- and 5-Year-Old Children—Curriculum Goals

Inappropriate Practice:
Experiences are narrowly focused on the child's intellectual development without recognition that all areas of a child's development are interrelated.

Children are evaluated only against a predetermined measure, such as a standardized group norm or adult standard of behavior. All are expected to perform the same tasks and achieve the same narrowly defined, easily measured skills.

Appropriate Practice:
Experiences are provided that meet children's needs and stimulate learning in all developmental areas—physical, social, emotional, and intellectual.

Each child is viewed as a unique person with an individual pattern and timing of growth and development. The curriculum and adults' interaction are responsive to individual differences in ability and interests. Different levels of ability, development, and learning styles are expected, accepted, and used to design appropriate activities.

Interactions and activities are designed to develop children's self-esteem and positive feelings toward learning.

SOURCE: Bredekamp 1986, p. 54.

---

developmentalists, he also was a strong believer that schools and teachers should serve as agents of social reform.

Among educators, George Counts and Harold Rugg are perhaps the best-known advocates of this position. As early as the 1920s Counts had advocated that educators act as agents of social change. The Great Depression, however, gave impetus to his stance. In his book *Dare the School Build a New Social Order?* (1932), Counts encouraged teachers to organize in order to bring about social justice and reform through the educational process. Like John Dewey and others, he viewed the public school curriculum as a tool for correcting social and economic injustices.

Rugg's social studies curriculum in American History was first published in 1929 and was very popular throughout the 1930s. However, an indication of how subversive social meliorism can seem to vested interests is that this program, which addressed issues of racism, class conflict, and the struggles of oppressed people, was forced off the market in the 1940s by conservative political action groups (Spring 1988a). In some towns Rugg's materials were even burned.

Currently the educators most closely allied with the kind of social meliorist curriculum presented by Kliebard are those known as feminist or critical theorists and pedagogues (cf. Apple 1986; Britzman 1991; Ellsworth 1989; Giroux 1983a, 1983b, 1988; Gitlin and Smyth 1989; McLaren 1989; Weiler 1988). The core concern of both feminist and critical theorists is an examination of patterns of subordination and domination in society: Who has access to power and why? As a consequence, stimulating the struggle against oppression based on gender, race, ethnicity, and social class is an essential element in such a curriculum.

At the center of the social meliorist curriculum is the notion of conflict and struggle. Students are provided with different perspectives on events and are encouraged to engage in critical examinations rather than merely reading texts and accepting the viewpoint of the author. A variety of texts are used to analyze all sides of an issue. For example, in a social studies discussion of the nineteenth-century "Western expansion" of white settlers into Indian lands, texts could include original documents, oral histories, diaries, novels, and treaties as well as talks by Native Americans. The term "Western expansion" could be deconstructed to determine whose interests are served by this label, and alternatives, including "Western colonization" or "conquest of indigenous peoples," could be chosen to describe the point of view of American Indians. Social meliorists believe that active student engagement through project-centered instruction is crucial to developing meaningful dialogue, critical thinking, and various perspectives of historical events. The underlying assumption of critical and feminist theorists is that by actively grappling with issues of struggle, domination, and oppression in the curriculum, students will work toward building a more democratic society.

The Formal Curriculum in Schools Today

The influence of all four of these curricula is likely to be visible in public schools, but social efficiency theorists have had the strongest influence. Their emphasis has been on efficiency, testing and measurement, and differentiated curricula. Administrators are still taught to be scientific managers of their schools. Public schools in the United States today continue to organize knowledge into discrete subjects to be taught in 50-minute blocks of time. Secondary school teachers still are subject matter specialists who work alone in isolated rooms with little time to develop different pedagogical strategies or to discuss professional issues with colleagues. Even at the elementary and middle-school level, departmentalized teaching, with children moving to different teachers' rooms for various subjects, is common.

Team teaching, project-based learning, flexible scheduling, whole language instruction, constructivist approaches to mathematics, integrated curricula, and cooperative approaches to schooling are currently in use by innovative teachers and administrators but are not the norm. Schools continue to base the stratified curriculum on standardized assessments of academic ability, rather than creating a curriculum based on research on child and adolescent development, the effects of ability grouping and tracking, or differences between school culture and the community cultures of children. Individual teachers or groups of teachers may be guided by social meliorist or developmentalist theories, but at the institutional level there is little systematic evidence of social meliorism or developmentalism in the standard curricula of public schools.

WHAT IS TAUGHT: THE HIDDEN CURRICULUM

The term **hidden curriculum** was first used by Edgar Z. Friedenberg in a conference in the late 1960s. This term called attention to the fact that students learn more in school than is included in their formal instruction. Giroux defines the hidden curriculum as "those unstated norms, values, and beliefs embedded in and transmitted to students through the underlying rules that structure the routines and social relationships in school and classroom life" (Giroux 1983b, p. 47). The hidden curriculum consists of the implicit messages given to students about differential power and social evaluation as they learn how to work in schools, what kinds of knowledge exist, which kinds are valued by whom, and how students are valued in their own right. These messages are learned informally and are sometimes, but not always, unintentional outcomes of the formal structure and curriculum of schooling. Giroux further suggests that in addition to information about the social relationships in school life, the hidden curriculum conveys messages both through the "form and content of school knowledge" and through the "silences," or what is left out.

For example, over the course of the school year a typical American high school history class would include very little formal curricular content that addressed the history of women and/or people of color. There would, however, be much text and discussion devoted to the white male military history of the United States. These omissions and inclusions give students a clear but implicit message about what knowledge society considers to be valuable and what is not.

Further, the hidden curriculum can be observed in social interaction. For example, traditional sex roles are reinforced by the way the teachers assign classroom tasks. Girls may be asked to clean up the room while boys may be asked to carry books or other heavy items out of the classroom. Middle-class children may be challenged by teachers to "try harder" while poor or working-class children are urged to "do the best they can." Girls may be discouraged from enrolling in advanced math and science classes, or teased when they enroll in them anyway (Holland and Eisenhart 1990).

While most writers have viewed the hidden curriculum primarily as the unintended outcome of the schooling process (McLaren 1989), we think it is important to understand that the hidden curriculum is often intended and considered desirable by school personnel. In fact, children can flunk out of school more readily by failing to behave in accordance with the hidden curriculum than they can by doing poor academic work. Teachers reward a hard-working slow student but penalize a high-achieving troublemaker or nonconformist.

The purpose of the hidden curriculum is to produce specific outcomes for later life, particularly to prepare students to accept as legitimate specific patterns of social behavior, positions in the social class structure, attitudes toward gender roles, and occupational placement. Functionalists and some interpretive theorists who view these behaviors, attitudes, and values as necessary for participation in society consider the hidden curriculum to be a necessary part of schooling. On the other hand, reproduction and critical theorists are more likely to examine the hidden curriculum for the extent to which it reinforces gender, social class, and minority group inequalities.

The Hidden Curriculum and Work Roles

Jackson (1968) argued that the hidden curriculum prepares students for the world of work by emphasizing such skills as learning to wait, accepting authority, coping with evaluation, and adhering to the demands of institutional conformity:

> Yet the habits of obedience and docility engendered in the classroom have a high pay-off value in other settings. So far as their power structure is concerned, classrooms are not too dissimilar from factories or offices, those ubiquitous organizations in which so much of our adult life is spent. Thus, school might really be called a preparation for life, but not in the usual sense in which educators employ that slogan. Power may be abused in school as elsewhere, but its existence is a fact of life to which we must adapt. The process of adaptation begins during the first few years of life but it is significantly accelerated, for most of us, on the day we enter kindergarten. (1968, p. 3)

LeCompte (1978b) has argued that these attitudes and values are embodied in a core of activities which teachers require of students as minimal behavior standards in the belief that without these behaviors, learning cannot take place. In the typical classroom today we see students sitting quietly at individual desks placed in straight rows or tidy clusters, with the teacher's desk in the front of the room. Students are expected to work individually from textbooks or worksheets without talking to each other. They are supposed to raise their hands to answer or ask questions and wait to be called on by the teacher. In striving to achieve these ideals, teachers provide hidden messages whose intent is to prepare the students for appropriate behavior in later work roles. The model of work embodied in these messages resembles the hierarchical working of a factory or other large-scale industrial enterprise, and it may be appropriate for some kinds of occupations. However, when it persists throughout pre-baccalaureate training, it is archaic, because it is incongruent with the working conditions and training required in most high-status and professional jobs, where employees are organized into teams, which work creatively and cooperatively with each other. Even today the factory model still predominates for most students; only high-status children systematically receive training whose hidden curriculum prepares them for professional work (Anyon 1990).

The organizational structure of schools teaches children that the social world of adults is hierarchical. Even in so-called restructured and site-based schools, administrators still manage teachers, teachers manage children, and children manage their assigned tasks. Teachers determine what children do in school, when, and how. Children learn that school knowledge comes from the teacher and from the textbook and that teachers evaluate how much they have learned by their performance on tests and classroom assignments. The evaluation process is external and performed by someone in a higher position. Anyon explains that daily life in this type of organizational structure provides practical ideological support for unequal distributions of power in society. . . . [T]he present unequal organization of authority in classrooms and schools not only indicates unequal power in society, but may reify and legitimate this in consciousness, thus fostering the impression that unequal power is natural, logical, or merely "in the order of things" and inevitable. (1988, pp. 178–179)

Children quickly discover that learning takes place individually and in quiet settings. It is "good" classroom behavior to sit quietly and "do your own work." "Keep your eyes on your own paper" helps to reinforce this message. Even cooperative groups most often mean those who sit still, not those who collaborate. Working together is discouraged except in groups organized by teachers. Even in classrooms where cooperative learning activities are stressed, children learn that there is a particular time period set aside by the teacher in which to engage in cooperation with peers. In such an individualistic school culture, it is not surprising that cooperative groups often become internally competitive, in a way that, as Deering's study of a middle-school classroom documents, derails the whole process.

CINDY: We got everything in!

KENNY: Yeah! You shoulda seen! We made Aaron do his work instead of fooling around. We kept telling him to work!

CINDY: Every time he'd goof around we'd call the teacher over and we'd get him in trouble! So he actually behaved himself for once! (1992, p. 141)

Schools require that students be punctual, clean, and neat, make efficient use of their time, take care of their equipment, work individually, and learn how to wait if they need something. Absenteeism is frowned upon and generally noted on evaluations. Classroom interaction conveys the message that there are different roles and expectations according to social class, race/ethnicity, and gender (for more detail see Chapters 5, 7, 8, and 9). Students who exhibit appropriate behavior in response to these school expectations are rewarded and displayed as role models to others. These rewards are both at the school and district level in the formal presentations at assembly programs and at the classroom level through teachers' evaluative comments. For example, here are several typical comments made by teachers:

- "I like the way Mary is waiting."
- "I like the way you wrote your name so neatly on the top of the page, Sally. Could you try to do that next time, John?"
- "You are really working hard on that math sheet, Sam."

The Hidden Curriculum and Perceptions of Knowledge

The organization of schools implies that both the structure of knowledge and social relationships are hierarchical. Knowledge is organized according to its perceived difficulty and its social value. Students who are expected to learn quickly are given lessons containing information that is more complex, higher on the cognitive scale, and more culturally valuable than are children who are deemed less able. Working-class children are less often placed in classes of higher mathematics and foreign languages and more often placed in vocational and industrial training than are middle-class children (Oakes 1985). The effect is to prepare the latter for college and professional careers, and the former for life in factories and blue-collar jobs of less status.

Despite the close interrelationship of many academic subjects, knowledge often is broken up into discrete courses, compartmentalized, and given to students as pieces of knowledge to be assimilated within certain periods or time slots. For example, students may have 30 minutes for reading, 30 minutes for language arts, and 15 minutes for handwriting. They are taught art divorced from history and mathematics devoid of science.

As a result, children fail to become seekers of information. They learn that knowledge comes from an external source such as the teacher or the selected textbook for the course, that there is usually one way to learn a skill, and that skills are taught by specialists. For example, in many classrooms reading is synonymous with phonics. A good reader comes to be perceived by other children as one who can "sound out words," not necessarily one who understands what the sounds mean. Deyhle, for example, describes how Navajo students who can't read nevertheless "act reading" during a silent reading period (1992). They turn pages and look attentive, even when their books are upside down or covering a well-disguised comic book.

Students learn that information is structured around multiple choice and true–false answers. They become uncomfortable with ambiguity—responses are either right or wrong rather than involving complex and often contradictory perspectives. The tasks assigned and the types of questions asked in classrooms reinforce this notion. Knowledge is seldom presented as complex, ambiguous, or something to be questioned; rather it is presented as "objective" fact. This approach is reinforced by standardized testing programs, which may drive the curriculum. Students are seldom encouraged to think that "knowledge" might be subjective, based on a particular historical context or social setting.

The Hidden Curriculum, Perceptions of Competency, and Self-Concept

Children who master the messages in the hidden curriculum, as Amber has (see box), learn how to "do school" successfully. Those who have difficulty understanding the instruction of the hidden curriculum, for whatever reason, often are perceived by teachers as less than competent students. In a study of reading in a first-grade classroom, K. P. Bennett (1986) discovered a hidden curriculum for measuring reading performance, one that had little to do with how well students understood what they read. Instead it addressed issues of *performance* in reading, including learning to (1) use the correct reading posture by sitting straight, still, and quietly; (2) watch and listen to the teacher when she spoke; (3) use a paper "marker" to keep the place in the book; and (4) demonstrate "comprehension" of the reading material by restating *verbatim* what was read in answer to questions the teacher took directly from the

Amber's Story

I came to this school from the city. We went on this choir trip back to Denver, and I, like I knew all the places and where the "jects" [housing projects] were and what they were called and the College City kids just like, wow! How do you know all that? I'm Hispanic. And the teachers, they were afraid I was going to bring my friends from Denver to visit the school and they said I couldn't. My best friend came from Denver, like me. We just hang out together. And the teachers are always watching us. We were out in the school yard under a tree and just talking, and the assistant principal came up and said we had to be smoking! He even smelled our breath . . . and we were just talkin'! I dress different, too [see "Amber's Dress Code" in Chapter 3]. I got good grades in my old school, but here it's a lot more advanced. It's hard and I had to study pretty hard. At first the teachers were always on my case. I hugged a boyfriend in the library and I had to go see the assistant principal. They were always watching me. The other kids could do things and nobody would notice. Then they tried to put me in a different class [a lower ability track]. I *know* how to write for school work, but when I talk, I just talk like I do, and the teachers listen and think I don't know anything. They were always watching me. But now I think they know me better and they're more used to me. I don't have so much trouble now.

text. Children who could exhibit these skills consistently were considered "good readers" and were put in the top reading groups. Those who had difficulty meeting these behavioral expectations or who refused to conform were considered to be less competent readers and placed in lower-ability groups, often without reference to standardized test scores which indicated that the placements were inappropriate. "She can't keep her place" or "He doesn't listen" or "She won't sit still in reading group" was enough to label a child a poor reader. Research by Eder and Felmlee (1984) and Grant and Rothenberg (1986) support these findings. How many adults could conform to such standards? One need only watch the behavior of adult teachers in faculty meetings to question whether adults can be as quiet, sit as still, and listen as well as children are expected to do.

Social standing in the peer group also is affected by academic placement. Children tend to choose for friends classmates who are in the same ability group or track as their own, so the social organization of schools comes to reflect the academic organization (Borko and Eisenhart 1986). This grouping has a profound effect upon self-concept. Children internalize the teachers' evaluations of them as well as their standing in the social organization of the classroom. Since they see the teacher as the authority figure and expert, they blame themselves for their lack of ability and low status. Anyon argues that the individualistic focus and evaluation structure of schools teach children that they are responsible for their own failures and academic shortcomings. Schools teach students that the reason for failure lies in their own "lack of motivation, low ability, disadvantage or inattention." Schools foster "blaming the victim" by shifting the terms of failure to the student rather than to the "failure of the institution to meet the student's needs by providing successful pedagogy" (Anyon 1988, p. 179).

Observe a classroom of your choice. Take extensive notes on what is happening there, trying to write down verbatim as much classroom dialogue as possible. What activities are the students and teacher engaged in? Analyze your observations according to the notion of a hidden curriculum. What are the implicit messages given to students in this classroom?

STRATIFICATION OF THE CURRICULUM

When sociologists talk about social stratification, they are referring to the hierarchy in society in which people are arranged according to how much they have of goods valued in that society. For example, in American culture, wealth, power, and prestige are highly valued. People who have more of these things are considered to be more valuable and therefore occupy the upper levels in the hierarchy. Both the formal and the hidden curriculum are similarly stratified. Today's schools are organized so that children are assigned to curricula according to the location and resources of the school, the age of the children, the number of children per classroom and—most important—the school's expectations of how well those children will perform both in school and in future occupations.

When we discuss the stratification of the curriculum, we are also talking about a hierarchy of power. Underlying this stratification is the notion that some types of knowledge and some types of instructional practices are considered superior to others. Similarly, some curricular programs are more valued than others. For example, a college preparatory program is considered superior to a vocational program, both because the former is believed to lead to more desirable occupations and because the children assigned to them tend to be more valued and have more social power in school. These placements are often based on perceived levels of ability, but, as we indicate in Chapters 7 and 8, they also are based on teachers' expectations of the children's academic performance, as mediated by the teacher's knowledge of their socioeconomic backgrounds, effective interaction with teachers and other students, behavior, appearance, use of language, and other markers of cultural capital.

In the next section we will discuss how stratification of the curriculum affects the school life of children. Questions to be considered include the following:

1. Which kinds of knowledge have more prestige in the school curriculum and why?
2. Who is eligible for inclusion in these programs?
3. Who is eligible to teach in the more prestigious courses and programs?

Choose a textbook in your field of study. Analyze the content and format of the text for the implicit messages provided to students and teachers.

Ability Grouping

Students at all levels of schooling are placed in groups according to their abilities as perceived by school personnel. This type of organization at the elementary school level is called **ability grouping.** It begins at least as early as kindergarten, but studies of nursery schools and day-care centers indicate that it may begin much earlier (Cox 1980; Woodhouse 1987). Students are most commonly grouped for instruction in reading and math. Throughout the kindergarten year classroom teachers and administrators assess their students' abilities, both formally and informally, and students begin to be identified as having different levels of ability or as being different kinds of learners. Some seem to "catch on" faster than others; some need a lot of extra individual help. Ability grouping is continued throughout the school years. Even through middle and high school children may remain in the groups that were established in their first year of school, for all subjects, as Jennifer's story documents (see box on p. 214).

Ability grouping even has echoes in higher education, as institutions themselves are stratified. The most able students are recruited for elite private schools. The next echelon consists of elite public state universities and private liberal arts colleges. Following those schools are a range of multipurpose state and private colleges and universities. At the bottom are two-year community and junior colleges, whose enrollment consists, for the most part, of less affluent or less able students who were not able to attend more prestigious institutions (Karabel and Halsey 1977).

Think back to when you were in elementary school. What reading group were you in? Were you ever changed from one to another? Why? What do you remember about learning to read in these groups? What did you think about the students in other groups?

Tracking

High school course offerings are differentiated both horizontally and vertically (Powell, Farrar, and Cohen 1985). Horizontal differentiation refers to diversity in content, or the number of disciplines in which courses are offered. The horizontal differentiation increased dramatically, for example, when vocational programs and a variety of electives were added. Vertical differentiation refers to the number of levels at which individual courses are offered. Vertical differentiation creates tracking. It occurs when, for example, senior high school physics is offered at the advanced, general, and remedial level, or when requirements for English can be met either by remedial reading classes or by advanced placement literature courses that include Chaucer and

Jennifer's Story

Hello. My name is Jennifer and I am in seventh grade, and I just turned 13 a little while ago. I have a teacher who puts us into groups, and the groups are smart group and dumb group.

She doesn't say they're smart group and dumb group, but they are the smart group and dumb group. All the smart people are in the smart group, and all the other people are in the dumb group, and I'm always in the dumb group because I always have been in the dumb group. Anyway, the other day we were all joking around because all the smart group people were downstairs doing algebra, and we were all joking around and saying, "Hey, you're the president of the dumb group," and we were just fooling around, and the teacher called me over to her desk and said, "There's no smart group or dumb group, it's all equal," and I said, "No, it's not." I said, "Listen, you don't give us any credit for what we do. We know this stuff like the back of our hand" and she said, "No, I just taught it to you today, you don't know this stuff," and I said, "Yes, we do. We learned this like a month ago." She said, "No, you didn't" and I said, "Yes, we did." She said, "When did I put you in groups? I just put you in groups today and you just learned it today." I said, "No, Ms. Jones, we did this last night in homework." I was getting really mad at her and she was like, "No, you didn't," and I was like, "Yes, I can take it out of my book right now, I did it last night for my homework." Well, to make a long story short, she was yelling at us and all, and she was telling me how I needed reinforcement or I was gonna fail, and I said, "Ms. Jones, I worked really hard this year and I got on the honor roll, and I got a B+ in math, and I don't need this reinforcement." I guess she was upset at me and I was really upset at her. She teaches us like we don't know anything and that we are really stupid. I know I'm not the smartest person in the world but I'm not the stupidest, either, and I can't believe she could say something like that, and do stuff like that, in front of the smart and dumb groups, if the groups are even equal. They're not equal. The teacher may think they're equal. They are not equal. They're smart and dumb. It may not be smart and dumb; maybe it's fast and slow. Well, that's smart and dumb. And if you're dumb, you're always dumb. I have always been put in the lower reading group and the lower math groups ever since first grade. I may not have read very well in first and second grade, but I did pretty good, and ever since then I was always put in the stupid groups and I don't think it's fair because I worked really hard this year to get a B+ in math, and I got a B+ in reading and I got on the honor roll, and I'm pretty proud of myself, I don't think it's fair at all that you should be put into groups.

Beowulf. A single high school can have as many as six or seven levels of basic academic courses. These courses share similar titles but their content and intellectual challenge differ significantly (Cusick 1983; Oakes 1985).

Vertical differentiation actually creates a vertical curriculum (Powell, Farrar, and Cohen 1985) when entire programs are created of courses at a given level. The vertical curriculum organizes students into tracks according to their perceived abilities, as determined by school personnel on the basis of standardized and nonstandardized testing and classroom performance. Allison and Bennett (1989) describe an example of a vertical curriculum in a high school. The tracking system contains five levels with admittance into each determined by the district's Language Arts supervisor and based on students' scores on the Stanford Test of Academic Skills, administered in the eighth grade. Level One, the Adaptive Program, contains those who read at a third-grade level or below, including nonreaders. Level Two, called Fundamental, was designed for those who read at fourth-, fifth-, and sixth-grade levels. Level Three, the Basic Program, is for students reading at seventh- and eighth-grade levels, and Level Four, Standard or College Preparatory, is for those reading "on grade" level. Level Five is an Honors Program to which students are invited if they scored at or above the 88th percentile on their achievement test.

This is fairly typical of the way high schools are organized, although some schools may be more explicit about the tracking system than others. Students who perform well academically in elementary school generally go on to the tracks that prepare them for college. Those who are not as academically talented are scheduled for classes in the basic or adaptive tracks.

Tracking is a common management strategy for organizing students in secondary schools. However, a growing body of literature as well as public concern raises questions about the practice (cf. Oakes 1985), because it labels children so early in their academic career as a success or a failure, and it contributes to the underachieving of students in what Jennifer describes as the "dumb group."

Analyze your high school experience in relation to the discussion on tracking systems. Which track were you in? How did this track differ from others? Did you have friends from other tracks? Were students from different tracks labeled with distinctive names? How many of the members of your track did the same things you did after high school?

Research on Ability Grouping and Tracking

Much current research indicates that ability grouping and tracking have detrimental effects on students. Studies about reading instruction report substantive differences in the content, delivery, and amount of instruction in reading in ability-grouped classes. Higher-level groups read more actual text than the lower-ability groups and also receive more direct instructional time. They are provided with more opportunities for independent silent reading, in contrast to the public oral reading required of the lower-level groups, a practice that limits the amount of actual reading practice

---

Rachel's Story

My most vivid experiences with ability grouping and tracking occurred in high school. There were three levels of all academic classes: low (remedial), average, and advanced. Some people had all their classes in one level, such as all low, or all advanced, but the majority of the people were mixed between the levels. I, for instance, had one of the lowest-level math classes, but I also took AP [Advanced Placement] English, AP Chemistry II, and AP American History. Many of my friends who took the highest math classes available were in the average English classes. One girl I knew who took four hours of cosmetology, which was considered by all students—the ones who took it and the ones who didn't—to be something you took if you weren't smart enough to go to college, also took advanced English and math. In spite of all this mixing, teachers and other students carried specific opinions about students. I think this had to do more with the lifestyle and social class background of the student rather than the classes they managed to get into. I lived in a small town; my teachers saw my mom and dad at City Council and Chamber of Commerce meetings. I came from a "good family," so they didn't think too much about the fact that I was extremely slow in math. Becky, who in spite of her four hours of cosmetology, and fighting her way into advanced English and math, was still a "redneck." Teachers knew where Becky lived, and they knew where she hung out on weekends. So, even though Becky could greatly outscore me on any math test around, I was "a good, smart girl," while Becky was just "one of those vo-tech kids."

---

received. Lower-ability groups are provided with fewer opportunities to read text (Allington 1977, 1980a, 1980b, 1983, 1984; Barr 1974, 1975, 1982; K. P. Bennett 1986; Borko and Eisenhart 1986; Borman and Mueninghoff 1982, 1983; Dreeben 1984; Featherstone 1987; Gambrell, Wilson, and Gantt 1981; McDermott 1976, 1977; Shavelson and Stern 1981). According to the *Harvard Education Letter,* "there is no persuasive evidence that ordinary elementary schoolers benefit from tracking" (July 1987, p. 1). In fact, some evidence (Barr 1982) indicates that tracking creates an achievement gap between children who had begun first grade with similar initial capabilities.

Interview a teacher (supervisor, principal, school board member, parent, student) about ability grouping and tracking practices. How do they support their views on these practices?

Research findings are much the same for tracking at the high school level. Oakes's *Keeping Track* (1985, and Page 1987) found that students' school experiences in more academic tracks were far different from those in lower tracks. There were significant differences in teacher expectations, academic content, and student achievement based on the level of the class. High-track classes involved more complex concepts, critical thinking, and discussion. Higher expectations were placed on these students because teachers understood that they were "college bound." Notwithstanding this evidence, many middle- and upper-class parents assume the high performance of their children and favor tracking for them. They argue that heterogeneous grouping with slower students, who also are more likely to be disadvantaged or minority students, will retard the learning of their ostensibly more advanced offspring.

Present a case for or against ability grouping and tracking. Support your arguments with evidence from scholarly journals.

The "Catholic School Effect"

In the 1980s attention was focused on the impact of Catholic schools on disadvantaged students. Studies indicated that Catholic schooling seemed to "push" achievement in these students, regardless of their social class standing (Coleman, Hoffer, and Kilgore 1982; Greeley 1982). However, Lee and Bryk (1988) have demonstrated that the supposed "Catholic School Effect" is a consequence of the less differentiated curricula in Catholic schools. Because they usually are smaller and have fewer resources than public schools, Catholic schools are unable to support the number of tracks commonly found in public school. Their students are therefore forced to enroll in the only classes available: solid academically oriented courses. As a consequence, most receive a more rigorous instructional program than public school students. Catholic school students were twice as likely as public school students to be assigned to an academic track, and a far greater proportion of Catholic school students who *wanted* to go to college were enrolled in the requisite preparatory program. Even general-track students in Catholic schools took more academic courses than similar students in the public schools.

Lee and Bryk repeat the findings that disadvantaged students in public schools are more often found in nonacademic tracks (Bowles and Gintis 1976; Cicourel and Kitsuse 1963; Oakes 1985). They also point out that the differentiated curriculum was initially developed as an equitable means to serve the presumed needs of a highly diverse public school enrollment (Cicourel and Kitsuse 1963; Heyns 1974; Powell, Farrar, and Cohen 1985). However, because the public schools offer so many nuances in courses, they amplify the initial differences in socioeconomic status and achievement that students bring with them to school. The reverse seems to be true for Catholic schools. The more constrained the curriculum, the greater is the academic rigor for all students. Hence student achievement is higher and the effects of poor background tend to wash out.

We believe that these findings demonstrate that activities initiated under the aegis of an ideology of democracy and egalitarianism can actually have the unintended effect of reducing equality. We will discuss these implications in Chapter 9.

SUMMARY

In this chapter we have looked at the ideologies underlying the formal and hidden curriculum of public schooling. We have also looked at the ways in which schools stratify this curriculum. We hope that you have begun to examine your own beliefs and values regarding what is taught in school. On the basis of this critique of current school practices, you may now be wondering what alternatives there are to the way we "do school" now. Chapter 9 will explore various possibilities for alternative, more appropriate ways to organize school curricula for both teachers and students.

chapter 7

Ethnic Minorities: Equality of Educational Opportunity

INTRODUCTION

In previous chapters we defined culture as a way of life shared by a group of people. In this chapter we are concerned with those cultural groups perceived in this society to be different from the "mainstream" dominant European American culture—ethnic minorities. Although membership in ethnic minority groups cannot really be considered apart from social class status (see Chapter 5), for our purposes here we will focus on group membership based on racial and ethnic identification. However, we urge you to keep in mind that one's identification is not related solely to ethnic group but is complicated by gender and social class. Each of us has multiple identities based on our gender, social class, ethnicity, sexual orientation, abilities, and other features. These identities play crucial roles in our interactions with individuals and institutions, and we continually reinterpret them on the basis of our interactions with others. For example, experiences of a working-class African-American female are profoundly different from those of an upper-middle-class African-American male, and the experiences of a white working-class Appalachian male are quite different from those of a middle-class Chinese-American female.

After an initial discussion about the labels given to or chosen by groups of people, we will define the terms *race, ethnicity, ethnic minority, prejudice,* and *discrimination.* We will then summarize the federal legislation related to equal educational opportunities for minorities. Next we will identify how social scientists have explained the question of school success and failure in minority student populations over the past two decades. Finally, we will address a question we consider to be the core issue in our discussion of equality of educational opportunity for minorities: What is the purpose of schooling for minorities, anyway?

What are your ethnic backgrounds? Many of us can trace our roots from several ethnic backgrounds. What values, beliefs, and behaviors have you learned as part of your cultural backgrounds? What biases do you think you would bring to the classroom as a teacher?

A Note about Labels

Terms used to refer to groups of people are constantly changing in response to political, economic, and social realities. For example, the term *African Americans* is currently used to describe people who have been labeled *Black, Afro-American,* and *Negro* during different historical periods. Often labels are ascribed by the dominant group in society but, particularly in recent decades, ethnic groups have selected their preferred labels. We have tried to use terms currently preferred or accepted by the particular groups we are discussing. In this chapter we use the terms *Anglo* and *European American* to describe people commonly referred to as "whites" in the United States. You may be more familiar and comfortable with the term *white* as a category to describe people from European backgrounds. We believe it is important to deconstruct this term. In her article, "White Is a Color! White Defensiveness, Postmodernism, and Anti-racist Pedagogy," Leslie Roman (1993a) reminds us that being white is not "colorless" and that people who are considered white in this society have their own racial subjectivities, interests, and privileges. She argues that the term *people of color,* which has been used as an alternative to more pejorative labels and as a celebration of multicultural diversity, "still implies that white culture is the hidden norm against which all other racially subordinate groups' so-called 'differences' are measured" (1993a, p. 71). By using the terms *Anglo* and *European American,* we emphasize that all people have ethnic backgrounds. *Anglo* or *Anglo American* is generally used to describe people from English heritage. *European American* refers to people from one or more European cultures. Since many "white" Americans can trace their roots to several European cultures, this is a broader term.

Considering themselves "American," European Americans in this society often do not self-identify as having ethnic backgrounds. We challenge the European American readers of this book to think about their beliefs, values, and behaviors as culturally based. As Nieto notes, "because whites in U.S. society tend to think of themselves as the 'norm,' they often view other groups as 'ethnic' and therefore somewhat exotic and colorful" (1992, p. 16).

Labels change frequently and not all labels are universally accepted by all members in a particular group. For example, we know people of African descent who prefer the descriptor *Black* to *African American.* We need to recognize that people may have multiple ethnic backgrounds and that they may or may not choose to be identified by one or all of these backgrounds. As we will see in this chapter, ethnicity is not static but quite complicated and always evolving—and so are the labels used to describe it.

What Is Race?

Race was the earliest term used by social scientists to address differences in group membership. Early anthropologists and some sociologists have used the term to describe a group of people with common ancestry and genetically transmitted physical characteristics. Although many complicated classification systems were developed in the nineteenth century to categorize different races, three racial groups traditionally were recognized in early anthropological writings: Caucasian, Mongoloid, and Negroid (Ember and Ember 1985). These classifications, based on traits such as amount and texture of hair, skin color, and other physical attributes believed to characterize each group, are no longer accepted in the scientific community. However, people in the United States today continue to have labels imposed on them or to identify themselves as members of a racial group primarily on the basis of skin color, even though many people do not fit easily into these rigid categories.

The term *race* is too vague to have much meaning for contemporary scientists, since biologists have found few genetic or real differences between members of so-called racial groups. Nevertheless the term *race* has social meaning in that what people *believe* about race determines how they relate to other groups of people. Often mistaken beliefs about racial and ethnic identities serve as the basis for prejudice, discrimination, and racist behavior.

Vivian's Story

My mother tells this story all the time . . . [about] when I first realized there was black and white. I had a very good [white] friend named Mary Adams. This was at the Christian school when this happened. . . . One day she [my friend Mary] came to school and told me she couldn't play with me any longer. I was in about the first grade, and I said, "Well why can't you play with me?" So she took me by my hand and she told me, "It's because you're black." . . . I said, "Oh, I'll fix that." I said, "When I go home, I'll tell my mother to wash me real clean."

SOURCE: Quoted in Etter-Lewis, 1993, p. 106.

In summary, *race,* a term with no scientific meaning, is a concept that has been used historically to categorize people in the ethnocentric belief that one race is superior to others. Cashmore and Troyna explain:

> . . . race is arbitrary. It's a convenient label applied to some groups to legitimate, justify or explain treating them unequally. And, while it refers, often explicitly, to biological differences, our interpretation of race is as something quite independent of physical phenomena. Race exists in the mind of the believer only. . . . Humans possess a striking faculty for defining not only their confederates, but also those who clearly don't belong. Physical characteristics are as reliable indicators of "them" as they are of "us." This is a worldwide, historical pattern: it seems to recognize no boundaries nor time limits. Human beings simply have this proclivity for dividing up the world in this way. (1990, p. 20)

What Is Ethnicity?

Ethnicity involves "ways of thinking, feeling, and acting that constitute the essence of culture" (Steinberg 1989). In other words, ethnicity is composed of shared values, cultural traits, behavior patterns, and a sense of peoplehood (Banks 1979; Spradley and McCurdy 1972). Smith defines ethnicity as being characteristic of people who "conceive of themselves as being alike, by virtue of their common ancestry and . . . are so regarded by others" (M. G. Smith 1982, p. 4). Irish Americans, Jewish Americans, Polish Americans, African Americans, Mexican Americans—all can be identified as distinct ethnic groups.

Ethnic identity is particularly useful in facilitating our understanding of who we are as people. There is an element of choice to ethnicity in that we can choose to identify ourselves according to particular groups. For example, an individual of Irish heritage may or may not choose to self-identify as Irish American. It is important to remember that ethnicity is not fixed but may change within the larger cultural context. It is also important to remember that people commonly have their cultural roots in several different ethnic backgrounds.

However, the term *ethnicity* is insufficient for our purposes because it is too broad and inclusive and does not address the question of the group's relative power in the society. It simply refers to common cultural ties. Each of us can claim ties to a particular ethnic group or groups, but not all of us experience discrimination on that basis. Cohen's definition of ethnicity as "fundamentally a political phenomenon as the symbols of the traditional culture are used as mechanisms for the articulation of political alignments" (1974, p. 97) comes closer to addressing power issues in society. In other words, people, including the dominant group, use cultural symbols, language, and behaviors to identify who is affiliated with the group and who is not.

What Is an Ethnic Minority?

The term *ethnic minority* is a more precise way to describe groups of people of concern in this chapter. What does the term mean? We already have defined what an ethnic group is, so we just need to look at the word *minority*. If our only concern is comparative numbers, all of us could be considered part of a minority group, given a particular set of circumstances. For example, a few Republicans at a national Democratic convention is a minority group. Because they are a small percentage within the total, women engineering professors or women high school principals can be considered minority groups. Male teachers in elementary schools could be considered a minority group for the same reason.

Christina's Story

I have always felt American, and learning about my Japanese background would not hinder me from being "American." However, part of who I am is partly Japanese. This doesn't make me less American. My mother brought me up with some different ideals because that is all she knew, but that doesn't make me an inferior American. It simply allows me the luxury of knowing two ways of thinking. In school I did feel some apprehension about telling anyone I was half Japanese, because it made me feel different and that is the last thing I wanted. When a child is that age, they simply want to blend in, not stick out. It is funny when I remember back because when I would have trouble pronouncing a certain word, I thought it was because I was half Japanese and therefore couldn't pronounce it correctly. It did not occur to me that it might have been a hard word for me or that other children may have the same problem. In the beginning I was very quiet about my background and sometimes felt angry at my mother for making me different. I guess I was afraid that everyone would treat me differently if they knew. It is completely different now. I appreciate my differences and appreciate my mother much more. It also has made me very open-minded and I hope to encourage this in my own classroom. If I can model an appreciation for diversity, hopefully my students will be more tolerant and open-minded about other cultures.

However, for our purposes we use the terms *minority* or *ethnic minority* to denote groups whose common characteristics go beyond mere numbers. Sociologists continue to struggle to find a definition for the term *minority* precise enough to be used by social scientists. Dworkin and Dworkin offer four qualities that characterize a minority group: (1) identifiability, (2) differential power, (3) differential and pejorative treatment, and (4) group awareness (1982, p. 16).

Identifiable characteristics of minority groups include patterns of language or dialect, religion, behavior or dress, and such physical characteristics as gender, complexion, or eye shape. In Western societies, despite scientific rejection of biologically determined racial characteristics, people continue to use complexion shade as the most crucial factor in group identification. The social and political power of ethnic minorities often depends upon how identifiably different they are from the dominant groups. The degree of difference generally determines where they are placed in the social class structure, how much prestige, power, and respect they are accorded, and how they are treated. For example, African Americans, Hispanics, and American Indians may be identifiable by distinctive physical characteristics, language, and cultural practices. On this basis, they are often subjected to discriminatory treatment. They occupy less powerful positions than do European Americans. Their subordinate position is reflected in their relative lack of educational attainment, less prestigious occupational placement, and lower level of participation in social and political life. Much of this is a product of discriminatory patterns of exclusion.

Discriminatory treatment by others often acts as a catalyst for the development of increased awareness, a sense of group identification, and solidarity among group members. In recent years we have seen some movement of oppressed groups into fuller participation in our society, but certainly not to an extent equitable with that of the dominant group.

Banks (1979) affirms these four qualities of minority groups. He defines ethnic minorities as those groups that often are a numerical minority, constituting a small part of the total population, but that also are easily distinguished physically and/or culturally from "white" Americans and are treated in a discriminatory way. Today in the United States the ethnic minority groups most likely to be defined in these terms are Latinos, African Americans, Asians, and American Indian/Alaskan Natives. These groups can be subdivided further. For example, Japanese, Filipinos, Chinese, Vietnamese, Hmong, and Asian-Indian Americans are all subsumed by the larger category of Asian Americans.

Identification of ethnic minorities is contextual: Whether a group is labeled by itself or others as an ethnic minority depends on the historical period and geographic location. For example, Irish immigrants in Boston in the nineteenth century were a distinct ethnic minority group, but today they tend to be assimilated into mainstream European-American culture. Although they can still be considered an ethnic group, Irish Americans cannot be considered an *ethnic minority*. Many Irish, Italians, Greek, Germans, and other European immigrant minorities have adopted much of the culture of mainstream Americans and blend into the majority population (Dworkin and Dworkin 1982). We need to remember, however, that many people from these ethnic groups became bicultural by maintaining their cultural beliefs and practices while participating in mainstream culture.

Pilar's Story

I was born in Colombia, South America, which is where all of my family is from. I lived in Colombia until I was one and then my family and I moved to the United States. Even though I have lived in the United States all of my life, my parents have instilled in me many Latin customs and have raised me with various Latin values and traditions. Although now I am extremely proud of my heritage and my family background, I can remember times when I was in grade school when being Latin was a hindrance. Even though my Latin-American background has enabled me to be bilingual, which is a very big asset to me now, it was something I avoided. I can remember wanting to be just like everyone else in my class, "American," and I wanted to ignore the fact that I was Colombian. At times I did not appreciate my culture because it was different from everyone else's, but now I realize how fortunate I am to have grown up exposed to two such rich cultures and I am so thankful for this experience.

I think that if my elementary school classroom would have been more multiculturally centered, I would have been able to feel more comfortable expressing my culture. If my peers and I would have been positively introduced to other cultures outside our own, they would have been intrigued by my culture and the culture of others, enabling them to be more accepting.

Ethnic minority status also depends upon where one lives. The impact of geographic location is illustrated by the experience of approximately 3 million Appalachians from the mountains in West Virginia, Kentucky, and Tennessee, who moved to northern cities in the Midwest between 1940 and 1970 in search of employment. Appalachians were viewed socially as ethnic minorities despite their Anglo ancestry in England, Scotland, and Wales. They were subjected to considerable discrimination and prejudice (Obermiller 1981), even though they had no physical characteristics that would distinguish them from other white Americans. This lack of physical distinctiveness also precluded them from being categorized politically as an ethnic minority group, so they were not eligible for federally funded programs for minorities. In the 1970s Appalachians began a movement to identify themselves politically as a minority group in order to qualify for certain governmental funding (Obermiller 1981; Zigli 1981).

Prejudice and Discrimination

Humans tend to categorize people into racial, ethnic, and minority groups and evaluate them using their own groups as the norm. This type of evaluation is known as *ethnocentrism* when it results in seeing other groups of people as inferior to one's own. Ethnocentric attitudes toward other groups of people are the basis for prejudice. Banks defines prejudice as a set of rigid and unfavorable attitudes toward a particular group or groups that is formed in disregard of facts. Prejudiced individuals respond to members of these groups on the basis of preconceptions, tending to disregard behavior or personal characteristics that are inconsistent with their biases. (1988, p. 223)

Prejudice usually results in two forms of behavior: stereotyping and the establishment of social distance.

Stereotyping. Stereotyping is depicting people on the basis of preconceptions and limited information. When stereotyping, we create caricatures, exaggerations of beliefs about the characteristics of a group, and then apply them unquestioningly to all members of that group. Hence all Chinese women are described as shy, all Italians are expected to be excitable, and all feminists are man-haters.

While Banks defines stereotypes only as negative, Dworkin and Dworkin (1982) assert that stereotypes can be both negative and positive. They also become part of the dominant ideology, serving to justify patterns of oppression and social differentiation, as well as differences in treatment. People use stereotypes to explain why some groups are greedier or lazier, more prone to irreligious or immoral behavior, more honest or sneakier, better lovers or more adept at mathematics than others. Stereotypes are the basis for and reinforce patterns of prejudice and are difficult to dislodge by logic or new information.

Social Distance. Stereotypes help to define how people relate to others because they determine the amount of social distance groups require from each other. Social distancing describes the degree of intimate interaction people can maintain without discomfort or repugnance. People feel little need to avoid those whose stereotype is positive. In fact, such a stereotype encourages social interactions. By contrast, a negative stereotype fosters social avoidance and even the desire for physical distance. If you agree with stereotyping that characterizes a particular group as intelligent, hardworking, and interesting, you are likely to want to become socially involved with its members. In contrast, if you view a group of people as lazy, dirty, lacking in intelligence, and untrustworthy, you probably would prefer to avoid them.

In 1993 in a rural, predominantly white school in Indiana, girls wearing clothes associated with young blacks—baggy clothes, braids, and other "hip-hop" fashions—have been harassed since mid-November by boys accusing them of "acting black." At least five of the girls have withdrawn from school. "It's gotten to the point where you can't think in your classes because all you can think about is what they are going to do to you in the halls" said one of the girls.

SOURCE: *New York Times*, December 8, 1993, p. B8.

One of our European-American middle-class female students was placed, as part of her teacher education program, in an inner-city school with a predominantly African-American student population. Her stereotypes about African-American young men became evident when she became frightened while walking by two young men smoking in an empty corridor between school buildings. The incident frightened her so much that she asked to be moved to a school she considered "safer." Like this young woman, we are unlikely to be easily convinced that members of groups can behave in ways that do not fit our stereotypes of them.

Racism

Race is the root word for the term *racism*. Racism in the United States refers primarily to ethnocentric beliefs and behaviors based on the notion that European Americans are superior to African Americans, Asians, Latinos, and other ethnic groups. Categorization according to race and other ethnic identification has provided a means for

---

Theresa's Favorite Breakfast

Having breakfast before going to school was a promise my mom never broke. Every morning she would get up at five and begin the day cooking. She would make tortillas and potatoes which filled the house with a delicious aroma. She would also make avena for me and my brothers. This was a favorite of ours and we ate it often with buttered toast and orange juice.

We had just moved to Michigan from New Mexico and my parents enrolled my brothers and me in a local elementary school. Even though our routine was somewhat altered, we still had our breakfasts before going to school. Since my parents are bilingual, my mother coded some words in Spanish. So when my teacher asked the class what we had for breakfast that morning, I didn't hesitate to raise my hand and say *"avena."*

However, after I said "oatmeal" in Spanish, there was silence. My teacher looked at me with a puzzled expression and asked me to repeat my answer. I did and there was even more silence. Then she said, "I've never heard of that." I believe my expression was more puzzling than hers because I just ate it that morning. Only, I did not know how to say *avena* in English. Not probing my mind any further, she went on to another child and I was left confused and wondered why she didn't understand what I was saying.

Being a first grader, this had an impact on me. It pointed out that I was different. This is perhaps the first time where I absolutely felt like I did not belong. We eventually moved back to New Mexico and I was happy to be back in our home state where just about everyone knows what *avena* is.

setting up a hierarchy in which some groups are relegated to social and economic positions dominated by others.

We can distinguish between the *individual racism* of people in their daily lives and *institutional racism,* which is so deeply embedded in the curriculum, policies, and practices in schools and other institutions that it often goes unrecognized. Institutional racism may be seen in the form of ability grouping and tracking, differential disciplinary practices, uneven representation in special education classes, and the like. This institutional racism perpetuates the differential educational and economic achievement of many minority people.

Think of examples of individual and institutional racism you have experienced or witnessed in your own life.

THE FEDERAL GOVERNMENT AND EQUALITY OF EDUCATIONAL OPPORTUNITY

A primary concern among sociologists of education is the impact of individual and institutional prejudice and racism on the schooling experiences and achievement of ethnic minority students. At first sociologists simply noted that minorities seemed to be less successful in school than other students. Then they began to ask *why* minority students fared so poorly. Was it because, in a land of supposedly equal opportunity, these children somehow were treated unequally?

Equality of Educational Opportunity

Equality of educational opportunity requires giving everyone the same initial opportunity to receive an education (Spring 1989). The history of U.S. social reform is replete with attempts by European-American policy makers to direct attention away from inequities in the economy by reforming the educational system rather than by redistributing wealth and eliminating oppression. Rather than creating policies ensuring that everyone had an equal chance to compete for jobs, policy makers have concentrated on equality of educational opportunity. Addressing this problem has proven to be very complicated. First, even if everyone had the chance to receive an equal education, societal discrimination on the basis of race precludes equality in the job market. Second, the roots of racism and unequal treatment in schools are so deep, and the practices so subtle, that it has been difficult to identify them, much less change their course.

In the next few pages we will discuss how policy makers have tried to manipulate the educational system to ameliorate racial inequality. We will present a short history of the pertinent major federal legislation and court cases over the last century. This discussion sets the stage for our later examination of minority student failure in schools.

Equal Access

American schools foster a powerful ideology about the existence of individual free-dom and opportunity. Young children are indoctrinated in the belief that anyone can be successful, given enough ambition and hard work. These myths are belied, how-ever, by reality. Equal opportunity requires and begins with equal access to the same facilities, and historically ethnic minority groups have less access to economic and social opportunities (LeCompte and Dworkin 1988).

Ask your local board of education for its most recent figures on minority student enrollment, achievement, and dropout rates. Do some schools in the district have higher proportions of minority students than others? Do some schools have higher dropout rates than others? How do you account for the differences? Compile your findings and present them to your class.

The Role of the Federal Courts

In 1895 the U.S. Supreme Court heard a case, *Plessy* v. *Ferguson,* in which Homer Plessy (one-eighth black and seven-eighths white) refused to ride in a separate "col-ored coach" of a train in Louisiana as required by law and was arrested. The Supreme Court decided that as long as the facilities were equal, they could be separate. This decision came to be known as the "separate but equal doctrine" and was used until 1954 to justify segregated facilities for African Americans and whites. Then a land-mark Supreme Court decision, *Brown* v. *Board of Education of Topeka, Kansas* (1954), overturned *Plessy* v. *Ferguson,* stating that separate facilities are inherently unequal and therefore illegal under the Fourteenth Amendment of the U.S. Constitu-tion. The Brown ruling states in part:

in the field of public education the doctrine of "separate but equal" has no place. Separate educational facilities are inherently unequal. . . . We hold that the plaintiffs and others similarly situated . . . are, by reason of the segre-gation complained of, deprived of equal protection of the laws guaranteed by the Fourteenth Amendment.

In *Brown* v. *Board of Education* sociological data were used by the Supreme Court for the first time as the basis for its decision. This research demonstrated to the satisfaction of the justices that separate treatment is inherently unequal treatment. This 1954 decision began the desegregation process of American schools, justified on the basis of providing *access* to equality of educational opportunity. Minority students would have to attend the same schools as European Americans in order to have equal access. Despite the Enforcement Decree of 1955, which required that federal district courts be used to end segregation of public schools at the local level, the process was and continues to be painfully slow.

One Lonsdale man recalls that opportunities were often closed to black students. In the days before integration, this young man wanted to attend summer school. But he could not go because there was no summer school for blacks.

"I received a letter from the Superintendent of the Knoxville public schools. He had written me this nice form letter, the superintendent of public schools, explaining why I couldn't go. That I couldn't go because I was black."

SOURCE: The Lonsdale Improvement Organization 1992.

Busing of students

After the 1950s African Americans finally obtained legal access to equal schooling. Additional court cases, often on a district-by-district basis, began to ensure that a legal right became an educational reality. While African Americans no longer were legally segregated, the fact of residential segregation often meant that most children still attended racially isolated schools. The emphasis of subsequent legislation was on providing *equal access* for all children. Soon, however, research results began to show that even after segregated schools were legally banned, equal access did not necessarily guarantee equal outcomes for minority children (Hess 1989; Metz 1978; Murnane 1975). Equal treatment for people who started out unequal did not permit disadvantaged people to "catch up." Subsequent legislation then began to provide *unequal* or *compensatory education* in order to offset the effects of economic and educational disadvantage. We will discuss these programs later in this chapter.

This legislation has been part of a continuing struggle to ensure the civil rights of all U.S. citizens, regardless of ethnic affiliation. *Civil rights* refers to the rights of individuals by the fact of their status as citizens. These rights are guaranteed by the Fourteenth Amendment, which provides "equal protection under law" for all citizens. This means that all citizens are to have equal access to opportunities for economic and social gain despite their racial or ethnic background, gender, age, sexual orientation, or disabling condition. Civil rights are guaranteed by the Constitution — the right to an education is not. Since education was a responsibility left to state governments, opportunities for schooling, particularly for ethnic minorities, varied from state to state.

Create an ethnic map of your neighborhood. First define the neighborhood and list all institutions—churches, stores, schools, places of entertainment—and classify them according to their ethnic group of origin. Were they initially begun or once used by a specific ethnic group? Determine if the clients who use them live in the neighborhood or elsewhere. Then try to determine the ethnic breakdown of the residences in your area.

The 1964 Civil Rights Act was passed by Congress to speed up the desegregation of public schools. Title IV of the Civil Rights Act gave the U.S. Commissioner of Education the power to help desegregate schools and the U.S. Attorney General the power to initiate lawsuits to force school desegregation. This power was enforced by Title VI, which denied federal funds to schools with racially discriminatory programs. For many school districts, this threat was effective.

School districts were given a clear message from the federal government that they must take steps to provide equal educational opportunities for minority students through both desegregation and compensatory education programs. These were closely linked, because schools were required to desegregate in order to receive federal funds for the compensatory programs.

Using a map of your school district, code the schools according to the ethnic composition of their students. What are your findings?

Desegregation and the Coleman Report

The unequal performance of minority students indirectly gave impetus to school desegregation. Conventional wisdom argued that inequalities of performance must be a consequence of inequalities in the schools, and therefore schools with high-achieving students must be spending more money on them than those whose students did poorly. To test that theory, Section 402 of the 1964 Civil Rights Act authorized the Commissioner of Education to examine "the lack of availability of equal educational opportunities for individuals by reason of race, color, religion, or national origin in public educational institutions at all levels in the United States." A survey, conducted by James Coleman and his associates, was entitled *Equality of Educational Opportunity* (1966). It looked at material differences between districts, comparing such things as school and class size, the background and level of training of teachers, provision of facilities such as libraries and laboratories, and per-pupil expenditure. These data were aggregated at the district level; Coleman did not look at differences among schools *within* districts.

Coleman expected to find that poor schools produced poor students. What he found out was surprising. First of all, the differences between school districts were not large enough to explain the differences in student performance among the six racial groups in the study. Second, he found that differences between minority and majority students' test scores greatly increased from the first to the twelfth grade. Third, minority and majority children did not differ in the value they attached to school and academic achievement (Borman and Spring 1984, p. 204). What he did find was that minority students who attended school with European-American students seemed to have higher levels of academic achievement than those who attended all-minority schools.

This research finding was a catalyst to mix students racially to improve the performance of minorities. And, while the impetus for desegregation certainly was congruent with American social ideology, it unfortunately was based upon a misinterpretation of Coleman's research; subsequent reanalyses showed that the real effect was not racial, but socioeconomic. What really seemed to have an effect on students was the peer group. Students whose classmates were from a higher socioeconomic group did better in school. Since minority students usually were poorer than their majority classmates, it appeared that going to European-American schools made the difference.

Different methods have been used to desegregate American schools in response to the 1954 Supreme Court decision, the 1964 Civil Rights Act, and the Coleman Report. U.S. schools have tried to comply in a variety of ways, some more effective than others. A few complied only under court order. A few refused to disband racially segregated systems and closed down the public schools until ordered to reopen by the courts. Many schools postponed compliance. Some districts still are fighting court battles over desegregation, under continued threats from the government to cut off federal funding and institute lawsuits (Borman and Spring 1984; Hughes, Gordon, and Hillman 1980; Kirby, Harris, and Crain 1973; P. E. Peterson 1976; Rogers 1968; Tatel, Lanigan, and Sneed 1986).

Bussing was one of the most widely used and controversial plans for achieving racial balance. Students from one neighborhood school—usually minority dominated—would be bussed to another, usually in European-American neighborhoods. Where this method is enforced by law, it is referred to as *involuntary desegregation* and has been met with resistance and hostility by both African-American and European-American parents. It has been argued that forced bussing encourages European Americans to flee from the districts affected, that it destroys neighborhoods and disrupts parents' involvement with their children's schooling. Parents objected to the long bus rides to which their children were subjected, especially since the majority bussed were minority children (Borman and Spring 1984; Crain 1977; Pettigrew and Green 1976; Reynolds 1986; Rist 1973).

A recent example of community tensions over bussing occurred in Wausau, Wisconsin, during the 1993–1994 school year. In accordance with a bussing program to distribute poor and/or Southeast Asian children across the district, 600 children were bussed up to 2.2 miles so that no school would have more than a 32 percent minority enrollment. This plan was in response to concern by teachers and principals overwhelmed by the needs of immigrant children, mostly from Hmong refugee families that settled in the area with the help of church groups. The group made up 16 percent of the district's enrollment and were concentrated in just a few schools, which also had disproportionate numbers of low-income European-American children. Parents rebelled against the bussing and collected 10,000 signatures to hold a recall election for the local school board. In December five school board members who had helped to implement the bussing program were voted out of office. At this writing the community continues to be in controversy over the bussing plan (Schmidt 1994).

In another district the school board used a lottery to institute a policy of involuntary transfers of teachers in an attempt to provide a racially balanced faculty. The names of European-American teachers and the names of African-American teachers in schools with predominantly African-American student populations were placed in separate sets of containers grouped according to grade level. At a public meeting the names of African-American teachers and corresponding European-American teachers were drawn, according to grade level. These teachers switched places for the next three years. Little in the way of in-service training was provided for these transferred teachers. The program was somewhat effective in desegregating faculties but caused major upheaval for the teachers and children whose lives were changed by the move. Four years after the transfer, one teacher captured her experience. "I've never been so angry in my entire career. I felt so powerless."

Voluntary desegregation plans use programs such as magnet schools, minority-to-majority transfers, metropolitan redistricting, and school pairing to improve ethnic balance. Magnet schools, usually inner-city schools with a history of minority enroll-ment, historically are transformed into centers offering programs designed to attract students from all over the district. In many cities ordered to desegregate, these mag-net schools have been developed as an alternative to bussing. Schools specializing in arts, languages, computer science, applied arts, medicine, math and sciences, physi-cal education, and programs for the gifted have replaced inner-city segregated schools. Students voluntarily apply to these schools and may even be required to audi-tion, as in Cincinnati and Houston, where inner-city high schools were transformed into schools for the creative and performing arts or programs for the gifted and tal-ented. The assumption is that if the school, despite its location, can offer an excellent program, students from outside the immediate neighborhood will be attracted to it, thus reducing the effects of de facto or residential segregation (Borman and Spring 1984; Ferrell and Compton 1986). However, magnet schools have been criticized for drawing away the best students and resources from other schools. Some magnet schools housed within larger schools have been criticized for "in-school segrega-tion," since locating the program in one portion of the building discourages interac-tions between students within and outside of the program.

The impact of social life on children in desegregated schools also has been dis-puted. The organization in some of these schools facilitates the development of cross-racial friendships (Damico, Bell, and Green 1980; Schofield 1982). All of them have made the development of such friendships more possible. However, desegregation has not always meant social integration, especially since the bussed children usually arrive and leave in intact groups on a scheduled bus and have little time to socialize with others. Sometimes the children even remain segregated in distinct classrooms. Especially where ability grouping and tracking reinforce racial differences, students tend to remain in racially segregated groups in the lunchroom, on the playground, in classes, and on the bus. Differences in cultural styles also impede the formation of friendships. European-American children tend to be intimidated by African Americans and to feel threatened by the noise and movement natural among African Americans (Clement, Harding, and Eisenhart 1979; Hanna 1987; St. John 1975; Schofield 1982; Wax 1980).

Despite the Supreme Court rulings requiring the desegregation of schools and federal legislation denying funding to racially discriminatory districts, the majority of American schools today continue to be relatively segregated, in large part because of persistent racial and economic residential segregation. Enforcement is a problem. In many cases federal funding has not been withheld despite serious, continuing viola-tions of the Civil Rights Act. Giving control over federal funds to state and local authorities, as happened in the early 1980s with the "block grant" program, has affected the dispersion of funds. Fred Hess, executive director of the Chicago Panel on Public School Policy and Finance, explained that "more than 80 percent of all minority students in Chicago continue to attend segregated schools and receive no significant compensatory education to offset the effects of this segregation" (1989). In fact, the neediest schools in Chicago often get fewer funds than those in more affluent neighborhoods. (See also Knapp and Cooperstein 1986; Lecompte and Dworkin 1988.) Hess and his associates called for shifting more resources from wealthier schools to deal with this problem.

In large part these inequities exist because the ethnic composition of schools parallels the ethnic composition of neighborhoods. Most of the major cities in the United States have racially and economically segregated patterns of residence which have been enforced by custom and legal statute, a situation that is becoming worse rather than better—despite Civil Rights legislation (W. J. Wilson 1987).

A recent study by the Harvard Project on School Desegregation (Orfield 1993) describes the increased segregation of African-American students across the United States. The study found that, after a rather dramatic decline of segregation in the South from the mid-1960s through the early 1970s and a period of stability until 1988, segregation significantly increased from 1988 to 1991. In addition the study reports the following findings:

- The proportion of black students in schools with more than 50% minority students increased from 1986 to 1991, reaching the level that had existed before the Supreme Court's first busing decision in 1971. The share of black students in intensely segregated (90–100% minority) schools— which had actually declined during the 1980s—rose. (Orfield 1993, p. 7)

- During the 1991 school year, Latino students were more likely than African American students to be in predominantly minority schools and slightly more likely to be in intensely segregated schools. (Orfield 1993, p. 7)

- African American and Latino students are much more likely than white students to find themselves in schools of concentrated poverty. Segregation by race is strongly related to segregation by poverty. (Orfield 1993, p. 7).

- Minority students are much more likely to be in high poverty schools. They face not only discrimination and stereotypes about minority schools but schools struggling with the much greater concentration of health, social, and neighborhood problems that are found in high poverty schools. (Orfield 1993, p. 1)

Forty years after the *Brown* v. *Board of Education* ruling called for the abolition of school segregation, communities and school districts continue to struggle over the issue of desegregation as large numbers of poor and minority children continue to attend schools that offer separate and unequal educational opportunities.

Compensatory Legislation

As we have described, the findings of the Coleman Report contradicted policy makers' expectations. Differential student achievement was strongly related, not to school characteristics, but to family background of students and aspirations of peers. Coleman's work led to theories linking poor academic achievement to the "cultural deprivation" of poor families. It gave scientific credence to the popular belief that children from ghetto families live in a "culture of poverty" (Valentine 1968) which puts them at a disadvantage in school. Federal policy makers used this argument to implement programs that would compensate for the home environment and facilitate equality of *results* rather than just equality of *access* (Baratz and Baratz 1970; Karabel and Halsey 1977). Initiated in the 1960s as part of the federally funded War on Poverty, these programs became known as "compensatory education." The Elementary and Secondary Education Act (ESEA), passed in 1965 as part of President Lyndon B. Johnson's "War on Poverty," provided approximately $1 billion in federal funding for programs and services beyond the regular school offerings (Ballantine 1983). These programs targeted preschool and elementary school children from poor and minority families and were predicated upon the assumption that early intervention would compensate for the disadvantages resulting from their family background. While the various titles of the ESEA provided funds for a wide variety of programs, the most important for instructional programs was Title I. It provided programs such as Head Start for preschoolers and remedial reading and math programs for school-aged children considered to be educationally deprived.

The importance of the ESEA to the issue of equality was that it improved opportunities for children by improving their education. It also reinforced the Civil Rights Act by linking federal funding for Title I programs to compliance with desegregation requirements.

These programs still exist under the 1981 Education and Consolidation and Improvement Act (ECIA); however, lumping federal funds into state-disseminated "block grants" gives control of the program and its funding to local districts. These Chapter I federal funds can be used for a wide variety of programs, not just those aimed at poor children. As Hess (1989) pointed out, local districts can structure programs so as to divert funds from those most in need, thereby weakening their impact. In 1994 congressional debates over federal funds for education, Senator Edward M. Kennedy called this block grant funding program "a slush fund for states" (Pitsch 1994).

Currently as of this second edition, the Clinton administration is working toward congressional reauthorization of the Elementary and Secondary Act. The Democratic administration has pushed Congress to eliminate the block grant funding of the 1980s and replace it with categorical aid directly to school districts serving the poorest children. Clinton's controversial plan would increase funds for the neediest districts through "concentration grants" for counties with high concentrations of poor students. His proposal also calls for increasing from 15 percent to 18 percent the proportion of poor students needed for a county to qualify for the grants. Clinton's proposal requires states to set standards for student performance and curriculum content in order to participate in Chapter I (Pitsch 1994). This change in the funding of compensatory education will require more accountability from school districts on their use of federal funding and is a step toward a national system of standards for performance in academic areas.

Special Needs Legislation

In the late 1960s and early 1970s lawmakers continued attempts to provide federal funding for specific student populations that had not yet received special educational services. The 1966 Education of Handicapped Children (Title VI) and the 1967 Bilingual Education Programs (Title VII) were added to the Elementary and Secondary Act. The Education of Handicapped Children Act provided for free public education for all handicapped children. It provided at public expense services previously available only in the private sector and too costly for poor families. The purpose of the Bilingual Act was to meet "the special educational needs of the large number of children of limited English speaking ability in the United States." An Indian Education Act of 1972 provided funds for health and nutrition programs for American Indians as well as innovative and bilingual programs. The Ethnic Heritage Act was passed in 1972 to assist in the establishment of ethnic studies programs. All of these programs were aimed at providing poor and minority students with the same educational opportunities that middle-class white students had.

Nura's Story

I still try to improve my reading ability, but since I came to this country and started learning English I have a hard time differentiating between the rules of reading the two languages. I keep getting mixed up by the rules of reading and writing Oromo versus English. English is a difficult language to learn. The other students use dictionaries to translate new words but there is no Oromo/English dictionary. If my husband doesn't know the words, then I will never find out. And sometimes even after they are translated they don't make much sense. Even worse, some words in English don't even exist in the Oromo language and vice versa.

My teacher says that we should be in contact with Americans to practice our English, but I hardly come in contact with Americans. There aren't any in my neighborhood. The only time I see them is when I watch television or go to the store. But at the store they have no time for discussions. My husband and I were advised to talk to one another in English, which we tried for a while. But since we kept running out of English words, we cut down on communicating with one another. That made us feel even worse, so we gave up on the idea of communicating with one another in English.

SOURCE: Center for Literary Studies 1992.

Underlying these programs was the assumption that if minority students could acquire the same cultural capital that mainstream European Americans had, they would have the same opportunities for economic success as whites. In other words, if you could teach them to "act white" (Fordham and Ogbu 1986), they would be equal. This is, however, an individualistic solution to what really is a problem generated by structural inequities in the society. It ignores the reality of how unequally distributed economic resources are in this country and how difficult it is for minority groups to gain access to them.

RESEARCH ON SCHOOLING FOR MINORITY STUDENTS

Research on the performance of minority students over the last three decades has attempted to explain why these children do not succeed in school in the same way that European-American children do. Three distinct theories have been developed: unequal resources and treatment, cultural background, and the labor market.

A Theory of Unequal Resources and Treatment

This approach to school failure examines the imbalance of financial resources available to minority students and the differential treatment they receive in school. Jencks, in his work *Inequality* (1972), examined this theory, testing it at the macro or structural level by reanalyzing Coleman's data from the mid-1960s. Since it had been determined that schools were not unequal enough to produce the observed differences in achievement, Jencks introduced what essentially was a class-conflict explanation: Poverty and poor performance were a function of social class rather than race (Scimecca 1980). He argued that family background was the most important determining factor in students' educational achievement. Students from families with higher incomes are more likely to acquire more education than those from lower-income families. According to Jencks, equalizing the resources for schools and the time spent in school would not be enough to reduce economic inequality. He argued:

> There is no evidence that school reform can substantially reduce the extent of cognitive inequality, as measured by tests of verbal fluency, reading comprehension or mathematical skill. Neither school resources nor segregation has an appreciable effect on either test scores or educational attainment. (1972, p. 8)

He argued that large-scale redistribution of wealth, not school reform, was the key to a more equitable society. He criticized the legislation of the 1960s for concentrating on children rather than directly attacking adult inequality.

Unfortunately, though economic reform is certainly a necessary strategy in reducing inequality in the society, this argument was interpreted to mean that because of the determining power of family background, schools made no difference and could be ignored as sites for social change.

Rist, by contrast, examined inequality in the treatment of children at the microlevel—inside schools and classrooms. Rist (1970) studied the school experiences of African-American primary-aged children from a poor, urban neighborhood. He found that teachers' perceptions of students' home lives made a significant difference in the way they treated students. Students perceived to come from poor homes—as determined by their appearance as well as informal knowledge of family background—were placed in lower-ability reading groups and provided with less direct instruction. Rist also observed that students in the top groups came from middle-class homes. Kindergarten teachers spent two to three times more time instructing these children than they did children in the slower, lower-class groups. Consequently, the "fast" group was able to complete the kindergarten curriculum while the "slower" groups did not. The slow group entered first grade already far behind their peers academically.

Theories of Cultural Background

Cultural Deprivation. In the 1960s researchers began to look away from the schools and toward the home to explain why minority and poor children failed in school. Educators from this perspective argued that a "culture of poverty" (Valentine 1968) explained the poor performance of minority children. The core of this explanation was the alleged "cultural disadvantage" of the children's home environment.

Children thought to be culturally deprived were described as those who lived in ghettos where they were not provided with proper nutrition or adequate health care. They attended poor schools, were not adequately prepared for jobs, and if and when they finished school, they repeated this "cycle of poverty" to the next generation. The homes in which they grew up—primarily the ethnic minorities—did not provide them with the tools they needed to succeed in school. It was believed that their parents did not read to them, did not encourage the kinds of home learning activities used by middle-class parents, and generally did not provide an intellectually stimulating environment. Minority children often came to school with a language or dialect different from middle-class or standard English (Bernstein 1977). Commonly referred to during the 1960s—and even sometimes today—as "culturally deprived" or "socially disadvantaged," these children were believed to be deprived of the cultural or social advantages necessary to succeed in school (Baratz and Baratz 1970; Erickson 1987).

Cultural deprivation theory was in large part responsible for the development of the compensatory education program. Schools were called upon to break this "cycle of poverty" through Head Start and the other preschool programs described above, including bilingual education and health and nutrition programs. Politicians and educators believed that if schools could intervene prior to entry into kindergarten, some of the effects of the home environment could be alleviated and the students would have a better chance to succeed in school.

The use of the term *culture* in this theory is misused in the anthropological sense. What was documented was not so much a culture per se, but a response to oppressive conditions of racial isolation, powerlessness, and poverty. Anthropologists argue that growing up in one culture does not mean being deprived of another and that the children described as "culturally deprived" actually functioned quite well in their own milieu. European-American middle-class youngsters in a barrio setting would be found similarly "culturally deprived."

The cultural deprivation theory was strongly criticized by scholars in the mid-1960s as ethnocentric. Rather than looking to the structure of schools or societal forces, blame was placed on the victims: individual children or minority groups (Ryan 1976). Educators, "frustrated by their difficulties in working with minority children, [were able] to place the responsibility for school failure outside the school" (Erickson 1987, p. 336).

Cultural Differences.   To counter cultural deprivation theory, social scientists began to look at differences or discontinuities between the cultures of the school and the home, particularly in communication and other interactions. Researchers working with Appalachian, African-American, Hawaiian, and American Indian students found that interactional difficulty in schools can be related to cultural differences in communication styles (Au and Mason 1981; Cazden, John, and Hymes 1974; D'Amato 1988; Erickson and Mohatt 1982; Heath 1983; Jordan 1984; Labov 1972; S. U. Phillips 1972; Piestrup 1973; Rist 1973).

According to the cultural difference explanation, school failure is a result of differences between the culturally derived white-middle-class communication patterns of the school and those of the students' home culture. Dissonance can be reduced if teachers are familiar with the verbal and nonverbal communication patterns of both the school and home culture. If educators can enhance classroom interaction and communication by adapting to and respecting the culture of minority students, they may be able to increase feelings of comfort and communicative competence in these students. As Erickson suggests:

> it may be that culturally congruent instruction depoliticizes cultural difference in the classroom, and that such depoliticization has important positive influences on the teacher–student relationship. Such a situation in the classroom might prevent the emergence of student resistance. (1984, p. 543)

These researchers believe that if classroom settings were structured so that cultural differences in communication patterns were reduced, achievement of minority students might be improved (Au and Mason 1981). Several examples of this type of research are presented here to give us a better understanding of this theory.

The work at the Kamehameha Early Education Program (KEEP) in Hawaii is a primary example of this research. On the basis of research in the local community, a team of teachers and researchers developed a way of teaching reading based on the communication style of the Hawaiian "talk story," in which conversational exchanges overlap rapidly in the cooperative building of a story. The basal reading program was reorganized so the everyday pattern of communication used by Hawaiian children replaced the Western structure in which children wait to be called on and speak one at a time. Researchers at the KEEP center documented increased academic achievement in reading through this more culturally congruent style (Au and Mason 1981).

The structures used in the KEEP program were then transplanted to a school with a Navajo population. Vogt (1985) reports that although the increased cultural congruency led to increased effectiveness in the reading programs for both groups of students, the original KEEP program had to be rather dramatically changed because participation structures were different for each group. What was culturally congruent

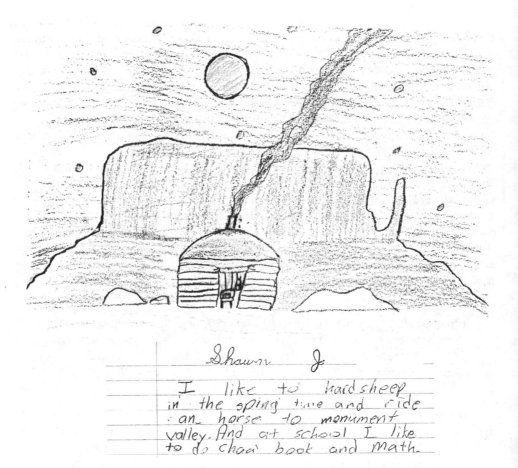

Shawn J.

I like to hard sheep in the sping time and ride an horse to monument valley. And at school I like to do chaa' book and math.

FIGURE 7.1 The Navajo student refers to his chaa' book, the Navajo equivalent of an English language vocabulary workbook. The chaa' book was introduced as a means of revitalizing and incorporating the Navajo language and culture in the Kayenta Intermediate School.

SOURCE: Shawn Johnson, Third Grade, Kayenta Intermediate School, Kayenta, AZ. (Teachers: Sylvia Dugi, Ruth Bradley; Principal: Debbie Braff; Superintendent: Joe Martin)

Jenny's Story

It's hard not knowin' how to read. A lot of these women, you know, they think it ain't that hard to read. Just sit down and read. . . . It's not easy. . . . That's why it was a little hard for me startin' to like . . . sound my words out . . . 'cause I talk different . . . 'cause I'm, you know . . . countrified. And my words don't come out the way they're supposed to.

SOURCE: Jenny is an urban Appalachian woman whose story of learning to read is beautifully portrayed by Victoria Purcell-Gates (1993).

---

for Hawaiian students didn't fit the cultural patterns of the Navajo students. (Figure 7.1 shows a drawing with a brief story by a Navajo student.)

In a study of Native Alaskan schools, Van Ness (1981) found that the interactional smoothness of lessons taught by a native teacher could be attributed to the teacher's cultural knowledge of the social situation. He argued that since social behavior is culturally organized, cultural congruency between the teacher and students allowed for smooth interactions even at the kindergarten level.

In a study of African-American children in two first-grade reading programs, Piestrup (1973) reported differences in reading achievement which she attributed to the way in which each teacher responded to the use of Black English Vernacular (BEV). The children whose use of dialect was often corrected during lessons obtained lower scores on reading tests and actually used more BEV than children who were permitted to use BEV in reading groups without correction. The uncorrected children actually scored higher in standardized reading tests, many above the national norms. Piestrup argued that when the dialect was treated as a barrier to communication, more time was spent in correcting the dialect than in actual reading.

Theories about cultural differences call for educators to understand the differences of minority students so as to establish a more culturally congruent classroom situation. However, critical theorists argue that doing this might be viewed as co-optation. Under the guise of cultural appropriateness, teachers can use a culturally congruent curriculum taught in culturally sensitive ways to lead students gradually into adopting the ideology of the dominant class. This is a less painful or coercive way to colonize the minds of students (McLaren 1989) and, for this reason, may be even more effective than force.

It is important to realize that its developers did not intend the cultural differences theory to be seen as the only way to view the problem or as a means to co-opt minority students. This explanation is restricted to the microlevel: a classroom view of factors in schooling that lead to minority student failure. It does not address the political and economic societal forces at the macrolevel which influence these students outside the structure of schools.

Examine a textbook in your subject area. Analyze the treatment of minority groups by examining the number of minority group members depicted in the text, the way in which they are described, and the extent to which they are integrated into the text rather than "highlighted" in a special section.

Labor Market Theory

A macrolevel or societal view of minority student failure is central to the work of John Ogbu. A core element in his theory is student perception of their chances in the labor market. Ogbu argues that the school performance of minority students is rooted in the connection they see between schooling and how successful they will be in the job market. If they see school as a means to become economically mobile, they are more likely to participate in the schooling process. If they do not consider school a viable avenue to employment, they will resist the experience.

Ogbu argues that minority students vary in their reactions to school according to their status as subordinated or migrant groups. Ogbu (1987) categorizes minority students into three groups: (1) autonomous minorities, (2) voluntary or immigrant minorities, and (3) involuntary or castelike minorities. *Autonomous minorities* are those who are born in the United States and who do not (or no longer) experience systematic discrimination, despite cultural differences from the mainstream such as religion or culture. Examples of autonomous minorities are Jews and Mormons.

Voluntary or immigrant minorities are groups who voluntarily moved to the United States from all parts of the globe for economic, political, or religious opportunities. They exhibit *primary cultural differences* from mainstream groups, including differences in language use, dress, food preferences, child-rearing, marital practices, and patterns of socializing and leisure. Despite these primary cultural differences, they view schooling as a way to advance socially and economically in this society, and they internalize "folk theories of success" congruent with those of dominant groups. These include viewing hard work and success in school as primary

---

Oliver's Story

Oliver, a 17-year-old from Nicaragua, describes his first day in a California school:

> That first day I went to Westmont, I didn't know what to do because everybody was speaking English and I didn't saw no one or I didn't heard no one speaking Spanish. . . . I saw a teacher, he looked to me Spanish. So I talked to him. I told him that I was looking for my classroom and he took me to my classroom and everything. He helped me a lot.

SOURCE: Center for Literary Studies 1992.

means for getting ahead economically. In addition, the immigrants' faith in "the system" is bolstered by the fact that most immigrants can favorably compare their present status in America with their past. No matter how bad their present situation here, life in the United States offers significantly more hope than life in their country of origin. These beliefs are fostered and reinforced among immigrant children by their families and communities.

Involuntary or castelike minorities were incorporated into the society forcibly either through conquest or colonization. African Americans who were enslaved and brought to this country, Mexican Americans who were conquered, American Indians who were conquered and forced onto reservations, and Puerto Rican Americans who were colonized in their own country are all examples of castelike minority groups. Involuntary or castelike minority groups exhibit *secondary cultural differences* from dominant groups. These are not as visible as primary differences; they developed *after* the castelike minority was forced into a subordinate status and can be thought of as coping mechanisms developed to address the psychological, political, economic, and social conflict inherent in interaction with the dominant culture.

Groups such as American Indians and African Americans have a long history of subordination and oppression in this society. They have had few opportunities to develop the favorable comparisons with U.S. society that immigrants construct; already at the bottom of the socioeconomic ladder, they can only compare up, to the unattainable status of more favored ethnic groups. Even though they may pay lip service to American myths about the efficacy of hard work and success in school, their actual experience of racism and oppression prevents them from believing that these efforts lead to socioeconomic success.

Their schooling experiences have involved deculturalization and forced assimilation, including stripping away of their primary language and culture. In place of indigenous ethnic identities, Ogbu suggests that castelike minorities

> appear to develop a new sense of social identity in opposition to the social identity of the dominant group after they have become subordinated, and they do so in reaction to the way that dominant-group members treat them in social, political, economic, and psychological domains. (1987, p. 323)

Fordham and Ogbu (1986; Fordham 1991) argue that involuntary minority students may engage in "cultural inversion," or resistance to the cultural behaviors and language forms of the dominant culture. They adopt cultural behaviors that specifically differentiate them from the dominant group. Getting good grades, speaking standard English, and listening to "white" music may be construed by their peers as "acting white"; speaking Black vernacular English, listening to rap music, being truant, and failing classes are oppositional behaviors which could be classified as secondary cultural differences. They also constitute a form of habitus (Bourdieu and Passeron 1977), or way of justifying why they do or do not succeed in the white man's world.

Fordham and Ogbu state that involuntary minority groups face a "job ceiling" constructed by a racist American society, which puts a limit on their economic opportunities, even if they are academically successful. In her ethnographic study of "Capital High School," located in a predominantly African-American section of Washington,

D.C., Fordham (1991) found that many students did poorly because they had difficulty reconciling school achievement and maintenance of African-American cultural identity. She found that the "fictive kinship" or sense of peoplehood of the African-American students she studied was a compelling reason for them to assign more importance to success with their peers and community than to success in the school community. Fordham said she was "flabbergasted" by the amount of resistance to "acting white" she found among the African-American students in her study. "I never believed it would be so pervasive, and so pronounced, and so academically stifling," she said in an interview (Schmidt 1993).

Although some researchers believe that Ogbu's typology does not fully characterize all minority groups (Deyhle 1991), his categorization nonetheless is useful because it provides a viable explanation why some groups succeed in school despite vast differences in language patterns and cultural understandings and why others with languages and cultures closer to those of European Americans fail. Also it is important to recognize that the negative responses of some minority students do not necessarily apply to all individuals. We would be stereotyping if we thought that all African Americans resisted schooling because it could be considered "acting white," or if we expected all immigrant minority students to succeed in school. These theories merely provide us with a way to consider the sociocultural and historical background students bring to school.

School Success through Accommodation

Some minority students succeed in school through *accommodation,* a process by which they maintain their ethnic identity while at the same time adopting whatever behaviors of the mainstream society they see as appropriate.

This process is illustrated in Gibson's (1988) study of a California high school where the Punjabi Sikh immigrant students were more serious about school and attained higher academic achievement than their European-American classmates. Gibson attributes their success to parental expectations as well as to cultural values that placed respect for family and authority at a premium. Punjabi parents urged their children to do well in school so they could compete in American society, but at the same time insisted that they maintain the home cultural values. Maintaining Punjabi cultural traditions earned them ridicule and harassment from non-Punjabi school peers, but family life provided a meaningful haven which not only buffered the prejudice at school but offered a viable cultural alternative to mainstream American life. Thus they were able to be accepted in their home milieu while accommodating to school life.

Student Resistance to School

In Chapter 3 we discussed resistance as a way for students to oppose the culture of the school. Resistance, in the form of acting out, tuning out, or dropping out of school, can be a way for minority students to reject degrading and racist experiences in school. Kunisawa (1988, pp. 62–63) found that the ten states with the highest

---

Jean's Story

People of rural Appalachia have been discriminated against for decades. I am one of these people. There is a distance between the poor whites and upper class whites that exists even today. As a child I knew these differences existed, but it was not until I started to school that I learned I was different. I lived in a rural area with no other children to identify with. Going to school in town, the only school in town, was a big step for me. There I learned about culture. Culture, I gathered, was something only the rich could attain or had a right to. I had a culture all my own but did not know this. My culture was not respected by my teachers or peers. Maybe they did not know that I lived in abject poverty not more than ten miles from the school. Maybe they did, but instead of bringing my family's lifestyle to light, I believe now that I was deculturalized. Soon I began to fit the mold, or tried to, although I never did. I had very few friends throughout school who understood my way of life. I could not have friends home from school to sleep over. I could not ask them to sleep in a cold house or to eat what food we had—food they were not used to like fried potatoes, gravy, and biscuits, when we were out of other staples such as beans and meal. I cannot deny that living in poverty has left its scars on me. Had I lived in Kentucky near the Appalachian coal mines, I would have fared better, no doubt, but living in rural Appalachia in east Tennessee, I was a fish out of water.

---

dropout rates all had minority enrollment exceeding 25 percent, six of them greater than 35 percent. A labor market explanation of these figures would be that these are students from castelike minority groups who do not see school as a viable avenue to economic success.

Resistance is also a way in which minority youth establish their own cultural identity while rejecting dominant-class ideologies embedded in schooling. Social scientists have documented resistance to school through the establishment of peer group cultures in working-class Caribbean, European-American, and African-American communities (e.g., McLaren 1980; McLeod 1987; Willis 1977). Deyhle's (1986) work with Navajo youth illustrates how minority youth resist the imposition of the dominant culture on their lives by forming a peer group centered on break dancing. This group became successful break dancers in an

> indifferent or negative school and community environment. As one young breaker explained with a smile, "It used to be cowboys and Indians. Now it is breakers and cowboys." With break dancing they had the motivation to assert themselves and prove to themselves and their peers that they were successful individuals. They worked hard, performed to the delight of many peers, and created a "space," even though it placed them on the fringe. (Deyhle 1986, p. 11)

Through this clique, Navajo youth were able to build self-confidence, achieve success through dancing, and establish an identity that challenged the type encouraged by school personnel.

Critical theorists view this active refusal to adopt the dominant group's beliefs as culture, class, and race resistance to a school-imposed culture which is contrary to their lives (McLaren 1989). They explain school failure of minority students, then, not from the standpoint of individual incompetencies, but from the perspective of a school system that attempts to impose on youth a culture they do not accept as a viable alternative to their own way of life. McLaren argues:

> Teachers must be aware of how school failure is structurally located and culturally mediated, so they can work both inside and outside of schools in the struggle for social and economic justice. Teachers must engage unyieldingly in their attempt to empower students both as individuals and as potential agents of social change by establishing a critical pedagogy that students can use in the classroom and in the streets. (1989, p. 221)

CONFLICTING PURPOSES OF SCHOOLING FOR MINORITY STUDENTS: CULTURAL ASSIMILATION OR CULTURAL PLURALISM?

Throughout the history of American schooling there has been a constant tension between those who believe in schooling for *assimilation* and those who believe in *cultural pluralism*.

Assimilationists believe that schools should teach all groups a common language, cultural heritage, and set of values that are distinctly American. In most cases the notion of the "melting pot" means following a European-American middle-class and upper-class model. As different cultural groups relinquish their ethnic identity, they are assimilated into American culture. The Americanization programs at the turn of the century tried to teach new immigrants the language, customs, and skills needed to fit into mainstream society. That notion is still current, evidenced in the "English only" legislation and the debate over the ongoing Anglocentric versus multicultural curricula.

Those who value cultural pluralism believe that minority groups can maintain their cultural identity while at the same time developing an allegiance to the nation. For example, a cultural pluralist believes that African Americans, Vietnamese, Irish, and Mexicans can retain the supporting benefits of their cultural groups while considering themselves part of a larger American culture. Rather than a "melting pot," one might envision this process as a "stew pot" or a "salad bowl" in which each ingredient maintains its own distinctive characteristics but enriches the final product. Cultural pluralists believe in affirming and celebrating diverse cultures in school policies, practices, and the curriculum. The whole issue of multiculturalism is one that challenges the definition of what it means to be an "American." Schools have long been the contested sites where people struggle with notions of ethnic and national identi-

> Did you ever think of what it feels like choosing a Barbie doll at Toys 'R Us? You know, white girls can choose from thirty Barbie models and black girls have only one.
>
> SOURCE: Teacher education student in children's literature class, quoted by her instructor.

ties. In the final chapter we will explore the issue of multicultural education more fully as we consider alternatives to the way we "do school."

These tensions between assimilationist and pluralist purposes of schooling are crucial to understanding minority student failure. Those who espouse assimilationist views explain this failure in terms of individual incompetency or a failure to take advantage of the educational system. They fail to recognize the limitations of schooling for minority students and end up "blaming the victim." Consequently, they do not question the structure and practices of schooling. Cultural pluralists, on the other hand, attempt to understand minority student culture and alter school practices to meet the needs of all students. Their goals are equality of educational opportunity as well as of economic opportunity. There are also those extremists who believe in neither cultural pluralism nor assimilation. These groups believe that there is no accommodation or compromise possible between their beliefs and those of other groups. They remain a challenge to societies which, however poorly, retain an ideology of tolerance (Burtonwood 1986).

SUMMARY

In this chapter we discussed key terms: race, ethnicity, ethnic minority group, racism, prejudice, and stereotyping. We then traced the development of the role of the federal government in schooling for minority students. In a discussion of research on schooling for minority children, we examined a theory of unequal resources and treatment, a cultural deprivation theory, a cultural differences theory, and a labor market explanation. Recent research illustrates how minority students respond to their schooling experiences through assimilation, accommodation, or resistance.

As you continue your explorations into cultures—your own as well as those of others—you might want to immerse yourself in the literature of various groups. There are wonderful novels and films available that can engage you in the lives of others, portraying the complexities of race/ethnicity, social class, gender, and sexual orientation. You may want to use the lists of multicultural books for children and adults available in current journals (cf., *Democracy and Education,* Winter 1991).

chapter **8**

Gender Equity in Schooling

Chapter Overview

INTRODUCTION

Children's identity as well as their school experiences are shaped by their membership in socioeconomic and/or ethnic minority groups. In Chapters 5 and 7 we demonstrated that students from ethnic minority or low socioeconomic groups have less access to equal educational opportunities than whites and/or students from more privileged social classes. Professionals concerned with equity in education generally direct their attention to the ways in which race, ethnicity, and socioeconomic class affect access and treatment. However, gender also directly affects the experiences children have in schools.

It has been common for researchers to investigate only the separate effects of race, class, and gender on children. More recently, scholars have called for examinations of the ways in which these three categories combine to affect school experiences. While it is impossible to separate out the effects of any of these three factors with real people in real schools, we have organized this book to examine each category separately. It is essential, therefore, to remember as you read that each student comes to school *both* as an engendered person *and* with membership in a particular ethnic and social class group.

Equality of Educational Opportunity or Gender Equity?

When we talk about equality of educational opportunity for girls and boys, women and men, we are referring to providing the same educational opportunities, support, and expectations regardless of gender. The implication that school programs will provide for females what they have been providing for males means that women's progress and the excellence of programs for them has been judged in terms of what has been thought standard and good practice for men. It does not examine the unique experiences of boys and girls in order to provide programs, structures, and practices that are geared toward the differing needs of both genders but that are nevertheless fair. This is certainly a beginning, but not nearly enough. The term *gender equity* goes beyond equality of educational opportunity. Maxine Greene argues:

> To work for sex equity in education and the social order as a whole is to move to alter the oppressiveness that makes individual autonomy antithetical to social concern. It is to rediscover what it signifies to be a person and a woman, while discovering what it signifies to transform. (1985, p. 42)

Understanding the Terms *Sex* and *Gender*

As a prelude to our discussions of school experiences based on gender, we need to clarify some terms. **Sex** and **gender** do not carry the same meaning and therefore are not interchangeable. *Sex*, a visible and usually permanent identifying attribute which is acquired at birth, refers to the physical characteristics associated with being male or female. *Gender* is a more inclusive term which refers not only to physiological characteristics but to learned cultural behaviors and understandings. Historian Joan Wallach Scott reminds us that usage of the word *gender*

> seems to have first appeared among American feminists who wanted to insist on the fundamentally social quality of distinctions based on sex. The word denoted a rejection of the biological determinism implicit in the use of such terms as "sex" or "sexual difference." . . . Instead, gender becomes a way of denoting "cultural constructions"—the entirely social creation of ideas about appropriate roles for women and men. It is a way of referring to the exclusively social origins of the subjective identities of men and women. Gender is, in this definition, a social category imposed on a sexed body. (1988, pp. 31–32)

Another useful perspective on the differences between sex and gender is quoted in *A Feminist Dictionary:*

> Gender is often used as a synonym for *sex*, i.e. biological male or femaleness. However, it is also used, particularly by contemporary writers, to refer to the socially imposed dichotomy of masculine and feminine roles and character traits. Sex is physiological, while gender, in the latter usage, is cultural. The distinction is a crucial one, and one which is ignored by unreflective supporters of the status quo who assume that cultural norms of masculinity and femininity are "natural," i.e. directly and preponderantly determined by biology. (Warren 1980, p. 181, quoted in Kramarae and Treichler 1985, pp. 173–174)

Recent scholarship has used *gender* as a synonym for "women" (Scott 1988). The title of this chapter, "Gender Equity in Schooling," may be seen as an example of this use. Though much of our discussion here is centered on the experiences of girls and women, we need to remember that these experiences are in relation to those of boys and men, so as you read the chapter, be sure to consider what the research shows for *all* children in school settings.

Gender Socialization and Differential Treatment

Children's gender determines the ways in which they are socialized, first by their families and later by school personnel, to learn what are considered to be appropriate male and female roles. Different patterns of behavior are learned by boys and girls through interaction with their primary caretakers and peers. Sex role stereotyping occurs when children are socialized to behave primarily in ways that are considered to be gender appropriate. For example, girls may be encouraged to be nurturing and cooperative, while boys may be encouraged to be aggressive and competitive. These socialization patterns lead to different and unequal expectations for males and females in this society.

The differential patterns of socialization and treatment in schools puts females in a position very similar to that of disadvantaged minority groups. Although females constitute 51 percent of the U.S. population, they do fit our definition of minority status. You will recall that attributes of minority group status were identifiability, differential power, differential treatment, and group awareness (Dworkin and Dworkin 1982). Hacker (1951), one of the first sociologists to utilize an understanding of race relations to create a theoretical framework for examining gender relationships, argued for the inclusion of women in minority group studies. Similarities between women and ethnic minorities in terms of group visibility, discrimination in the labor market, stereotypes attributed to them by majority members, and their accommodation to such treatment suggest that knowledge from other minority groups could be helpful in understanding women (Dworkin and Dworkin 1982).

Research data clearly illustrate that the treatment females receive in schools is neither the same as nor equal to that given males, just as other categories considered to be minorities—the socioeconomically disadvantaged, handicapped, and culturally different—also receive unequal treatment from members of the mainstream, able-bodied middle class. Despite a growing body of literature detailing sexist practices in schools, gender is a sorely neglected category in recent reform literature calling for equity and excellence in schooling. Tetreault and Schmuck (1985) report that gender is virtually ignored as an equity issue in schooling by at least eight of the major commission reports. They argue:

> Gender is not a relevant category in the analysis of excellence in schools. When gender was considered, it appears to merely embellish the traditional—and male—portrait of the school. The proposed vision for excellence in the schools is of education for the male student in the public and productive sphere. Because gender, as a relevant concept, is absent, even Title IX is ignored. Issues of gender in relation to policy, students, curricula, and faculty are not identified nor treated as educational problems to be solved. The goal of excellence does not even have the female student in mind. (1985, p. 63)

An analysis of 35 reports issued by commissions and special task forces regarding education reform revealed that 60 percent had a female membership of less than 30 percent. In addition, few of the reports defined educational issues in terms of gender or suggested recommendations for changes regarding women's issues (AAUW 1992).

This chapter focuses on gender issues related to equality of educational opportunity, gender equity, and differential outcomes in academic achievement and economic opportunities for men and women. We will first discuss how the socialization process acts to construct gender roles in American society. Next is a discussion of sexism and the legislation designed to fight sexist practices in educational institutions. We will then provide an overview of how sexist practices are still evident in both the formal and hidden curricula of schooling. Finally we will discuss how sexism makes the outcomes of schooling—academic achievement and occupational place-ment—different for males and females. Despite two decades of feminist activism, re-search detailing discriminatory practices in schools, and legislation designed to en-sure equality of access and treatment, females in this society do *not* have equal access to educational and economic opportunities because of their status as women. The chapter ends with a discussion of feminism and the ways we can use feminist theories to understand schooling.

THE DEVELOPMENT OF GENDER ROLES

Children learn what it means to belong to any society through a socialization process which begins in infancy. Interacting verbally and nonverbally with family members and other caretakers, they learn behavior appropriate to the cultural norms. As part of this process, they learn how to be males and females (Maccoby 1966; Maccoby and Jacklin 1974).

In a summary of research on sex role differences, Lee and Gropper (1974) report that males and females are socialized to different lifestyles through child-rearing prac-tices which entail differential expectations. Despite learning a common language, they differ in their verbal and nonverbal expressions. They are socialized to belong to sex-segregated social groups, wear gender-appropriate clothing, prefer activities and toys associated with one sex or another, and develop different competencies based on those activities. As we see from Lisa's story (see box on p. 254), by the age of 4, children see the sexes as opposite and understand concepts of "girls' things" and "boys' things." In preschool and kindergarten, even in the 1980s, girls are more likely to be found playing in the doll corner while boys spend their time with the building blocks and trucks. By 6 or 7, children have a clear idea about gender roles, prefer sex-segregated play, and tend to strive to conform with stereotypic gender roles. In children between 8 and 10, researchers have found more flexibility in notions about occupational roles for men and women. There is somewhat less sex segregation in their play during this period, but they still tend to prefer same-sex play. In early adoles-cence girls and boys tend to adhere more rigidly to stereotypic gender roles (AAUW 1992).

Television and other media play a crucial role in transmitting the culture's sex role behaviors and values. Children watch television and movies, listen to popular music, and are confronted daily with advertisements—in magazines, in newspapers, on TV, on buses. Popular culture transmits messages about the values, behaviors, and communication styles of men and women, generally in stereotyped and often deroga-tory forms. We need only flip through the pages of popular magazines to see the gender models offered to young people.

Find images of gender roles in current examples of popular culture. Com-pare them to examples found in media from the 1940s, 1950s, and 1960s.

Lisa's Story

I overhead the following conversation between two four-year-old male children at the local child development center. The first child has very liberal parents and they allow him to dress himself in the morning for school. This child has an older female sibling and decided to wear one of her pink shirts. The second child looked at the first child's shirt and said, "You have on a pink shirt and I know that is a girl color. You look like a girl! Boys wear blue." The first child argued, "No, I am not a girl." At this point I casually mentioned that all different kinds of people like different colors. I added, "Look, my shirt is blue and I'm a girl, and Joey (my husband) has a pink shirt that is one of his favorites." The children listened to what I had to say and then decided to play in a different area of the classroom.

Children's literature has always played a crucial role in the socialization process as well. Those of us who grew up in the 1950s and 1960s vividly remember the Nancy Drew mysteries, with Nancy fearlessly stepping into dangerous situations. Nancy provided a courageous, intelligent female role model for young women. In contrast, in a recent study about a current series of children's books, The Baby-sitters Club Books, Jill Goodman (1993) found that the girls there were depicted as selfless, capable of balancing untold family burdens and responsibilities, and constantly nagged by guilt. Since the series was first printed in 1986, over 78 million Baby-sitters Club Books have been printed, most sold to girls between 8 and 12. Goodman captures the main message of the series: "Life's work is assigned according to gender, and women's work is caring, nurturing, worrying about relations, making things right, and feeling guilty" (p. 10). In addition to reading the books, children caught up in the world of the Baby-sitters Club can watch Baby-sitters Club videos, play with Baby-sitters Club dolls, and use Baby-sitters Club cosmetics, backpacks, and sleeping bags (Goodman 1993). This bombardment of values is a powerful socializer for young women.

How were you socialized to become a man or woman? What toys did you play with as a child? What books did you read? Were there gender messages in these? What messages about gender roles were you given from parents, teachers, and other adults as you were growing up? What messages do you receive today from the media and popular culture about men's and women's roles in society?

Lyn Mikel Brown and Carol Gilligan (1992), along with colleagues at the Harvard Project on the Psychology of Women and the Development of Girls, have made major contributions to our understanding of ways girls are socialized from childhood through adolescence. In *Meeting at the Crossroads: Women's Psychology and Girls' Development,* Brown and Gilligan explore the lives of young girls through extensive interviews, documenting a silencing of their voices as they move through adolescence.

> For girls at adolescence to say what they are feeling and thinking often means to risk, in the words of many girls, losing their relationships and finding themselves powerless and all alone. Over the years of our study, even as they became more sophisticated cognitively and emotionally, young girls who had been outspoken and courageous in both an ordinary and a heroic sense became increasingly reluctant to say what they were feeling and thinking or to speak from their own experience about what they knew. Honesty in relationships began to seem "stupid"—it was called "selfish" or "rude" or "mean." (1992, p. 217)

The researchers found that as young girls begin to understand the relational cost of expressing real thoughts and feelings, they respond by silencing themselves and behaving in ways considered more appropriate for "good little girls." They may hide their thoughts or feelings so as to avoid hurting people or risking relationships.

> [As] girls mature and enter mid-adolescence, their voices become more tentative and conflicted. Their responses reveal a sometimes debilitating tension between caring for themselves and caring for others, between their understanding of the world and their awareness that it is not appropriate to speak or act on this understanding. (AAUW 1992, p. 12)

What are the implications of the Brown and Gilligan study for girls in middle and high schools? How can this information about girls' development influence classroom interactions and expectations of young women?

A national survey by the AAUW in 1990 addressed the issue of self-esteem in children and adolescents and found that 69 percent of males and 60 percent of girls in elementary schools reported being "happy the way I am." The same question given to high school students produced a significant drop in the positive response—46 percent of males and 29 percent of females. These data varied across ethnic lines at both elementary and high school levels. In the elementary group 55 percent of white girls, 65 percent of African-American girls, and 68 percent of Hispanic girls reported being "happy the way I am." In high school the numbers declined, with 22 percent of white girls, 30 percent of Hispanic girls, and 58 percent of African-American girls agreeing with the statement. The authors are quick to point out that the African-American girls did not have high levels of self-confidence when it came to academics (AAUW 1992).

EQUALITY OF EDUCATIONAL OPPORTUNITIES FOR WOMEN

Differential socialization patterns in the society lead to differences in the goals of schooling for males and females. Men and women are expected to play different roles and are trained to fulfill these roles. These roles change with social and economic changes in society. One way to examine changes in the purposes of schooling for women is to look at the dramatic changes that have taken place in educational practices since the turn of the century. The following fictional vignettes, based on actual experiences, provide a sense of what schools were like for American women since the early part of the twentieth century. The stories, which span three generations of one family, describe school experiences for white, working-class women and consequently do not capture the experiences of women from other social class or cultural backgrounds.

Changes in Twentieth-Century American Schools for Women

Time: *1912*

Place: *A Small Rural High School in East Tennessee.*   Emily, the 15-year-old daughter of a farmer, attends a school which was established in 1903 as a "model" rural school. The school was funded with the help of northern philanthropists for the purpose of training young men in the art of agriculture. The school is expected "to make better and wiser husbandmen of the country boys and more economical and skillful housewives of the farmers' daughters" (local newspaper, July 24, 1903). Emily is very happy attending this school, which offers the skills she will need later in her role as a housewife. There is a department of domestic economy for the girls "consisting of a cooking school and instruction in good substantial and fancy needlework," and in the second-year sewing classes the girls learn "the use of the needle, the highest of the feminine arts."

A U.S. Bulletin report about this school states that "if the subject to be discussed deals with technical phases of agriculture in which they are not interested, the women will meet in another room and discuss some problem of housekeeping. The discussions are made as practical as possible" (Allison 1989). Emily attends many classes in the department of domestic economy with her female classmates. They are becoming proficient in sewing, cooking, and the general management of the household. Emily hopes that soon she will meet a man who will make a good husband and provide a comfortable life for her in this community. She wants her life to revolve around the farm, the home, and the children.

Time: *1956*

Place: *A Neighborhood Elementary School in a Small New Jersey Town.*
Emily's granddaughter, Jennifer, lives in a small New Jersey town across the

---

river from Philadelphia. Emily's daughter had moved from East Tennessee with her husband looking for work in the 1940s and settled here. Jennifer is in the third grade at the elementary school just three blocks away from her home. Each day she walks back and forth from school to home twice. Like the rest of the children, she goes home at noon to eat lunch. When she arrives at the school yard in the morning and again after lunch, she uses the entry on the girl's side. The girls' playground is separate from the boys' and about one third the size. The boys usually play football and baseball on their side and the girls jump rope and play hopscotch on theirs. When the bell rings, announcing the time for classes to begin, the girls line up according to class in front of the door on their side of the school yard. The first-grade girls are on the far right and sixth-grade girls on the far left. The boys do the same on the other side of the building.

Jennifer is in the top reading group. She knows this because her group is always called to read first and reads more stories than the other groups. Like everyone who lives in this town, all the characters in Jennifer's reading books have white skin. The boys in the stories play outside, running, playing, and building things. They often help the girls when they get in trouble. The girls tend to play inside quietly with their dolls. Jennifer and her brothers and sisters tend to play much like this at home. She likes to play school and fantasizes about being a teacher when she grows up.

Time: *1962*

Place: *A Junior High School in a Small New Jersey Town.*   Jennifer is now in eighth grade at the local junior high school, which is about a mile from her home. In addition to her "regular" school subjects such as English, math, history and science, she takes home economics and physical education. These subjects she takes with other girls. In seventh grade the girls take cooking and in eighth grade they take sewing. The boys take "shop" or industrial arts at this time. The males and females are separated for their gym classes, with girls engaged in such activities as field hockey, lacrosse, and tennis and the boys engaged in football, baseball, and track. Jennifer has joined an after-school club in industrial arts for girls. She has enjoyed making several projects from plastic and wood using the tools and machinery available in the shop. She feels that it isn't fair for the girls in the school to be excluded from the regular shop classes during the school day and petitions the administration to open these classes to both sexes. Unfortunately, despite the support of other students and the shop teacher, Jennifer's request is denied on the basis that females do not need to learn the skills offered in the industrial arts program.

Time: *1966*

Place: *A High School in the Same Town of New Jersey.*   Jennifer dreams of becoming an elementary school teacher. She believes that teaching and nursing are the occupations open to her. In teaching, she would be able to have a career and still marry and raise a family. Jennifer's parents, who did not attend college, have never talked with her about going on for further educational or career pursuits. They expect that she will marry and raise a family as her mother did. Jennifer would like to go to a state teacher's college but doesn't know how to begin the process. She talks with the guidance counselor at her school, Mr. Jones, who is surprised at her interest in college. He discourages her from this pursuit, knowing that her parents do not have the money to support a college education. Jennifer is surprised and hurt that Mr. Jones does not seem willing to help her. She knows that her grades are good; she has earned high scores on her SATs and has been a member of the National Honor Society. She has not been involved in school activities because she worked four hours every day after school and six hours each Saturday. She remembers last year when her sewing teacher gave her a "D" one grading period for not modeling a knitted sweater she made in the school fashion show. It was an evening she was committed to work.

Jennifer decides to apply to college without help from the counselor. She uses the money she has saved for the five applications she sends and is pleased that spring to receive acceptances from those colleges.

Time: *1988*

Place: *A Large Suburban High School in East Tennessee.*   Jennifer's daughter, Susan, is now a senior at a sprawling suburban high school in East Tennessee, the home of her maternal grandmother. Jennifer decided to move the family back to Tennessee following her divorce. Her love of the family's original home place precipitated this move. Susan attends the same school that her great-grandmother attended in the early part of the century, but there is now a newly built, consolidated high school in its place. Much has changed since her great-grandmother attended classes here. Susan is offered the same choices as the male students. All students are able to take whatever subjects they choose and join whatever clubs and sports they want. Susan is the editor of the school newspaper and is also involved with a variety of school activities. She intends to go on to college but has not decided on a field of study. She was encouraged by the recruiters on College Night to pursue studies in law, medicine, computers, veterinary science, and engineering. Whatever she decides, she looks forward to a profession that will be challenging and rewarding.

Time: *1994*

Place: *A Large University in the Southeast.*   Last year Susan completed a B.A. degree in Liberal Arts. She began college with a major in the sciences, hoping to go to veterinary school after completing her undergraduate degree. After the first two years she took courses in several different programs and finally switched her major to anthropology. She felt that she didn't belong in the sciences. She enjoyed some of the coursework but seemed to have difficulty making connections with her teachers. She met with her professors only when it was time to get advice on her schedule. Susan had little contact with the one woman professor in the program. In anthropology she was excited about the courses and felt that the professors were supportive and interested in her.

Now Susan is in a Master's program in anthropology, but doesn't really know what she wants to do with this degree. She has been toying with the idea of going into education. She has always liked working with young children and believes that her anthropology and sociology courses have helped her become interested in people who come from a wide variety of backgrounds. She thinks she would like to try teaching in an inner-city school but hasn't had much experience working with kids from the city. Since she relied on her mother's support all through college, she feels increased pressure to be financially independent. She has heard that teachers don't make much money, but teaching would be a challenge.

What do you think Susan will decide to do about her career? What are some possible explanations for Susan's change in major in undergraduate school? How do your experiences compare with Susan's?

These short vignettes illustrate some of the changes that have taken place for women. Does this mean that discrimination based on gender differences no longer exists? Unfortunately, although sexism is less explicitly practiced, it is still evident in American society. Female students like Susan often *believe* that they will have complete and equal access to educational and economic opportunities. Expectations about the role of men and women have changed considerably since the turn of the century. Particularly as a result of the feminist movement of the 1970s and 1980s, there is greater consciousness about gender-based inequity and subsequent expansion of opportunities for women. However, sexism is still evident in this society; it has just become more subtle.

What Is Sexism?

Sexism refers to "a social relationship in which males denigrate females" (Humm 1990, pg. 202) or to "discrimination against women, as in restricted career choices, job opportunities, etc." (Webster's New Universal Unabridged Dictionary 1992). Sexism, analogous to racism, is the belief that women are inferior to men and justifies discrimination based on gender. Sexism is generally used to describe prejudice against females, although it "indicates any arbitrary stereotyping of males and females on the basis of their gender" (Guidelines . . . in McGraw-Hill . . . Publications 1980, p. 346).

It is important for us as educators to understand and confront sexism in the structures, practices, and curricula of schooling. Researchers in the past three decades have examined how sexist practices affect girls' and women's experiences in school settings. We explore this research in more detail through the chapter.

Think about your own schooling experiences. How did being a female or male play a role in these experiences? Have you had experiences in which you felt sexism was involved? You might want to share some of these experiences with classmates.

Federal Legislation Related to Gender Discrimination

In 1972 Congress passed Title IX of the Education Amendments to the Civil Rights Act to address issues of sex discrimination in educational programs that received federal funding. This legislation begins by stating:

> [N]o person in the United States shall, on the basis of sex, be excluded from participation in, be denied the benefits of, or be subjected to discrimination under any education program or activity receiving federal financial assistance.

In other words, any educational institution receiving federal funds must provide equal opportunity for both sexes to participate in all programs and activities of that institution. According to Title IX, practices once common in schools, such as subject area segregation based on gender, are no longer legal. In our story above, the policy that excluded Jennifer from participating in "male" classes such as industrial arts was prohibited by federal legislation after 1972. This legislation was an important force in changing explicit sexist practices in public schools. It has given students like Susan more freedom of choice in their academic and extracurricular programs than their mothers and grandmothers had. Susan's male colleagues likewise are able to enroll in once "female" courses such as cooking.

Despite Title IX, researchers have found that sexist practices still exist in schools. Tetreault (1986) noted that research on sex-role biases in schools in combination with the movement for gender equity in the 1970s and 1980s have resulted in significant changes in the past fifteen years. These changes include increased enrollment of women in science and mathematics, increased expenditures for women's athletic programs, and a higher number of female elementary principals. The use of gender-inclusive language (see Appendix) and inclusion of women in textbooks are also a result of a movement toward sex equity. However, Tetreault argues that despite equal access, separate provisions for male activities continue to be the norm. The different educational needs of men and women are ignored and women are implicitly socialized into "the behaviors of men in the public sphere" (Tetreault 1986). Shakeshaft supports this view:

> [U]nfortunately, few schools provide an equitable culture in which all students and faculty members can grow. Most offer white males more options in an environment that is hospitable to their needs. Females and members of minority groups, on the other hand, must obtain their education in systems

that are at best indifferent and at worst hostile to them. Women and members of minority groups learn that their concerns, their lives, their cultures are not the stuff of schooling. They discover that school is not a psychologically or physically safe environment for them and that they are valued neither by the system nor by society. (Shakeshaft 1986, p. 500)

Women's athletics was particularly affected by Title IX, since it required the funding of athletics programs to be changed significantly. Acosta and Carpenter (1990) reported that the number of sports programs had increased over the intervening eighteen years, enabling more women to participate at all levels. The number of young women participating in high school athletics rose from 4 percent in 1972 to 26 percent in 1987 (AAUW 1992).

However at the collegiate level women's programs consistently receive less funding and have less adequate facilities than those of men. There has also been a significant decrease in the number of women coaches. Prior to Title IX 90 to 100 percent of coaches on women's teams were female, but by 1990 the percentage had dropped to 47.3 percent. In 1972, 90 percent of women's intercollegiate sports programs were under the directorship of a female athletic director; in 1990 this percentage had dropped to 5.9 percent. Women today hold only about 32 percent of the administrative positions in women's collegiate sports programs (Acosta and Carpenter 1990). Veri argues:

This decrease was marked by the removal of previously established female coaches and administrators and fewer opportunities for women to enter the field in those capacities. These opportunities decreased because colleges and universities chose to instead place men in those positions. In essence, it was male sports leaders' reactions to women's increased athletic participation that caused women to become victims of yet another backlash. (1993, p. 15)

GENDER DIFFERENCES IN THE FORMAL CURRICULUM

The formal school curriculum serves as the core for the daily activities of teachers and students. Earlier in this chapter we described a school in 1903 which proudly prescribed a separate curriculum for males and females so that they could be prepared for the work they would be doing after high school. Girls were taught homemaking and needlecrafts and boys were schooled in the science of agriculture. This separate curriculum reflected the supposed needs and values of the community at that time. Today, because of changed perceptions of gender roles, Title IX of the Elementary and Secondary Education Act mandates that schools must permit males and females to study the same curriculum. However, in reality, gender-based differential patterns of enrollment in courses, different patterns of treatment for men and women in classes, and inequities in how women are portrayed in the formal curricular content still exist.

Gender-Identified Subject Matter

Tradition categorizes curricular content areas by gender. Math, science, and many of the vocational areas (auto shop, woodworking, drafting) historically have been considered by educators, parents, and students as more appropriate for males. The humanities and a few vocational courses (bookkeeping, typing, shorthand, cosmetology) are perceived to be more relevant for females. Gender differences according to subject matter continue, particularly in math and the sciences.

Although there is little gender difference in enrollment in beginning science and math, these differences do emerge at the more advanced levels. More men than women take higher-level courses (AAUW 1992). Fewer women enroll in the most advanced math courses in secondary schools (Fennema and Leder 1990). A 1991 survey by the Council of Chief State School Officers reported that 60 percent of the high school students enrolled in first-year physics and 70 percent of the second-year students are male. A 1987 report prepared for the Committee on Research in Mathematics, Science, and Technology Education reports that males spend more time on microcomputers and are more likely to participate in after-school computer-related activities. More males than females take computer programming courses and go on to high-paying positions in the computer industry. The authors of this report attribute these inequalities to a belief that quantitative fields are a male domain.

Sorensen and Hallinan (1987) studied 1,477 students in 48 fourth- to sixth-grade classes in ten public schools to determine the effects of gender on ability-grouped math classes. Analyzing standardized achievement test scores, the researchers found that females are more likely to be assigned to the wrong ability group than males. Girls with high aptitude in math were less likely to be assigned to high-ability math groups than boys with similar aptitudes. Sorensen and Hallinan suggest that the teachers' placement decisions "may reveal" discrimination based on gender expectations. This study supports the notion that quantitative subjects "belong" to males.

Girls tend to have less confidence in their math abilities than do boys (AAUW 1992). Fennema and Sherman (1977) found a drop in girl's confidence in math during middle elementary school, preceding a decrease in their academic achievement. It is not difficult to understand how lack of confidence would be a serious obstacle to continued pursuit of a subject.

In a Michigan study on physical education, students reported gender bias in their perceptions of sports activities. All sports were seen as male domains with the exception of gymnastics, jumping rope, figure skating, and cheerleading. Despite legal requirements for gender equity in programs, this study found that 70 percent of the school districts surveyed did not provide girls with athletic opportunities comparable to those available for boys (AAUW 1992).

Gender-Based Staffing

Segregation of the curriculum along gender lines is evident in the staffing of these courses. Since more men than women go into areas of quantitative subject matter, more men teach in these areas. Kelly and Nihlen (1982) report that teaching staffs are segregated by subject matter, with women predominant in language arts, foreign languages, and to some extent social sciences, while men dominate the math, science, computer, and engineering courses. Gender differences by subject matter reinforce to students the already clear message about what is "appropriate" knowledge for males and females.

In higher education, college classrooms are still predominantly taught by men, particularly at the senior ranks. Recent figures show that 90 percent of the full professors on U.S. campuses are male, compared with 91 percent a decade ago (Sadker, Sadker, and Klein 1986). Women at the post-secondary level find fewer female role models in the college classroom or curriculum.

Portrayal of Women in Curricular Materials

The way in which females have been depicted in textbooks has changed since the early 1970s. Feminist criticism of curricular materials has pushed publishers to portray female characters in more diverse roles. Whereas Jennifer was provided with a limited number of female role models in her texts—teachers, nurses, and housewives—her daughter Susan was more likely to read texts depicting women as doc-

---

Ten Quick Ways to Analyze Children's Books for Sexism and Racism

1. *Check the illustrations.* Look for stereotypes. Look for tokenism. Who's doing what (active, leadership roles versus passive, subservient roles)?
2. *Check the story line.* Standard for success (via "white" behavior or extraordinary abilities). Resolution of problems (are minorities the "problem" or are problems solved by Anglos)?
3. *Look at the lifestyles.* Check for inaccuracies, inappropriate or oversimplified depictions of other cultures such as American Indians.
4. *Consider the relationships between people.* Who has power, exhibits leadership, and solves problems, and how are families depicted?
5. *Note the heroes.* Whose interest is a particular hero serving?
6. *Consider the effects on a child's self-image.*
7. *Consider the author's or illustrator's background.* Assess his or her qualification to write about the topic.
8. *Examine the author's perspective.* Look for a particular ethnocentric perspective.
9. *Watch for loaded words.* Look for words with offensive overtones.
10. *Look at the copyright date.* Older books are often more laden with racism than those published more recently.

SOURCE: Council on Interracial Books for Children 1980.

tors, telephone repair personnel, and scientists. However, although change in the portrayal of women in textbooks can be observed, "rarely is there dual and balanced treatment of women and men, and seldom are women's perspectives and cultures presented on their own terms" (AAUW 1992, p. 62).

In an evaluation of recent editions of six popular basal reading texts, Hitchcock and Tompkins (1987) determined the number of male and female main characters as well as the range and frequency of occupations for female characters. Out of 1,121 stories, females were portrayed in 37 occupations, compared with 5 occupations in 1961–1963 readers and 23 occupations in 1969–1971 readers. In the recent editions males were main characters in 18 percent of the stories; females, in 17 percent. Surprisingly, the main characters in three times as many stories were now categorized as "other"—neutral characters such as talking trees or neutered characters such as animals. Although there has been some effort to portray women in a variety of occupational roles, Hitchcock and Tompkins argue that textbook publishers appear to be avoiding questions of sexism by creating neutral characters.

A 1989 national study of book-length works used in high school English courses found only one woman author and no minority authors in the ten most frequently assigned books. Applebee (1989) argues that there has been little change from similar lists in 1907 and 1963, on which required books were dominated by white, male authors.

Tetreault (1986) reported that although publishers have responded to pressure to include women in textbooks, they depict "outstanding women who contributed in areas or movements traditionally dominated by men" (p. 230). She argues that women have been tacked on to a history which continues to be dominated by men's values and perspectives. She calls for a gender-balanced curriculum which also looks at ordinary women's everyday lives in traditional roles as well as their efforts to move beyond these boundaries.

Peggy McIntosh (1983) provides the following curricular typology that we can use to analyze the treatment of women and minorities in texts:

Phase I: Womanless and All-White History

Phase II: Exceptional Women and Persons of Color in History

Phase III: Women and People of Color as Problems, Anomalies, Absences, or Victims in History

Phase IV: Women's Lives or the Lives of People of Color *as* History

Phase V: History Redefined and Reconstructed to Include Us All

Gretchen Wilbur (1991) gives us another way to think about curricula that are gender fair. She argues that a gender-fair curriculum has the following six attributes:

1. It *acknowledges* and affirms variation within and across groups of people.
2. It is *inclusive* in that both females and males can find and identify positive messages about themselves.
3. It is *accurate,* presenting data-based, verifiable information.

4. It is *affirmative* in that it values the worth of individuals and groups.
5. It is *representative* with a balance of multiple perspectives.
6. It is *integrated* in that the experiences, needs, and interests of men and women are woven together. (AAUW 1992)

Using these approaches as well as others may help you analyze your own work as a teacher in providing equitable school experiences for your students.

Choose several 1990s texts at different levels—elementary, middle school, high school, and college. Analyze these texts using McIntosh's typology or Wilbur's list of attributes for gender-fair curricula. You may want to compare them with earlier editions of the texts.

Silences in the Curriculum

In an examination of the formal curriculum, the most important aspect is not what is *presented* about women, but what is omitted. Curricular silences, that is, what is left out of the text, sends a clear message to students about what is important and what is peripheral knowledge. Research on the portrayal of women in texts indicates that females, rather than sharing central roles with men, are either ignored or relegated to domestic roles (Kelly and Nihlen 1982). A view of women as home workers profoundly affects what is taught, since the focus of the curriculum is to prepare students for future work roles. Schools will never be able to broaden instructional opportunities for women as long as cultural beliefs that men work and women stay at home prevail.

An example of how women are portrayed is found in an analysis of social studies texts for courses such as World and American History. Males dominate these texts. Women's contributions to the labor union or suffrage movement are minimized. Females are portrayed as wives, social workers, nurses, and helpmates to men (Kelly and Nihlen 1982; Treckler 1973), despite the long history of female participation in the professions and even the industrial labor force, especially in wartime. Men are *never* portrayed as caretakers or seen in traditionally female roles, such as secretaries, nurses, or day-care workers. Feminists sardonically note that the word used to describe the course is *his*-tory rather than *her*-story. They call for a rewriting of such courses to include the roles women have played (Scott 1987).

Although more recent textbooks have made efforts to incorporate women's roles, history remains the study of male military matters. Students learn American political history as a chronology of the various wars that were waged from the American Revolution through the Vietnam War. The "failure to integrate female experiences into general curriculum drives home the message that girls and their experiences are somehow 'other,' that they are not part of general literature and history" (Shakeshaft 1986, p. 501).

Select a new social studies textbook at any grade level. Analyze the content of the text for gender differences. How is the text organized? What are the major topics covered? How does the text portray women and women's issues? Compare your findings to a social studies text that is ten or twenty years old.

GENDER IN THE IMPLICIT CURRICULUM

The question of gender equity in the curriculum goes beyond the formal curriculum to incorporate implicit or hidden messages given to students (see Chapter 6 for discussion on the hidden curriculum). This section examines how ideas about sex roles are transmitted every day in schools.

Implicit Messages in the Patriarchy of Schooling

The structure of schooling has been described by educational historians as an "educational harem" (Tyack 1974) because it relies heavily on a hierarchical system in which male administrators manage female teachers and support staff. This harem-like structure remains the norm today, as we have noted in earlier chapters. Principals dominate the policy decisions that affect the daily running of the school, and women often find themselves in subordinate positions. This administrative structure clearly tells students that men hold positions of authority and power in society while women play subordinate roles, having control only over the children in their classrooms.

Implicit Messages in Classroom Organization

The sex of students is often used as an organizational tool for structuring activities. In elementary schools boys and girls are lined up separately to walk to lunch or to the restrooms. Some teachers ask children to read aloud in groups according to gender. Classroom and playground games pit the girls against the boys. Although this practice may seem innocuous, separation by gender as an organizational strategy is unnecessary and results in differential treatment based on gender.

Classroom jobs may be distributed on the basis of teachers' perceptions of appropriate sex roles. In one first-grade classroom (K. P. Bennett 1986) male students were asked to perform the tasks that would take them out of the room, such as delivering messages to the principal's office. These jobs were highly valued by the children and were considered by the teacher to require a higher level of responsibility. Female students were asked to perform chores inside the classroom such as picking up papers, straightening library books, or erasing the blackboard—traditional roles for women. A principal who comes into a classroom asking for "four strong boys" to carry some books is providing a message that boys play active roles and can handle chores that require physical strength, while girls do not.

Shakeshaft reports that research on gender and schooling provides us with two messages: "First, what is good for males is not necessarily good for females. Second, if a choice must be made, the education establishment will base policy and instruction on that which is good for males" (Shakeshaft 1986, p. 500). She argues that the school organization would better fit the needs of females if single-sex rather than coeducational schools were available. This argument is based on research findings that females perform better in single-sex schools than in coeducational ones. They exhibit higher self-esteem, are more involved in the academic life of the school, and have greater involvement in a broad range of social and leadership activities. Males do well in both single-sex and coeducational schooling (Shakeshaft 1986).

Shakeshaft argues that both the structure and curriculum of schools mirror male rather than female development. Although females mature earlier, are ready for verbal and math skills at a younger age, and have control of small motor skills sooner, classrooms are structured to meet the needs of males, who tend to develop at a slower pace. This pattern, coupled with research that shows that male students get a larger proportion of attention from and interaction with the teacher (Sadker and Sadker 1985; Shakeshaft 1986), puts female students in a difficult position. "Some grow bored, others give up, but most learn to hold back, be quiet, and smile" (Shakeshaft 1986, p. 500).

Implicit Messages in Instructional Techniques

Schools rely on what Goldman and McDermott (1987) refer to as a "culture of competition." This competition can be in the form of grades, classroom games and activities, or simply the amount of time it takes to finish a task. Despite a recent emphasis on peer tutoring and cooperative learning techniques, classrooms are usually structured so that children work individually. The stress on individual accomplishment sets up a culture of competition in which there is constant comparison of students' abilities by teachers and by students themselves. A hierarchy based upon achievement is established as classmates interact with each other and develop an understanding of others' work habits, skills, and abilities. If you were to ask first graders to name the best and worst readers in their classroom, they would have little difficulty in so doing. As we have indicated earlier, this hierarchy is duplicated in friendship groups and the organization of high school peer structures. The use of competition in schools is taken for granted by educators as the way to "do school."

In a study of high school extracurricular activities, Eder and Parker (1987) found that athletic programs encouraged males to be aggressive, achievement oriented, and competitive. Cheerleading, which was more highly valued for women than athletics, served to remind girls of the importance of being attractive. Traditional male and female roles—competition for men and emotional management (caretaking) for women—were the values integral to these activities.

Competition as an instructional strategy is problematic for female students, who tend to prefer connection and collaboration and to value relationships with others as central to their activities (Shakeshaft 1986). Competition is a threat to these relationships. Since so much of what is done in schools is based on competition, females often find themselves in an uncomfortable or alienating environment. Belenky et al. (1986) emphasize the need for building patterns of connection and collaboration into learning environments in order to facilitate women's development.

Implicit Messages in Classroom Interactions

Research on gender differences in classroom interaction demonstrates that males verbally dominate classrooms at all levels of schooling, despite the gender of the teacher (Brophy and Good 1970; Martin 1972; Sikes 1971). In a study by Sadker and Sadker (1985) a team of researchers observed more than a hundred fourth-, sixth-, and eighth-grade classes in four states and Washington, D.C. Half of these classes were in English and language arts and the other half were in science and math. The researchers found that teachers, regardless of gender and ethnic background, asked more questions of white males, and male students talked more than female students at a ratio of three to one. The Sadkers found that as the school year progressed, the participation and assertiveness of the males in the classrooms increased. Boys would ''grab teachers' attention'' by calling out answers, which then were accepted by teachers. When girls called out answers, they were more likely to be reprimanded for inappropriate behavior. As a consequence, girls sat patiently with their hands raised waiting to be called on. The study reports that males were eight times more likely to call out answers to teachers' questions. The Sadkers argue that through this type of interaction, teachers socialize males to be academically assertive and girls to assume a more traditional role of sitting quietly.

The Sadkers use the term ''mind sex'' (as opposed to ''mind *set*'') to describe the pattern of teachers' repeatedly calling on students of the same sex. For example, if the teacher asks a question of a male student, the next several questions will be likely to be addressed to male students. They found this serial pattern to be more pronounced for male students and suggested that this practice may be influenced by the self-selected sex segregation in seating patterns in more than half the classes they observed.

Male students receive more attention of all kinds by teachers—more praise, more time, but also more reprimands and harsher discipline (LaFrance 1985; Lippitt and Gold 1959; Sikes 1971). The attention given to males is much different from that given to females. For example, the Sadkers found that teachers were more likely to assist boys performing a difficult task, but more likely to do the entire task for the girls. As a consequence, girls learn not to confront challenging work. Also teachers give more criticism to males, so they learn to handle it better.

Female students are neither reprimanded nor praised but tend to be ignored in classrooms. This is particularly true of high-achieving females, who receive the least attention of all students. As both majority and minority females learn that their opinions are not valued and their answers are not worthy of attention, they come to believe they are not smart or important (Grant 1984; Hall and Sandler 1982; LaFrance 1985). If they do well in school, they attribute their success to luck or hard work rather than to their own abilities. School interactions ''reinforce societal messages that females are inferior'' (Shakeshaft 1986, p. 501).

Bonnie's Observations

During a classroom curriculum development class, we were shown a video meant to display a particular method of teaching. In one of the segments a female teacher was presenting a lesson to elementary school students. The teacher called on three boys in a row. My interest was piqued and I began to take a tally of how many times the female teacher called on male versus female students—things I've begun doing since I started your class! The results amazed and saddened me. Boys and girls alike raised their hands to all questions. A total of fourteen boys were called on, versus four girls. To make matters worse, the boys were encouraged and asked multiple questions; girls were not. I know this has been discussed in class and I have always agreed with the findings of teacher preference toward male students. However, I have never observed this behavior. Seeing this did make a strong impression on me. I am sure the teacher was completely unaware of her favoritism. The class viewing the video was oblivious to this behavior.

Observe a classroom. Count the number of males and females, and note the gender of the teacher. Keep track of the number of times the teacher calls on males and females. Note the types of questions asked of male and female students. Try to document how much time is provided to students according to gender. What are some of the gender-related patterns you see in this classroom?

Gender differences also exist in the ways men and women interact in social settings outside the academic world. Men speak more often than women and frequently interrupt them. Women are less active verbal participants in conversations, but they provide supportive and passive nonverbal cues by smiling and gazing at the speaker (Duncan and Fiske 1977; LaFrance and Mayo 1978). Researchers found that listeners recall more from male speakers than from females even when the content is identical and the style is similar.

Women may seem unsure or less competent in their comments because they often transform a declarative statement into a tentative comment by adding a tag question such as "isn't it" or qualifiers such as "I guess." To listeners this habit signals lack of power and influence (Sadker and Sadker 1985). Another interesting interpretation of this practice was provided by McIntosh (1988), who argues that such qualifiers serve to signal equality or the lack of a power differential between the speaker and the listener. By not appearing to be an all-knowing authority, the woman can encourage an equal exchange of information between the listener and the speaker.

Sociolinguist Deborah Tannen argues that conversation between men and women is cross-cultural communication. In her book, *You Just Don't Understand* (1990), she provides detailed accounts of the ways we miscommunicate or misunderstand one another because men and women live in two different worlds. Tannen differentiates between the "report talk" of men and the "rapport talk" of women. In report talk, the purpose of the conversation is to maintain independence, to establish social status, and to convey information directly and concisely. In the rapport talk of women, the purpose of the conversation is to build rapport, develop relationships, and establish connections, with little emphasis on status.

Read Tannen's book. How do the communication style differences she describes help you understand your own communication across gender lines?

Sexist Language in Schools

Sexist language is one way in which gender stereotypes continue to affect beliefs and attitudes about women. Although educators have become more aware of sexist language, it persists in many American schools. It is not uncommon for elementary bulletin boards to portray community helpers as "firemen" and "policemen." Social studies and science courses refer to "mankind" or "man's contributions to science." LaFrance argues:

[O]ne of the more subtle ways teachers contribute to female invisibility in classrooms is by reliance on the generic "he" to refer to both men and women. . . . Theoretically, the generic "he" includes females as well as males, but recent studies show its exclusionary properties. (1985, p. 43)

Many institutions have implemented policies that discourage the use of sexist language, but these guidelines are often ignored. The use of sexist language in schools at any level is unnecessary and potentially debilitating to females. It is another way in which women are socialized to see themselves as subordinate to males.

When a sexist word is scrawled across the lockers or when a male student uses sexist language, the silence can be deafening. Few teachers even code it as a problem, and many of the insults and put-downs of girls come from teachers and administrators themselves. After all, boys will be boys and girls will continue to receive their schooling in a hostile environment. (Shakeshaft 1986, p. 502)

Sexual Harassment in Schools

The pervasiveness of sexual harassment was dramatically highlighted in the televised hearings over Judge Clarence Thomas's fitness for confirmation as a Supreme Court Justice. His former associate, Professor Anita Hill, accused him of sexual harassment and the Senate Judiciary Committee held hearings on the matter. Attention to the issue has continued, particularly in relation to schools and the work place. Sexual harassment is defined by the Equal Employment Opportunity Commission as:

> Unwelcome sexual advances, request for sexual favors, and other verbal or physical conduct of a sexual nature constitute sexual harassment when (1) submission to such conduct is made either explicitly or implicitly a term or condition of an individual's employment, (2) submission to, or rejection of such conduct by an individual is used as the basis for employment decisions affecting such individual or (3) such conduct has the purpose or effect of unreasonably interfering with an individual's work performance or creating an intimidating, hostile, or offensive working environment. (Eskenazi and Gallen 1992, p. 63)

Sexual harassment, or unwelcome sexual attention, is a form of discrimination that violates Title VII of the 1964 Civil Rights Act, Title IX of the 1972 Education Amendments, and the Civil Rights Act of 1991 (Eskenazi and Gallen 1992). Sexual harassment in school creates an adverse environment for students and can result in embarrassment, fear, inability to concentrate on studies, poor grades, absenteeism, and physical symptoms (Bogart and Stein 1987; Bogart et al. 1992). Researchers Bogart and Stein provide us with several examples of teacher/student sexual harassment:

> A science teacher measured the craniums of the boys in the class, and the chests of the girls. This lesson in skeletal frame measurements was conducted one by one, at the front of the class, by the teacher.
>
> A classroom teacher asked one junior high school girl, in front of the whole class, how far she had gone with her boyfriend, specifically if she had gone to "second" or "third" base with him, and if they had "French kissed."
>
> A group of teachers suspected that one of their younger colleagues had been displaying excessive and inappropriate affection toward some of his students. Included among the behaviors they were concerned about was driving the students in his car, inviting them to his apartment on weekends, and generally doing a lot of touching and group hugging. Although no one had complained, they requested that the headmaster provide some staff training and discussion on appropriate and inappropriate behaviors between staff and students. (Bogart and Stein 1987, p. 151)

In June 1993 the Educational Foundation of the American Association of University Women (AAUW) released a groundbreaking study, *Hostile Hallways: The AAUW Survey on Sexual Harassment in America's Schools.* The study, conducted in February and March of 1993, surveyed representative samples of Hispanic, white, and African-American students in grades 8 through 11 from 79 schools across the United States. One of the primary questions asked is instructive for this discussion because it provides a listing of the types of behaviors considered to be sexual harassment.

During your whole school life, how often, if at all, has anyone (this includes students, teachers, other school employees, or anyone else) done the following things to you *when you did not want them to?*

- Made sexual comments, jokes, gestures, or looks in your presence.
- Showed, gave, or left you sexual pictures, photographs, illustrations, messages, or notes.
- Wrote sexual messages/graffiti about you on bathroom walls, in locker rooms, etc.
- Spread sexual rumors about you.
- Said you were gay or lesbian.
- Spied on you as you dressed or showered at school.
- Flashed or "mooned" you.
- Touched, grabbed, or pinched you in a sexual way.
- Pulled at your clothing in a sexual way.
- Intentionally brushed against you in a sexual way.
- Pulled your clothing off or down.
- Blocked your way or cornered you in a sexual way.
- Forced you to kiss him/her.
- Forced you to do something sexual, other than kissing. (AAUW 1993, p. 5)

AAUW researchers found that sexual harassment is widespread in schools, with *four* out of *five* of the students surveyed reporting some form of sexual harassment experience in school. Reports of harassment by girls across ethnic groups was similar: 82 percent of Hispanics, 84 percent of African Americans, and 87 percent of whites. The percentage of African-American boys (81%) reporting harassment was higher than of whites (75%) and Hispanics (69%). Sexual comments, jokes, gestures, or looks were the most common forms of sexual harassment reported. Touching, grabbing, and/or pinching in a sexual way were the second most common forms. Fifty-seven percent of girls as compared with 36 percent of boys reported having been intentionally brushed up against in a sexual way.

According to the survey, peer harassment is much more common than harassment by adults in school settings. Of the students who reported harassment incidents, only 18 percent were harassed by a school employee, one in four girls (25%) and one in ten boys (10%). More African-American girls (33%) reported being sexually harassed by an adult school employee than Hispanics (17%) or whites (25%). One interesting finding concerned students that were perpetrators of sexual harassment. Thirty-seven percent of them reasoned: "It's just part of school life/A lot of people do it/It's no big deal." Very few of the students had reported any incidents of harassment to adults. Only 7 percent said they told a teacher about the experience. Students were far more likely to confide in their peers—63 percent of sexually harassed students told a friend (49% boys and 77% girls).

Nan Stein argues that peer harassment in schools is often overlooked by teachers and administrators, who view it as "flirting" or as a normal stage of adolescent development. She explains:

> Sexual harassment in schools operates in full and plain view of others. Boys harass girls with impunity while people watch. Examples of sexual harassment that happen in public include attempts to snap bras, grope at girls' bodies, pull down gym shorts, or flip up skirts; circulating "summa cum slutty" or "piece of ass of the week" lists; designating special weeks for "grabbing the private parts of girls"; nasty, personalized graffiti written on bathroom walls; sexualized jokes, taunts, and skits that mock girls' bodies performed at school sponsored pep rallies, assemblies, or half-time performances during sporting events; and outright physical assault and even rape in schools. (Stein 1994, p. 2)

Stein argues that teasing and bullying behaviors learned and practiced in elementary school are antecedents to peer harassment in high school. She is currently developing a bullying and teasing curriculum for elementary schools that will help teachers engage students in confronting the problem by developing a vocabulary to talk about what are appropriate and inappropriate or hurtful behaviors. These discussions can serve as springboards for later understanding about sexual harassment in middle and high school (Stein 1994).

Sexual harassment in school seems to take a greater toll on girls than on boys. The AAUW survey indicated that 33 percent of the girls reported that they did not want to attend school after an experience of harassment. The finding varied by ethnicity; more African-American girls (39%) than Hispanics (29%) or whites (33%) responded in this way. Only 12 percent of the boys surveyed responded that a harassment incident made them want to stay away from school. Authors of the study conclude that "parents, teachers, and administrators must acknowledge that sexual

---

Sexual Harassment by Peers in a Public High School

It came to the point where I was skipping almost all of my classes, therefore getting kicked out of the honors program. It was *very* painful for me. I dreaded school each morning, I started to wear clothes that wouldn't flatter my figure, and I kept to myself. I never had a boyfriend that year. I'd cry every night I got home, and I thought I was a total loser. . . . Sometimes the teachers were right there when it was going on. They did nothing. . . . I felt very angry that these arrogant, narrow-minded people never took the time to see who really was inside. . . . I'm also very angry that they took away my self-esteem, my social life, and kept me from getting a good education.

SOURCE: 16-year-old from mid-sized city in Illinois, quoted in Stein 1994, p. 1.

harassment in school is creating a hostile environment that compromises the education of America's children'' (AAUW 1993).

Sexual Orientation in Schools

Since our last edition of this book (1990) educational researchers have been giving more attention to gay and lesbian teachers and students. What once was a subject of little research has now become an area with a considerably larger knowledge base. However, many educators continue to avoid the issue of sexual orientation as it relates to schooling because it is such a volatile societal issue. As an example of how fearful heterosexual people are of homosexuality, note that in the previous section being called gay or lesbian was listed as a form of sexual harassment. Of those who responded in that survey that they had experienced sexual harassment, 17 percent said they were called gay or lesbian when they didn't want to be. Boys were more likely than girls to report this form of harassment. Open discussion in classrooms regarding homosexuality or gay and lesbian concerns continues to be met with resistance and homophobia. By homophobia we mean the "irrational fear of sexual expression between people of the same gender" (Steinem, in Kramarae and Treichler 1985, p. 195). This section will explore literature on homosexuality as related to school settings.

In a thorough and timely overview of the equity issues of homosexuality in relation to education in *Sex Equity and Sexuality in Education* (Klein 1992), Delores Grayson quotes Audre Lorde, saying, "if we truly intend to eliminate oppression, heterosexism and homophobia must be addressed" (Grayson 1992, p. 172). It helps to understand the scope of sexual orientation issues if we realize that there are an estimated 150,000 gay and lesbian teenagers in the New York city metropolitan area, 10,000 in Philadelphia public high schools, 24,000 in Washington, D.C., and between 50,000 and 70,000 in Los Angeles. In Los Angeles and San Francisco, where school dropout rates exceed 40 percent, a disproportionate number of dropouts are gay or lesbian youth. In Los Angeles an estimated one-third of the homeless youth are those with a gay or lesbian orientation who have left home voluntarily or have been thrown out (Grayson 1992). Although these data are from urban centers only, we need to remember that what we will term sexual minority youth—as well as teachers, administrators, and counselors—live in communities of all sizes and descriptions.

The invisibility of this minority group is a central issue for gays and lesbians, as well as for those who are concerned with justice for oppressed groups. Where the culture is rigidly heterosexual, it often is not safe for gay and lesbian students or teachers to be open about their sexuality. As we saw, sexual harassment of students includes being labeled gay or lesbian (usually in more derogatory forms like dyke, faggot, wimp, sissy), whether or not the students actually are homosexual. Any behavior that may be perceived as a departure from the traditional male and female roles can set students up for this type of harassment. Grayson explains:

> Schools have depended on rigid sex-role definition to control their students. Homophobia helps keep boys and girls "in their place" better than any written rule. The fear of being accused of being gay or lesbian influences deci-

sions to stay in traditional shop and home economics classes, avoid inappropriate sport teams and student activities, and hide "too exclusive" same-sex relationships. (1992, p. 173)

In this oppressive culture, sexual minority youth, as well as their lesbian and gay teachers, remain "in the closet," where they are excluded but perhaps are safer from discrimination and abuse. As long as homosexuals are invisible, heterosexual educators are able to deny the contributions of this group of people.

Researchers have demonstrated that the personal cost for gay and lesbian educators can be high, particularly when they must adopt a "dual identity." In fear that they will damage themselves personally or professionally, homosexual educators change names of partners to the opposite gender or engage in so-called gender-appropriate behaviors to "pass" as heterosexual. For example, a single young female teacher might endure other teachers' well-intentioned efforts to arrange dates with eligible males. There are many documented incidents of harassing phone calls and letters, threats of violence, and violent actions against gays and lesbians whose sexual orientation becomes known in a community (Grayson 1992). We do not mean to imply here that all gay and lesbian educators respond to their school contexts in this way; some settings are more accepting than others of a range of lifestyles.

Assumed heterosexuality is a norm which pervades school practices. For example, on a form requiring the names of the father and mother, lesbian mothers crossed out "father" and wrote in "co-mother" (Casper, Schultz, and Wickens 1992). Virtually nothing in the curriculum deals with homosexuality as an alternative lifestyle. Children with gay parents do not see their type of family represented in any way in their schools because the heterosexual family is held up as the norm. In 1993 the Rainbow Curriculum, a multicultural curriculum introduced in New York City, created a controversy by its portrayal of gay families. After heated debate and the removal of the school superintendent, the controversial curriculum was removed as a district-wide mandate.

Given the climate of homophobia in society today, many gay parents are hesitant to discuss their personal life with teachers or school administrators for fear of repercussions for their children. A lesbian raising a six-year-old son explained:

No, there's no way I would come out. If you tell them, they might . . . change their attitude against you, and you're gonna feel, like rejected. So let them find out on their own. (Casper, Schultz, and Wickens 1992, p. 118)

Researchers Casper, Schultz, and Wickens (1992) call for educators to engage in open discussion in their teacher preparation programs and in their schools about lesbian and gay families. They argue that it is essential for educators to become more comfortable with the words *lesbian* and *gay*. They remind us that "clear and nonbiased understandings of family, gender, and culture will require the actions of teachers, parents, administrators, and activists (1992, p. 134).

Think about the content of popular songs, advertisements, and leisure activities. What are some messages gay and lesbian youth get about homosexuality from popular culture, media, and school experiences? How can teachers provide equitable school experiences for sexual minority youth?

GENDER-BASED DIFFERENTIAL OUTCOMES IN SCHOOLING

We have presented data about the different treatment of males and females particularly as related to the structure, curriculum, instructional strategies, and interactions in schools. The differential treatment young men and women receive in elementary and secondary school leads to differential academic and occupational outcomes based on gender. This section will present data showing the clear differences in these outcomes. Culturally induced differences also exist. Carol Tavris (1992) summarizes some of what she believes are the "real" differences between male and female behavior; "real" differences tend to focus on the different experiences men and women have rather than on allegedly innate sex-linked characteristics.

Differences in Academic Performance

What gender differences exist in student performance on academic tasks? Female students achieve higher grades throughout public school and do better on language-related courses such as reading, writing, and literature, while males do better in math and science. Although high school girls make better grades than boys, males tend to take more computer science and science courses involving math which would prepare them for careers in science-related areas (Ballantine 1989). Males are more likely to take physics and calculus courses than females (AAUW 1992). Females are less likely to participate in special or gifted programs and less likely to take math and science courses—even if they are academically talented—because they are less likely to believe themselves capable of pursuing these fields in college.

Females tend to attribute their failures to internal factors, such as lack of intellectual ability, while attributing successes to external factors such as luck (Sadker and Sadker 1985). In a study of college retention and attrition in mathematics and science courses, McDade (1988) found differences in how men and women dealt with their failures in these fields. Men were more able to disengage their self-image from their academic performance; rather than question their own abilities, they viewed their failure as a lack of fit with the field of study. Women internalized their failures, questioning their competence as learners not only in the specific area, but in general. Holland and Eisenhart's work with African-American and white college women (1988) corroborates McDade's findings. When confronted by teachers, parents, or boyfriends who told them they lacked the drive or ability to pursue "hard" subjects, they tended to give up or lower their career aspirations rather than to question the validity of negative judgments.

An interesting longitudinal study, the Illinois Valedictorian Project, issued a first-

Do Men and Women Differ?

Where the differences aren't	Where the differences are
Attachment, connection	Care-taking
Cognitive abilities	Communication
Verbal, mathematical,[a] reasoning,	▪ interaction styles
rote memory, vocabulary,	▪ uses of talk
reading,[b] etc.	▪ power differences
Dependency	Emotions
Emotions	▪ Contexts that produce them
▪ Likelihood of feeling them	▪ Forms of expression
Empathy	▪ "Feminization of love"
Moods and "moodiness"	▪ "Feminization of distress"
Moral reasoning	Employment, work opportunities
Need for achievement	Health and medicine
Need for love and attachment	▪ medication and treatment
Need for power	▪ longevity differences
Nurturance[c]	Income
Pacifism, belligerence	Life-span development
(e.g., depersonalizing enemies)	▪ effects of children
Sexual capacity, desire, interest	▪ work and family sequence
Verbal aggressiveness, hostility	Life narratives
	Power and status at work, in
	relationships, in society
	Reproductive experiences
	Reproductive technology and its
	social/legal consequences
	"Second shift": housework, child
	care, family obligations
	Sexual experiences and concerns
	Violence, public and intimate
	Weight and body image

[a]Males excel at highest levels of math performance; in general population, females have slight advantage.

[b]Males are more susceptible to some verbal problems. However, many alleged sex differences seem to be an artifact of referral bias: More boys are *reported* for help than girls, but there are no sex differences in the *actual* prevalence of dyslexia and other reading disabilities (see Shaywitz et al., 1990).

[c]As a capacity; in practice, women do more of the actual care and feeding of children, parents, relatives, friends.

SOURCE: Tavris 1992.

decade report documenting the academic and nonacademic lives of 82 valedictorians and salutatorians graduating from Illinois schools in 1981. The group, predominantly white, includes five African-American students, three Hispanic students, and one Asian-American student. The study found that although the men and women received equally high college entrance examination scores and grade point averages, the women had lowered estimates of their intelligence over the course of their college years. Attrition of women from math and science started in college and continued through graduate school and postdoctoral training. The researchers found that as college seniors, women's professional expectations were less well-defined than those of the men. The men's occupational levels were slightly higher than those of the women. The study reported that females were "well represented at the highest career levels among the group, with half of the female participants working in traditionally male-dominated career fields such as law, medicine, science, engineering, accounting, and computer science" (North Central Regional Educational Laboratory [NCREL] 1993, pp. 1-2). However, the remaining female valedictorians were disproportionately employed in clerical work and jobs that did not require a college degree (NCREL 1993).

What factors might account for the differences in self-perceptions, expectations, and occupational outcomes for these Illinois valedictorians?

Gender Differences in the SAT.   The Scholastic Aptitude Test (SAT) published by the Educational Testing Service (ETS) serves as a major measure of student achievement in the United States. The Project on Equal Education Rights (PEER) of the National Organization for Women, an advocacy program for equal educational opportunities for women, monitors the progress of females in schools. In their 1986 Report Card PEER found that in 1985 male SAT scores were 59 points higher than females'. The national average (of a possible 1600) was 936 for males and 877 for females, the largest gap in twenty years. Women scored lower than men on both verbal and math sections. The 1985 national average math score was 499 for men and 452 for women; the verbal score was 437 for men, 425 for women. Although the Educational Testing Service was unable to explain this discrepancy, it reported that SAT scores underpredict the grades women can expect to earn in college. The test is not an accurate predictor of women's college performance as based on grades.

Researchers suggest that there is sex bias in both the construction and the content of the SAT test. More of the test questions are set in a science context than in the humanities, where women traditionally have been encouraged to excel. The Educational Testing Service also removed both the essay writing portion of the verbal test and the data sufficiency question on the math test—items on which female students had excelled. A new version of the SAT was recently developed in an attempt to rectify the gender bias in the test. While there is some evidence that the "gender gap" in achievement test scores is diminishing on tests other than the SAT (the College Board achievement tests, the National Assessment of Educational Progress, graduate school admissions tests, the Armed Forces Qualification Tests, and the College

Boards), the reason may be that while women are improving their performance in math, their verbal performance is slipping, given the change in the test (Kolata 1989).

Studies by the College Board, by ETS, and by independent research consistently report that women "receive higher grades than men in every subject in high school and college, but lower average SAT scores by approximately 60 points" (Rosser, in Kelly-Benjamin 1990). Rosser reports that in 1989 women's average scores were 13 points lower on the verbal portion and 46 points lower on the math portion of the test. Women at all social class levels, as measured by parental income and education, scored lower than men in their groups. She argues that the test, which is designed to predict students' grades in their first year of college, *underpredicts* the performance of 780,000 young women every year. If the SATs were actually predictive, women would receive higher average scores than men by 10 or 20 points.

Women of color are especially disadvantaged in the SAT process; their average scores are lower than those of both white men and men in their own ethnic group. For example, combined verbal and math scores of high school seniors in 1989 indicated that Latin-American females averaged 63 points lower than Latin-American men and 172 points lower than white men; African-American women averaged 27 points lower than African-American men and 243 points lower than white men (Rosser, in Kelly-Benjamin 1990).

Underpredicting of their ability limits the chances of young women to get into the colleges that require SAT scores. In addition, women are disadvantaged in the competition for merit scholarships offered by corporations, foundations, professional organizations, unions, and governmental agencies because those scholarships are based largely on SAT scores. In 1989, for example, only 32 percent of the National Merit Semifinalists were women. Since the SAT scores of women of color are consistently lower, they are even less likely to be selected for these SAT-based scholarships.

In February 1994 the American Civil Liberties Union filed a federal civil rights complaint charging bias against women in the use of SAT tests to award the $25 million per year National Merit Scholarships. The ACLU argued that 60 percent of the semifinalists and finalists are boys despite the fact that only 45 percent of those who take the test are male. A spokesperson for the College Board denied any gender bias in the test, explaining that the difference reflects differential academic preparation, including the fact that women take fewer high school math courses (*Education Week* 1994).

The American Association of University Women's (AAUW) 1992 study, *How Schools Shortchange Girls: A Study of Major Findings on Girls and Education,* reports that women perform better on the verbal portion of the SAT when the material is abstract and general rather than concrete and specific. They also tend to do better when asked to deal with concepts and ideas rather than facts and things. On mathematics items, women generally do more poorly than men on word problems, even when the problems relate to stereotypic female contexts such as food preparation. Females answer fewer test items than males. They tend to score higher on open-ended or essay type items, whereas boys tend to score higher on multiple choice items (AAUW 1992).

The Educational Testing Service requests that students supply information about

My daughter had straight As in high school and my son's record was indifferent. Then they took their SATs. My daughter's four years of achievement were wiped out by her low SAT score and my son's high score suddenly made him a brain. It had a tremendous psychological impact. My daughter began to set up barriers. She couldn't apply to certain places because her scores were not as good as the books say they should be. When she entered college she didn't study hard enough at first because she thought she couldn't get As. [Eventually she realized she could and brought her grades up to her previous standards.]

SOURCE: Prominent feminist leader quoted by Phyllis Rosser in Kelly-Benjamin 1990, p. 1.

their academic goals when they take the SAT. PEER found that in 1985, 10.6 percent of the high school senior women taking the SAT reported that their goal was to major in physical sciences, compared with 34 percent of the male seniors. In 1980–1981 only 3 percent of the women graduates received a Bachelor's degree in physical sciences, mathematics, or engineering, while 23 percent of them earned degrees in education and 11 percent graduated in nursing and health-related professions—both traditionally female.

Differences in Educational Attainment

Since the 1960s women have made significant gains in education. We owe much of this progress to the work of feminist women and men. Currently over half of undergraduate college students are women. The student population also has become increasingly diverse, with nearly one out of every five students a person of color in 1988. In 1989, women earned the majority of college degrees at all levels except doctorate. Although they have continued to concentrate in traditional undergraduate majors such as social sciences, the arts, and education, in 1988 one out of every five women college graduates majored in business. Women have earned increasing numbers of undergraduate degrees in science and engineering since 1960. In fact, one-half of the biological science degrees in 1989 were earned by women—almost double the 1970 percentage. In 1989 women earned more than one-fourth of the dentistry degrees, one-third of the medical degrees, one-half of the veterinary degrees, and two-fifths of the law degrees (Ries and Stone 1992).

Despite these gains, problem areas persist. Although women *have* moved into traditionally male-dominated fields such as science and engineering, Randour, Strasburg, and Lipman-Blumen (1982) found that at the Bachelor's degree level they continue to be concentrated in education, fine and applied arts, foreign languages, health professions, home economics, and library science—all traditionally female professions. In addition, although greater numbers of women are now earning Master's degrees and doctorates, over half of the women at the Master's level and over one-third of those at the doctoral level are earning degrees in education. In traditionally male-dominated fields women are still the minority. For example, in 1989 only 15 percent of Bachelor's degrees in engineering were earned by women, and women earned only 36 percent of the doctorates awarded in that year (Ries and Stone 1992). Women continue to outnumber men significantly in undergraduate education programs. Goldin reported in 1990 that 76 percent of all education majors are women. You need only look around your class to confirm this figure.

Women have made striking advances in educational attainment since the early 1960s, when most women had two basic options—teaching and nursing. As we have seen, many more options are open to today's young women. In the next section we will examine both women's progress in occupational attainment and the subtle and not-so-subtle glass ceiling.

Occupational Attainment, Economic Rewards, and the Glass Ceiling

The existence of a "glass ceiling"—analogous to the "job ceiling" for ethnic minorities—in the labor market means that despite being highly educated, well-qualified, and extremely motivated, women still may rise only so far in their career hierarchies.

Many women who have worked their way into professional positions across a range of fields find themselves hitting their heads against the "glass ceiling." This means that despite appropriate and even exceptional qualifications, they are not promoted to the highest levels possible. Women high school principals and school superintendents are few. As we have seen, women are not well represented on the faculties or in administrative posts of colleges and universities. Women attorneys are often prevented from rising to the top of the legal profession. The Honorable William S. Russell, a Tennessee judge, using data from the Harvard Law School Class of 1974, reported that "ten years after graduation, 59 percent of the male graduates were full partners in law firms, but only 23 percent of the female graduates had obtained that status" (Fretz 1990).

Some encouraging trends are that from 1975 to 1987 the number of higher education institutions headed by women increased 100 percent, and the number of businesses owned by women also increased. By 1987, 30 percent of U.S. companies were owned by females.

However, in 1982 Kelly and Nihlen reported:

[W]omen earn less than 56 percent of male income, regardless of job categories; they are concentrated in the lowest-paying jobs in both service and industrial sectors of the economy; they are segregated into occupations which permit very little upward mobility; and they are concentrated in the "marginal" areas of the workforce. (1982, p. 165)

This statement still holds true today. Women continue to be concentrated in the traditional service industries. In 1990 more than two-thirds of working women were in service sector industries, in wholesale and retail trade, and in protective service fields such as teaching and nursing (Ries and Stone 1992). In the same year 46 percent of

"Construction of the glass ceiling begins not in the executive suite but in the classroom."

SOURCE: Alice McKee, president of the American Association of University Women, 1992.

female workers were in low-paying service and administrative-support occupations such as health aides, secretaries, and waitresses. African-American women were more likely than white women to work in these service jobs. Overall, most jobs tend to be gender segregated along traditional lines. For example, only 19.3 percent of physicians, 8 percent of engineers, 13.9 percent of police and detectives, and 36 percent of computer programmers were women in 1990. According to a 1989 survey the Fortune 500 companies continue to be male dominated; only one out of eight of their board members was a woman.

In higher education, as in the corporate world, women are depressingly underrepresented. They comprised only 28 percent of college faculty in 1985, up from 20 percent in 1910. In 1985 only 3 percent of the college faculty were women of color. Current women faculty tend to be clustered at the bottom ranks in assistant or associate professorships rather than at the full professor rank. Only one of ten top executive posts in colleges and universities were held by women in 1989 (Ries and Stone 1992).

Women also continue to lag behind men in earnings. In 1980 females earned 64 cents for every dollar earned by men. By 1990 they were earning 72 cents to a man's dollar, but African-American women continued to earn 62 cents for every dollar earned by white men (Ries and Stone 1992).

Thus we can see that unequal educational treatment in schools coupled with culturally determined notions of what constitutes appropriate women's work continue to produce inequities in the economic structure.

Think about the reasons for the glass ceiling. Why is it that women are not promoted to the highest positions in their fields or do not serve on corporate boards? Talk to some women professionals about their experiences with the glass ceiling.

We have discussed equality of educational opportunities in two ways: equal access to education and equal treatment of students in schools. By law, women, like minority groups, have achieved equal access to educational opportunities through Title IX. However, equitable treatment of women in schools is not a reality. Differences in the treatment of men and women in schools mirror cultural beliefs about appropriate roles for males and females. In the United States, as in Western countries, men are politically, economically, and socially dominant. Although there have been significant improvements in both educational and economic opportunities for women, the work force continues to be sex-segregated so that women hold subordinate positions in the economy.

> I myself have never been able to find out precisely what feminism is; I only
> know that people call me a feminist whenever I express sentiments that differ-
> entiate me from a doormat.
>
> SOURCE: Rebecca West, 1913, *The Clarion*, Nov. 14, quoted in Kramarae & Treichler, 1985.

I'M NOT A FEMINIST, BUT . . .

When we talk in our classes about women's issues, our students often will preface
their comments with the phrase, "I'm not a feminist, but. . . ." If you recall our earlier
discussion of stereotypes, it is clear that such students may be harboring a stereotype
about feminists. Feminists are often portrayed in the media as man haters, aggressive
bitches, as well as aging and bitter leftovers from the 1960s. Feminists also are never
portrayed as male. Rush Limbaugh is currently building his career by bashing feminists with his label "feminazi." Given this backdrop, it isn't surprising that some students try to establish some distance from such a label. However, we believe it is important for both women and men in education to consider themselves feminists so
they can provide equitable and appropriate practice for all children and young adults.

In this section we will consider what it means to be a feminist. There is no *one*
feminism, but a range of political and theoretical feminist positions. Our discussion
here is merely a cursory introduction to several of the major feminist positions in
current writing and debate, rather than a detailed analysis of each position. We will
briefly discuss liberal feminism, radical feminism, socialist feminism, poststructural
feminism, and black feminism or womanism and the perspectives of these positions
on gender and schooling. You will see a common thread throughout these discussions
which serves as a backdrop for our subsequent discussions of girls' and women's
experiences in school settings. As you read, consider where you stand on these issues.
What do you agree with? What makes you uncomfortable? Why?

In your view, what is feminism? Do you consider yourself a feminist? Why or
why not?

What Is Feminism?

Feminism is both a theory of women's position in society and a political statement
focused on gaining equal rights and opportunities for women and changing existing
power relations between men and women. Feminism by definition implies social action, as we see in the following. A feminist is

> a person, female or male, whose worldview places the female in the center
> of life and society, and/or who is not prejudiced based on gender or sexual
> preference. Also, anyone in a male-dominated or patriarchal society who

works toward the political, economic, spiritual, sexual, and social equality of women. (*The Wise Woman* 1982, p. 7)

And another framing of the definition of feminism:

> Feminism is the political theory and practice to free all women: women of color, working-class women, poor women, physically challenged women, lesbians, old women, as well as white economically privileged heterosexual women. Anything less than this is not feminism, but merely self-aggrandizement. (B. Smith 1979, quoted in Morage and Anzaldua 1981, p. 61)

Although we often think of the feminist movement of the 1960s as the beginning of contemporary feminism, the roots of feminist thinking go back centuries to individual men and women and groups of women and men who worked to free women from the oppression of patriarchy.

Feminist Theories

The way in which people understand feminism depends on their view of the larger society. *Liberal feminists* focus on the *rights* of individual women; they work to transform traditional beliefs about femininity and masculinity as well as to achieve full equality of opportunity in all spheres of life. Liberal feminists do not criticize the basic structure of the nuclear family but place stress on an individual woman's right to decide how she wants to participate in that family. Liberal feminists work to transform understandings of male and female roles at home and in the workplace; they advocate individual choice rather than biological sex differences as the factor that determines what men and women do in their families and in the work place (Weedon 1987). The liberal feminist position has been crucial in achieving equality of educational opportunities for women; it opened doors for young women to careers that were once the exclusive domain of white males. Much of the research cited in the sections about gender differences in the formal and hidden curriculum was done by liberal feminists who believed that traditional or stereotypic notions of male and female roles were debilitating for all people.

Radical feminists argue that the roots of women's oppression lie in the biological differences between men and women; the patriarchal family is seen to be the primary means by which women have been controlled by men. Radical feminists work to reclaim women's bodies from male control and to celebrate their life-giving abilities. Rather than attempting to transform patriarchy, they argue for women's separation from men in order to assert autonomy and develop a women's culture independent of men (Weedon 1987). Hawthorne explains that "separatism is a politically motivated strategy for empowering women and undermining patriarchy. It varies in its manifestations within women's lives" (1991, p. 312). She argues that separatism is a feminist strategy that challenges the oppressive societal structures, providing a continuum of choices whereby women can establish separate spheres from men. Her choices begin with participating in dialogue with other women in a variety of groups (such as consciousness-raising groups, study groups, or political action groups), to working in an all-female environment, to becoming woman-identified in emotional and sexual ways, or at the end of the continuum, to living in an all-woman environment (Hawthorne 1991). Radical feminists would view single-sex schools as a way to begin to develop an empowering woman's culture.

The *socialist feminist* position also criticizes the dominant structures of Western society. Socialist feminists view family as historically constructed. They believe race, social class, and gender oppression to be the interrelated consequence of a patriarchal, capitalist system. Socialist feminists call for total transformation of the social system to emphasize the following:

> . . . full participation of men in childrearing; reproductive freedom for women, that is, the right to decide if and when to have children and under what conditions, together with the provision of the conditions necessary for the realization of the right of women to make these choices; the abolition of the privileging of heterosexuality, freedom to define one's own sexuality and the right of lesbians to raise children; the eventual abolition of the categories "woman" and "man," and the opening up of all social ways of being to all people. (Weedon 1987, p. 18)

Social feminists would challenge the historically constructed patriarchy in today's schools, calling for total transformation in the structures, policies, and practices for women and men.

Recent writings by *feminist poststructuralists* play a key role in discussions of feminism. Weedon (1987) explains that poststructuralism isn't just one theory but rather a range of positions developed in the work of Derrida, Lacan, Dristeva, Althusser, and Foucault. Language is the common element in the analysis of our individual consciousness, power, and social organizations. Through language we are able to think, speak, and attach meaning to the world around us. All social meaning is constructed within, not apart from, language. Feminist poststructuralists examine the ways competing language patterns produce our notions of gender. Rather than having a static understanding of ourselves in the world, we are constantly engaged in constructing and deconstructing, interpreting and reinterpreting ourselves and the way we understand our worlds through language (Weedon 1987). Since language is the principal focus of the poststructuralists, they would deconstruct the competing discourses found in school settings—including the policies, practices, and interactions among those who participate in school life. The feminist poststructuralist would attempt to examine schools through social, cultural, and historical lenses, analyzing the relations of knowledge and power. By understanding whose interests are served in the language of schools, they would discover whose interests are marginalized, silenced, or excluded, so they could begin work toward changes and transformations in those settings.

Black feminism or *womanism* defines African-American women's struggles around the issues of race, social class, and gender. For African-American women, the feminist movement has symbolized a struggle for equity based on a universal notion of women, with little recognition of the distinction of race. Alice Walker captures the relationship of black women to the white feminist movement: "Womanist is to feminist as purple is to lavender" (Walker 1983, p. xi). The history of African Americans in the United States has been a history of oppression. For black women, sexual abuse and harassment began with the institution of slavery, so it is impossible to separate the experience of being a woman from the experience of being an African-American woman (Brown 1994). In *Black Feminist Thought* (1990) P. H. Collins describes the grounding of black feminism in the experience of African-American women: "all African American women share the common experience of being Black women in a society that denigrates women of African descent" (Collins 1990, p. 22). The struggle against both racism and sexism is a core theme for womanists. Through their efforts, black feminists work to replace denigrated images of black women with self-defined images, to give voice to the experiences of black women, and to take action in the struggle for human freedom. Collins argues that black feminist thought "cannot flourish isolated from the experiences and ideas of other groups" (1990, p. 35); she describes the necessity of forming coalitions with others whose goals are to challenge relations of domination in the society. The Combahee River Collective characterizes this struggle:

> We are actively committed to struggling against racial, sexual, heterosexual, and class oppression and see as our particular task the development of integrated analysis and practice based upon the fact that the major systems of oppression are interlocking. The synthesis of these oppressions creates the conditions of our lives. As Black women we see Black feminism as the logical political movement to combat the manifold and simultaneous oppressions that all women of color face. (Combahee River Collective, 1977, in Morage and Anzaldua 1981, p. 210)

We have provided a brief taste of several of the primary feminist theories currently used to explain and transform societal institutions and practices. Although these theories have different key points or elements, all are concerned with equal rights for women and a transformation in the ways both women and men experience their lives. We urge you to read about each of these feminist theories in more depth.

Which of the feminist theories expresses views most like yours? Why?

SUMMARY

In this chapter, we've addressed the major issues related to gender equity in schools. It is clear, a few decades after the passage of Title IX, that women have more alternatives in schools and more equitable access to educational opportunities. The gender differences are no longer as explicit as they were in the school that Emily attended in 1903. Emily's granddaughter, Susan, has been given access to many educational alternatives and career options. However, schools continue to reproduce a patriarchal society through subtle (and often not-so-subtle) messages embedded in their organizational structure, curriculum, and social interaction patterns. "The achievement of sex-and-gender-equitable education remains an elusive dream. The time to turn dreams to reality is now" (AAUW 1992, p. 84). The following AAUW recommendations for action were proposed to address the critical gender equity issues in schools:

1. Strengthening and reinforcement of Title IX is essential.
2. Teachers, administrators, and counselors must be prepared and encouraged to bring gender equity and awareness to every aspect of schooling.
3. The formal school curriculum must include the experiences of women and men from all walks of life. Girls and boys must see women and girls reflected and valued in the materials they study.
4. Girls must be educated and encouraged to understand that mathematics and the sciences are important and relevant to their lives. Girls must be actively supported in pursuing education and employment in these areas.
5. Continued attention to gender equity in vocational education programs must be a high priority at every level of educational governance and administration.
6. Testing and assessment must serve as stepping-stones, not stop signs. New tests and testing techniques must accurately reflect the abilities of both girls and boys.
7. Girls and women must play a central role in educational reform. The experiences, strengths, and needs of girls from every race and social class must be considered in order to provide excellence and equity for all our nation's students.
8. A critical goal of education reform must be to enable students to deal effectively with the realities of their lives, particularly in areas such as sexuality and health. (AAUW 1992, pp. 84–88)

Up to this point in the book we have tried to paint a realistic picture of the way schools work—at times a rather gloomy picture. It is important for you to understand the realities of schooling so you can help transform schools into better places for teachers and children. In the next chapter we will describe some of the ways schools are currently trying to address the problems and issues raised here.

chapter 9

Alternatives to the Way We "Do School": A Critical Perspective

Chapter Overview

INTRODUCTION

CHANGING THE BALANCE OF POWER
    Alternative Possibilities for School Structures
    Alternative Ideologies of Schooling: Transformative Pedagogies
    Alternative Possibilites for Teacher Education and Practice

A CLOSING NOTE

INTRODUCTION

What have we learned about schooling from sociology? We have attempted to provide an overview of how sociologists look at students and teachers. We have presented the major sociological interpretations used to explain the purposes of school and the experiences of students in schools. Using these interpretations, particularly a critical/feminist framework, we have examined the complex nature of work within educational institutions and the ways social class, ethnicity, and gender impact the experiences of students.

    You might wonder, since we know so much about schooling from a sociological perspective, why we still "do school" in ways that clearly contradict our research findings. Why are so many schools still organized and operated in much the same manner they were a hundred years ago? Why do we ignore research on individual differences and continue to educate children in batches, like cookies? Why do we say we venerate and respect teachers and then refuse to pay them well or trust their judgment about what they teach? Why do we still believe that education is necessary in order to get ahead economically? Why—when it is clear that benefits from schooling are directly proportional to how close one is to being white, male, and middle class—do we continue to urge children who differ from white males by race, class, and gender to believe that "education pays off"? Given demographic shifts so that by the year 2000 the majority of public school students will come from non-European (African, Asian, or Latin-American) backgrounds (Hodgkinson 1985), why do those who plan and administrate educational programs ignore the needs of a growing multicultural student population?

Part of the answer can be found in Tom Robbins's delightful novel *Jitterbug Perfume.* Robbins writes: "The Universe does not have laws. It has habits. And habits can be broken" (1984, p. 283). Schools, like Robbins's universe, run on old habits. For example, when you ask teachers why they put children into three groups for reading, they may tell you that they've always done it that way. The practice is reinforced and legitimated by district supervisors who require such a structure, as well as by the teachers' guides for basal readers. Much of what happens in and to schools is done because of habit.

Another part of the answer lies in the expectations that parents and communities hold for schooling and their resistance to new systems. Almost everyone has attended school for some long period of time. Almost everyone feels that she or he "knows about" schools and what they are like. Parents who benefited from school tend to want schools to be run in much the same way as when *they* were children, and to have the same supposed effects. You might hear them say, "It was good enough for me; it ought to be good enough for my kids, too." Disadvantaged parents express the same kind of conservatism, but for different reasons: They have observed the benefits that schooling seems to have provided for the children of the middle and upper classes and fear that innovative programs will be inferior. They want their children to have the same advantages—hence the same kinds of schooling—that traditionally have benefited the dominant groups in society.

Imagine what would happen if all schools suddenly were to discontinue compensatory education, ability grouping, and academic tracking. Many administrators and some teachers would be up in arms, ignoring research findings that tracking widens the differences between children and benefits only those in the highest tracks. They would feel overwhelmed with the wide range of ability in their classrooms. Middle-class parents would storm the barricades, protesting that their children's life chances had been impaired because teachers would be spending all their time on "slow" learners at the expense of the more able. Despite evidence that many so-called compensatory education programs are not targeted to instruction, that the programs often don't raise achievement, and that often they actually benefit students other than the target populations, disadvantaged parents would complain that without this special treatment their children would slide even farther behind.

Imagine further that all standardized testing was eliminated and that schools were no larger than 400 students, as has been recommended by us (Dworkin and LeCompte 1989; LeCompte and Dworkin 1988; LeCompte and Goebel 1987) and by a Carnegie Commission Report (1989). Imagine that the requirements for employment were a demonstrated background in the arts, humanities, literature, and mathematics, not a diploma. Imagine that it would be impossible to find an all-European-American classroom.

If people, particularly teachers and administrators, were able to distance themselves from their long-cherished notions about schools and take a moment to contemplate the adverse consequences that their activities have for poor and minority children, they most likely would ask: "How else can you do it? What are the alternatives?" In this final chapter we will engage in some intellectual play with these questions. On the basis of what we have learned from the sociologists of education, we will present a few alternatives to the way we "do school."

At this point in our courses our students are usually ready for action. You may be frustrated that we haven't answered certain questions: What can we as teachers and administrators do about the issues and problems you've raised here? How can we do schools better? Many sociologists, anthropologists, and educators are now addressing these questions. In this last chapter we cannot provide you with a "cookbook" for ways to improve school experiences, but we can introduce you to views of educators concerned with alternatives to traditional school structures, policies, and practices. We must remember that each context is different and what works in one setting may not be appropriate in another. We present these alternatives in three separate but interrelated categories: (1) the structure of schools, (2) alternative ideologies of schooling with an emphasis on transformative pedagogies, and (3) teacher education and classroom practice. We offer these suggestions as a mere beginning—a way for students and teachers to think in new ways about schooling and to raise questions about their own teaching and learning practices, as well as about policies that have been implemented in their own school districts.

We have tried not to be Utopian. We have restricted our own suggestions to things that are now in practice in innovative schools or that we feel current school districts might be able to accomplish. We hope your thinking and questioning will not end with the suggestions in this chapter. We challenge you to use the knowledge you have gained in this text to examine critically your own beliefs, practices, policies, and structures throughout your professional life. We hope you will work to transform your own setting into one that is culturally affirming, developmentally appropriate, intellectually challenging, and socially just.

CHANGING THE BALANCE OF POWER

Sociologists have been criticized for the terribly gloomy portrait they paint of the role of schools in social transformation. This is particularly true of reproduction theorists. In suggesting that schools have no power to act upon the source of the problems that they are called upon to solve, sociologists seem to have left educators with little to do but wish for a more humane society. While it is true that schools more reflect than shape the economic and social foundations of society—to a greater extent than educators or reformers would like to believe—there is nevertheless much that schools can do.

Since the first edition of this book, educators have challenged the traditional structures of schooling whereby classrooms are organized by age, subjects are taught in segregated units in 50-minute periods, and teachers work in isolation. Today we can find many examples of multi-age grouping, integrated curricula, changes in the scheduling of classes, and teachers immersed in transformative practice. Educators have proposed and implemented alternative and transformative pedagogies. The educational community has called for a reconceptualization of teachers' work and the way teachers are educated.

What is at the core of all these changes is a change in power relationships. Traditional hierarchies of power have come under serious critique. The traditional role of teachers and students is in question. School administrators are being asked to participate in very different ways. The whole notion of the construction of knowledge and whose knowledge is taught in schools, as well as whose knoweldge is omitted, continues to be debated by educators and policy makers. Educators have formed powerful networks across schools, districts, and states to share knowledge and to support transformative projects. As critical/feminist theorists, we are excited about the critique of these traditional structures and practices and the ways in which power is currently shifting to those who have long been on the bottom of the hierarchy—women, minority groups, teachers, and students. In this next portion of the chapter we will examine the ways the balance of power is changing in (1) school structures, (2) pedagogies, and (3) teacher education.

Alternative Possibilities for School Structures

How could schools be organized to better meet the needs of a diverse population? What issues of power in schools need to be addressed? Who should determine how schools are structured? In this section we examine some of these questions and offer several suggestions.

> Visit a school (or classroom) where alternative practices and structures are the norm. How does this school compare with a more traditionally organized school? Talk with some of the students and teachers about their experiences in this setting.

Keeping Schools Small. As was described in Chapter 2, schools and school districts are currently organized into large, consolidated bureaucratic organizations, having replaced the smaller community schools which were the norm until the early twentieth century. With more students, consolidated schools could offer more curricular and extracurricular options. However, in schooling, big is not necessarily better. Increased size has come at the expense of the sense of community and belonging which schools often created. Schools also have lost the capacity for flexibility, a characteristic that enables them to accommodate to the varied needs and capabilities of students. In our opinion, schools have become so big and complex that teachers, students, and administrators can no longer perform in them the work that large schools were designed to do. Recent research indicates that the bigger the school, the higher the dropout rates, especially for minority students (R. Turner 1989). Sociological analyses consistently show that students are happier and have a higher level of participation in smaller schools.

Regardless of their size, schools that can conform to overall structural rules while still bending them enough to engage their students socially and academically tend to have lower dropout rates, even among students who are learning disabled and from minority backgrounds (Miller, Leinhardt, and Zigmond 1988). Similarly, teachers feel more competent and satisfied when they feel that they have some control over their work. They feel more alienated and less in control when they do not feel that they have supportive administrators and when they work in impersonal, highly bureaucratized school districts (Dworkin 1986; Dworkin, Lorence, and LeCompte 1989). Schools must be small enough to enable teachers, administrators, and other school staff to build strong, lasting relationships with their students. Teachers in smaller schools working with children over longer periods of time can get to know their students and respond to their needs more quickly. It is much more difficult to lose students in the bureaucracy when the bureaucracy is small.

Teaching and learning are not only *social* acts, but *intimate* social acts, facilitated by the close personal attention of the participants. Intimacy and large contemporary schools are virtually mutually exclusive, but one structural variable over which schools *do* have control is size. We propose that the school consolidation clock be rolled back so that the optimum size for elementary schools be about 300 students, and for secondary schools, 200 per grade level with a maximum of 600 students. This means that a school with four grades would have a grade level limit of 150. With innovative scheduling, these configurations can be accomplished within existing buildings. Any existing old buildings can be reopened or new ones can be constructed on a much smaller scale.

Some experiments in reducing school size, particularly at the secondary level, are being attempted. For example, the Coalition Campus Schools Project in New York City, a three-year initiative, is implementing twelve new, small high schools in an "effort to humanize urban school education and transform large failing inner-city schools into successful learning environments for all students" (National Center for Restructuring Education, Schools, and Teaching [NCREST] 1994, p. 1). The plan is to phase out two large, comprehensive high schools and replace them with twelve smaller schools on the same campuses, consisting of approximately 400 students each. The schools will emphasize personalized instruction, close school–family communications, rigorous intellectual standards for all children, and shared decision making. Deborah Meier, co-director of Central Park East Secondary School, explains: "Most human beings need to be known, and it is more critical when other things are also fragile. Kids are dying in these large schools" (NCREST 1994, p. 4). This type of innovation illustrates the potential for large urban and suburban school districts to reorganize into smaller communities or units to meet the needs of students while staying within budget constraints and maintaining the size necessary to provide the educational alternatives offered by a consolidated high school.

Flexible Groupings of Students.   Even more critical to overall school organization would be a radical departure from age-grading. We now "batch-process" children. From the elementary school level on, children are categorized by age and locked into movement through the grades one year at a time, with complete disregard for what we have learned from sociologists and psychologists about the most appropriate ways to organize learning for children.

The National Association for the Education of Young Children has consistently urged districts to adopt "developmentally appropriate practice," which gears schools to the developmental rather than the chronological age of children. This structuring permits children to learn through activities appropriate for their developmental stage and to move through the curriculum in accordance with their readiness. This type of teaching and learning has been termed a *multi-graded unit* or *multi-aged grouping*. The emphasis shifts from didactic teaching of content to providing appropriate learning activities through which children acquire content. Not only does this arrangement change the way children learn, it drastically alters the role of the teacher. They can no longer "rule" from the top down but must preside over a multitude of activities, using their expertise to work with students in a wide range of ways. You can find schools that use multi-age groupings in most communities in the United States today.

Changing the School Schedule.   Perhaps the most important act schools might perform is to take a serious look at school conditions and to arrange the school day, the types of training, and the services available so that they more closely correspond to what students need. One consideration might be the recognition that the 12-year limit on elementary and high school attendance — reinforced by state funding formulas — is unrealistic. Some students are slower learners, some must work for a living, and some just need extra time for a particularly difficult program. Students who are gifted in music, the performing arts, or athletics may need time off for competitions or for extra practice; they lose out when they must choose between missing class work or giving up their competitions. Often these are the students who are pushed out of school. Precedent for changing this arrangement exists; "special" or handicapped students can take additional years to finish their program, to age 21.

There also exist precedents for arranging the school year to correspond with labor needs of society. The long public school summer vacations are a relic from an agricultural past, when student labor was needed on the farms during the growing season. Changes in the school calendar according to the needs of the community could promote better working relationships with parents and could provide for continuous educational services for that community's students.

School schedules can be transformed to recognize that most parents or guardians work and can neither come to school during the day for conferences nor be at home after school to baby-sit or help with homework. With these accommodations, parent involvement programs would be less of an excuse for teachers to pass on blame and less of a source of guilt for parents.

Further, day care needs to be found for the *children* of schoolchildren, the babies of teenagers who must otherwise drop out of school. Most teenage mothers choose to keep their babies, and most find few incentives and little assistance to remain in school (Hess and Green 1988). Infant care programs established on public school campuses have been notably helpful in ensuring continued school attendance as well as better child care. Funds for these programs might come from redirection of vocational education monies, about which we comment below.

Schools schedules can be designed around students' learning rather than around a factory model of discreet 50-minute periods. Humans simply don't learn in neatly organized 50-minute blocks with bells ringing to signal movement to the next subject. Some schools currently provide expanded periods so teachers can work in teams with groups of students over longer time blocks, thus allowing for thematic organization and integration of subject matter. At the elementary level students are being kept together in a classroom for the entire day, so the schedule is more flexible. In his book *Schools that Work* (1992) George Wood describes how progressive schools have restructured their schedules to provide a better learning environment for children and more time for teachers to work in teams. For example, in one school Wood visited, the staff shared a 75-minute lunch period during which they planned curriculum and worked on collaborative projects. Another school staff arranged to work together one morning a week while their students were involved in community service projects.

Schools and the Labor Market.   We need to look more closely at the skills needed in the labor market, particularly those related to vocational training. Most public schools cannot afford to offer the state-of-the-art training required for technical and industrial jobs. Employers often prefer to find literate job candidates and do their own training. Vocational students, then, find themselves doubly short-changed; not only are they insufficiently trained in the basic cognitive skills, but they have spent years in training that is outdated and leads only to dead-end jobs. We have argued elsewhere that the best vocational training possible is a good liberal arts education (LeCompte 1987a, 1987b; LeCompte and Dworkin 1988). We recommend eliminating the vocational track altogether and having *all* students study health, nutrition, personal finance, automobile mechanics, carpentry, data processing, and small engine repair as everyday living skills — in addition to reading, mathematics, science, the arts, and social studies.

School Governance and Leadership.   Whereas sociologists have been criticized for being too gloomy about the prospects for reform of schooling, educational researchers have been criticized for being naive or Utopian. Regardless of how insightful their work has been, much of it remains unused. Ernest Boyer of the Carnegie Foundation for the Advancement of Teaching says:

> We've made remarkable breakthroughs in understanding the development of children, the development of learning, and the climate that enhances [them, but too often] what we know in theory and what we're doing in the classroom are very different. (Quoted in Kantrowitz and Wingert 1989, p. 51)

The issue is, how does what we know get translated into what we do? How does our sociological knowledge of schooling help us to bring about change?

A key element is an understanding of how power affects processes of change in organizations. Sociological insights have made clear that schools are not apolitical institutions in which the exercise of power is irrelevant. People who have power are not interested in giving it away, whether they are school administrators, government bureaucrats, or old-line teachers. Many people prefer to work in hierarchical structures where roles are governed by traditional habits. However, despite the deeply entrenched nature of conventional practice, we believe that redistribution of power is necessary for teachers to gain control over their work and their work place. Implicit in our thinking, and that of critical theorists, is that change needs to begin at the bottom of the hierarchy. Confrontation also needs to occur at the level of policy and power as well.

In the past several years educators have moved into the era of school restructuring. As Darling-Hammond reminds us, "over the last decade the rhetoric of school improvement has changed from a language of school reform to a language of school restructuring" with the aims of fundamentally redesigning schools and approaches to teaching and learning (1993, p. 753). At all levels of education, faculties and administrators have been called on to restructure their schools and programs to create places where people learn at a high level, develop their talents, evaluate and develop alternatives to complex problems, and construct their own knowledge (Darling-Hammond 1993). This form of restructuring demands input from teachers and communities about programs and policies. Site-based management and local community school boards have been instituted in many districts, changing more traditional hierarchical and patriarchal forms of financial and curricular control.

Perhaps the best known example of such restructuring is in Chicago, where in December 1988 the Illinois State Legislature passed the Chicago School Reform Act which fundamentally changed the governance structure of Chicago's public schools. The law created Local School Councils consisting of two community representatives, six parents, two teachers, and the principal. For high schools a nonvoting student sat on the board. With the establishment of these Local Schools Councils, principals, rather than being responsible to the central office, are chief executive officers responsible to and working with a managing board, which oversees the total running of the school and which has the power to hire and fire the principal, regardless of tenure. These councils construct school budgets, evaluate existing staff, and select new personnel. After consultation with members of the Council and the Professional Personnel Advisory Committee (PPAC) made up of school faculty, principals develop school improvement plans. The PPAC creates a mechanism where shared decision making can take place and teachers' voices are heard regarding issues that affect them. The Chicago Reform Act significantly changed the involvement and power of teachers and community members in the governance of the city's schools (Hess 1991).

Explore the Chicago school reform or current statewide reforms such as that begun by the Kentucky Education Reform Act (KERA). What changes are being made in these reform movements? How have the governance and structure of schooling changed?

While some decentralization and site-based management are touted as important reform efforts, they can also sabotage innovations, lead to fragmentation in educational policy, and create conflict between different levels of governance

(Goldwasser 1994). A number of years ago New York City, the largest school district in the United States, decentralized into a number of subdistricts, several of which have become notorious for poor student achievement and corruption in both financial and personnel matters, In one of the poorest districts, number 9, at least nine school board members were arrested within five years. Its students have repeatedly scored lower than any other district on citywide tests. In 1994 District 9 became a test case for the power of the city superintendent to enforce improvement upon a local school board. Under its new superintendent, Felton Johnson, District 9 became a model for corporate involvement in public schools. Johnson persuaded local foundations and corporations to buy computers, provide tutors, increase parent involvement, and engage in a number of other charitable projects. However, the local board decided not to renew Mr. Johnson's contract, whereupon the private-sector benefactors announced that they were ending their support, citing the district's instability and lack of commitment to reform. New York City Superintendent, Mr. Cortines countered by ordering the local board to reinstate Mr. Johnson in the interests of consistent reform and educational stability. The local district sued Cortines, stating that he had no legal right to overrule the decisions of locally elected school officials. The state courts upheld the firing of Johnson, a ruling that considerably weakened the city superintendent's power to root out corruption and institute districtwide reform (Dillon 1994).

At the same time that restructuring efforts have decentralized power, the increased standardization in statewide testing, standardized teacher evaluation, and standardized curricula have worked against restructuring efforts. The tensions between decentralization and standardization set up situations where two very different types of teachers are desired. On one hand, restructuring efforts call for teachers who share in decision making, collaborate with colleagues, develop challenging curricula to meet the developmental and intellectual needs of their students, and evaluate student outcomes through measures such as portfolio assessment. This view of teaching/learning requires teachers who have extensive professional expertise and are empowered to engage in policy decisions. On the other hand, standardized tests and curriculum, as well as more sanctions and rewards, require teachers who can work within a top-down hierarchy where decisions are made above the classroom level.

Empowered teachers working within these competing ideologies may find such conditions difficult at best. These are the teachers who have constructed classrooms where they engage children in meaningful learning activities but who must subvert the required curriculum to fit into what they know is best for their students or must interrupt their programs to administer state-mandated tests. Many examples of these competing ideologies can be found in schools today. Perhaps they occur most commonly where ability grouping is required for basal reading instruction but teachers implement the remainder of their programs through a whole language/integrated curricular approach.

School Choice.   The term *choice* has been applied to a number of approaches to school governance and structure. *Choice* is a word that has positive ideological power in the United States. As a consequence, it has been appropriated by political action groups, especially in education, from a variety of quite different and often conflicting perspectives (Lawrence 1994). In contemporary educational debates, *choice* has become a synonym for providing alternatives to the neighborhood public schools to which children ordinarily would be assigned.

The simplest way to give parents choices about the schools their children attend has been to relax the requirements that students attend the school closest to their home, that is, to eliminate attendance zones. Magnet schools have used this strategy, as have open-enrollment policies. Open enrollment plans have been criticized as advantaging only those children whose families have the ability to evaluate schools and transport their children to often distant campuses.

A rather restricted use of the term *choice* has been applied to giving teachers considerable autonomy in selecting curricular materials and instructional strategies. This approach changes governance only insofar as centralized curriculum directives are localized to the classroom and teachers are empowered to become more forceful decision makers in their own classrooms.

Another alternative to existing schools is to set up new ones at public expense. We have already discussed the multiple constituencies whose agendas compete for control of public schools. Over the years some of these constituencies have set up schools of their own. In the 1960s proponents of progressive "free" schools established a number of these institutions as private, tuition-charging alternatives. Private schools were also set up as "segregation academies" to avoid court-ordered desegregation of schools. The 1980s saw a tremendous increase in the number of Christian academies.

Current moves toward privatization differ in that they advocate the use of publicly funded alternative schools which, unlike magnet schools, do not further a socially mandated public policy. These plans exist under several rubrics. The first is a kind of fiscal reform that permits the allocation of school tax monies to parents in the form of vouchers. Advocates of this form of choice argue that if parents are allowed to use their vouchers to pay for at least part of their children's education, inferior schools would go bankrupt because no children would be sent to them. Critics argue that only the more affluent parents would have the means to provide transportation to out-of-neighborhood schools, which would persist despite their shortcomings because impoverished parents would have no choice at all. Furthermore, affluent parents could personally subsidize their voucher amount, thereby enhancing the quality of their children's schools in a way less affluent parents would be unable to do.

Choice can also encompass "charter schools," which have been established in limited numbers in several states. Charter schools resemble the magnet schools which were established to help maintain racially integrated schools, but they focus on a particular approach, theme, or curriculum, such as schools for outdoor experiences, music and the arts, and science and mathematics. They are financed by public funds, just as the magnet schools are, but they are established and governed by interested groups of parents and educators, who are given considerable autonomy. Although parents do not pay tuition, enrollment can be limited to students with certain qualifications.

A final form of privatization is allowing corporations and other institutions to set up schools which would run for profit—ostensibly more efficiently and effectively than the public schools. You may recall the arguments by the Scientific Management movement about making schools more effective by applying the tenets of corporate practice. The Whittle Corporation's Edison Project is an example. Some advocates of privatization argue that this alternative is the best one, just as they also argue for privatization of the penal system. However, as of this writing, several very ambitious attempts by well-funded corporate entities, such as Whittle Enterprises, have had second thoughts about their ability to run schools more cheaply and better than the public schools and have scaled back their efforts considerably. No examples of these efforts are currently available for assessment.

Alternative Ideologies of Schooling: Transformative Pedagogies

In this section we will examine four major approaches to transformative pedagogy currently being debated in educational literature: democratic education, critical pedagogy, multicultural education, and feminist pedagogy. These approaches in many ways encompass or overlap one another. For example, democratic educators would see multicultural education as an important part of their work. Multicultural educators would view democratic education and often critical and feminist pedagogies as processes for working with students. We have presented them separately here so as to explain briefly the main focus of each approach in the hope that you will explore them all in more detail.

All four approaches use similar specific pedagogical strategies. They all engage students in the construction of their own knowledge through methods such as whole language, an integrated curriculum, project-centered learning, Foxfire, process approaches to math and science, the use of student narratives, manipulatives, collaborative learning, peer tutoring, and authentic assessments. (See Table 9.1 for a summary of the four transformative pedagogies.)

Democratic Education. A primary theme of democratic education is the belief that children develop democratic ideals of equality, liberty, and community by living them in their daily lives. Proponents of democratic education use John Dewey's works as a theoretical base. Writing in the late nineteenth and early twentieth centuries with a concern for the negative effects of urbanization and industrialization, Dewey believed schools could serve as social centers where people could build a spirit of cooperation and community as well as a sense of interdependence as they learned the critical thinking skills necessary for a democratic society. Heavily reliant on Dewey's notion of building community, democratic educators are concerned with constructing learning environments where children can participate in the democratic process. Lehman (Lappe and DuBois 1993) reminds us that "a sense of community is at the heart of any democratically run organization" (p. 9). There are many ways teachers and administrators can work toward democratic education. Table 9.1 gives a sense of democratic education in a real school setting.

For this example we have relied heavily on Dave Lehman (1993), principal of

TABLE 9.1   Transformative Pedagogies

Pedagogy	Focus
Democratic Education	Democratic education is concerned with constructing learning communities where children can participate actively and fully in the democratic process. Students learn democratic ideals of equality, liberty, and community by living them in their daily lives.
Critical Pedagogy	Language of critique challenges the economic and political power structures in society and the ways people are exploited and oppressed. It asks questions about whose interests are served. Through democratic classroom processes, curriculum relies on sociocultural/political analysis challenges. Through language of possibilities, it empowers students to work toward social transformation.
Multicultural Education	Focus is on knowledge and affirmation of pluralism in all forms (ethnic, linguistic, gender, religious, sexual orientation, abilities). Centering the experiences of marginalized groups in society provides a more holistic, multidimensional perspective of society as a replacement for the Western curriculum usually privileged in schools. Openly challenges and rejects racism, sexism, and other forms of discrimination and oppression through critical pedagogy; works toward social justice.
Feminist Pedagogy	Focus is on the experiences of women, particularly as related to patriarchal structures and language. Notions of student voice, alternatives to hierarchical classroom structures, and emotional connectedness to each other and to the course content are important aspects of this pedagogy. Central strategies emphasizing personal experiences are journals, narratives, and autobiography. It works toward social action and transformation.

Ithaca's Alternative Community School, a public school housing 230 students and governed through a participatory democracy that includes all students. The school community is built on Family Groups consisting of approximately ten students and a teacher who meet together at least twice a week. Four separate but interrelated governing bodies provide the mechanisms through which the democracy works: (1) An Advisory Board consisting of student, staff, parent, and community representatives meets once monthly. (2) There are 15 to 20 staff-facilitated Committees—concerned with much of the business of the school such as curriculum, discipline, appeals, school lunch, agenda for the All School Meeting, and so on—which meet twice weekly for two class periods. (3) The Staff Meeting, held weekly for at least two hours, is a collaborative effort of the school's professional staff. (4) A weekly All School Meeting attended by students and staff work through school decisions. All decisions and policies are discussed and decided in the governing bodies. Extensive in-service training for staff helps them develop skills in group processes. A democratic process also takes place in classrooms, where the teacher presents a course plan and students participate in setting the course goals and designing the structure and means to evaluate their learning.

As can be seen from this limited description, democracy is accomplished by full participation of students and staff.

Think of your own classroom, school, or college setting. Is it a participatory democracy? What would you need to do to transform it into one?

Critical Pedagogy.   Critical pedagogy has grown out of the work of the critical theorists writing in the 1980s and 1990s. You may want to refer back to the discussion of critical theory in Chapter 1. Critical pedagogy is concerned, on one hand, with a critique of the society, particularly around issues of power, and on the other hand with developing students' critical abilities in order to work toward the transformation of society. This pedagogy involves a "language of critique" as well as a "language of possibilities." Teachers using this approach engage students in critical questioning of their own beliefs and assumptions, as well as the assumptions in their text materials. By *text* we mean anything used in the education process: textbooks, original source materials, popular culture, and so on. The deconstruction of textual language is especially important for critical pedagogy. What are the underlying assumptions, for example, in the phrase *manifest destiny?* Critical pedagogy attends to the question: "Whose interests are served?"

Student voice and resistance are central components of critical pedagogy. In these classrooms all students are encouraged to explore and express their own positions. Through active questioning and critique, students develop the ability to understand how people are manipulated by the economic and political power structures in society and can become empowered to work toward social change for a more democratic society in which human oppression and exploitation are not tolerated. Henry Giroux (1988) sees both teachers and students as transformative intellectuals who are able to engage in these critical dialogues of the ways power is

> understood as an embodied and fractured set of experiences that are lived and suffered by individuals and groups within specific contexts and settings. . . . First they need to analyze how cultural production is organized within asymmetrical relations of power in schools. Second, they need to construct political strategies for participating in social struggles and designed to fight for schools as democratic public spheres. (1988, pp. 101–102)

Think about a class in which you are either a teacher or a student. How could that class be transformed into one that uses critical pedagogy? What changes would be made in the way the class is structured, in the curriculum, or in the way the teacher(s) and students interact?

Multicultural Education.   Multicultural education has been woven through discussions in the professional education literature since the 1960s, when social activists struggled against racial and gendered oppression. Multicultural education means quite different things to different people. Some educators have chosen the "tacos on Tuesday" approach, which is limited to celebrating the foods and customs of "ethnically different" groups. At the other end of the continuum, educators view multicultural education as anti-racist, anti-sexist education that critiques both individual and structural forms of racism, sexism, and other forms of discrimination and that works toward social transformation. Suzuki explains the consequence of this variation:

> [M]any widely differing conceptualizations of multicultural education have been formulated. As a consequence, the various programs in the field often appear to have conflicting purposes and priorities. Many educators have come to view multicultural education as ill defined, lacking in substance, and just another educational fad. (1984, p. 294)

In *Empowerment through Multicultural Education* Christine Sleeter (1991) gives a concise history of multicultural education in the United States, explaining five approaches that had been used in school pedagogy over the previous three decades:

1. A *human relations approach* is aimed toward sensitivity training, with people's interpersonal relationships and attitudes being central. A key understanding is that "we are all the same because we are all different." People are taught that through the power of love and harmony we can change insensitive or prejudiced attitudes. The human relations approach does not attend to oppression at the structural level.
2. *Teaching the culturally different* has grown out of research we reviewed in Chapter 7, which examined culturally congruent approaches to schooling. It argues that learning environments must be constructed so that culturally different children can use their abilities and knowledge for educational success.
3. *Cultural democracy* is a form of multicultural education whereby classrooms model an equal and unoppressive society that is culturally diverse. The notion here is that by experiencing this democratic, pluralistic setting, students can be empowered to work for social change in a society that does not practice these values. This approach uses an implicit rather than explicit approach to teach about oppression.
4. *Single group studies,* such as African-American studies, Chicano studies, or Women's studies, emphasize the history of the target group and the way the group's culture has formed and changed within oppressive circumstances. This form of multicultural education emphasizes group solidarity and identification for target members.
5. Education that is multicultural and *social reconstructionist* explicitly teaches about oppression and discrimination of historically marginalized groups and promotes social action to fight oppression through a coalition of oppressed and dominant groups. (1991)

Current educational literature continues to provide us with examples of all these approaches to multicultural education. We believe multicultural educators *cannot* stop at the individual or group level but must teach explicitly about ways in which racist and sexist practices are permeated through our institutions. A social action

---

Seven Basic Characteristics of Multicultural Education

Multicultural education is anti-racist education.

Multicultural education is basic education.

Multicultural education is important for all students.

Multicultural education is pervasive.

Multicultural education is education for social justice.

Multicultural education is a process.

Multicultural education is critical pedagogy.

SOURCE: Nieto 1992, p. 208.

---

component is a critical one for multicultural education. We support multicultural education as described by Nieto:

> Multicultural education is a process of comprehensive school reform and basic education for all students. It challenges and rejects racism and other forms of discrimination in schools and society and accepts and affirms the pluralism (ethnic, racial, linguistic, religious, economic, and gender, among others) that students, their communities, and teachers represent. Multicultural education permeates the curriculum and instructional strategies used in schools, as well as the interactions among teachers, students and parents, and the very way that schools conceptualize the nature of teaching and learning. Because it uses critical pedagogy as its underlying philosophy and focuses on knowledge, reflection, and action (praxis) as the basis for social change, multicultural education furthers the democratic principles of social justice. (1992, p. 208)

Think of teachers you know who are multicultural educators. What approach does each take to this form of pedagogy?

Carefully examine your own knowledge of the history of oppressed groups. Do you need to expand your knowledge in order to be able to infuse your curriculum with multicultural content?

Feminist Pedagogies.   As Chapter 8 noted, there is not just one feminism or one feminist theory. Similarly, there are many forms of feminist pedagogies. This section will provide a brief overview of the central components of feminist pedagogies; we urge you to explore this literature. Consistent with feminism and feminist theory, feminist pedagogies are concerned with the experiences of women in societies, particularly as related to differential power structures. Feminist teachers critique the cultural patriarchal structures and language which continue to place women in oppressive, exploited positions. Shrewsbury explains:

> At its simplest level, feminist pedagogy is concerned with gender justice and overcoming oppressions. It recognizes the genderedness of all social relations and consequently of all societal institutions and structures. (1987, p. 7)

Using bell hooks's (1989) notions, this pedagogy moves traditional curricular content to the margins, as that which has been silenced or marginalized is moved to the center of exploration. The experiences of women and marginalized groups are the focus of class readings and discussion. Feminist teaching

> moves people and topics ordinarily defined as "marginal" into focus in the classroom and it invites people who ordinarily occupy the center of attention (i.e. white males) to notice what it's like to not be the center of attention. Students then have the opportunity to examine how power and status are used among them. (Thompson and Disch 1992, p. 5)

Concerned with hierarchical relations in their schools, feminist teachers interrupt these relations by using strategies to share the power with students. Teachers collaborate with other teachers and students in the construction of the structure, content, and interactions in the class. Therefore, like other forms of transformative pedagogies, feminists rely on democratic decision-making processes and community building. Thompson and Disch explain:

> We continually think about how our classes are going as communities. Other teachers obsess about their lectures; we obsess about both the content we teach as well as the relationships among students and our relationships with both individuals and the group as a whole. We think carefully about how to express our anger when the class isn't taking responsibility to carry on meaningful discussion of the readings. We think carefully about how to address or resolve conflicts among particular pairs or groups of students. No two semesters are alike. The results of this kind of teaching cannot be predicted because the students have power, and we never know how they're going to use it, how they're going to challenge us, or how they're going to challenge each other. (1992, p. 9)

Teachers assume roles of co-learner and facilitator rather than authority. However, because of institutional structures, feminist teachers are positioned in the role of those who have ultimate authority for student evaluation, and they struggle to find ways to engage students in making decisions about their own evaluations and grades.

Clearly, student voice is central to the feminist classroom, as are the personal experiences of teachers and students. Feminist teachers believe that students construct their own knowledge by using their personal experiences to connect with the course content. The use of journals, biography, autobiography, and narratives enhances this process. Berry and Black explain:

> We encourage them [students] to look for connections between their personal experience and the theoretical and historical concerns addressed in class; we push them to examine their own lives in the context of larger cultural, social and economic issues relating to women. (1987, p. 59)

Because of the emotional nature of sharing personal experiences in the classroom, there is often a sense of emotional connectedness among participants. These emotions are not always positive, but rather they reflect the struggle among participants as they make sense of their differing views and experiences. Feminist teachers expect a range of emotions because of both the content and the pedagogical strategies used in the teaching/learning process. Feminist pedagogy requires us to accept and explore these emotions as part of classroom life. Teachers understand that in order to really struggle with the knowledge, students must feel this emotional connectedness to the experience:

> We assume that learning needs to be close to the heart, meaning that the course must move the learner and make a lasting impact on her or his life. (Thompson and Disch 1992, p. 4)

Have you ever participated in feminist pedagogy? Share your experiences with others in the class.

A Note about Networks.   Since the last edition of this book, networks of individuals, schools, and colleges have proliferated and serve to share knowledge, support one another's efforts, and discuss their issues and concerns. These networks are coalitions of individuals and institutions, variously supported by public and foundational monies, that work to support transformative educational projects. As we end this section, we urge you to explore the work of these networks.

Just a few of the many examples are the Coalition for Essential Schools, the Institute of Democracy in Education, the Foxfire Network, Rethinking Schools, the San Diego State Multicultural Infusion Center (MEIC), the Urban Network for the Improvement of Teacher Education (UNITE), the Center for Collaborative Education (CCE), the National Coalition of Education Activists, and the National Center for Restructuring Education, Schools, and Teaching (NCREST). In addition, many local and state teachers' support groups are actively engaged in exploring new forms of teaching and learning. Some of these networks have established electronic mail discussion groups that are usually open to anyone interested in participating. We invite you to explore these networks of innovative educators.

Select a network whose efforts are centered on a project that interests you, and become part of its electronic mail discussion group. Write for the network's literature, find out about its funding agencies, and explore its purposes and activities. Write to us, through Longman, Inc., to share your findings. Maybe for our next edition we will compile a list of these networks.

Alternative Possibilities for Teacher Education and Practice

What types of teachers are needed to provide quality schooling in a multicultural world? How should these teachers be educated? What is the role of teachers in schools today? The 1980s brought a new reform movement in teacher education calling for complete restructuring of the profession. One set of critics was based in universities and colleges of education; the other found its impetus in school districts and state legislatures. The former provided their central arguments in two documents: The Holmes Group's *Tomorrow's Teachers* (1986), and *A Nation Prepared: Teachers for the 21st Century* by the Carnegie Task Force on Teaching as a Profession (1986). Both call for a more highly educated professional teaching force.

The Holmes Group proposed a five-year program, with students pursuing a fifth year of teacher education after completing a Liberal Arts degree. The underlying assumption is that a Liberal Arts degree in a specific academic field would provide preservice teachers with the necessary knowledge base and then the fifth year would furnish the pedagogical knowledge and experience for teaching of that subject matter. These reforms leave control of entrance to the teaching profession in the hands of the university teacher training programs.

A counterproposal, calling for a different route to certification, has been spearheaded largely by school district personnel who feel that college teaching is out of touch with the realities of public school life and who resent the poor preparation given to many teachers. While the content of such routes to certification does not differ from that proposed by the Holmes Group, the control mechanisms do. They seek to weaken or even eliminate the role of colleges of education in teacher preparation. One approach places teacher certification in the hands of school districts. It calls for the establishment of district-level "teacher centers," where methods courses and other requirements would be provided. People who already have degrees would enter a teacher center and, while taking courses, would begin an apprenticeship under the supervision of the school district. A variation calls for the teacher center to be located in a local teachers' college but for all other activities to be carried out by the district. Other proposals call for centers to be established and examinations to be given under state supervision, with districts providing the supervised apprenticeships.

These plans differ substantially from traditional teacher training programs which have been in place in colleges of education throughout most of the twentieth century. The extreme case is in elementary education, where in some programs a teacher trainee is limited to two years of academic training, a year and a half of methods—or "Mickey Mouse"—courses, and student teaching, leaving college with no real specialization whatsoever. Currently teacher training often does not prepare students for the political arena, either on the microlevel or on the macrolevel. By retaining what we call a "psychocentric" focus on individual differences and cognition, teacher training has avoided confronting the social and political context of schooling altogether. This gap makes new teachers exceedingly vulnerable to pressure, prone to sliding into teaching at the lowest common denominator for survival and to accepting the conventional wisdom of senior teachers about "how it's always been." This is why we have advocated explicit training and practice in the critical and political for pre-service teachers. In-service activities for practicing teachers could also make good use of such instruction.

The demand for a more rigorously educated teaching force has gained support from both the radical left and neoconservative right. The call for raising entrance standards, increasing the number and rigor of classes, and establishing tests for exit-level competencies conforms to the neoconservative "back to the classics" excellence movement propounded by William Bennett, Secretary of Education under President Reagan. These proposals argue from the "top down" for more centralized state control over the training and evaluation of students and teachers. They are based upon a deep suspicion that teachers cannot be trusted to work competently and the belief that only a program of tight, centralized control will put things right.

Teachers as Intellectuals.   On the left, critical theorists such as Henry Giroux (1988) argue for the concept of "teachers as intellectuals." Contrary to the neoconservatives, critical theorists argue for less rather than more control over teachers. In fact, they wish to shift the locus of power from state, university, and district administrators to the classroom teacher.

Giroux argues that current demands for reform in teacher education are at variance with the democratically informed schooling needed in a pluralistic society. Giroux states that these proposals lead to de-skilling of teachers—the process by which teachers lose the ability to utilize professional training, judgment, and autonomy. He argues that a "teacher-proof" standardized curriculum, uniform text adoptions, centralized and test-driven systems of student evaluation and placement, routinized classroom management systems, and reduction in decision-making power all act to reduce teachers to mere technicians. He further calls for a complete restructuring of teachers' work so that they are viewed as valued intellectuals, not barely competent, mindless technicians. The first step in this process would be to transfer instructional control from administrators, state bureaucrats, and textbook publishers to teachers. As intellectual leaders, teachers would be responsible for determining the goals of schooling—what should be taught, how these goals would be translated into curricular materials, and how the materials should be presented.

Central to Giroux's argument is the concept of the teacher as a critical pedagogue or transformative intellectual. To be intellectually critical educators, teachers must not only be intellectuals in the sense that they reflect seriously on the meaning and consequences of their practice, but be critical in the sense that they question the taken-for-granted assumptions—the "that's the way it's always been"—of school practice and societal organization. Critical pedagogues have the *responsibility* to question political motives and social inequities with their students in an ongoing effort to create a more democratic and equitable society. Giroux is worth quoting at length on the role of teachers as transformative intellectuals:

> Transformative intellectuals need to develop a discourse that unites the language of critique with the language of possibility, so that social educators recognize that they can make changes. In doing so, they must speak out against economic, political and social injustices, both within and outside of schools. At the same time, they must work to create the conditions that give students the opportunity to become citizens who have the knowledge and courage to struggle in order to make despair unconvincing and hope practical. As difficult as this task may seem to social educators, it is a struggle worth waging. To do otherwise is to deny social educators the opportunity to assume the role of transformative intellectuals. (1988, p. 128)

There are limitations in Giroux's critique. First, neither neoconservatives nor critical theorists have addressed the impact of their proposals on the participation of minorities in the teaching profession. On the one hand is a concern that raising standards and increasing the length—and cost—of teacher training would make it more difficult for minority individuals to become teachers (Halcon and Reyes 1989). On the other is a concern that minority teachers who advocate radical change would threaten their legitimacy and acceptance. Standing too far from conventional practice might well place such teachers, already in the minority on most faculties, in danger of being fired—or at least ostracized professionally—as troublemakers.

Another concern is that it is difficult to imagine how today's teachers could be critical, intellectual pedagogues given the limits of their preparation, the structural constraints on their activities, and their largely oppressive working environments. Implicit in Giroux's notion of the teacher as transformative intellectual is a critique of the entire system of schooling. Clearly, a complete restructuring is required if teachers are to be reflective, to have their skills, expertise, and creativity celebrated, and to work in situations that do not denigrate their sense of professionalism.

Unfortunately, both the neoconservative right and the radical left calls for reform focused primarily on teachers. This may be so because blaming teachers is relatively easy. This stance may be due to an optimistic hope that only through a "grass roots" community-based organization of teachers will significant changes be accomplished. Much more difficult is addressing the structural and political constraints which have created the radically alienating conditions prevalent in many schools. However, as we've described above, present alternatives for the structure of public schools empower teachers to begin to function in the ways prescribed by critical theorists.

Teachers as Feminists.   We have earlier discussed how hegemony consists of the practices and thinking that justify existing patterns of domination and subordination in society. In this section we look at ways in which the educational system might begin to question these patterns.

We demonstrated in Chapter 4 that teaching is a predominantly female activity, that schools resemble "pedagogical harems" where women teach and men supervise and administrate. Increasing the professional status of teaching—in our view as well as that of scholars like Apple, Blau, Kelly, Lortie, Simeone, Weiler, Weis, and others cited in previous chapters—cannot be discussed without a consideration of the engendered nature and patriarchal structure of schooling. The unequal distribution of power among men and women is one of the most salient features of the profession, one that undermines its status. As long as teaching is considered to be "women's work," neither it nor its participants (male and female) will enjoy the power and prestige they seek.

Through feminist critiques, teachers can question the legitimacy of the male-dominated hierarchy of schools in order to gain a voice in the decision-making process. Feminist teachers are those who are sensitive to and directly address issues of gender inequality in the curricular content, instructional methods, and organization of schools. Their knowledge of gender and power issues enables them to assess their own and their students' experiences in schools, question the oppressive aspects of these experiences, and provide more democratic alternatives. Weiler (1988) suggests that feminist teachers, both male and female, are more sensitive to and respectful of the racial, cultural, and class identities of their students because they have been made sharply aware of patterns of gender discrimination.

Recruitment to Teacher Education.   What would teacher education look like from critical theoretical and feminist perspectives? If you were to walk through the halls of most colleges of education in the United States today, you would find a fairly homogeneous population of white, middle-class, female students being taught by a fairly homogeneous population of white, middle-class, male professors—despite an increasing number of young female and minority assistant professors. A salutary change would occur if the ranks of both professors and students in these colleges more closely resembled the general population of public schools.

Although minority recruitment programs have been in place in most colleges for some years, the number of actual recruits is small and decreasing, especially in colleges of education. The continued low status and salary of teachers as well as the lack of scholarship funds limit the number of minority students interested in pursuing teaching as a career. In addition, as colleges move toward five-year degree plans, tuition costs soar, and financial aid continues to diminish, the hardships of attendance as well as the opportunity costs of becoming a teacher become overwhelming to minority students.

Despite these barriers, it is essential for colleges of education to be sensitive to the type of students they are admitting. With the current reform movement's emphasis on "excellence," concerns about race, ethnicity, class, and gender balance may be obscured by concerns over "quality." It will be easy for insensitive teacher educators to mistake being white, middle-class, and comfortable with school culture for academic quality. A college of education committed to preparing intellectual teachers for a multicultural world will work to ensure the comparable diversity of the student body. These colleges must be committed to recruiting and educating a multi-ethnic, gender-balanced teaching population.

Multicultural Infusion.   A college committed to social justice and to training teachers for today's multicultural schools will place emphasis on courses and experiences that prepare students to function among those who are ethnically, culturally, and economically different from themselves. These materials should not be "ghettoized" into isolated courses or parts of courses, nor taught only by minority faculty. The multicultural emphasis achieves legitimacy only when it becomes part and parcel of everyday life in every subject—infused throughout the programs.

Teaching in teams so that faculty become familiar with each other's subject areas and work toward integrating each into their instruction—including material relevant to other ethnicities, classes, and genders—would help normalize the currently exotic nature of both the multicultural content and the faculty who teach it. We suggest also that colleges go beyond advocating and teaching sensitivity to cultural differences. Colleges should also establish a "minimum competency" for affirming diversity, such that candidates who demonstrate bigoted attitudes do not receive certification. Such a competency is no more subjective than demonstrated competence to evaluate visual art or poetry.

Watch the movie *Stand and Deliver,* an illustration of alternative teaching methods in a barrio school in Los Angeles. What worked for the teacher and students in this film? How was the teacher able to engage his students effectively? Do you think these methods would work in other settings?

An Interdisciplinary Perspective.   Teachers can be neither critical, intellectual, nor competent if they have never experienced intellectual challenges nor been exposed to the world of content and ideas. With this in mind, we conform to certain aspects of the neoconservative reform, which calls for basing the curriculum on a Liberal Arts education. At the same time, it is important to remember the multicultural curriculum. Liberal Arts does not mean a return to a traditional androcentric and ethnocentric emphasis on classics of the Western European heritage. Rather, it means that students would specialize in a particular discipline of their choice for the requisite four-year program and only then enter a teacher education program.

This preparation would be based upon an experiential study of schooling within its social context. Departing from the heavily cognitive teacher training programs, we propose to place greater emphasis on child and adolescent development, on the historical and philosophical antecedents of current practice, and on the social, political, and cultural context within and outside of the schools. These studies derive from what have come to be known as the foundations of education—history, philosophy, psychology, anthropology, and sociology.

At the present time, despite the fact that whole children are the primary focus in what teachers do, teacher trainees take only an introductory course or two in human growth and development; their study of psychology is narrowly limited to experimental and behavioral studies of cognition. Similarly, they get only the barest smattering of the other foundational studies, usually crammed into a single survey course covering the history, philosophy, sociology, anthropology, and politics of education. Graduate programs are rarely more rigorous. The program we propose would have a much stronger psychological and social foundation in order to prepare teachers to examine critically current practices and procedures, to analyze patterns of control and governance in education, and to critique text materials, instructional techniques, and classroom management strategies.

Form small groups or committees in your class to design a school based on the research knowledge presented in this text. Share your ideas in a general group discussion. How could you incorporate some of these ideas into your real world of school practice?

A CLOSING NOTE

The suggestions above are just a beginning. Professional journals as well as the popular press are full of articles calling for reform and describing successful innovative programs purporting to resolve some or all of the crisis in education. Yet the innovations, like cream, still float to the top, serving the most advantaged students; programs for the most disadvantaged seem remarkably ineffective. We believe that the insights offered in this text provide a way of beginning a new kind of thinking about schools. What *are* the purposes of schooling in contemporary society? What *should* they be? Are the two compatible? How will the characteristics of the students change in the next few years? What will the teaching force look like? How would this work force, as well as curricula, school structures, forms of control, and instructional practices, have to change to be congruent with the incoming population of children—and teachers? What can *you* do about it?

appendix

Do's and Don'ts for Non-Sexist Language

"Relax...it's only a <u>man</u>-eating tiger."

GENERAL PRINCIPLES

■ *De*gender, don't *re*gender (e.g. degender *chairman* to *chair*, don't regender it to *chairwoman).*

■ Create gender-neutral terms: convert adjectives to nouns by adding *ist* (e.g. active: activist).

■ Replace occupational terms in *man* and *boy*, if possible, with terms that include members of either sex.

■ Avoid occupational designations having derogatory *-ette* and *-ess* endings.

NAMES AND TITLES

■ When Mr. is used, Ms. is the equivalent. Use Ms. to designate both a married and unmarried woman. A woman should be referred to by name in the same way that a man is. Both should be called by their full names, by first or last name only, or by title.

⟋ Miss Lee, Ms. Chai and Mrs. Feeney ♦ Ms. Lee, Ms. Chai and Ms. Feeney or Lee, Chai and Feeney.

⟋ Governor Burns and Anna Kahanamoku ♦ Governor Burns and Representative Kahanamoku.

■ Forms for using a woman's name before marriage should be gender-neutral.

⟋ maiden name ♦ pre-marital name, birth name.

■ Issue invitations or notices, bills, financial statements, etc. in the name of each of the individuals concerned.

⟋ Mr. and Mrs. John Tanaka ♦ Ellen and John Tanaka (if both names are known), or (if the name of spouse is not known) Ellen Tanaka and spouse.

SALUTATIONS IN LETTERS

■ If the name of the addressee is unknown, start the letter immediately without a salutation. Alternatively, especially in letters of recommendations or memos not addressed to a specific person, start with "To Whom It May Concern."

⟋ Dear Sir/Madam/Gentlemen:
♦ Aloha: (Use only in Hawaii.)
♦ Dear Customer/Colleague/Subscriber:
♦ Dear Editor/Manager/Account Executive/(other job title):
♦ Dear Representative/Senator/Delegate/(other honorary title):
♦ Dear Friend(s):

⟋ indicates DON'T, a sexist expression to be avoided.
♦ indicates DO, a non-sexist alternative.

PRONOUNS

■ Avoid the pronoun *he* when both sexes are meant. Alternative approaches are:

● Recast into the plural.

⟋ Give each student *his* paper as soon as *he* is finished. ♦ Give students *their* papers as soon as *they* are finished.

● Reword to eliminate the pronoun.

⟋ The average student is worried about *his* grades. ♦ The average student is worried about grades.

● Replace the masculine pronoun with *one, you,* or (sparingly) *he* or *she* as appropriate.

⟋ If the student is dissatisfied with *his* grade, *he* can appeal to the instructor. ♦ A student who is dissatisfied with *her* or *his* grade can appeal to the instructor.

● Alternate male and female expressions.

⟋ Let each student participate. Has *he* had a chance to talk? Did *he* feel left out? ♦ Let each student participate. Has *she* had a chance to talk? Did *he* feel left out?

● Use plural indefinite pronoun.

⟋ Anyone who wants to go to the game should bring *his* money tomorrow. ♦ All those who want to go to the game should bring *their* money tomorrow.

● Use the double-pronoun construction.

⟋ Every person has a right to *his* opinion. ♦ Every person has a right to *his or her* opinion.

● Use *he/she, his/her,* etc. in printed contracts and other forms so the inapplicable pronoun can be crossed out.

SPORTS

■ Let language usage reflect the fact that sports do not exclusively concern males.

■ Use gender-free terms in writing or talking about sports events.

⟋ sportsmanship ♦ fair play, team play, sporting attitude.

⟋ baseman (as in first baseman) ♦ base (as in first base), baseplayer.

⟋ crewman ♦ crew, crew member.

⟋ ironman (event and participant) ♦ (iron) triathlon, triathlete.

⟋ tinman (event and participant) ♦ (tin) triathlon, triathlete.

EXAMPLES OF DEGENDERED USAGE

actress ♦ actor.

anchorman ♦ anchor, anchorperson.

authoress ♦ author.

average or common man ♦ average person, ordinary people, typical worker.

bachelor ♦ single (or unmarried) man.

bachelorgirl, spinster ♦ single (or unmarried woman).

brotherhood (unless only men are meant) ♦ community, amity, unity.

businessman ♦ business executive, business person, business manager, manager, entrepreneur.

cameraman ♦ camera operator, photographer.

career girl ♦ professional woman.

chairman, chairwoman ♦ chair (for both sexes).

Chinamen ♦ the Chinese.

cleaning lady/woman, maid ♦ housekeeper, housecleaner, office cleaner.

clergyman ♦ clergy, minister, priest.

coed ♦ student.

congressman ♦ member of Congress, representative, legislator.

copy boy, copy girl ♦ messenger, runner.

councilman, councilwoman ♦ councilmember.

countryman, countrymen ♦ people of the country, country's citizens.

craftsman ♦ craftsperson, artisan, crafter.

draftsman ♦ drafter, drafting technician.

Dutchmen ♦ the Dutch.

early man, caveman ♦ early humans, early societies.

Esquire ♦ Attorney at law, lawyer.

executrix ♦ executor.

fellow worker ♦ colleague, co-worker, peer.

fireman ♦ firefighter.

forefathers ♦ ancestors, precursors, forebears.

foreman ♦ supervisor.

founding fathers ♦ the founders, pioneers.

gal or girl Friday ♦ assistant or secretary.

gentlemen's agreement ♦ personal agreement, informal contract.

great men in history ♦ great figures in history, people who made history, historical figures.

heroine ♦ hero.

hostess ♦ host.

hula girl ♦ hula dancer.

insurance man ♦ insurance agent.

Irishmen ♦ the Irish.

lady doctor ♦ doctor, physician.

layman ♦ layperson, lay, laity, lay people, lay member.

libber ♦ feminist, liberationist.

mailman, postman ♦ mail carrier, letter carrier, postal worker.

male nurse ♦ nurse.

(to) man ♦ to staff, run, operate.

man and his world ♦ world history, history of peoples.

manhood ♦ adulthood, maturity.

man-hours ♦ work hours, staff hours, hours worked, total hours.

manhunt ♦ a hunt for . . .

mankind ♦ humanity, human race, human beings, people, human family.

man-made ♦ artificial, hand made, of human origin, synthetic, manufactured, crafted, machine made.

manned flight ♦ piloted flight.

manned orbital flight ♦ piloted orbital flight.

manning chart ♦ staff chart.

man-on-the-street ♦ ordinary person, ordinary citizen, average voter, average person.

manpower ♦ work force, human resources, labor force, human energy, personnel, workers.

man's achievements ♦ human achievements.

man-sized job ♦ big or difficult (job), requiring exceptional abilities.

men of science ♦ scientists.

middleman ♦ go-between, liaison, agent.

Mr. Chairman! Madam Chairwoman! ♦ Chair! (for both sexes).

one-man band or show ♦ soloist, performer, artist, individual, individual show.

poetess ♦ poet.

policeman ♦ police officer.

police matron ♦ police officer.

primitive man ♦ primitive people, primitive human beings, a primitive.

repairman ♦ repairer.

right hand man ♦ assistant, helper.

rise of man ♦ rise of the human race or humanity, rise of civilization, rise of cultures.

salesman ♦ salesperson, sales representative, salesclerk, seller, agent.

salesman ♦ sales staff, sales personnel.

showman ♦ performer.

spokesman ♦ representative, spokesperson.

statesman ♦ official, diplomat.

tradesman ♦ shopkeeper, trader, merchant, entrepreneur, artisan.

tradesmen ♦ trades people, tradespersons.

weatherman ♦ forecaster, weathercaster.

woman lawyer ♦ lawyer.

working man ♦ workers, typical worker.

workman ♦ worker, laborer, employee.

workman like ♦ competent.

■ The following assumptions are obsolete and should be avoided.

● That only men hold influential jobs. E.g. ⊘ Congressional representatives urged the President to find the right *man* for the job. ◆ Congressional representatives urged the President to find the right *person*.

● That children are cared for by their mothers only. E.g. ⊘ *Mothers* should note that a nutritious breakfast is more important for a child than it is for an adult. ◆ A nutritious breakfast is more important for a child than . . .

● That men head all families and are the major wage earners. E.g. ⊘ The average worker with a wife and two children pays 30 percent of *his* income to taxes. ◆ An average family of four pays 30 percent of *its* income . . . *or* an average worker with three dependents pays 30 percent of income . . .

● That certain professions are reserved for one sex. E.g. ⊘ Sometimes a nurse must use *her* common sense. ◆ Sometimes nurses must rely on common sense . . .

● That women perform all work related to homemaking. E.g. ⊘ The family grocery shopper wants to get all *her* shopping done in one stop. ◆ The family grocery shopper wants to get all the shopping done in one stop.

● Housewives are not using the new truth-in-weight information. ◆ *Homemakers* (*shoppers, customers*) are not using the new . . .

● That women are possessions of men and are not responsible for their actions. E.g. ⊘ Henry *allows* his wife to work part time. ◆ Odette Lee works part time.

■ Describe the appearance of a woman only in circumstances in which you would describe the appearance of a man.

⊘ The *attractive well-dressed* interior minister fielded questions from reporters. ◆ The interior minister fielded . . .

■ Do not report the marital status of a woman or a man, unless marital status is the subject of the story.

⊘ Divorcee Judy Petty lost her bid to unseat Representative Wilbur Mills. ◆ Candidate Judy Petty lost her bid . . .

■ An employed person should be identified by his or her occupation, when relevant. Do not use the terms "homemaker" and "mother" unless his or her homemaking role and family relationship, respectively, are the subject of discourse.

● Mrs. Marion Chong, *wife* of Dr. Allan Chong, gave a report on recent zoning variances. ◆ Marion Chong, *member* of the Zoning Board, gave a report on . . .

■ Use title, terms and names in parallel construction, with females mentioned first sometimes to avoid stereotyping.

⊘ Man and wife ◆ Wife and husband (or husband and wife)

■ Do not suggest that women are immature, adolescent and emotional and hence inferior to men.

⊘ Sports stories and pictures that portray females merely as spectators. ◆ Sports stories and pictures that portray females as active participants

⊘ The term *girl* for a female over 18 ◆ The term *woman*

⊘ Fair sex, weaker sex ◆ Women

⊘ The little woman or better half ◆ Wife

⊘ Housewife ◆ Homemaker

⊘ ALSO AVOID: Stories that emphasize exceptions to stereotypes (examples: John Kealoha is glad his mother-in-law is visiting); and expressions that demean women (example: distaff, women's work, woman driver, weak sister, sissy, old-maidish, spinsterish, womanish).

■ Avoid stories, photographs, captions, or phrases that imply:

⊘ That the sole or primary interest of an unmarried woman is "catching a man."

⊘ That certain categories of women are shrewish or overbearing. (Examples: mothers-in-law, feminists.)

⊘ That certain categories of women are scatterbrained, incompetent, or excessively dependent upon men to manage their lives. (Example: young, pretty, or blond-haired women.)

⊘ That women are incompetent in areas once considered "man's domain." (Example: Leilani is mechanically inept.)

⊘ That career women generally lack homemaking skills, do not have children, or are not good parents if they do have children.

⊘ That all or nearly all female homemakers are unsympathetic to the objectives of the women's movement. [Surveys and articles indicate the contrary.]

⊘ That men have the active roles, women have the passive roles.

⊘ That men are brutish, violent, crude, harsh or insensitive.

⊘ That women are fearful, squeamish, passive, dependent, weepy, frivolous, weak, shrewish, nagging, easily defeated, hysterical, scatterbrained.

This material has been adapted from *Women, Men and the Changing Language,* a 13-page brochure produced by the Media Task Force of the Honolulu County Committee on the Status of Women. Produced by HCCSW. Cover art by David Friedman. Edited by John Defrancis, Laudra B. Eber, Gerald H. Ohta, Katsue Akiba Reynolds, 1988. Additional copies of the brochure are available. Send stamped, self-addressed envelope to Office of Human Resources, 650 S. King St., Honolulu, HI 96813 (phone 523-4073).

Glossary

Ability grouping is the practice, used in elementary schools, of organizing students into instructional groups according to their abilities as assessed by school personnel on the basis of classroom performance and standardized test scores. These groups are used primarily for math and reading instruction.

Adolescence refers to the transition stage in one's life which usually begins at puberty and ends when one participates in activities normally associated with adulthood: economic independence from parents, marriage, or the birth of a child.

Alienation is a sociological word for the more popularly used term *burnout*. It occurs when the social and cultural context in which individuals live changes so drastically that personal goals that were once valued and desired cannot be achieved. As a result, the individuals lose faith in the institutions that structure their lives. Alienation is manifested in six types of feelings: *powerlessness,* or the sense that people have no control over their personal or work lives; *meaninglessness,* or a sense that the world has become absurd or incomprehensible; *normlessness,* or the feeling that the rules that structure the world have disappeared or become ineffective; *personal isolation,* or feeling apart from other human beings; *cultural isolation,* or being in opposition to or isolated from values held by one's community; and *self-estrangement,* or being forced to engage in activities that are intrinsically unrewarding or counter to one's beliefs and self-definition. (LeCompte and Dworkin 1991, p. 5)

Bureaucracy is a sociological term referring to a large, hierarchically structured formal organization whose purpose is to carry out some complex task. Both work and administration in bureaucracies are rationally subdivided and supervised by career professionals specifically trained for their jobs.

Caste refers to a social group or class whose membership is fixed by hereditary rules and defined by occupational status. In societies where castes exist they are the primary means by which society is stratified.

Caste-like minority (Ogbu 1978) is a native-born stigmatized group whose destiny is caste-like because it has experienced so many generations of systematic economic discrimination that its poverty becomes virtually hereditary.

Civil rights refers to those rights belonging to individuals because of their status as citizens; all citizens are guaranteed equal protection under the law by the Fourteenth Amendment of the U.S. Constitution.

Class refers to a category of things grouped together because they share common characteristics.

Cohort is a demographic term identifying a category of people who share a characteristic such as age or the date of entering an institution. Sociologists frequently refer to an *educational* or *age cohort*, people who are of the same generation or who entered the educational system or other social institution at the same time.

Compensatory education refers to school programs funded by the federal government to provide additional, individualized education to compensate for disadvantages resulting from a poor environment.

Conflict theory uses the same general systems analysis as does functionalism but focuses on conflict, change, and inequality, which it views as a consequence of unequal resource distribution within society (Coser 1956; Marx 1955; Simmel 1955; J. Turner 1978). Conflict theorists believe that conflict, rather than equilibrium, is natural and inherent to social systems and that it in fact contributes to the healthy adaptations of social systems.

Correspondence refers to society's economic organization being mirrored in its institutions and vice versa. Thus if schools and churches resemble factories, this is so because the factory is the dominant form of economic organization in industrial society.

Critical theory asserts that existing societal structures derive from historically generated patterns of domination and subordination. Many critical theorists state that patterns of oppression derive from inequalities in the distribution of economic resources; others focus on the unequal distribution of knowledge and skill in society. These theorists are concerned with the power of language and control of information, and so they often give particular attention to curriculum. Still others emphasize asymmetries such as race, gender, religion, age, gender preference, and region. Critical theorists make two different critiques of the existing social order. The first views the hegemony of the existing order as inescapably rigid and inegalitarian, dooming most of the human race to slavery or rule by autocrats. The second and less pessimistic critique emphasizes human "agency" or self-determination in the face of institutional rigidity. The latter provides a basis for social transformation insofar as it uses social critique as a way to escape the control of the dominant classes (Tar 1985).

Cultural capital consists of the knowledge base possessed by individuals; it includes general cultural knowledge and preferences, patterns of language use, leisure activities, manners, and skills. Some kinds of cultural capital are more valuable than others, and people who possess valuable cultural capital have more social power.

Curriculum is what is taught to children in schools, whether or not the instruction is intended.

De-skilling refers to a process by which the level of specialized, professional knowledge and skill needed to carry out a task is progressively reduced until workers' autonomy over their work is shifted upward to supervisors.

Education broadly refers to the process of learning over the span of one's entire life. Education begins at birth and continues in a wide variety of both formal and informal settings.

Empowerment refers to the ability to become conscious of oppression and to learn to implement strategies to overcome it.

Ethnicity refers to a group of people bound by a sense of peoplehood based on shared cultural traits such as religion, ancestry, national origin, or language. All people can trace their roots to an ethnic background.

Ethnocentricity is the tendency to evaluate others using your own group as the norm or standard.

Feminism is both a theory or explanation about women's position in a society and a political statement focused on gaining equal rights and opportunities for women and on changing power relations between men and women.

Formal organization is one that has a legally established identity and is organized for some specific long-term purpose. Formal organizations are distinguished from informal friendship groups, associations, and families in that the former are governed by charters, bylaws, or rules and regulations. They exist independently of the identities of individual participants, and their life span exceeds the tenure of individual members.

Functionalism views societies as systems made up of interrelated components. It uses the analogy of the human body with its interrelated organs. Functionalism argues that all societies consist of systems which perform the basic functions necessary for the society to survive. Functionalism seeks to identify the basic functions that systems need to survive as well as the relationships between different functions within a society. Functionalists believe that a social system seeks its natural state of equilibrium. They assume that change tends to occur through growth or by stimulation from outside forces, rather than through internal conflict or contradictions. Functionalists suggest that societies must continually face and solve problems that threaten its survival. Consequently, those elements in society that persist are those that have contributed to its continued viability. Societies continue to organize formal schooling because doing so helps societies to survive (Dworkin 1989; Merton 1967; Parsons 1963; J. Turner 1978).

Gender, in addition to physiological traits, refers to the cultural understandings and behaviors associated with maleness and femaleness. Gender is learned through a process of socialization at birth.

Hegemony is a form of social control. It exists in the form of a social consensus created by dominant groups who control socializing institutions such as the media, schools, churches, and the political system; these institutions prevent alternative views from gaining an audience or establishing their legitimacy (McLaren 1989). Hegemony maintains the power of the existing social and political structure without the use of force because it creates a consensus in which all groups agree that the status quo is satisfactory, even if it is inequitable.

Hidden curriculum refers to the implicit and sometimes unintentional messages transmitted to students through the content, routines, and social relationships of schooling.

Ideology is a system of values and beliefs which provide the concepts, images, and ideas by which people interpret their world and shape their behavior toward other people. It is accepted as the natural and common-sense explanation of the way the world operates. Ideologies often act to reinforce the power of dominant groups in society.

Ideology of schooling refers to values and beliefs held by educators and students that inform and determine how we "do school."

Intensification refers to an increase in the amount and kind of work required on a job, without concomitant additional rewards or time in which to accomplish it.

Interpretive theory states that social structures are based upon webs of meaning created by individuals in their interaction with others. Meaning—and hence reality—is constructed during social interaction; because it is based upon interpretation of objects and events, it is flexible and negotiated rather than fixed. The meanings with which participants enter a setting affect the course of social interaction, but these meanings change in the course of interaction as they are negotiated and renegotiated. Among the most important contributions of interpretive researchers has been their shift of attention from systems to individuals; they also pioneered observational research in schools and classrooms.

Liminality refers to the time after leaving one clearly identified social identity and before entering another. Adolescence is a liminal state between childhood and adulthood.

Line offices are the positions in an organization located in the vertical supervisory structure. People in lower-line offices report to and are supervised by those directly above them, who in turn report to and are supervised by those above them. These workers carry out the actual tasks for which the organization exists. In schools, the teachers, principals, and superintendents hold line offices.

Loose coupling refers to the degree to which units within a school system are not closely linked to one another in the authority structure. It is a consequence of geography and training. Supervision is difficult in school systems because the units are geographically isolated and so the work—especially that of teachers—takes place out of the sight of supervisors. Supervisors also have little special claim to authority because the training they receive is similar to that undergone by teachers.

Minority refers to a group of people who comprise a small proportion of the total population and who are easily distinguished by physical or cultural characteristics; they often suffer discrimination because of their differences.

Peer group refers to people who share relationships because of special characteristics such as age, race, gender, or professional or social status.

Professional organizations and unions are established to further the status and power of a particular occupational or professional group. They are distinguished mostly by the characteristics of their members and the degree to which they see the interests of their members as opposed to the interests of management. *Professional organizations* are white-collar associations, while *unions* were established for blue-collar workers. Unions traditionally have viewed political activity and collective action, especially strikes, as legitimate ways to secure benefits for their members. Professional organizations have been more conservative and reluctant to engage in conflict with dominant groups in society.

Purposes of schooling can be viewed primarily as training in the cognitive, intellectual, political, economic, or social realms. Researchers, communities, politicians, educators, and others interested in schools differ in their beliefs of how these purposes should be carried out and how much emphasis should be accorded to each.

Race is a term with no scientic meaning that has been used historically to categorize people based on beliefs about their common ancestry and/or physical characteristics.

Racism refers to ethnocentric beliefs and behaviors based on the notion that one race is superior to others.

Rationalization or technical rationalization in the sociological sense refers not to the making of excuses but rather to the application of principles of reason to a task or course of action. In practice, technical rationalization means applying methods of efficiency to the work and organization of industrial and service institutions. Efficiency takes precedence over other factors in decision making. For example, efficiency is more important than what is morally right and wrong, what is esthetically desirable, or in the case of schoolchildren, what is developmentally appropriate. Technical rationalization places responsibility for institutional decision making in the hands of the management rather than the workers who are closest to the process.

Reconceptualist curriculum theory refers to the work of those who challenge the notions of traditional curricular theorists. Their work is informed by critical theory, phenomenology, and feminist theory.

Reproduction is a process by which existing patterns of social and cultural domination and subordination are duplicated from one generation to another. Schools are important in this process because they help to reproduce both the existing values and ideologies and the social class structure. Reproduction processes suggest that schools do not necessarily promote democracy, social mobility, and equality, as is widely believed and hoped in America. Conflict theorists state that reproduction takes place as members of disadvantaged groups resist or drop out of school, realizing that schools serve only the needs of elites. The disadvantaged come to believe that their lack of success lies in their own inadequacy rather than the system's inequity (Carnoy 1972; Giroux 1983a, 1983b; Karabel and Halsey 1977).

Resistance is behavior that takes a conscious, principled, and active stand contrary to the dictates of authority figures or social systems.

Restructuring refers to reforms involving reorganization of schools' authority and accountability systems. The term probably was coined in the 1986 report of the National Governors' Association, "A Time For Results: The Governors' 1991 Report on Education," which suggested that existing school practices and structures had to be changed fundamentally if any substantive reform of the U.S. educational system was to succeed.

Schooling is the process by which members of a society, particularly youth, acquire norms, values, and specific skills by participating in formal educational institutions.

Scientific management is a way to improve the operation of industrial organizations by analyzing how workers use time, machinery, and resources. It was invented by an industrial engineer, Frederick W. Taylor, who pioneered the use of "time and motion" studies to improve the efficiency of organizing and carrying out work.

Sex refers to the physiological traits of maleness or femaleness.

Sexism refers to prejudice and/or discrimination based on gender.

Sex role stereotyping refers to exaggerated beliefs about "appropriate" roles for males and females in a society. For example, girls are cooperative and nurturing; boys are competitive and aggressive.

Social class refers to groups of people who share certain characteristics of income, occupational status, educational levels, aspirations, behavior, and beliefs. Social classes are arranged in hierarchies based upon prestige, power and status, and how their members obtain a livelihood.

Socialization refers to the process of teaching and learning behaviors, values, roles, customs, and the like considered appropriate in a society.

Social mobility refers to the movement of people and groups from one social class to another.

Sociology of curriculum is the study of the content and organization of school knowledge with emphasis on the relationships between school curriculum, students, educators, and the political/economic structure of society.

Sociology of knowledge is the study of knowledge and how we construct and organize it through our social relationships. Power and hierarchy of knowledge are central to this study.

Staff offices occupy horizontal positions in the reporting structure; their tasks are ancillary or consultative to the overall work of the organization. In schools, counselors, secretaries, curriculum staff, and media specialists are examples of staff. While the supervisory structure of their own departments may be hierarchical, they can only assemble information and give advice to line personnel in the organization; they have no direct power to enforce their suggestions.

Stratification refers differentiation into levels, which usually are arranged into a hierarchy. Stratification of social classes refers to a class hierarchy based on the prestige or power possessed by each social class.

Stratification of the curriculum refers to the organization of curriculum according to a hierarchy of levels in which different types of knowledge are considered more or less valuable than others.

Structural functionalism is an important variant of functionalism. Based upon the assumption that human systems have an underlying but unobservable coherence based upon formal rules, signs, and arrangements, structuralists seek to understand human phenomena, such as systems of meaning, language, and culture, by identifying these underlying structures. Structuralists make inferences about underlying social structure based upon patterns observed in human life. Central to structural functionalism is the conviction that social systems are like living bodies. Structures, like bodily organs, evolve to carry out vital functions in society, and they must maintain an equilibrium with each other in order for societal health to be maintained.

Theoretical framework is a set of related theories which serve as an overall way to explain, interpret, or investigate the social world. Some major theoretical frameworks that inform sociological perspectives in education include functionalism, conflict theory, interpretive theory, symbolic interactionism, reproduction or transmission, and critical theory.

Theory is a statement of interrelated sets of assumptions and propositions which help us to explain our worlds. Theories are like mental road maps, guiding the way we perceive the world.

Tracking is the practice of categorizing students and placing them in classes at various levels of difficulty at the high school level. School personnel do this on the basis of the students' ability, as measured by classroom performance and standardized test scores. The resulting organization usually differentiates college preparatory, general, remedial, and vocational tracks. In British literature tracking is referred to as *streaming*.

Womanism or black feminism defines African-American women's struggles around the issues of race, social class, and gender. The struggle against both racism and sexism is a core theme for womanists. Through their efforts, black feminists work to replace denigrated images of black women with self-defined images, to give voice to the experiences of black women, and to take action in the struggle for human freedom

Youth culture is a broader term than *peer group* and refers to the total way of life, the distinctive behavior patterns and beliefs of, in this case, young people.

References

Abercrombie, N., Hill, S., and Turner, B. S. (1984). *The Penguin dictionary of sociology*. Hammondsworth, Middlesex, England: Penguin Books.

Abington School District v. *Schempp*, 374 U.S. 203 (1963).

Acosta, R. V., and Carpenter, L. (1990). Women in intercollegiate sport: A longitudinal study — 13-year update. Unpublished manuscript.

Adams, R. S., and Biddle, B. J. (1970). *Realities of teaching*. New York: Holt, Rinehart & Winston.

Albjerg, P. G. (1974). *Community and class in American education, 1865-1918*. New York: John Wiley.

Allington, R. L. (1977). If they don't get to read much, how they ever gonna get good? *Journal of Reading, 21*(1), 57-61.

Allington, R. L. (1980a). Poor readers don't get to read much in reading groups. *Language Arts, 57*, 872-877.

Allington, R. L. (1980b). Teacher interruption behaviors during primary grade oral reading. *Journal of Educational Psychology, 72*, 371-377.

Allington, R. L. (1983). The reading provided readers of differing abilities. *Elementary School Journal, 83*, 548-559.

Allington, R. L. (1984). Content coverage and contextual reading in reading groups. *Journal of Reading Behavior, 16*(2), 85-96.

Allison, C. B. (1989). Life history of MacArthur School. Unpublished paper, University of Tennessee-Knoxville.

Allison, C. B., and Bennett, K. P. (1989). *Life in MacArthur High School: A case study*. Paper presented at the Southwest Philosophy of Education Society Meeting, Padre Island, Texas.

American Association of University Women. (1992). How schools shortchange girls: A study of major findings on girls and education. Washington, DC: AAUW/NEA.

American Association of University Women. (1993). Hostile hallways: The AAUW survey on sexual harassment in America's schools. Washington, DC: AAUW/NEA.

325

American heritage dictionary. (1983). New York: Houghton Mifflin.

Anderson, B. D., and Mark, J. H. (1977). Teacher mobility and productivity in a metropolitan area: A seven-year case study. *Urban Education, 12,* 15–36.

Anderson, G. L. (1989). Critical ethnography in education: Its origins, current status and new directions. *Review of Educational Research, 59*(3), 249–270.

Anyon, J. (1983). Workers, labor and economic history, and textbook content. In M. W. Apple and L. Weis (Eds.), *Ideology and practice in schooling* (pp. 37–60). Philadelphia: Temple University Press.

Anyon, J. (1988). Schools as agencies of social legitimation. In W. F. Pinar (Ed.), *Contemporary curriculum discourses* (pp. 175–200). Scottsdale, AZ: Gorsuch Scarisbrick.

Anyon, J. (1990). Social class and the hidden curriculum of work. In F. Hammack and K. Dougherty (Eds.), *Education and society* (pp. 464–438). San Diego: Harcourt, Brace & Jovanovich.

Apple, M. W. (1978). The new sociology of education: Analyzing cultural and economic reproduction. *Harvard Educational Review, 48,* 495–503.

Apple, M. W. (1979). *Ideology and curriculum.* Boston: Routledge & Kegan Paul.

Apple, M. W. (1982). *Education and power.* Boston: Routledge & Kegan Paul.

Apple, M. W. (1986). *Teachers and texts: A political economy of class and gender relations in education.* New York: Metheun.

Apple, M. W. (1988). *Teachers and texts.* New York: Routledge & Kegan Paul.

Apple, M. W. (1992). Do the standards go far enough: Power, policy and practice in mathematics education. *Journal for Research in Mathematics Education, 23*(5), 412–431.

Apple, M. W. (1993). *Official knowledge: Democratic education in a conservative age.* New York: Routledge & Kegan Paul.

Apple, M. W., and Weis, L. (Eds.). (1983). *Ideology and practice in schooling.* Philadelphia: Temple University Press.

Applebee, A. (1989). *A study of book-length works taught in high school English courses.* Albany: Center for the Learning and Teaching of Literature, State University of New York School of Education.

Aries, P. (1962). *Centuries of childhood: A social history of family life.* New York: Vintage Books.

Armor, D. (1969). *The American high school counselor.* New York: Russell Sage Foundation.

Aronowitz, S., and Giroux, H. (1985). *Education under siege.* South Hadley, MA: Bergin & Garvey.

Ashcroft, L. (1987). Diffusing "Empowering": The what and the why. *Language Arts, 64*(2), 142–156.

Atkinson, P., Delamont, S., and Hammersley, M. (1988). Qualitative research traditions: A British response. *Review of Educational Research, 58*(2), 231–250.

Au, K. H. (1979). Using the experience-text relationship with minority children. *The Reading Teacher, 32,* 677–679.

Au, K. H. (1980). Participant structures in a reading lesson with Hawaiian children: Analysis of a culturally appropriate instructional event. *Anthropology and Education Quarterly, 11,* 91–115.

Au, K. H., and Jordan, C. (1981). Teaching reading to Hawaiian children: Finding a culturally appropriate solution. In H. Trueba, G. P. Guthrie, and K.H. Au (Eds.), *Culture and the bilingual classroom: Studies in classroom ethnography* (pp. 139–152). Rowley, MA: Newbury House.

Au, K. H., and Mason, J. (1981). Social organizational factors in learning to read: The balance of rights hypothesis. *Reading Research Quarterly, 17,* 139–152.

Ayella, M. E., and Williamson, J. B. (1976). The social mobility of women: A causal model of socioeconomic success. *The Sociological Quarterly, 17,* 334–354.

Ballantine, J. H. (1983). *The sociology of education: A systematic analysis.* Englewood Cliffs, NJ: Prentice Hall.

Ballantine, J. H. (1989). *The sociology of education: A systematic analysis* (2nd ed.). Englewood Cliffs, NJ: Prentice Hall.

Banks, J. A. (1979). *Teaching strategies for ethnic studies* (2nd ed.) Boston: Allyn & Bacon.

Banks, J. A. (1988). *Multiethnic education: Theory and practice* (2nd ed.). Boston: Allyn & Bacon.

Banks, J. A., and McGee Banks, C. A. (Eds.). (1993). *Multicultural education: Issues and perspectives* (2nd ed.). Boston: Allyn & Bacon.

Baratz, S. S., and Baratz, J. C. (1970). Early childhood intervention: The social science base of institutional racism. *Harvard Educational Review, 40,* 29-50.

Barker, R. G., and Gump, P. V. (1964). *Big school, small school.* Stanford, CA: Stanford University Press.

Barnhart, C. (1982). "Tuning-in": Athabaskan teachers and Athabaskan students. In R. Barnhardt (Ed.), *Cross-cultural issues in Alaskan education, Vol. 2* (pp. 144-164). Fairbanks, AK: University of Alaska Center for Cross-Cultural Studies.

Barr, R. C. (1974). Instructional pace differences and their effect on reading acquisition. *Reading Research Quarterly, 9,* 526-554.

Barr, R. C. (1975). How children are taught to read: Grouping and pacing. *School Review, 83,* 479-498.

Barr, R. C. (1982). Classroom reading instruction from a sociological perspective. *Journal of Reading Behavior, 14,* 375-389.

Basso, K. H. (1984). "Stalking with stories": Names, places and moral narratives among the Western Apache. In E. M. Bruner (Ed.), *Text, play and story: The construction and reconstruction of self and society* (pp. 19-56). Washington, DC: Proceedings of the American Ethnological Society.

Bastian, A., Fruchter, N., Gittell, M., Greer, C., and Haskins, K. (1985). *Choosing equality: The case for democratic schooling.* Philadelphia: Temple University Press.

Bayes, J. (1988). Labor markets and the feminization of poverty. In H. Rodgers, Jr. (Ed.), *Beyond welfare: New approaches to the problem of poverty in America* (pp. 86-114). Armonk, NY: M.E. Sharpe.

Becker, G. (1964). *Human capital: A theoretical and empirical analysis with special reference to education.* New York: Columbia University Press.

Becker, H. S. (1953). The teacher in the authority system of the public school. *Journal of Educational Sociology, 27,* 128-141.

Becker, H. S., Geer, B., Hughes, E. C., and Strauss, A. L. (1961). *Boys in white: Student culture in medical school.* Chicago: University of Chicago Press.

Belenky, M. F., Clinchy, B. M., Goldberger, N. R., and Tarule, J. M. (1986). *Women's ways of knowing: The development of self, voice, and mind.* New York: Basic Books.

Bennett, E. W. (1988). *James Madison High School.* Washington, DC: U.S. Office of Education.

Bennett, K. P. (1986). Study of reading ability grouping and its consequences for urban Appalachian first graders. Unpublished doctoral dissertation, University of Cincinnati.

Bennett, K. P. (1988). *Yup'ik women's ways of knowing.* Charleston, WV: ERIC Clearinghouse on Rural Education and Small Schools (Eric Document Reproduction Service No. ED 301 401).

Bennett, K. P. (1991). Doing school in an urban Appalachian first grade. In C. Sleeter (Ed.), *Empowerment through multicultural education* (pp. 27-47). Albany, NY: State University of New York Press.

Bennett, K. P., Nelson, P., and Baker, J. (1992). Yup'ik Eskimo storyknifing: Young girls at play. *Anthropology and Education Quarterly, 23*(2), 120-144.

Bensman, J., and Vidich, A. J. (1971). *The new American society: The revolution of the middle class.* Chicago: Quadrangle Books.

Benson, C. S. (1982). The deregulation of schools: Views from the federal, state and local levels. [Editor's introduction]. *Education and Urban Society, 14,* 395–397.

Berger, J. (1989). New York study of welfare clients: False practices of trade schools. *New York Times,* June 18, p. 14.

Berger, P. L., and Luckmann, T. (1967). *The social construction of reality: A treatise in the sociology of knowledge.* New York: Anchor Books.

Bernardi, B. (1952). The age system of the Nilotic Hamitic people. *Africa, 22,* 316–332.

Bernardi, B. (1985). *Age class systems, social institutions and policies based on age.* New York: Cambridge.

Bernstein, B. (1970). *Class, codes and control. Vol. I: Theoretical studies towards a sociology of language.* London: Routledge & Kegan Paul.

Bernstein, B. (1977). *Class, codes and control. Vol. III: Towards a theory of educational transmission.* London: Routledge & Kegan Paul.

Berry, E. and Black, E. (1987). The integrative learning journal (or, Getting beyond "True Confessions" and "Cold Knowledge"). *Women's Studies Quarterly, XV*(3–4), 59–64.

Betz, M., and Garland, J. (1974). Intergenerational mobility rates of urban school teachers. *Sociology of Education, 47,* 511–522.

Bidwell, C. E. (1965). The school as a formal organization. In J. G. March (Ed.), *The handbook of organizations* (pp. 972–1022). New York: Rand McNally.

Binder, F. H. (1974). *The age of the common school, 1830–1865.* New York: John Wiley.

Blau, P. M. (1955). *The dynamics of bureaucracy.* Chicago: University of Chicago Press.

Blau, P. M., and Duncan, O. D. (1967). *The American occupational structure.* New York: John Wiley.

Blau, P. M., and Scott, W. R. (1962). *Formal organizations: A comparative approach.* San Francisco: Chandler.

Blaug, M. (1970). *An introduction to the economics of education.* London: Allen Lane.

Blaug, M. (1976). Human capital theory: A slightly jaundiced survey. *Journal of Economic Literature, 14,* 827–856.

Bloom, A. (1987). *The closing of the American mind.* New York: Simon & Schuster.

Bluestone, B., and Bennett, H. (1982). *The de-industrialization of America.* New York: Basic Books.

Blumberg, A. (1985). *The school superintendent: Living with conflict.* New York: Teachers College Press.

Blumer, H. (1969). *Symbolic interactionism: Perspectives and method.* Englewood Cliffs, NJ: Prentice Hall.

Bobbitt, F. (1912). The elimination of waste in education. *The Elementary School Teacher, 12,* 259–271.

Boehnlein, M. M. (1985). *Children, parents, and reading: An annotated bibliography.* Newark, DE: International Reading Association.

Bogart, K., Simmons, S., Stein, N., and Tomaszewski, E. P. (1992). Breaking the silence: sexual and gender-based harassment in elementary, secondary, and postsecondary education. In S. S. Klein (Ed.), *Sex equity and sexuality in education* (pp. 192–221). Albany: State University of New York Press.

Bogart, K., and Stein, N. (1987). Breaking the silence: Sexual harassment in education. *Peabody Journal of Education, 64*(4), 146–163.

Bogdan, R. (1972). *Participant observation in organizational settings.* Syracuse University Division of Special Education and Rehabilitation and the Center on Human Policy.

Boggs, C. (1976). *Gramsci's Marxism.* London: Pluto Press.

Boocock, S. (1980). *Sociology of education: An introduction* (2nd ed.). Boston: Houghton Mifflin.

Borko, H., and Eisenhart, M. (1986) Students' conceptions of reading and their reading experience in school. *The Elementary School Journal, 86,* 589-612.

Borman, K. M. (1988). The process of becoming a worker. In J. Mortimer & K. Borman (Eds.), *Work experience and psychological development through the lifespan* (pp. 51-75). Boulder, CO: Westview Press.

Borman K. M., and Mueninghoff, E. (1982). Work roles and social roles in three elementary school settings. Paper presented at the meeting of the American Educational Research Association, New York.

Borman, K. M., and Mueninghoff, E. (1983). Lower Price Hill's children: Family, school and neighborhood. In A. Batteau (Ed.), *Appalachia and America* (pp. 210-224). Lexington: University Press of Kentucky.

Borman, K. M., and Spring, J. H. (1984). *Schools in central cities.* New York: Longman.

Bossert, S. T. (1979). *Tasks and social relationships in classrooms: A study of instructional organization and its consequences.* Cambridge, England: Cambridge University Press.

Bottomore, T. (1984). *The Frankfurt School.* New York: Tavistock.

Boudon, R. (1974). *Education, opportunity, and social inequality: Changing prospects in Western society.* New York: John Wiley.

Bourdieu, P., and Passeron, J. (1977). *Reproduction in education, society and culture.* London: Sage.

Boutwell, G. S. (1859). *Thoughts on educational topics and institutions.* Boston: Phillips, Sampson and Company.

Bowers, A. W. (1965). Hidatsa social and ceremonial organization (Bulletin 194). Washington, DC: Smithsonian Institution Bureau of American Ethnology.

Bowles, S., and Gintis, H. (1976). *Schooling in capitalist America: Educational reform and the contradictions of economic life.* New York: Basic Books.

Boyd, W. (1966). *The history of Western education* (8th ed.). New York: Barnes & Noble.

Boyd, W. L., and Crowson, R. L. (1981). The changing conception and practice of public school administration. In D. C. Berliner (Ed.), *Review of Research in Education. Vol. 9* (pp. 31-37). Washington, DC: American Educational Research Association.

Braddock, J. H., Crain, R. L., and McParland, J. M. (1984). A long-term view of school desegregation: Some recent studies of graduates as adults. *Phi Delta Kappan, 66,* 259-264.

Braroe, N. W. (1975). *Indian and white: Self-image and interaction in a Canadian plains community.* Stanford, CA: Stanford University Press.

Bredekamp, S. (Ed.). (1986). *Developmentally appropriate practice.* Washington, DC: National Association for the Education of Young Children.

Bredo, E. (1989). After positivism, what? Paper presented at the meeting of the American Educational Research Association, San Francisco.

Brenton, M. (1974). Teachers' organizations: The new militancy. In E. A. Useem and M. Useem (Eds.), *The education establishment* (pp. 60-69). Englewood Cliffs, NJ: Prentice Hall.

Britzman, D. (1991). *Practice makes practice: A critical study of learning to teach.* Albany: State University of New York Press.

Brookover, W. B., and Erickson, E. L. (1975). *Sociology of education.* Homewood, IL: The Dorsey Press.

Brophy, J. E., and Good, T. L. (1970). Teachers' communication of differential expectations for children's classroom performance: Some behavioral data. *Journal of Educational Psychology 61,* 365-374.

Brouillette, L. R. (1993). A geology of school reform: An ethnohistorical case study of the successive restructurings of a school district. Unpublished doctoral dissertation, School of Education, University of Colorado–Boulder.

Brown D. (1991). The effects of State-mandated testing on elementary classroom instruction. Unpublished doctoral dissertation, University of Tennessee–Knoxville.

Brown, L. M., and Gilligan, C. (1992). *Meeting at the crossroads: Women's psychology and girls' development.* Cambridge, MA: Harvard University Press.

Brown, R. (1986). State responsibility for at-risk youth. *Metropolitan Education, 2,* 5–12.

Brown v. *Board of Education of Topeka, KS,* 349 U.S. 294 (1955).

Brown, V. E. (1994). Unititled paper presented in session. "Sexual harassment and power politics in higher education," American Educational Research Association, New Orleans.

Burtonwood, N. (1986). *The culture concept in educational studies.* Philadelphia: Nfer-Nelson.

Butts, R. F. (1978). *Public education in the United States: From revolution to reform.* New York: Holt, Rinehart & Winston.

Butts, R. F., and Cremin, L. A. (1953). *A history of education in American culture.* New York: Holt.

Callahan, R. (1962). *Education and the cult of efficiency.* Chicago: University of Chicago Press.

Campbell, R. T. (1983). Status attainment research: End of the beginning or beginning of the end? *Sociology of Education, 56,* 47–62.

Carnegie Council of Adolescent Development. (1989). Turning points: Preparing American youth for the 21st century. New York: Carnegie Corporation.

Carnegie Task Force on Teaching as a Profession. (1986). *A nation prepared: Teachers for the 21st century.* New York: Author.

Carnoy, M. (Ed.). (1972). *Schooling in a corporate society: The political economy of education in America.* New York: McKay.

Carnoy, M., and Levin, H. M. (1976). *The limits of educational reform.* New York: McKay.

Carnoy, M., and Levin, H. M. (1985). *Schooling and work in the democratic state.* Stanford, CA: Stanford University Press.

Carroll, T. G. (1975). Transactions of cognitive equivalence in the domains of "work" and "play." *Anthropology and Education Quarterly, 6,* 17–22.

Cashmore, E., and Troyna, B. (1990). *Introduction to race relations* (2nd ed.). New York: Falmer Press.

Casper, V., Schultz, S., and Wickens, E. (1992). Breaking the silences: Lesbian and gay parents and the schools. *Teachers College Record, 94*(1), 109–137.

Cazden, C. B., John, V. P., and Hymes, D. (Eds.). (1974). *Functions of language in the classroom.* New York: Teachers College Press.

Center for Literacy Studies, University of Tennessee, Knoxville. (1992). *Life at the margins: Profiles of adults with low literacy skills.* U.S. Congress Office of Technology Assessment, Contract #H3.5365.0. Washington, DC: National Technical Information Service, March.

Chafetz, J. S., and Dworkin, A. G. (1986). *Female revolt: Women's movements in world and historical perspective.* Totowa, NJ: Rowan & Allanheld.

Chandler, J. (1981). Camping for life: Transmission of values at a girl's summer camp. In R. T. Sieber and A. J. Gordon (Eds.), *Children and their organizations: Investigations in American culture* (pp. 122–137). Boston: G. K. Hall.

Charters, W. W., Jr. (1970). Some factors affecting teacher survival in school districts. *American Educational Research Journal, 7,* 1–27.

Cherryholmes, C. H. (1988). *Power and criticism: Poststructural investigations in education.* New York: Teachers College Press.

Children's Defense Fund. (1988). *A call for action to make our nation safe for children: A briefing book on the status of American children in 1988.* Washington, DC: Author.

Chowdorow, N. (1978). *The reproduction of mothering.* Berkeley: University of California Press.

Christian-Smith, L. (1988). Romancing the girl: Adolescent novels and the construction of femininity. In L. Roman, L. Christian-Smith, and E. Ellsworth (Eds.), *Becoming feminine: The politics of popular culture* (pp. 76–102). Philadelphia: Falmer Press.

Cicourel, A. V. (1964). *Method and measurement in sociology.* New York: The Free Press.

Cicourel, A. V., and Kitsuse, J. (1963). *The educational decision makers.* Indianapolis: Bobbs-Merrill.

Cleary, E. L. (1985). *Crisis and change: The church in Latin America today.* Maryknoll, NY: Orbis Books.

Clement, D. C., Eisenhart, M. A., and Harding, J. R. (1979). The veneer of harmony: Social-race relations in a southern desegregated school. In R. C. Rist (Ed.), *Desegregated schools: Appraisals of an American experiment* (pp. 15–52). New York: Academic Press.

Cohen, A. (1974). *Two-Dimensional Man.* Berkeley: University of California Press.

Cohen, J., and Rogers, J. (1983). *On democracy: Toward a transformation of American society.* Middlesex, England: Penguin Books.

Cole, M., and Griffin, P. (Eds.). (1987). *Contextual factors in education: Improving science and mathematics for minorities and women.* Madison: Wisconsin Center for Education Research.

Coleman, J. S. (1961). *The adolescent society.* Glencoe, IL: The Free Press.

Coleman, J. S. (1965). *Adolescents and the schools.* New York: Basic Books.

Coleman, J. S. (1966). *Equality of educational opportunity.* Washington, DC: U.S. Government Printing Office.

Coleman, J. S., and Hoffer, T. (1987). *Public and private schools: The impact of communities.* New York: Basic Books.

Coleman, J. S., Hoffer, T., and Kilgore, S. (1982). *High school achievement: Public, Catholic and private schools compared.* New York: Basic Books.

Collins, G. (1987). Day care for infants: Debate turns to long term effects. *The New York Times,* November 25, p. B9.

Collins, P. H. (1990). *Black feminist thought: Knowledge, consciousness, and the politics of empowerment.* London: HarperCollins Academic.

Collins, R. (1977). Functional and conflict theories of educational stratification. In J. Karabel and A. H. Halsey (Eds.), *Power and ideology in education* (pp. 118–136). Cambridge, England: Oxford University Press.

Combahee River Collective. (1977). "A Black feminist statement." Quoted in C. Morage and G. Anzaldua (Eds.), (1981), *This bridge called my back: Writings by radical women of color* (pp. 210–218). New York: Kitchen Table: Women of Color Press.

Conant, J. (1988). Alaska's suicide epidemic. *Newsweek,* February 15, p. 61.

Connell, R. W. (1985). *Teachers' work.* North Sydney, Australia: George Allen & Unwin.

Connors, N. A., and Irvin, J. L. (1989). Is "middle-schoolness" an indicator of excellence? *Middle School Journal, 21,* 12–14.

Corwin, R. G. (1965). *Sociology of education.* New York: Appleton.

Corwin, R. G. (1970). *Militant professionalism: A study of organizational conflicts in high school.* New York: Appleton-Century-Crofts.

Coser, L. A. (1956). *The functions of social conflict.* Glencoe, IL: The Free Press.

Council on Interracial Books for Children, Inc. (1980). In M. K. Rudman (1984), *Children's literature: An issues approach* (2nd Ed.), p. 126. White Plains, NY: Longman.

Counts, G. (1932). *Dare the school build a new social order?* New York: John Day.

Cox, T. V. (1980). Kindergarten: A status passage for American children: A microethnography of an urban kindergarten classroom. Unpublished doctoral dissertation, Department of Anthropology, University of Georgia.

Crain, R. L. (1977). Racial tension in high schools: Pushing the survey method closer to reality. *Anthropology and Education Quarterly, 8,* 142–151.

Crow, M. L. (1985). The female educator at midlife. *Phi Delta Kappan, 67,* 281–284.

Cuban, L. (1984). *How teachers taught: Constancy and change in American classrooms, 1890–1980.* New York: Longman.

Cull, D. (1989). Elected officials proliferate. *New York Times,* January 14, p. 6.

Curti, M. (1971). *The social ideas of American educators.* Totowa, NJ: Littlefield, Adams & Company.

Cusick, P. A. (1983). *The egalitarian ideal and the American high school.* New York: Longman.

Dahrendorf, R. (1959). *Class and conflict in industrial society.* Stanford, CA: Stanford University Press.

Dalton, G. W., Barnes, L. B., and Zaleznik, A. (1968). *The distribution of authority in formal organizations.* Boston: Harvard University, Division of Research, Graduate School of Business Administration.

Dalton, G. W., Barnes, L. B., and Zaleznik, A. (1973). *The distribution of authority in formal organizations.* Cambridge, MA: M.I.T. Press.

D'Amato, J. D. (1987). The belly of the beast: On cultural differences, castelike status and the politics of schools. *Anthropology and Education Quarterly, 18,* 357–360.

D'Amato, J. D. (1988). "Acting": Hawaiian children's resistance to teachers. *The Elementary School Journal, 88,* 529–544.

Damico, S. B., Bell, N. A., and Green, C. (1980). Friendship in desegregated middle schools: An organizational analysis. Paper presented at the meeting of the Social Contexts of Education Conference, sponsored by Division G of the American Educational Research Association, Atlanta.

Darling-Hammond, L. (1984). *Beyond the commission reports: Coming crisis in teaching.* Santa Monica, CA: Rand Corporation.

Darling-Hammond, L. (1993). Reframing the school reform agenda: Developing capacity for school transformation. *Phi Delta Kappan, 74*(10), 752–761.

Davis, J. A. (1965). *Undergraduate career decisions.* Chicago: Aldine.

Deering, P. (1992). An ethnographic study of cooperative learning in a multiethnic working class middle school. Unpublished doctoral dissertation, School of Education, University of Colorado–Boulder.

Delamont, S. (1989). *Knowledgeable women: Structuralism and the reproduction of elites.* New York: Routledge & Kegan Paul.

Delgado-Gaitan, C. (1988). The value of conformity: Learning to stay in school. *Anthropology and Education Quarterly, 19,* 354–382.

Delgado-Gaitan, C. (1990). *Literacy for empowerment.* New York: Falmer Press.

Dellinger, D. (1991). "My Way or the Highway": The Hawkins County Textbook Controversy. Unpublished doctoral dissertation, University of Tennessee–Knoxville.

Delpit, L. D. (1988). The silenced dialogue: Power and pedagogy in educating other people's children. *Harvard Educational Review, 3,* 280–298.

Dewey, J. (1916). *Democracy and education: An introduction to the philosophy of education.* New York: Macmillan.

Dewey, J. (1929). *The quest for certainty.* New York: Putnam.

Dewey, J. (1938). *Experience and education.* New York: Macmillan.

Deyhle, D. (1986). Break dancing and breaking out: Anglos, Utes and Navajos in a border reservation high school. *Anthropology and Education Quarterly, 17,* 111-127.

Deyhle, D. (1987). Empowerment and cultural conflict: Navajo parents and the schooling of their children. Unpublished manuscript.

Deyhle, D. (1988). Dropouts cite reasons for leaving school. *Farmington (Utah) Daily Times* (American Indian News Section), October 27.

Deyhle, D. (1989). Pushouts and pullouts: Navajo and Ute school leavers. *Journal of Navajo Education, 6,* 36-51.

Deyhle, D. (1991). Empowerment and cultural conflict: Navajo parents and the schooling of their children. *International Journal of Qualitative Studies in Education, 4*(4), 277-297.

Deyhle, D. (1992). Constructing failure and maintaining cultural identity: Navajo and Ute school leavers. *Journal of American Indian Education,* January, 24-47.

Deyhle, D., and LeCompte, M. D. (in press). Cultural differences in child development: Navajo adolescents in middle schools. *Theory into Practice.*

Dillon, S. (1994). Superintendent's dismissal leads to loss of corporate grants. *The New York Times,* March 26, p. 16.

Domhoff, G. W. (1967). *Who rules America?* Englewood Cliffs, NJ: Prentice Hall.

Dreeben, R. (1968). *On what is learned in school.* Reading, MA: Addison-Wesley.

Dreeben, R. (1973). The school as a workplace. In R. M. W. Travers (Ed.), *The second handbook of research on teaching* (pp. 450-473). Chicago: Rand McNally.

Dreeben, R. (1984). First grade reading groups: Their formation and change. In P. L. Peterson, L. C. Wilkinson, and M. Hallinan (Eds.), *The social context of instruction: Group organization and group process* (pp. 69-83). New York: Academic Press.

Duncan, S., and Fiske, D. W. (1977). *Face-to-face interaction: Research, method and theory.* New York: John Wiley.

Durkheim, E. (1969). *The division of labor in society.* New York: The Free Press [first published in 1893].

Dworkin, A. G. (1974). Balance on the bayou: The impact of racial isolation and interaction on stereotyping in the Houston Independent School District. In A. G. Dworkin, R. G. Frankiewicz, and H. Copitka, *Intergroup Action Report* (pp. 7-51). Houston, TX: Houston Council on Human Relations.

Dworkin, A. G. (1980). The changing demography of public school teachers: Some implications for faculty turnover in urban areas. *Sociology of Education, 53,* 65-73.

Dworkin, A. G. (1985a). Ethnic bias in writing assignments. *American Sociological Association Teaching Newsletter, 10,* 15-16.

Dworkin, A. G. (1985b). *When teachers give up: Teacher burnout, teacher turnover and their impact on children.* Austin, TX: The Hogg Foundation for Mental Health.

Dworkin, A. G. (1986). *Teacher burnout in the public schools: structural causes and consequences for children.* Albany: State University of New York Press.

Dworkin, A. G., and Dworkin, R. J. (1982). *The minority report: An introduction to racial, ethnic, and gender relations* (2nd ed.). New York: Holt, Rinehart & Winston.

Dworkin, A. G., Frankiewicz, R. G., and Copitka, H. (1975). Impact and assessment on stereotype reduction activities in the public schools. Paper presented at the meeting of the Southwestern Sociological Association, San Antonio.

Dworkin, A. G., Haney, C. A., and Telschow, R. L. (1988). Fear, victimization and stress among urban public school teachers. *Journal of Organizational Behavior, 9,* 159-171.

Dworkin, A. G., and LeCompte, M. D. (1989). Giving up in schools: American public education in crisis. *Houston Update, 3*(12), 1, 2, 7. Houston, TX: Center for Public Policy, University of Houston.

Dworkin, A. G., Lorence, J., and LeCompte, M. D. (1989). Organizational context as determinants of teacher morale. Paper presented at the meeting of the Southwestern Social Science Association.

Ebaugh, H. R. F. (1977). *Out of the cloister: A study of organizational dilemmas.* Austin: University of Texas Press.

Eder, D. (1982). The impact of management and turn allocation activities on student performance. *Discourse Processes, 5*(2), 147-159.

Eder, D. (1985). The cycle of popularity: Interpersonal relations among female adolescents. *Sociology of Education, 58*(3), 154-165.

Eder, D., and Felmlee, D. (1984). The development of attention norms in ability groups. In P. L. Peterson, L. C. Wilkinson, and M. Hallinan (Eds.), *The social context of instruction: Group organization and group process* (pp. 189-207). New York: Academic Press.

Eder, D., and Parker, S. (1987). The cultural production and reproduction of gender: The effect of extracurricular activities on peer-group culture. *Sociology of Education, 60*(3), 200-213.

Education Week. (1988). NAEP: Results of the fourth mathematics assessment, June 15, p. 29.

Education Week, March 1, 1989, p. 7.

Education Week, February 23, 1994, p. 4.

Eisenhart, M. (1985). Women choose their careers: A study of natural decision making. *Review of Higher Education, 8*(3), 247-270.

Eisenhart, M., and Graue, E. (1990). Socially constructed readiness for school. *International Journal of Qualitative Studies in Education, 3,* 253-269.

Eisenhart, M. A., and Holland, D. C. (1988). Moments of discontent: University women and the gender status quo. *Anthropology and Education Quarterly, 19*(2), 115-138.

Eisenhart, M. A., and Holland, D. C. (1992). Gender constructs and career committment: The influence of peer culture on women in college. In T. L. Whitehead and B. Reid (Eds.), *Gender constructs and social issues.* Champaign, IL: University of Illinois Press.

Ekstrom, R. B., Goertz, M. E., Pollack, J. M., and Rock, D. A. (1986). Who drops out of school and why?: Finding from a national study. *Teachers College Record, 87,* 356-375.

Ellsworth, E. (1989). Why doesn't this feel empowering?: Working through the repressive myths of critical pedagogy. *Harvard Educational Review, 59*(3), 297-324.

Elmore, R. E., and Associates. (1990). *Restructuring schools.* San Francisco: Jossey-Bass.

Ember, C. R., and Ember, M. (1985). *Anthropology* (4th ed.). Englewood Cliffs, NJ: Prentice Hall.

Engel v. *Vitale,* 370 U.S. 421 (1962).

Epstein, J. L., and Karweit, N. (Eds.). (1983). *Friends in school: Patterns of selection and influence in secondary schools.* New York: Academic Press.

Erickson, F. (1984). School literacy, reasoning and civility: An anthropologist's perspective. *Review of Educational Research, 54,* 525-546.

Erickson, F. (1987). Transformation and school success: The politics and culture of educational achievement. *Anthropology and Education Quarterly, 18,* 335-356.

Erickson, F., and Mohatt, G. (1982). Cultural organization of participation structures in two classrooms of Indian students. In G. Spindler (Ed.), *Doing the ethnography of schooling* (pp. 132-174). New York: Holt, Rinehart & Winston.

Eskenazi, M., and Gallen, D. (1992). *Sexual harassment: Know your rights.* New York: Carroll & Graf.

Etaugh, C., & Harlow, H. (1974). The influence of sex of the teacher and student on classroom behavior. In E. Brophy & T. L. Good (Eds.), *Teacher-student relationships: Causes and consequences* (pp. 199-239). New York: Holt, Rinehart & Winston.

Etter-Lewis, G. (1993). *My soul is my own: Oral narratives of African American women in the professions.* New York: Routledge.

Etzioni, A. (Ed.). (1969). *The semi-professions and their organization: Teachers, nurses, social workers.* New York: The Free Press.

Evans Pritchard, E. E. (1940). *The Nuer: A description of the modes of livelihood and political institution of a Nilotic people.* Oxford, England: Clarendon Press.

Falk, W. W., Grimes, M. D., and Lord, G. F. (1982). Professionalism and conflict in a bureaucratic setting: The case of a teachers' strike. *Social Problems, 29,* 551-560.

Fantini, M., Gittell, M., and Magat, R. (1974). Local school governance. In M. Useem and E. L. Useem (Eds.), *The education establishment* (pp. 86-98). Englewood Cliffs, NJ: Prentice Hall.

Fantini, M. D. (1975). The school-community power struggle. *National Elementary Principal, 54*(3), 57-61.

Farnham, C. (1987). *The impact of feminist research in the academy.* Bloomington: Indiana University Press.

Fausto-Sterling, A. (1985). *Myths of gender:* Biological theories about women and men. New York: Basic Books.

Featherstone, H. (Ed.) (1987). Organizing classes by ability. *Harvard Education Letter, 3*(4), 1-9.

Feinberg, W., and Soltis, J. F. (1985). *School and society.* New York: Teachers College Press.

Feistritzer, C. E. (1983). *The condition of teachers: A state by state analysis.* Princeton, NJ: Carnegie Foundation for the Advancement of Teaching.

Feldman, R. S. (1985). Nonverbal behavior, race, and the classroom teacher. *Theory into Practice, 24,* 45-49.

Felmlee, D., Eder, D., and Tsui, W. (1985). Peer influence on classroom attention. *Social Psychology Quarterly, 48*(3), 215-226.

Fennema, E., and Leder, G. C. (1990). *Mathematics and gender.* New York: Teachers College Press.

Fennema, E., and Sherman, J. (1977). Sex-related differences in mathematics achievement, spatial visualization and affective factors. *American Educational Research Journal, 14*(1), 51-71.

Ferrell, B., and Compton, D. (1986). The use of ethnographic techniques for evaluation in a large school district: The vanguard case. In D. Fetterman and M. A. Pitman (Eds.), *Educational evaluation: Ethnography in theory, practice and politics* (pp. 171-192). Beverly Hills, CA: Sage.

Fine, M. (1986). Why urban adolescents drop into and out of public high school. *Teachers College Record, 87,* 393-410.

Fine, M. (1987). Silencing in public schools. *Language Arts, 64*(2), 157-174.

Finn, C. E., and Ravitch, D. (1987). *What do our 17-year-olds know? A report on the first national assessment of history and literature.* New York: Harper and Row.

Firestone, W. A., and Rosenblum, S. (1988). Building commitment in urban high schools. *Educational Evaluation and Policy Analysis, 10*(4), 285-299.

Fiske, E. (1986). Student debt reshaping colleges and careers [Education Life]. *New York Times,* August 30, p. 34.

Fiske, E. (1988). American test mania [Education Life]. *New York Times,* April 10, pp. 16-20.

Fordham, S. (1991). Peer-proofing academic competition among Black adolescents: "Acting White" Black American style. In C. Sleeter (Ed.), *Empowerment through multicultural education* (pp. 69-93). New York: SUNY Press.

Fordham, S., and Ogbu, J. U. (1986). Black students' school success: Coping with the "burden" of "acting white." *The Urban Review, 18*(3), 176-206.

Fortune, R. F. (1963). *Sorcerers of Dobu.* New York: E.P. Dutton.

Foucault, M. (1980). *Power/knowledge.* New York: Pantheon Books.

Freire, P. (1970). *Pedagogy of the oppressed.* New York: Continuum.

Freire, P. (1985). *The politics of education.* South Hadley, MA: Bergin & Garvey.

Freire, P. (1987). *A pedagogy for liberation.* South Hadley, MA: Bergin & Garvey.

Fretz, C. (1990). Gender bias plagues women lawyers—judge. *The Knoxville Journal,* June 9, p. 4A.

Fuller, M. (1980). Black girls in a London comprehensive. In R. Deem (Ed.), *Schooling for women's work* (pp. 56–65). London: Routledge & Kegan Paul.

Furlong, V. J. (1985). *Deviant pupil: Sociological perspectives.* Philadelphia: Open University Press.

Gaertner, K. N. (1978). Organizational careers in public school administration. Unpublished doctoral dissertation, University of Chicago.

Gambrell, L. B., Wilson, R. M., and Gantt, W. N. (1981). Classroom observations of task attending behaviors of good and poor readers. *Journal of Educational Research, 74,* 400–404.

Gamoran, A., and Berends, M. (1987). The effects of stratification in secondary schools: A synthesis of survey and ethnographic research. *Review of Educational Research, 57,* 415–437.

Garbarino, M. S. (1983). *Sociocultural theory in anthropology.* Prospect Heights, IL: Waveland Press.

Garcia, E. (1994). *Understanding and meeting the challenge of student cultural diversity.* Boston: Houghton Mifflin.

Garfinkel, H. (1967). *Studies in ethnomethodology.* Englewood Cliffs, NJ: Prentice Hall.

Geertz, C. (1973). *The interpretation of cultures.* New York: Basic Books.

Geertz, C. (1988). *Works and lives: The anthropologist as author.* Stanford, CA: Stanford University Press.

Gennep, A. van (1960). *The rites of passage.* Chicago: Chicago University Press.

Gerth, H., and Mills, C. W. (1953). *Character and social structure.* New York: Harcourt Brace & World.

Gibson, M. A. (1987a). Punjabi immigrants in an American high school. In G. Spindler and L. Spindler (Eds.), *Interpretive ethnography of education: At home and abroad* (pp. 281–310). Hillsdale, NJ: Lawrence Erlbaum Associates.

Gibson, M. A. (1987b). The school performance of immigrant minorities: A comparative view. *Anthropology and Education Quarterly, 18,* 262–276.

Gibson, M. A. (1988). *Accommodation with assimilation: Punjabi Sikh immigrants in an American high school and community.* Ithaca, NY: Cornell University Press.

Gilligan, C. (1982). *In a different voice.* Cambridge, MA: Harvard University Press.

Ginsburg, M. B. (1979). Colleague relations among middle school teachers. In A. Hargreaves and B. Tickle (Eds.), *Middle schools: Origins, ideology and practice* (pp. 277–296). New York: Harper & Row.

Ginsburg, M. B. (1988). *Contradictions in teacher education and society: A critical analysis.* New York: Falmer Press.

Giroux, H. (1983a). Theories of reproduction and resistance in the new sociology of education. *Harvard Educational Review, 53,* 257–293.

Giroux, H. (1983b). *Theory and resistance in education: A pedagogy for the opposition.* Hadley, MA: Bergin & Garvey.

Giroux, H. (1988). *Teachers as intellectuals: Toward a critical pedagogy of learning.* Hadley, MA: Bergin & Garvey.

Gitlin, A. D., Siegel, M., and Boru, K. (1988). Purpose and method: The failure of ethnography to foster school change. Paper presented at the meeting of the American Educational Research Association, New Orleans.

Gitlin, A. D., Siegel, M., and Boru, K. (1989). The politics of method: From left ethnography to educative research. *Qualitative Studies in Education, 2*(3), 237–253.

Gitlin, A. D., and Smyth, J. (1989). *Teacher evaluation: Educative alternatives.* New York: Falmer Press.

Gleick, J. (1989). After the bomb, a mushroom cloud of metaphors. *The New York Times Book Review,* May 29, p. 1.

Glesne, C., and Peshkin, A. (1992). *Becoming qualitative researchers: An introduction.* New York: Longman.

Goetz, J. (1981). Sex-role systems in Rose Elementary School: Change and tradition in the rural transitional south. In R. T. Sieber and A. J. Gordon (Eds.), *Children and their organizations: Investigations in American culture* (pp. 58–73). Boston: G. K. Hall.

Goetz, J. P., and Breneman, E. A. (1988). Desegregation and black students' experiences in two rural southern elementary schools. *The Elementary School Journal, 88,* 503–514.

Goetz, J. P., and LeCompte, M. D. (1984). *Ethnography and qualitative design in educational research.* Orlando, FL: Academic Press.

Goffman, E. (1959). *The presentation of self in everyday life.* Garden City, NY: Doubleday.

Goldin, C. (1990). *Understanding the gender gap: An economic history of American women.* New York: Oxford University Press.

Goldman, S. V., and McDermott, R. (1987). The culture of competition in American schools. In G. Spindler (Ed.), *Education and cultural process: Anthropological approaches* (2nd ed.) (pp. 282–299). Prospect Heights, IL: Waveland Press.

Goldwasser, M. L. (1994). Restructuring schools and the gap between policy and practice. Unpublished doctoral dissertation, School of education, University of Colorado–Boulder.

Goodlad, J. I. (1984). *A place called school.* New York: McGraw-Hill.

Goodman, J. L. (1993). Reading toward womanhood: The Baby-sitters Club Books and our daughters. *Tikkun, 8*(6), 7–11.

Gordon, C. W. (1957). *The social system of the high school.* Glencoe, IL: The Free Press.

Gottlieb, D. (1964). Teaching and students: The views of Negro and white teachers. *Sociology of Education, 37,* 345–353.

Gould, S. J. (1981). *The mismeasure of man.* New York: W.W. Norton.

Graham, P. A. (1974). *Community and class in American education, 1865–1918.* New York: John Wiley.

Gramsci, A. (1971). *Selections from the prison notebooks.* Q. Hoare and G. N. Smith (Eds.) New York: International.

Grant, C. A., and Sleeter, C. E. (1986). *After the school bell rings.* Philadelphia: Falmer Press.

Grant, L. (1984). Black females' "place" in desegregated classrooms. *Sociology of Education, 57*(2), 98–110.

Grant, L., and Rothenberg, J. (1986). The social enhancement of ability differences: Teacher–student interactions in first and second grade reading groups. *Elementary School Journal, 87,* 29–50.

Graue, E. (1994). *Ready for what?* Ithaca, NY: State University of New York Press.

Grayson, D. A. (1992). Emerging equity issues related to homosexuality in education. In S. S. Klein (Ed.), *Sex equity and sexuality in education* (pp. 171–189). Albany: State University of New York Press.

Greeley, A. M. (1982). *Catholic high schools and minority students.* New Brunswick, NJ: Transaction Books.

Greene, A. D. (1989). Yates valedictorian hoping success will dispel stereotype. *The Houston Chronicle,* April 30, p. 1C.

Greene, Maxine. (1985). Sex equity as a philosophical problem. In S. Klein (Ed.), *Handbook for achieving sex equity through education*. Baltimore: The Johns Hopkins University Press.

Groce, N. (1981). Growing up rural: Children in the 4-H and the Junior Granges. In R. T. Sieber and A. J. Gordon (Eds.), *Children and their organization: Investigations in American culture* (pp. 106–122). Boston: G.K. Hall.

Grow, J. (1981). Characteristics of access to the school superintendency for men and women. Unpublished doctoral dissertation, University of Chicago.

Guidelines for equal treatment of the sexes in McGraw-Hill Book Company publications. (1980). In A. M. Eastman (Ed.), *The Norton reader* (5th ed.) (pp. 346–358). New York: W. W. Norton.

Gumbert, E., and Spring, J. H. (1974). *The superschool and the superstate: American education in the twentieth century*. New York: John Wiley.

Hacker, H. M. (1951). Women as a minority group. *Social Forces, 30,* 60–69.

Halcon, J. J., and Reyes, M. (1989). Trickle-down reform: Hispanics, higher education and the excellence movement. Unpublished manuscript, University of Colorado–Boulder.

Hall, R. M., and Sandler, B. R. (1982). *The classroom climate: A chilly one for women?* Washington, DC: Project on the Status and Education of Women, Association of American Colleges.

Hammack, F. M. (1986). Large school systems; Dropout reports: An analysis of definitions, procedures and findings. *Teachers College Record, 87,* 324–342.

Hanna, J. L. (1987). *Disruptive school behavior: In a desegregated magnet school and elsewhere*. New York: Holmes & Meier.

Hare, D. (1988). Teacher recruitment in three rural Louisiana parishes: The development of recruitment materials. Paper presented at the meeting of the American Educational Studies Association, Toronto, November.

Hargreaves, A., and Woods, P. (1984). *Classrooms and staffrooms: The sociology of teachers and teaching*. Milton Keynes, England: Open University Press.

Hargroves, J. S. (1987). The Boston compact: Facing the challenge of school dropouts. *Education and Urban Society, 19*(3), 303–311.

Harris, M. (1981). *America now: The anthropology of a changing culture*. New York: Simon & Schuster.

Hart, A. W. (1990). Impacts of the school social unit on teacher authority during work redesign. *American Educational Research Journal, 25,* 503–532.

Hawthorne, S. (1991). In defence of separatism. In S. Gunew (Ed.), *Reader in feminist knowledge* (pp. 312–318). New York: Routledge & Kegan Paul.

Heath, S. B. (1983). *Ways with words: Language, life, and work in communities and classroom*. New York: Cambridge University Press.

Held, D. (1980). *Introduction to critical theory*. Berkeley: University of California Press.

Hernstein, R. J. (1973). *IQ in the meritocracy*. Boston: Little, Brown.

Hess, G. A. (1989). Panel finds school board misuses state Chapter I funds. *Newsletter of the Chicago Panel on Public School Policy and Finance, 6*(1).

Hess, G. A. (1991). *School restructuring, Chicago style*. Newbury, CA: Corwin Press.

Hess, G. A., and Green, D. O. (1988). Invisibly pregnant: A study of teenaged mothers and urban schools. Paper presented at the meeting of the American Anthropological Association, Phoenix, AZ.

Hess, G. A., Wells, E., Prindle, C., Liffman, P., and Kaplan, B. (1985). ''Where's room 185?'': How schools can reduce their dropout problem. *Education and Urban Society, 19,* 320–330.

Heyns, B. J. (1974). Social selection and stratification within schools. *American Journal of Sociology, 79,* 1434–1451.

Higham, J. (1969). Origins of immigration restriction, 1882–1897: A social analysis. In S. N. Katz and S. I. Kutler (Eds.), *New perspectives on the American past: Vol. 2/1877 to the present* (pp. 82–92). Boston: Little, Brown.

Hirsch, E. D., Jr. (1987). *Cultural literacy.* Boston: Houghton Mifflin.

Hirschman, C., and Wong, M. G. (1986). The extraordinary educational attainment of Asian-Americans: A search for historical evidence and explanations. *Social Forces, 65*(1), 1–27.

Hitchcock, M. E., and Tompkins, G. E. (1987). Are basal reading textbooks still sexist? *The Reading Teacher, 41,* 288–292.

Hodge, R. W., Siegel, P. M., and Rossi, P. H. (1966). Occupational prestige in the United States: 1925–1963. In R. Bendix and S. M. Lipset (Eds.), *Class, status and power: Social stratification in comparative perspective* (pp. 322–335). New York: The Free Press.

Hodgkinson, H. L. (1985). *All one system: Demographics of education, kindergarten through graduate school.* Washington, DC: Institute for Educational Leadership.

Holland, D. C., and Eisenhart, M. A. (1988). Women's ways of going to school: Cultural reproduction of women's identities as workers. In L. Weis (Ed.), *Class, race and gender in American education* (pp. 266–302). Albany: State University of New York.

Holland, D. C., and Eisenhart, M. A. (1990). *Educated in romance: Women, achievement and college culture.* Chicago: University of Chicago Press.

Holley, F. M., and Doss, D. A. (1983). *Momma got tired of takin' care of my baby.* Publication #82.44. Austin, TX: Office of Research and Evaluation, Independent School District.

Hollingshead, A. B. (1949). *Elmtown's youth.* New York: John Wiley.

Holmes Group, The. (1983). *Tomorrow's schools.* East Lansing, MI: Author.

Holmes Group, The. (1986). *Tomorrow's teachers.* East Lansing, MI: Author.

Hooks, B. (1989). *Talking back: Thinking feminist, thinking black.* Boston: South End Press.

Hughes, L. W., Gordon, W. M., and Hillman, L. W. (1980). *Desegrating America's schools.* New York: Longman.

Humm, M. (1990). *The dictionary of feminist theory.* Columbus: Ohio State University Press.

Jackson, P. (1968). *Life in classrooms.* Chicago: University of Chicago Press.

Jacob, E. (1987). Qualitative research traditions: A review. *Review of Educational Research, 57*(1), 1–50.

Jacob, E., and Jordan, C. (Eds.). (1987). Explaining the school performance of minority students (Theme issue). *Anthropology and Education Quarterly, 18*(4).

Jacobs, G. (Ed.). (1970). *The participant observer: Encounters with social reality.* New York: Braziller.

Jencks, C. (1972). *Inequality: A reassessment of the effect of family and schooling in America.* New York: Basic Books.

Jencks, C., Crouse, J., and Mueser, P. (1983). The Wisconsin model of status attainment: A national replication with improved measures of ability and aspiration. *Sociology of Education, 56,* 3–19.

Jensen, A. (1969). How much can we boost I.Q. and scholastic achievement? *Harvard Educational Review, 39,* 1–23.

Johnson, J. (1987). Death of unattended children spurs day care bills in Congress. *The New York Times,* November 25, p. B9.

Joint Center for Housing Studies, Harvard University. (1988). Cited by Paul Reeves. (1988). *The New York Times,* March 27, p. B9.

Jordan, C. (1984). Cultural compatibility and the education of ethnic minority children. *Educational Research Quarterly, 8*(4), 59–71.

Jordan, C. (1985). Translating culture: From ethnographic information to educational program. *Anthropology and Education Quarterly, 16,* 105–123.

Kaestle, C. F. (1983). *Pillars of the Republic: Common schools and American society, 1780–1860.* New York: Hill & Wang.

Kahl, J. A. (1953). Educational and occupational aspirations of "common man" boys. *Harvard Educational Review, 23,* 186–203.

Kantrowitz, B., and Wingert, P. (1989). How kids learn: A special report. *Newsweek,* April 17, pp. 50–56.

Karabel, J., and Halsey, A. H. (Eds.). (1977). *Power and ideology in education.* New York: Oxford University Press.

Katz, M. B. (1971). *Class, bureaucracy and the schools.* New York: Praeger.

Kaufman, P. W. (1984). *Women teachers on the frontier.* New Haven, CT: Yale University Press.

Keddie, N. (1971). Classroom knowledge. In M. F. D. Young (Ed.), *Knowledge and control* (pp. 133–160). London: Collier-Macmillan.

Kelly, G. P., and Nihlen, A. S. (1982). Schooling and the reproduction of patriarchy: Unequal workloads, unequal rewards. In M. W. Apple (Ed.), *Cultural and economic reproduction in education: Essays on class, ideology and the state* (pp. 162–180). London: Routledge & Kegan Paul.

Kelly-Benjamin, K. (1990). *The young women's guide to better SAT scores: Fighting the gender gap.* New York: Bantam Books.

Keniston, K. (1968). *The young radicals.* New York: Harcourt, Brace & World.

Keniston, K. (1971). The agony of the counterculture. *Educational Record, 52,* 205–211.

Kennedy, S. (1990). *Jim Crow guide: The way it was.* Boca Raton: Florida Atlantic University.

Kerr, N. (1973). The school board as an agency of legitimation. In S. D. Sieber and D. E. Wilder (Eds.), *The school in society: Studies in the sociology of education* (pp. 380–401). New York: The Free Press.

Kilbride, P. L., Goodale, J. C., and Ameisen, E. R. (1990). *Encounters with American ethnic cultures.* Tuscaloosa: University of Alabama Press.

Kirby, D., Harris, T. R., and Crain, R. (1973). *Political strategies in northern school desegregation.* Lexington, MA: Lexington Books.

Klein, S. (Ed.). (1985). *Handbook for achieving sex equity through education.* Baltimore: Johns Hopkins University Press.

Klein, S. S. (Ed.). (1992). *Sex equity and sexuality in education.* Albany: State University of New York.

Kliebard, H. M. (1986). *The struggle for the American curriculum: 1893–1958.* Boston: Routledge & Kegan Paul.

Knapp, M. S., and Cooperstein, R. (1986). Early research on the federal block grant: Themes and unanswered questions. *Educational Evaluation and Policy Analysis, 8,* 121–138.

Kolata, G. (1989). Gender gap in aptitude tests is narrowing, experts find. *The New York Times,* July 1, p. 1.

Kozol, J. (1991). *Savage inequalities: Children in America's schools.* New York: Crown.

Kramarae, C., and Treichler, P. A. (1985). *A feminist dictionary.* London: Pandora Press.

Kunisawa, B. (1988). A nation in crisis: The dropout dilemma. *National Education Association, 6*(6), 61–65.

La Belle, T. J. (1972). An anthropological framework for studying education. *Teachers College Record, 73,* 519–538.

Labov, W. (1972). *Language in the inner city: Studies in the Black English vernacular.* Philadelphia: University of Pennsylvania Press.

LaFrance, M. (1985). The school of hard knocks: Nonverbal sexism in the classroom. *Theory Into Practice, 24,* 40–44.

LaFrance, M., and Mayo, C. (1978). *Moving bodies: Nonverbal communication in social relationships.* Monterey, CA: Brooks/Cole.

Tappe, F. M., and Du Bois, P. M. (1993). Others study democracy—We do it. *Democracy and Education, 7*(3), 9–14.

Lather, P. (1986). Research as praxis. *Harvard Educational Review, 56,* 257–277.

Lau v. *Nichols,* 414 U. S. 563 (1974).

Lawrence, N. R. (1994). The choice of language and the language of choice: Public/private discourse about abortion and education in the early 1990s. Doctoral dissertation, School of Education, University of Colorado–Boulder.

Leap, W. L. (1978). American Indian English and its implications of bilingual education. In J. Alatis (Ed.), *International dimensions of bilingual education* (pp. 657–669). Washington, DC: Georgetown University Press.

Leap, W. L. (1993). *American Indian English.* Salt Lake City: University of Utah Press.

LeCompte, M. D. (1969). Dilemmas in inner-city school reform. Unpublished Master's thesis, Department of Education and the Social Order, University of Chicago.

LeCompte, M. D. (1972). The uneasy alliance between community action and research. *School Review, 79*(1), 123–132.

LeCompte, M. D. (1974). Teacher styles and the development of student work norms. Unpublished doctoral dissertation, University of Chicago.

LeCompte, M. D. (1978a). Culture shock: It happens to teachers, too. In B. Dell Felder et al. (Eds.), *Focus on the future: Implications for education* (pp. 102–112). Houston, TX: University of Houston.

LeCompte, M. D. (1978b). Learning to work: The hidden curriculum of the classroom. *Anthropology and Education Quarterly, 9,* 23–37.

LeCompte, M. D. (1981). The civilizing of children: How young children learn to become students. *The Journal of Thought, 15,* 105–129.

LeCompte, M. D. (1985). Defining the differences: Cultural subgroups among mainstream children. *The Urban Review, 17*(2), 111–128.

LeCompte, M. D. (1987a). The cultural context of dropping out: Why good dropout programs don't work. Paper presented at the meeting of the American Association for the Advancement of Science, Chicago.

LeCompte, M. D. (1987b). The cultural context of dropping out: Why remedial programs don't solve the problems. *Education and Urban Society, 19,* 232–249.

LeCompte, M. D., and Bennett, K. P. (1988). Empowerment: The once and future role of the Gringo. Paper presented at the meeting of the American Anthropological Association, Phoenix, AZ.

LeCompte, M. D., and Bennett, K. P. (1990). Empowerment: The once and future role of the Bilagaana. *Navajo Education, VIII*(1), 41–46.

LeCompte, M. D., and Bennett deMarrais, K. P. (1992). The disempowerment of empowerment: Out of the revolution and into the classroom. *Educational Foundations, 6*(3), 5–31.

LeCompte, M. D., and Dworkin, A. G. (1988). Educational programs: Indirect linkages and unfulfilled expectations. In H. R. Rodgers, Jr. (Ed.), *Beyond welfare: New approaches to the problem of poverty in America* (pp. 135–167). Armonk, NY: M. E. Sharpe.

LeCompte, M. D., and Dworkin, A. G. (1991). *Giving up on school: Teacher burnout and student dropout.* Newbury Park, CA: Corwin Press.

LeCompte, M. D., and Goebel, S. G. (1985). *Issues in defining and enumerating dropouts* [HISD dropout report #1]. Houston, TX: Department of Planning, Research and Evaluation, Houston Independent School District, June 6.

LeCompte, M. D., and Goebel, S. G. (1987). Can bad data produce good program planning?:

An analysis of record-keeping on school dropouts. *Education and Urban Society, 19,* 250–268.

LeCompte, M. D., and McLaughlin, D. (forthcoming). Witchcraft and blessings, science and rationality: Discourses of power and silence in collaborative work with Navajo schools. In A. Gitlin (Ed.), *Power and method: Political activism and educational research.* New York: Routledge & Kegan Paul.

LeCompte, M. D., and Preissle, J. (1992). Toward an ethnology of student life in schools: Synthesizing the qualitative research tradition. In M. D. LeCompte, W. Millroy, and J. Preissle (Eds.), *The handbook of qualitative research in education* (pp. 815–855). San Diego: Academic Press.

LeCompte, M. D., and Preissle, J. (1993). *Ethnography and qualitative research design in educational research.* Orlando, FL: Academic Press.

LeCompte, M. D., and Wiertelak, M. E. (1992). Constructing the appearance of reform: Restructuring, site-based management and shared decision-making in a Navajo public school district. Paper presented at the American Educational Research Association Meetings, San Francisco.

Lee, E. S., and Rong, X. (1988). The educational and economic achievement of Asian-Americans. *The Elementary School Journal, 88,* 545–560.

Lee, P. C., and Gropper, N. B. (1974). Sex-role culture and educational practice. *Harvard Educational Review, 44,* 369–409.

Lee, V. E., and Bryk, A. S. (1988). Curriculum tracking as mediating the social distribution of high school achievement. *Sociology of Education, 61,* 78–94.

Lesko, N. (1988). The curriculum of the body: Lessons from a Catholic high school. In L. Roman, L. Christian-Smith, and E. Ellsworth (Eds.), *Becoming feminine: The politics of popular culture* (pp. 123–143). Philadelphia: Falmer Press.

Lever, J. (1976). Sex differences in the games children play. *Social Problems, 23,* 479–488.

Liebow, E. (1969). *Tally's corner: A study of Negro streetcorner men.* Boston: Little, Brown.

Linton, R. (1945). *The cultural background of personality.* New York: Appleton-Century.

Lippitt, R., and Gold, M. (1959). Classroom social structure as a mental health problem. *Journal of Social Issues, 15,* 40–49.

Liston, D., and Zeichner, K. (1991). *Teacher education and the social conditions of schooling.* New York: Routledge & Kegan Paul.

Littwin, J. (1987). *The postponed generation: Why America's grown-up kids are growing up later.* New York: Morrow.

Lonsdale Improvement Organization. (July, 1992). *Remembering Lonsdale: Our community, our home.* Knoxville, TN: Author.

Lortie, D. (1969). The balance of control and autonomy in elementary school teaching. In A. Etzioni (Ed.), *The semiprofessions and their organization: Teachers, nurses, social workers* (pp. 1–53). New York: The Free Press.

Lortie, D. (1973). Observations on teaching as work. In R. M. W. Travers (Ed.), *The second handbook of research on teaching* (pp. 474–496). Chicago: Rand-McNally.

Lortie, D. (1975). *Schoolteacher: A sociological study.* Chicago: University of Chicago Press.

McCarthy, C. (1988). Rethinking liberal and radical perspectives on racial inequality in schooling: Making the case for nonsynchrony. *Harvard Educational Review, 58,* 265–279.

McCarthy, C. (1990). *Race and curriculum: Social inequality and the theories and politics of difference in contemporary research on schooling.* New York: Falmer Press.

Maccoby, E. (1966). *The development of sex differences.* Stanford, CA: Stanford University Press.

Maccoby, E., and Jacklin, C. (1974). *The psychology of sex differences.* Stanford, CA: Stanford University Press.

McDade, L. (1988). Knowing the "right stuff": Attrition, gender, and scientific literacy. *Anthropology and Education Quarterly, 19,* 93–114.

McDermott, R. P. (1976). Kids make sense: An ethnographic account of the instructional management of success and failure in a first grade classroom. Unpublished doctoral dissertation, Stanford University, CA.

McDermott, R. P. (1977). Social relations as contexts for learning in school. *Harvard Educational Review, 47,* 198–213.

McDill, E. L., Pallas, A. M., and Natriello, G. (1985). Uncommon sense: School administrators, school reform, and potential dropouts. Paper presented at the meeting of the National Invitational Conference on Holding Power and Dropouts, Columbia University, February.

McGivney, J. H., and Haught, J. M. (1972). The politics of education: A view from the perspective of the central office staff. *Educational Administrative Quarterly, 8*(3), 35.

McIntosh, P. (1983). Interactive phases of curricular re-vision: A feminist perspective. Working Paper No. 124. Wellesley, MA: Wellesley College Center for Research on Women.

McIntosh, P. M. (1988). Feeling a fraud (Keynote address). American Educational Studies Association, Toronto, November.

McLaren, P. (1980). *Cries from the corridor: The new suburban ghettos.* Toronto: Metheun.

McLaren, P. (1986). *Schooling as a ritual performance.* Boston: Routledge & Kegan Paul.

McLaren, P. (1989). *Life in schools.* New York: Longman.

McLeod, J. (1987). *Ain't no makin' it: Leveled aspirations in a low-income neighborhood.* Boulder, CO: Westview Press.

McNeil, J. D. (1985). *Curriculum: A comprehensive introduction* (3rd ed.). Boston: Little, Brown.

McNeil, J. D. (1992). *Kids as customers.* New York: Lexington Books.

McNeil, L. (1983). Defensive teaching and classroom control. In M. W. Apple and L. Weis (Eds.), *Ideology and practice in schooling* (pp. 114–142). Philadelphia: Temple University Press.

McNeil, L. M. (1986). *Contradictions of control: School structure and school knowledge.* New York: Routledge & Kegan Paul.

McNeil, L. M. (1988a). Contradictions of control, Part I: Administrators and teachers. *Phi Delta Kappan, 69*(5), 333–339.

McNeil, L. M. (1988b). Contradictions of control, Part II: Teachers and students. *Phi Delta Kappan, 69*(6), 432–438.

McNeil, L. M. (1988c). Contradictions of control, Part III: Contradictions of control. *Phi Delta Kappan, 69*(7), 478–485.

McRobbie, A. (1978). Working class girls and the culture of femininity. In Women's Studies Group, Centre for Contemporary Cultural Studies (Ed.), *Women take issue: Aspects of women's subordination* (pp. 96–108). London: Hutchinson.

Main, J. T. (1966). The class structure of revolutionary America. In R. Bendix and S. M. Lipset (Eds.), *Class, status and power: Social stratification in comparative perspective* (pp. 111–121). New York: The Free Press.

Malen, B., and Hart, A. W. (1987). Career ladder reform: A multilevel analysis of initial efforts. *Educational Evaluation and Policy Analysis, 9,* 9–23.

Malen, B., Ogawa, R. and Kranz, J. (1990). What do we know about school-based management? A case study of the literature. In W. McClune & J. Witte (Eds.), *Choice and control in education: The practice of choice, decentralization and school restructuring,* Volume 2 (pp. 289–342). Bristol, PA: Falmer Press.

Malinowski, B. (1963). Quoted in Intro to *Fortune,* p. xxix.

Maloney, M. E. (1985). *School dropouts: Cincinnati's challenge in the eighties* (Working Paper #15). Cincinnati: Urban Appalachian Council.

Mann, H. (1842). *Fifth annual report of the secretary of the board.* Boston: Board of Education.

Mark, J. H., and Anderson, B. D. (1978). Teacher survival rates—A current look. *American Educational Research Journal, 15,* 379–383.

Marotto, R. A. (1986). "Posin' to be chosen": An ethnographic study of in-school truancy. In D. A. Fetterman and M. A. Pitman (Eds.), *Educational evaluation: Ethnography in theory, practice and politics* (pp. 193–214). Beverly Hills, CA: Sage Publications.

Marrou, H. I. (1956). *A history of education in antiquity.* Madison: University of Wisconsin Press.

Martin, R. (1972). Student sex and behavior as determinants of the type and frequency of teacher–student contacts. *Journal of School Psychology, 10,* 339–347.

Marx, K. (1955). *The communist manifesto.* Chicago: H. Regney.

Marx, K. (1959). *Basic writings on politics and philosophy* (L. Feuer, Ed.). Garden City, NY: Anchor Books.

Marx, K. (1971). *Economy, class and social revolution.* New York: Scribner.

Marx, K. (1973). *On society and social change.* Chicago: University of Chicago Press.

Mason, W. S. (1961). The beginning teacher: Status and career orientations. Department of Health, Education and Welfare Publication. Washington, DC: U.S. Government Printing Office.

Massachusetts teacher, The. (1851). *Immigration, 4,* 289–291.

Mechling, J. (1981). Male gender display at a Boy Scout camp. In R. T. Sieber and A. J. Gordon (Eds.), *Children and their organizations: Investigations in American culture* (pp. 138–160). Boston: G. K. Hall.

Merton, R. K. (1967). *Social theory and social structure.* New York: The Free Press.

Mertz, N. T., and McNeely, S. R. (1988). Secondary schools in transition: A study of the emerging female administrator. *American Secondary Education, 17*(2), 10–14.

Metz, M. H. (1978). *Classrooms and corridors: The crisis of authority in desegregated secondary schools.* Berkeley: University of California Press.

Miles, M. W. (1977). The student movement and the industrialization of higher education. In J. Karabel and A. H. Halsey (Eds.), *Power and ideology in education* (pp. 432–456). Cambridge, MA: Oxford University Press.

Miller, S. E., Leinhardt, G., and Zigmond, N. (1988). Influencing engagement through accommodation: An ethnographic study of at-risk students. *American Educational Research Journal, 25,* 465–489.

Millett, K. (1977). *Sexual politics.* London: Virago Press.

Mills, C. W. (1956). *The power elite.* New York: Oxford University Press.

Mohatt, G. V., and Erickson, F. (1981). Cultural differences in teaching styles in an Odawa school: A sociolinguistic approach. In H. Trueba, G. P. Guthrie, and K. II. Au (Eds.), *Culture and the bilingual classroom* (pp. 105–119). Rowley, MA: Newbury House.

Moll, L. C., and Diaz, R. (1987). Teaching writing as communication: The use of ethnographic findings in classroom practice. In D. Broome (Ed.), *Literacy and schooling* (pp. 193–221). Norwood, NJ: Ablex.

Molner, A. (1987). *Social issues and education: A challenge and responsibility.* Alexandria, VA: Association for Supervision and Curriculum Development.

Morage, C., and Anzaldua, G. (Eds.). (1981). *This bridge called my back: Writings by radical women of color.* New York: Kitchen Table: Women of Color Press.

Morgenstern, J. (1989). Can "USA Today" be saved? *New York Times Magazine,* January 1, section 6, p. 13.

Morrow, G. (1986). Standardizing practice in analysis of school dropouts. *Teachers College Record, 87,* 342–356.

Murnane, R. J. (1975). *The impact of school resources on the learning of inner-city children.* Cambridge, MA: Ballinger.

Nadel, S. F. (1957). *The theory of social structure.* Glencoe, IL: The Free Press, pp. 35–41. Quoted in Charles E. Bidwell, The school as a formal organization. In James G. March (Ed.), *The handbook of organizations.* New York. Rand McNally, 1965,

Nash, R. (1976). Pupil expectations of their teachers. In M. Stubbs and S. Delamont (Eds.), *Explorations in classroom observation* (pp. 83–101). New York: John Wiley.

National Assessment of Educational Progress (NAEP) Report. (1988). *Science and Engineering Indicators—1987* (N.S.B. 87-1). Washington, DC: U.S. Government Printing Office.

National Center for Restructuring Education, Schools, and Teaching Newsletter (1994), p. 1.

National Commission on Excellence in Education. (1983). *A nation at risk.* Washington, DC: U.S. Government Printing Office.

National Education Association. (1963). Teachers in public schools. *NEA Research Bulletin, 41*(1), 23–26.

National Education Association. (1970). Teacher strikes. 1960–61 to 1970–71. *National Education Association Bulletin, 48*(1).

National Education Association. (1972). The American public school teacher, 1970–1971: More highlights from the preliminary report. *NEA Research Bulletin, 50*(1), 3–8.

National Institute of Education. (1978). *Violent schools—safe schools: The safe school study report to Congress* (Vol. 1). Washington, DC: Department of Health, Education & Welfare, U.S. Government Printing Office.

National School Boards Association. (1993). *Violence in the schools: How America's school boards are safeguarding your children.* Alexandria, VA: National School Boards Association.

Needle, R. H., Griffin, T., Svendsen, R., and Berney, C. (1980). Teacher stress: Sources and consequences. *The Journal of School Health,* February, pp. 96–99.

New York Times. (1993). White girls jeered for "acting black," *Education,* December 8, p. B8.

Nieto, S. (1992). *Affirming diversity: The sociopolitical context of multicultural education.* New York: Longman.

North Central Regional Educational Laboratory. (1993). Executive Summary: The Illinois Valedictorian Project. Oak Brook, IL: Author.

Oakes, J. (1985). *Keeping track: How schools structure inequality.* New Haven, CT: Yale University Press.

Obermiller, P. J. (1981). The question of urban Appalachian ethnicity. In W. W. Philliber (Ed.), *The invisible minority.* Lexington: University of Kentucky Press.

Ogbu, J. U. (1978). *Minority education and caste: The American system in cross-cultural perspective.* New York: Academic Press.

Ogbu, J. U. (1983). Minority status and schooling in plural societies. *Comparative Education Review, 27*(2), 168–190.

Ogbu, J. U. (1987). Variability in minority school performance: A problem in search of an explanation. *Anthropology and Educational Quarterly, 18,* 312–335.

O'Neill, D. M., and Sepielli, P. (1985). *Education in the United States: 1940–1983* [CDS-85-1]. Washington, DC: U.S. Department of Commerce, Bureau of the Census.

Orfield, G. (1993). *The growth of segregation in American schools: Changing patterns of separation and poverty since 1968.* Alexandria, VA: National School Boards Association Council of Urban Boards of Education.

Ortiz, F. I. (1981). *Career patterns in education: Men, women and minorities in public school administration.* New York: Praeger.

Ortiz, F. I. (1988). Hispanic-American children's experiences in classrooms: A comparison between Hispanic and non-Hispanic children. In L. Weis (Ed.), *Race, class and gender in American education* (pp. 63–87). Albany: State University of New York Press.

Orum, L. (1984). *Hispanic dropouts: Community responses*. Washington, DC: Office of Research, Advocacy and Legislation, National Council of La Raza.

Page, R. (1987). Lower-track classes at a college-preparatory high school: A caricature of educational encounters. In G. Spindler and L. Spindler (Eds.), *Interpretive ethnography of education at home and abroad*. Hillsdale, NJ: Lawrence Erlbaum.

Page, R. (1988). Interpreting curriculum differentiation. Unpublished manuscript, University of California–Riverside.

Page, R. (1989). The lower track curriculum at a "heavenly" high school: Cycles of prejudice. *Journal of Curriculum Studies, 21,* 197–221.

Parsons, T. (1951). *The social system*. Glencoe, IL: The Free Press.

Parsons, T. (1959). The school class as a social system: Some of its functions in American society. *Harvard Educational Review, 29,* 297–319.

Pavalko, R. M. (1970). Recruitment to teaching: Patterns of selection and retention. *Sociology of Education, 43,* 340–353.

Perrillo, V. (1980). *Strangers to these shores*. Boston: Houghton Mifflin.

Persell, C. H. (1977). *Education and inequality: The roots and results of stratification in America's schools*. New York: The Free Press.

Peterson, K. S. (1987). School cost can cut doubly deep: Scholarship meets hardship. *USA Today,* November 17, p. 1 [Section D].

Peterson, P. E. (1976). *School politics Chicago style*. Chicago: University of Chicago Press.

Pettigrew, T. F., and Green, R. L. (1976). School desegregation in large cities: A critique of the Coleman "white flight" thesis. *Harvard educational review report series No. 11. School desegregation: The continuing challenge* (pp. 17–69). Cambridge, MA: Harvard University Press.

Phillips, B. N., and Lee, M. (1980). The changing role of the American teacher: Current and future sources of stress. In C. L. Cooper and J. Marshall (Eds.), *White collar and professional stress* (pp. 93–111). New York: John Wiley.

Phillips, D. C. (1987). *Philosophy, science and social inquiry*. New York: Pergamon Press.

Phillips, S. U. (1972). Participant structures and communicative competence: Warm Springs Indian children in community and classroom. In C. B. Cazden, V. John, and D. Hymes (Eds.), *Functions of language in the classroom* (pp. 370–394). New York: Teachers College Press.

Piestrup, A. (1973). Black dialect interference and accommodation in first grade [Monograph No. 4]. Berkeley, CA: Language Behavior Research Laboratory.

Pinar, W. F. (Ed.). (1988). *Contemporary curriculum discourses*. Scottsdale, AZ: Gorsuch Scarisbrick.

Pinar, W. F. (1989). A reconceptualization of teacher education. *Journal of Teacher Education, 40*(1), 9–12.

Pitman, M. A. (1987). Compulsory education and home schooling: Truancy or prophecy? *Education and Urban Society, 19,* 280–290.

Pitman, M. A., and Eisenhardt, M. A. (Eds.). (1988). Women, culture, and education [Theme issue]. *Anthropology and Education Quarterly, 19*(2).

Pitsch, M. (1994). House poised to clear E.S.E.A. reauthorization. *Education Week,* March 9, p. 16.

Plessy v. Ferguson, 163 U.S. 537 (1895).

Popper, K. R. (1968). *The logic of scientific discovery*. New York: Harper & Row.

Powell, A. G., Farrar, E., and Cohen, D. K. (1985). *The shopping mall high school: Winners and losers in the educational marketplace*. Boston: Houghton Mifflin.

Project on Equal Education Rights. (1986). *1986 PEER report card: A state-by-state survey of the status of women and girls in America's schools* [PEER Policy Paper #5]. Washington, DC: Author.

Psacharaopoulos, G. (1973). *Returns to education: An international comparison.* San Francisco: Jossey-Bass.

Purcell-Gates, V. (1993). I ain't never read my own words before. *Journal of Reading, 37*(8), 210-219.

Randour, M. L., Strasburg, G. L., and Lipman-Blumen, J. (1982). Women in higher education: Trends in enrollments and degrees earned. *Harvard Educational Review, 52,* 189-202.

Reed, S., and Sautter, R. C. (1990). Children of poverty: The status of 12 million young Americans. *Phi Delta Kappan Special Report,* K1-K12.

Reeves, P. (1988). Rising rents squeeze lower-income families. *The Houston Chronicle,* March 27, p. 6.

Reisler, R., Jr., and Friedman, M. S. (1978). Radical misfits? How students from an alternative junior high school adapted to a conventional high school. *Educational Theory, 28*(1), 17-82.

Report of the Massachusetts Senate committee on establishing a reform school. (1984). Commonwealth of Massachusetts, Senate. (Doc. No. 86, 1846).

Resnick, D. P., and Resnick, L. B. (1985). Standards, curriculum and performance: A historical and comparative perspective. *Educational Researcher, 14*(4), 5-20.

Reyes, M., and Halcon, J. J. (1988). Racism in academia: The old wolf revisited. *Harvard Educational Review, 58,* 299-314.

Reyes, M., and Laliberty, A. (1992). A Teacher's "Pied Piper" Effect on Young Authors. *Education and Urban Society, 24*(2), 263-278.

Reynolds, W. B. (1986). Education alternatives to transportation failures: The desegregation response to a resegregation dilemma. *Metropolitan Education* (1), 3-15.

Richard, D. (1990). *Lesbian lists: A look at lesbian culture, history, and personalities.* New York: Alyson.

Richardson, V., Casanova, U., Placier, P., and Guilfoyle, K. (1989). *School children at-risk.* New York: Falmer Press.

Ries, P., and Stone, A. J. (1992). *The American woman 1992-93: A status report.* New York: Norton.

Rist, R. C. (1970). Student social class and teacher expectations: The self-fulfilling prophecy in ghetto education. *Harvard Educational Review, 40,* 411-451.

Rist, R. C. (1973). *The urban factory for failure.* Cambridge, MA: MIT Press.

Robbins, T. (1984). *Jitterbug perfume.* New York: Bantam.

Roberts, J. I., and Akinsanya, S. K. (1976). *Schooling in the cultural context: Anthropological studies of education.* New York: David McKay.

Robinson, V., and Pierce, C. (1985). *Making do in the classroom: A report on the misassignment of teachers.* Washington, DC: Council for Basic Education, American Federation of Teachers.

Rogers, D. (1968). *110 Livingston Street: Politics and bureaucracy in the New York City schools.* New York: Random House.

Roman, L.G. (1988). Intimacy, labor and class: Ideologies of feminine sexuality in the Punk slam dance. In L. G. Roman and L. Christian-Smith (Eds.), *Becoming Feminine: The politics of popular culture* (pp. 148-270). London: Falmer Press.

Roman L. G. (1993a). White is a color/white defensiveness, postmodernism, and anti-racist pedagogy. In C. McCarthy and W. Crichlow (Eds.), *Race, Identity, and Representation in Education.* New York: Routledge.

Roman, L. G. (1993b). Double exposure: The politics of feminist materialist ethnography. *Educational Theory, 43*(3), 278-309.

Rose, R. (1988). "Syntactic styling" as a means of linguistic empowerment: Illusion or reality? Paper presented at the meeting of the American Anthropological Association, Phoenix.

Rosenfeld, G. (1971). *Shut those thick lips.* New York: Holt, Rinehart & Winston.

Rosenfeld, R. A. (1980). Race and sex differences in career dynamics. *American Sociological Review, 45,* 583–609.

Ross, E. A. (1901). *Social control: A survey of the foundations of order.* New York: Macmillan.

Rosser, P. (1990). Introduction. In K. Kelly-Benjamin, *The young women's guide to better SAT scores: Fighting the gender gap.* New York: Bantam.

Rudolph, L., and Rudolph, S. (1967). *The modernity of tradition.* Chicago: University of Chicago Press.

Rumberger, R. W. (1987). High school dropouts: A review of issues and evidence. *Review of Educational Research, 57,* 101–122.

Ryan, W. (1976). *Blaming the victim.* New York: Random House.

Saario, T. N., Jacklin, C. N., and Tittle, C. K. (1973). Sex role stereotyping in the public schools. *Harvard Educational Review, 43,* 386–415.

Sadker, M. P., and Sadker, D. M. (1985). Sexism in the schoolroom of the '80's. *Psychology Today,* March, pp. 54–57.

Sadker, M. P., and Sadker, D. M. (1988). *Teachers, schools, and society.* New York: Random House.

Sadker, M. P., Sadker, D. M., and Klein, S. S. (1986). Abolishing misperceptions about sex equity in education. *Theory into Practice, 25,* 219–226.

St. John, N. H. (1975). *School desegregation: Outcomes for children.* New York: Wiley-Interscience.

Sanjek, R. (Ed.). (1990). *Fieldnotes: The makings of anthropology.* Ithaca, NY: Cornell University Press.

Sarason, S. B. (1971). *The culture of the school and the problem of change.* Boston: Allyn & Bacon.

Schildkrout, E. (1984). Young traders of Northern Nigeria. In J. P. Spradley and D. W. McCurdy (Eds.), *Conformity and conflicts: Readings in cultural anthropology* (pp. 246–253). Boston: Little, Brown.

Schmidt, P. (1993). *Education Week,* June 9, p. 7.

Schmidt, P. (1994). *Education Week,* January 12, p. 5.

Schmuck, P. A. (Ed.). (1987). *Women educators: Employees of schools in western countries.* Albany: State University of New York Press.

Schofield, J. (1982). *Black and white in school: Trust, tension or tolerance?* New York: Praeger.

Schultz, T. W. (1961). Investment in human capital. *American Economic Review, 51,* 1–17.

Schumacher, E. F. (1989). *Small is beautiful: Economics as if people mattered.* New York: Harper Colophon.

Schutz, A. (1972). *The phenomenology of the social world.* New York: Columbia University Press.

Scimecca, J. A. (1980). *Education and society.* New York: Holt Rinehart & Winston.

Scott, J. W. (1987). Women's history and the rewriting of history. In C. Farnham (Ed.), *The impact of feminist research in the academy* (pp. 34–50). Bloomington: Indiana Press University.

Scott, J. W. (1988). *Gender and the politics of history.* New York: Columbia University Press.

Seeman, M. (1959). On the meaning of alienation. *American Sociological Review, 24,* 783–791.

Seeman, M. (1967). On the personal consequences of alienation in work. *American Sociological Review, 32,* 273–285.

Seeman, M. (1975). Alienation studies. *Annual Review of Sociology, 1,* 91–123.

Sege, I. (1989). Children in poverty, Part Three. The inner city: Streets of children begetting children. *The Oregonian,* June 27, p. A2. Reprinted from *The Boston Globe.*

Sennett, R., and Cobb, J. (1973). *The hidden injuries of class.* New York: Vintage Books.

Sewell, W. II., Haller, A O., and Ohlendorf, G. W. (1970). The educational and early occupational attainment process: Replication and revision. *American Sociological Review, 34,* 82-92.

Sewell, W. H., Haller, A. O., and Portes, A. (1969). The educational and early occupational attainment process. *American Sociological Review, 34,* 82-92.

Sewell, W. H., and Shah, V. P. (1967). Socioeconomic status, intelligence, and the attainment of higher education. *Sociology of Education, 40,* 1-23.

Sewell, W. H., and Shah, V. P. (1977). Socioeconomic status, intelligence and the attainment of higher education. In J. Karabel and A. H. Halsey (Eds.), *Power and ideology in education* (pp. 197-215). New York: Oxford University Press.

Shaker, P., and Kridel, C. (1989). The return to experience: A reconceptualist call. *Journal of Teacher Education, 40*(1), 2-8.

Shakeshaft, C. (1986). A gender at risk. *Phi Delta Kappan, 67,* 449-503.

Shavelson, R. J., and Stern, P. (1981). Research on teachers' pedagogical thoughts, judgments, decisions and behavior. *Review of Educational Research, 51,* 455-498.

Shepard, L. A., and Kreitzer, A. E. (1987). The Texas teacher test. *Educational Researcher,* August/September, pp. 22-31.

Shrewsbury, C. M. (1987). What is feminist pedagogy? *Women's Studies Quarterly, 25,* 6-14.

Shultz, J., and Erickson, F. (1982). *The counselor as gatekeeper.* New York: Academic Press.

Sieber, R. T. (1981). Socialization implications of school discipline, or how first-graders are taught to "listen." In R. T. Sieber and A. J. Gordon (Eds.), *Children and their organization* (pp. 18-44). Boston: G. K. Hall.

Sikes, J. (1971). Differential behavior of male and female teachers with male and female students. Unpublished doctoral dissertation, University of Texas-Austin.

Silberman, C. E. (1973). *The open classroom reader.* New York: The Free Press.

Sills, D. L. (1970). Preserving organizational goals. In O. Grusky and G. A. Miller (Eds.), *The sociology of organizations: Basic studies* (pp. 227-236). New York: The Free Press.

Simeone, A. (1986). *Academic women: Working towards equality.* South Hadley, MA: Bergin & Garvey.

Simmel, G. (1955). *Conflict.* Glencoe, IL: The Free Press.

Simmel, G. (1968). *The conflict in modern culture and other essays.* New York: Teachers College Press.

Simpson, R. L., and Simpson, I. H. (1969). Women and bureaucracy in the semi-professions. In A. Etzioni (Ed.), *The semi-professions and their organization: Teachers, nurses, social workers* (pp. 196-266). New York: The Free Press.

Sizer, T. (1984). *Horace's compromise: The dilemma of the American high school.* Boston: Houghton Mifflin.

Sleeter, C. (1991). *Empowerment through Multicultural Education.* New York: SUNY Press.

Smith, B. (1979). Quoted in C. Morage and G. Anzaldua (Eds.), (1981), *This bridge called my back: Writings by radical women of color* (p. 61). New York: Kitchen Table: Women of Color Press.

Smith, L. M., and Geoffrey, W. (1968). *The complexities of an urban classroom: An analysis toward a general theory of teaching.* New York: Holt, Rinehart & Winston.

Smith, M. G. (1982). Ethnicity and ethnic groups in America: The view from Harvard. *Ethnic and Racial Studies, 5*(1), 1-22.

Smith v. *Board of School Commissioners* (82-0544-BH, 82-0792-BH), 11th Cir., March 4, 1987.

Smith v. *School Commissioners of Mobile, Alabama,* 827 F.2d 684 (1987).

Sorensen, A. B., and Hallinan, M. T. (1987). Ability grouping and sex differences in mathematics achievement. *Sociology of Education, 60*(2), 63–72.

Spencer, D. (1986). *Contemporary women teachers: Balancing school and home.* New York: Longman.

Spencer, H. (1851). *Social Statistics.* London: Chapman.

Spencer, H. (1967). *The evolution of society: Selections from Herbert Spencer's principles of sociology* (R. L. Carneiro, Ed.). Chicago: University of Chicago Press. (First printed 1898 as *First Principles.* New York: Appleton.)

Spindler, G. D. (1987). Beth-Ann: A case study of culturally defined adjustment and teacher perceptions. In G. D. Spindler (Ed.), *Education and cultural process: Anthropological approaches* (2nd ed.). Prospect Heights, IL: Waveland.

Spolsky, B., and Irvine, P. (1992). Sociolinguistic aspects of the acceptance of literacy in the vernacular. In F. Barkin, E. Brandt, and J. Ornstein-Galicia (Eds.), *Bilingualism and language contact: Spanish, English, and Native American languages* (pp. 73–79). New York: Teachers College Press.

Spradley, J. P. (1980). *Participant observation.* New York: Holt, Rinehart and Winston.

Spradley, J. P., and McCurdy, D. W. (Eds.). (1972). *The cultural experience: Ethnography in complex society.* Chicago: Science Research Associates.

Spring, J. H. (1976). *The sorting machine.* New York: David McKay.

Spring, J. H. (1985). *American education* (3rd ed.). New York: Longman.

Spring, J. H. (1986). *The American school, 1642–1985.* New York: Longman.

Spring, J. H. (1988a). *Conflict of interests: The politics of American education.* New York: Longman.

Spring, J. H. (1988b). The political structure of popular culture. Paper presented at the 10th Conference on Curriculum Theory and Classroom Practice, Bergamo Conference Center, Dayton, OH.

Spring, J. H. (1989). *American education* (4th ed.). New York: Longman.

Spring, J. H. (1992). *Images of American life: A history of ideological management in schools, movies, radio, and television.* Albany: State University of New York Press.

Spring, J. H. (1994). *American education* (5th ed.). New York: McGraw-Hill.

Srinivas, M. N. (1965). *Religion and society among the Coorgs of South India.* New York: Asia.

Stein, N. (1994). Seeing is not believing: Sexual harassment in public school and the role of adults. Paper presented at the American Educational Research Association Meetings, April.

Steinberg, L., Blinde, P., and Chan, K. (1984). Dropping out among language minority youth. *Review of Educational Research, 54*(1), 113–132.

Steinberg, L. D., Greenberger, E., Garduque, L., and McAuliffe, S. (1982). High school students in the labor force: Some costs and benefits to schooling and learning. *Educational Evaluation and Policy Analysis, 4*(3), 363–372.

Steinberg, S. (1989). *The ethnic myth: Race, ethnicity, and class in America.* Boston: Beacon.

Stern, S. P. (1987). Black parents: Drop-outs or push-outs from school participation. Paper presented at the meeting of the American Anthropological Association, Chicago, November.

Stinchcombe, A. (1964). *Rebellion in a high school.* Chicago: Quadrangle Press.

Suarez-Orozco, M. M. (1987). "Becoming somebody": Central American immigrants in U.S. inner-city schools. *Anthropology and Education Quarterly, 18,* 287–300.

Sumner, W. G. (1883). *What social classes owe to each other.* New York: Harper Brothers.

Suzuki, B. H. (1984). Curriculum transformation for multicultural education. *Education and Urban Society, 15,* 294–322.

Sykes, G. (1958). *The society of captives.* Princeton, NJ: Princeton University Press.

Tannen, D. (1990). *You just don't understand.* New York: William Morrow.

Tar, Z. (1985). *The Frankfurt School.* New York: Schocken Books.

Tatel, D. S., Lanigan, K. J., and Sneed, M. F. (1986). The fourth decade of Brown: Metropolitan desegregation and quality education. *Metropolitan Education* (1), 15-36.

Tavris, C. (1992). *The mismeasure of woman. Why women are not the better sex, the inferior sex, or the opposite sex.* New York: Simon & Schuster.

Tedford, D. (1988). Making the grade at HISD: It helps being White, well-off. *The Houston Chronicle,* October 16, p. 1.

Tetreault, M. K. (1986). The journey from male-defined to gender-balanced education. *Theory into Practice, 25,* 227-234.

Tetreault, M. K., and Schmuck, P. (1985). Equity, educational reform and gender. *Issues in Education, 3*(1), 45-67.

Thomas, K. (1990). *Gender and subject in higher education.* Buckingham, England, MK: The Society for Research into Higher Education and Open University Press.

Thompson, B., and Disch, E. (1992). Feminist, anti-racist, anti-oppression teaching: Two white women's experience. *Radical Teacher,* 41, 4-10.

Tiedt, S. W. (1966). *The role of the federal government in education.* New York: Oxford University Press.

Tierney, W. G. (1992). *Official encouragement, institutional discouragement: Minorities in academe—the Native American experience.* Norwood, NJ: Ablex.

Tinker v. *Des Moines School District,* 393 U.S. 503 (1969).

Tobier, E. (1984). *The changing face of poverty: Trends in New York City's population in poverty, 1960-1990.* New York: Community Service Society.

Today's numbers, tomorrow's nation. (1986). *Education Week,* May 14, p. 14.

Tong, R. (1989). *Feminist thought: A comprehensive introduction.* Boulder, CO: Westview.

Treckler, J. L. (1973). Women in U.S. history high school textbooks. *International Review of Education, 19,* 133-139.

Turner, J. H. (1978). The structure of sociological theory (rev. ed.). Homewood, IL: The Dorsey Press.

Turner, R. L. (1989). Organizational size effects at different levels of schooling. Paper presented at the meeting of the American Educational Research Association, New Orleans, April.

Turner, V. (1969). *The ritual process: Structure and anti-structure.* Ithaca, NY: Cornell University Press.

Turner, V. (1974). *Dramas, fields and metaphors: Symbolic action in human society.* Ithaca, NY: Cornell University Press.

Tyack, D. (1974). *The one best system.* Cambridge, MA: Harvard University Press.

Tyack, D. (1990). Restructuring in historical perspective. *Teachers College Record, 92*(2), 170-191.

Tylor, E. B. (1958). *Primitive culture.* New York: Harper Torchbooks (orig. pub. in 1871).

U.S. Bureau of the Census. (1986). *Statistical Abstract of the United States: 1987* (107th ed.). Washington, DC: U.S. Government Printing Office.

Valentine, C. A. (1968). *Culture and poverty: Critique and counterproposals.* Chicago: University of Chicago Press.

Valli, L. (1983). Becoming clerical workers: Business education and the culture of femininity. In M. W. Apple and L. Weis (Eds.), *Ideology and practice in schooling* (pp. 213-234). Philadelphia: Temple University Press.

Valli, L. (1988). The parallel curriculum at Central Catholic High School. Paper presented at the American Educational Research Association, New Orleans.

Valverde, S. A. (1987). A comparative study of Hispanic dropouts and graduates: Why do some leave school early and some finish? *Education and Urban Society, 19,* 311–320.

Van Galen, J. (1987). Maintaining control. The Structuring of parent involvement. In. G. W. Noblit and W. T. Pink (Eds.), *Schooling in social context* (pp. 78–90). Norwood, NJ: Ablex.

Van Ness, H. (1981). Social control and social organization in an Alaskan Athabaskan classroom: A microethnography of getting ready for reading. In H. Trueba, G. P. Guthrie, and K. H. Au (Eds.), *Culture and the bilingual classroom* (pp. 120–138). Rowley, MA: Newbury House.

Velazquez, L. (1993). Migrant adults' perceptions of schooling, learning and education. Unpublished doctoral dissertation, Department of Technological and Adult Education, University of Tennessee–Knoxville.

Veri, M. (1993). The backlash against women in sports. Unpublished paper, University of Tennessee–Knoxville.

Vogt, L. (1985). Rectifying the school performance of Hawaiian and Navajo students. Paper presented at the meeting of the American Anthropological Association, Washington, DC.

Walker, A. (1983). Quoted in P. H. Collins (1990). *Black feminist thought: Knowledge, consciousness, and the politics of empowerment* (p. 37). London: HarperCollins Academic.

Walker, S., and Barton, L. (1983). *Gender class and education.* Sussex, England: Falmer Press.

Waller, W. (1932). *The sociology of teaching.* New York: John Wiley.

Warren, M. A. (1980). Quoted in C. Kramarae and P. A. Treichler (1985). *A feminist dictionary* (pp. 173–174). London: Pandora Press.

Wax, M. (Ed.). (1980). *When schools are desegregated: Problems and possibilities for students, educators, parents and the community.* New Brunswick, NJ: Transaction Books.

Weber, M. (1947). *The theory of social and economic organizations* (A. M. Henderson and T. Parsons, Trans.). New York: Oxford University Press.

Weber, M. (1958). *From Max Weber: Essays in sociology* (H. Gerth and C. W. Mills, Eds. and Trans.). New York: Oxford University Press.

Weber, M. (1962). *Basic concepts in sociology.* New York: Philosophical Library.

Weedon, C. (1987). *Feminist practice and poststructuralist theory.* Oxford: Basil Blackwell.

Wehlage, G. G., and Rutter, R. A. (1986). Dropping out: What do schools contribute to the problem? *Teachers College Record, 87,* 374–392.

Weick, K. (1976). Educational organizations as loosely coupled systems. *Administrative Science Quarterly, 21,* 1–19.

Weiler, K. (1988). *Women teaching for change.* South Hadley, MA: Bergin & Garvey.

Weis, L. (Ed.). (1988a). *Class, race and gender in American education.* Albany: State University of New York Press.

Weis, L. (1988b). High school girls in a de-industrializing society. In L. Weis (Ed.), *Class, race and gender in American education* (pp. 183–209). Albany: State University of New York Press.

Whitty, G. (1985). *Sociology and school knowledge: Curriculum theory, research and politics.* London: Metheun.

Wilbur, G. (1991). Gender-fair curriculum. Research report prepared for Wellesley College Research on Women, August.

Wiles, J., and Bondi, J. (1981). *The essential middle school.* Columbus, OH: Merrill.

Williams, S. B. (1987). A comparative study of Black dropouts and Black high school graduates in an urban public school system. *Education and Urban Society, 19,* 303–311.

Williamson, R., and Johnson, H. J. (1991). *Planning for success: Successful secondary school principals.* Reston, VA: National Association of Secondary School Principals.

Willis, P. (1977). *Learning to labour.* Lexington, MA: D. C. Heath.

Wilson, M. (1963). *Good company: A study of Nyakyusa age villages.* Boston: Beacon.

Wilson, W. J. (1987). *The truly disadvantaged.* Chicago: University of Chicago Press.

Wirt, F. M., and Kirst, M. W. (1974). State politics of education. In E. L. Useem and M. Useem (Eds.), *The education establishment* (pp. 69-86). Englewood Cliffs, NJ: Prentice Hall.

The Wise Woman. (1982). 4(2) [June 21], 7. Quoted in C. Kramarae and P. A. Treichler (1985). *A feminist dictionary.* London. Pandora Press.

Wolcott, H. (1973). *Man in the principal's office.* Prospect Heights, IL: Waveland Press.

Woo, L. C. (1985). Women administrators: Profiles of success. *Phi Delta Kappan, 67,* 285-288.

Wood, G. (1992). *Schools that work.* New York: Dutton.

Woodhouse, L. (1987). The culture of the 4-year-old in day care: Impacts on social, emotional and physical health. Unpublished doctoral dissertation, University of Cincinnati.

Wright, E. O. (1978). *Class, crisis and the state.* London: New Left Books.

Wright, E. O., and Perrone, L. (1977). Marxist class categories and income inequality. *American Sociological Review, 42,* 32-55.

Young, M. F. D. (1958). *The rise of the meritocracy.* London: Thames & Hudson.

Young, M. F. D. (1971). *Knowledge and control: New directions for the sociology of education.* London: Collier-Macmillan.

Ziegler, S., Hardwick, N., and McGreath, A. M. (1989). Academically successful inner city children: What they can tell us about effective education. Paper presented at the meeting of the American Educational Research Association, San Francisco.

Zigli, B. (1981). A distinctive culture, but an identity crisis. In G. Blake (Ed.), *The urban Appalachians.* Cincinnati: The Cincinnati Enquirer.

Index